Too Many Lawyers?

The topic of "too many lawyers" is both timely and timeless. The future make up and performance of the legal profession is in contest, challenged by new entrants, technology and the demand for transparency; at the same time, lawyers long have participated in contests over professional boundaries. In this book, we take up several fundamental questions about the question of whether there are "too many lawyers". What do we mean by "too many"? Is there a surplus of lawyers? What sort of lawyers are and will be needed? How best can we discern this? These questions and more are addressed here in scholarly articles presented at the Onati International Institute for the Sociology of Law (Spain) by some of the best researchers in the field. The collection, with a chapter by Prof. Richard L. Abel, addresses methodological, normative and policy questions regarding the number of lawyers in particular countries and worldwide, while connecting this phenomenon to political, social, economic, historical, cultural and comparative contexts. This book was previously published as a special issue of the *International Journal of the Legal Profession.*

Eyal Katvan is Senior Lecturer at the Faculty of Law, College of Law & Business, Ramat-Gan, Israel. He specializes in the fields of bioethics, law and medicine, the legal and medical professions, legal history, and the history of medicine.

Carole Silver is Professor of Global Law & Practice, Northwestern Pritzker School of Law in Chicago, USA. Her research focuses on globalization and the legal profession, legal education, regulation of the legal profession and diversity and inclusion.

Neta Ziv is Professor at the Buchman Faculty of Law, Tel Aviv University, Israel. She teaches professional responsibility, legal ethics, law and poverty, and disability rights. Her book *Who Will Guard the Guardians of Law? Lawyers in Israel between the State Market and Civil Society* (2015) describes the Israeli legal profession from a historical, critical perspective.

Avrom Sherr is the founding Editor of the International Journal of the Legal Profession and is Professor and Director Emeritus at the Institute of Advanced Legal Studies, University of London. His work is on legal services, legal profession and legal education as well as human rights issues relating to religion and HIV and AIDS.

Too Many Lawyers?

The future of the legal profession

Edited by

Eyal Katvan, Carole Silver, Neta Ziv and Avrom Sherr

Routledge
Taylor & Francis Group
LONDON AND NEW YORK

First published 2017 by Routledge

2 Park Square, Milton Park, Abingdon, Oxfordshire OX14 4RN
711 Third Avenue, New York, NY 10017

Routledge is an imprint of the Taylor & Francis Group, an informa business

First issued in paperback 2018

British Library Cataloguing in Publication Data
A catalogue record for this book is available from the British Library

ISBN 13: 978-1-138-21279-4 (hbk)
ISBN 13: 978-0-367-03014-8 (pbk)

Typeset in Plantin
by diacriTech, Chennai

Publisher's Note
The publisher accepts responsibility for any inconsistencies that may have arisen during the conversion of this book from journal articles to book chapters, namely the possible inclusion of journal terminology.

Contents

Citation Information

The chapters in this book were originally published in the *International Journal of the Legal Profession*, volume 19, issue 2–3 (July–November 2012). When citing this material, please use the original page numbering for each article, as follows:

Introduction
Too many lawyers?
Eyal Katvan, Carole Silver and Neta Ziv
International Journal of the Legal Profession, volume 19, issue 2–3 (July–November 2012) pp. 123–129

Chapter 1
What does *and* should *influence the number of lawyers?*
Richard L. Abel
International Journal of the Legal Profession, volume 19, issue 2–3 (July–November 2012) pp. 131–146

Chapter 2
Too many lawyers? Or should lawyers be doing other things?
Carrie Joan Menkel-Meadow
International Journal of the Legal Profession, volume 19, issue 2–3 (July–November 2012) pp. 147–173

Chapter 3
Unauthorized practice of law and the production of lawyers
Neta Ziv
International Journal of the Legal Profession, volume 19, issue 2–3 (July–November 2012) pp. 175–192

Chapter 4
The flood of US lawyers: natural fluctuation or professional climate change?
Bruce A. Green
International Journal of the Legal Profession, volume 19, issue 2–3 (July–November 2012) pp. 193–207

Chapter 5
It's the law schools stupid! Explaining the continuing increase in the number of lawyers
Herbert M. Kritzer
International Journal of the Legal Profession, volume 19, issue 2–3 (July–November 2012) pp. 209–225

Chapter 6
Coping with the consequences of 'too many lawyers': securing the place of international graduate law students
Carole Silver
International Journal of the Legal Profession, volume 19, issue 2–3 (July–November 2012) pp. 227–245

Chapter 7
Effects of the acceleration in the number of lawyers in Israel
Limor Zer-Gutman
International Journal of the Legal Profession, volume 19, issue 2–3 (July–November 2012) pp. 247–263

Chapter 8
The new knowledge economy and the transformation of the law discipline
Margaret Thornton
International Journal of the Legal Profession, volume 19, issue 2–3 (July–November 2012) pp. 265–281

Chapter 9
Is access to the profession access to justice? Lessons from Canada
Avner Levin and Asher Alkoby
International Journal of the Legal Profession, volume 19, issue 2–3 (July–November 2012) pp. 283–299

Chapter 10
The 'overcrowding the profession' argument and the professional melting pot
Eyal Katvan
International Journal of the Legal Profession, volume 19, issue 2–3 (July–November 2012) pp. 301–319

Chapter 11
Setting the limits: who controls the size of the legal profession in Japan?
Kay-Wah Chan
International Journal of the Legal Profession, volume 19, issue 2–3 (July–November 2012) pp. 321–337

Chapter 12

Legal education in Spain: challenges and risks in devising access to the legal professions
Laura Carballo Piñeiro
International Journal of the Legal Profession, volume 19, issue 2–3 (July–November 2012) pp. 339–355

Chapter 13

The virtue of low barriers to becoming a lawyer: promoting liberal and democratic values
Russell G. Pearce and Sinna Nasseri
International Journal of the Legal Profession, volume 19, issue 2–3 (July–November 2012) pp. 357–378

Chapter 14

'I love my American job': professional prestige in the Indian outsourcing industry and global consequences of an expanding legal profession
Swethaa Ballakrishnen
International Journal of the Legal Profession, volume 19, issue 2–3 (July–November 2012) pp. 379–404

For any permission-related enquiries please visit:
http://www.tandfonline.com/page/help/permissions

Notes on Contributors

Richard L. Abel is Connell Distinguished Professor of Law Emeritus and Distinguished Research Professor at UCLA. His recent books are *Lawyers on Trial* (2010), *Lawyers in the Dock* (2008), and *English Lawyers between Market and State* (2003).

Asher Alkoby is Associate Dean at the Ted Rogers School of Management, Ryerson University, Toronto, Canada. His research interests include international law, global environmental governance, diversity and inclusion, and civil society engagement.

Swethaa S. Ballakrishnen is a Post Doctoral Associate at the Division of Social Sciences, New York University Abu Dhabi and an Affiliate Research Fellow at the Centre on the Legal Profession, Harvard Law School. Her research broadly investigates globalization, organizational innovation and labor market stratification in emerging markets. She is a graduate of the National Academy of Legal Studies and Research, India, and the Harvard Law School (LL.M'08). She received her PhD in Sociology from Stanford University in 2015.

Kay-Wah Chan is Senior Lecturer in the Faculty of Business and Economics, Macquarie University, North Ryde, Australia. His areas of expertise include Japanese law, Chinese law, comparative law, and legal professions. He is a co-author of *Commercial Law of the People's Republic of China* (2012) and a co-editor of *The Chinese Commercial Legal System* (2008).

Bruce A. Green is Louis Stein Chair at Fordham Law School, Fordham University, New York, USA, where he directs the Louis Stein Center for Law and Ethics. His research focuses on the areas of legal ethics and criminal law.

Eyal Katvan is Senior Lecturer in the Faculty of Law, College of Law & Business, Ramat-Gan, Israel. He specializes in the fields of bioethics, law and medicine, the legal and medical professions, legal history, and the history of medicine.

Herbert M. Kritzer is Professor and Marvin J. Sonosky Chair of Law and Public Policy at the University of Minnesota Law School, Minneapolis, USA.

A major portion of his research focuses on the empirical study of the legal profession. His two most recent books are *Lawyers at Work* (2015) and *Justices on the Ballot: Continuity and Change in State Supreme Court Elections* (2015).

Avner Levin is Professor, Law and Business Department, Ryerson University, Toronto, Canada. He studies the diversity of the legal profession, privacy, personal information and cyber-crime.

Carrie Menkel-Meadow is Chancellor's Professor of Law and Political Science at the University of California, Irvine and A.B. Chettle Professor of Law, Dispute Resolution and Civil Procedure. She is an international expert on dispute resolution and the legal profession and she has published 10 books and over 200 articles on these and other subjects.

Sinna Nasseri is an Associate at Latham & Watkins, New York, USA, where he focuses on technology transactions, intellectual property, and general corporate law.

Russell G. Pearce is Professor of Law and Edward & Marilyn Bellet Chair in Legal Ethics, Morality and Religion at Fordham University, School of Law, New York, USA. He researches and teaches in the areas of legal education and religious liberty.

Laura Carballo Piñeiro is Professor of Law at the Department of Common Law, University of Santiago de Compostela, Spain. Her research focuses on legal education, private international law, international civil procedure law and international insolvency law.

Avrom Sherr is the founding Editor of the International Journal of the Legal Profession and is Professor and Director Emeritus at the Institute of Advanced Legal Studies, University of London. His work is on legal services, legal profession and legal education as well as human rights issues relating to religion and HIV and AIDS.

Carole Silver is Professor of Global Law & Practice, Northwestern Pritzker School of Law in Chicago, USA. Her research focuses on globalization and the legal profession, legal education, regulation of the legal profession and diversity and inclusion.

Margaret Thornton is a Professor of Law at The Australian National University, Canberra, Australia. She researches in the legal profession, legal education, discrimination law and feminism. Her current project focuses on work/life balance in corporate law firms. Her books include *Privatising the Public University: The Case of Law* (Routledge, 2012).

Limor Zer-Gutman is Senior Lecturer in the Faculty of Law, COMAS, Rishon Lazion, Israel. She received her PhD from Stanford University, USA, in 1997.

She is the founder and the Head of the David Weiner Center for legal ethics and professional responsibility. Her research focuses on comparative legal ethics, the legal profession and the judiciary.

Neta Ziv is a Professor at the Buchman Faculty of Law, Tel Aviv University, Israel. She teaches professional responsibility, legal ethics, law and poverty, and disability rights. Her book, *Who Will Guard the Guardians of Law? Lawyers in Israel between the State market and Civil Society* (2015), describes the Israeli legal profession from a historical, critical perspective.

Introduction

Too many lawyers?

EYAL KATVAN, CAROLE SILVER & NETA ZIV

Introduction

> We have, it is computed, nearly 70,000 lawyers in the country. France, with a population of 40,000,000, has 6,000 lawyers and 2,400 other officials . . . and Germany, with a population of 45,000,000, has in the same category 7,000. Thus the proportion of the legal element is – in France 1 to 4,762; in Germany 1 to 6,423; in the United States 1 of 909. Taking all these figures together, is it any wonder that a cynic should say that we American lawyers talk more and speed less than any other equal number of men known to history?[1]

This passage appeared in the *Virginia Law Journal* in 1889, but the topic of 'too many lawyers' is as timely today. There is continuing concern with whether a surplus of lawyers exists and how best to discern it – including drawing comparisons among jurisdictions to highlight the problem at home.[2] This has animated debates among jurists, policymakers, professional associations, educators, students and the public that have recently been played out in the popular and legal press, bar journals and law reviews.[3] However, although the controversy is not new as a macro question, its particularities and perspectives have changed, influenced by the rapid transformations caused by globalization, the growing gaps between countries and forces of legal harmonization.

"Too Many Lawyers? Facts, Reasons, Consequences and Solutions" was the topic of an international workshop that took place in April 2012 in Onati, Spain, at the International Institute for the Sociology of Law. The workshop's objective was to address methodological, normative and policy questions regarding the number of lawyers in particular countries and worldwide, and to connect this phenomenon to political, social, economic, historical, cultural and comparative contexts.

The workshop served as a unique opportunity for scholars from a variety of countries and disciplines to unpack these issues relating to the perception of an overabundance of lawyers. The comparative framework highlighted issues of methodology and substance: what do we mean by 'lawyers' when we ask if there are too many? Why do certain countries have more lawyers than others? What is the role of legal education in the supply of lawyers? How does state regulation affect entry into the profession as well as professional ideology and structure? What is the relationship between the number of lawyers and access to justice? As reflected in the articles that follow, the workshop stimulated a lively discussion of the reasons for the profession's popularity among students, and the consequences for the profession as well as the public of a perceived 'flooding of the profession'. Interestingly, the discussion led to an understanding that the answer to the question of whether there are too many lawyers depends as much on preliminary questions of who is considered a lawyer, who is eligible to serve as a lawyer in particular contexts and who is eligible to provide legal services, as it does on the larger consideration of who is asking the question and the geographical, economic and political contexts of the debate.

Our objective was to address the issue of a lawyer surplus in a manner that would illuminate its connection with legal consciousness and culture, and to use data and facts to shed light on the reasons for the continuing popularity of the profession among aspiring entrants. We considered the role of legal education, including a discussion of the factors leading people to choose to study law and become lawyers,[4] differences among countries with regard to creating new law schools, and the link between the nature of legal education and the desire to study law.[5] We also examined the outcomes of both the fact and perception of a flooding of the profession, including whether this has any positive consequences, its impact on economic activity,[6] whether more lawyers increases or inhibits access to legal services, whether an abundance of lawyers changes what lawyers do and how it influences the image of the legal profession. Additionally, we considered whether a surplus of lawyers is a symptom of an ailing society, or of higher trends of litigiousness and legalization. Our inquiry extended to the impact of a surplus or perceived surplus on the profession itself, especially in an era of globalization, including evidence of an effect on professional choices and decisions about expertise, as well as about staying in the profession. Finally, we considered means of intervention and the possibility of drawing operative conclusions: is state regulation warranted, or should the matter be left to market forces? And what role should bar associations take with regard to controlling the number of lawyers in a particular jurisdiction?

The articles presented in this special IJLP issue, each of which addresses one or more of the themes identified above, benefitted from a discussion among workshop participants as well as from the thorough review provided by IJLP reviewers and editors. These are joined and complemented by Richard L. Abel's essay, "What does and should influence the number of lawyers?", which provides a temporal and contextual overview for the question of 'too many lawyers'. Abel reminds us that the topic seems to appear on the public agenda periodically and should be understood as part of the fluctuations and temporary imbalances between supply and demand faced by many professions. He argues that the terms of debate on the topic ought to be framed through two central paradigms – *controlling the production of producers* and *controlling the production by producers.* The first inquires into the type of external gatekeeping structures that determine entry into the profession, including state control, formal legal education, entry exams and apprenticeship, as well as market forces. The second focuses on measures employed by professions to restrict competition, such as unauthorized practice rules, fee caps and restrictions on advertisement. Abel's article thus situates the debate in a particular context and as part of a recurring discussion about lawyers and their societies.

Facts and reasons

In "Too many lawyers? Or should lawyers be doing other things?", Carrie Menkel-Meadow identifies the importance of considering who asks the question about an oversupply of lawyers in framing the consideration of consequences. She suggests that the identity of those asking the question whether there are too many lawyers is linked to the satisfaction of legal needs under the current regime, and conversely that those whose needs are not being met are not asking the question. In discussing why those currently under- and un-served are not invested in the debate about too many lawyers, she explains differences in ways of identifying problems as implicating law and the need for lawyers. Menkel-Meadow concludes that lawyers must reconceive their roles and services to satisfy the larger demands of society.

In "Unauthorized practice of law and the production of lawyers", Neta Ziv proposes an atypical explanation, at least as it pertains to Israel, for the saturation of lawyers.[7] Taking as her premise Israel's broad rules relating to the unauthorized practice of law and their enforcement by the Israel Bar Association, Ziv explains that this law, whatever its original intention, in fact serves to attract any person who wants to be involved in provision of legal services into becoming a lawyer. As a consequence, she finds a strong correlation between UPL rules and policies and the choices of individuals to become lawyers.

Bruce Green, in "The flood of US lawyers: natural fluctuation or professional climate change?", also considers the role of regulation in producing and supporting the current oversupply of lawyers. From the model of legal education to the bar exam as entry requirement and the role of unauthorized practice rules as a boundary regulation, Green considers the options that regulators might take to reduce the number of lawyers. These include raising the standard for passing the bar and recertification requirements, among others. In the end, Green suggests that the market is the only possible force for correction.

Herbert Kritzer also looks for the reasons for saturation of the legal market – but he focuses on a much earlier stage. In "It's the law schools stupid! Explaining the continuing increase in the number of lawyers", he asks why people turn to legal studies and presents national and comparative data about law schools' incentives. Kritzer's analysis also focuses on the mindset of prospective law students – who he suggests may suffer from "career delusions". With regard to both prospective students and law schools themselves – and particularly with regard to the schools' positions in the context of higher education – Kritzer explores the need for external control as well as the forces that might lead to self-correction.

In "Coping with the consequences of 'too many lawyers': securing the place of international graduate law students", Carole Silver places the issue of supply and demand in a global context by focusing on the role of international students in the patterns of producers, in this case, US law schools. Recruiting increasing numbers of international students may enable law schools to continue to finance their activities, despite the decline in enrollment of US law students in JD programs. But growing competition for international law students requires US law schools to reconsider their approaches to educating international students. Drawing on survey and interview research conducted with international law students and graduates, Silver highlights the need for US law schools to develop new approaches and attitudes towards international students.

Outcomes

Limor Zer-Gutman presents new and notable data about the consequences of the increase in the number of lawyers in Israel. In "Effects of the acceleration in the number of lawyers in Israel", she shows that at least in certain respects, such as diversity in the profession, growth may yield benefits. For example, the growth in the number of law students and lawyers enabled the entrance of women and minorities into the legal profession; at the same time, overall growth has led to specialization in new fields of law. Zer-Gutman finds that growth has not affected the rate of disciplinary procedures initiated against lawyers. She suggests that while this raises questions about the effectiveness of disciplinary rules to monitor lawyers' behavior, the increase in the number of lawyers does not necessarily indicate an increase in the rate of ethical misconduct.

In "The new knowledge economy and the transformation of the law discipline", Margaret Thornton addresses the reorientation of legal education in Australia towards the market for legal services. Thornton finds that neoliberalism's influence on higher education and legal education in particular has caused legal education to focus on the large law firm market. This risks undermining the work of law schools in reforming curricula in order to educate students to fill a variety of roles in society. Despite the influence of large and corporate-oriented firms, most law school graduates in Australia pursue work in fields other than legal practice. Consequently, Thornton suggests that the concern of an oversupply of lawyers is inapt for Australia.

Avner Levin and Asher Alkoby use the case of Ontario, Canada's legal education system to inquire about the consequences of a stable number of law schools over time, as well as about existing barriers at the gate of the profession, particularly the difficulty in finding a clerkship. In "Is access to the profession access to justice? Lessons from Canada", they claim that these structural features impair access to justice and prevent the creation of a more heterogenic and diverse profession. Notwithstanding, representatives of the profession continue to argue that it is overcrowded and 'flooded'.

In "The argument of 'overcrowding the profession' and the professional melting pot", Eyal Katvan argues that the notion of overcrowding is an artificial argument aimed at creating (perhaps unconsciously) a professional melting pot, animated by a wish to achieve and enhance the "lost homogeneity" which prevailed in the profession for decades and was interrupted in Israel by the establishment of new law colleges. Katvan draws on data from surveys of law students and lawyers to identify important social differences among students at the law colleges compared to those studying at universities. He finds that as successive cohorts join the profession, their expression of concern about too many lawyers facilitates new entrants taking on the identity of the profession. Katvan presents the history of the 'too many lawyers' argument in Israel and discovers that it is being periodically recycled as a repeating dynamic among professionals and institutions of legal education.

Kay-Wah Chan describes the forces at play in producing lawyers in Japan in his article, "Setting the limits; who controls the size of the legal profession in Japan?" Japan's system has been strictly controlled by a rigid quota for entry into the profession through state control over the number of candidates passing the professional entry exam. Chan describes the changes this system has undergone in the last decades, focusing on tensions within the profession between lawyers (*bengoshi*) on the one hand and judges and prosecutors on the other; on forces of globalization and their impact on the business sector which, in turn, demanded an increase in the number of lawyers; and on the role of political parties in the struggle over lawyers' quotas. He explains that each of these factors influences the public's willingness to turn to formal law – and lawyers – as redress for civil disputes.

Laura Carballo Piñeiro addresses the dramatic changes characterizing the legal profession in Spain. In "Legal education in Spain: challenges and risks in devising access to the legal professions", Carballo Piñeiro uses the context of the Bologna process, which aims to ensure comparability in the standards and quality of higher education qualifications, to situate Spain's consideration of the need to reform its system for qualifying lawyers. The major change resulted in the separation of legal education from entry into the profession. While this may lead to a more modern profession, Carballo Piñeiro suggests that it is also likely to change the accessibility of the legal profession because of increased costs associated with qualification.

In "The virtue of low barriers to becoming a lawyer: promoting democracy, human rights, and rule of law", Russell Pearce and Sinna Nasseri consider the appropriate barriers to entry to becoming a lawyer in light of the goals inherent in liberal democratic societies, drawing primarily on the US but also from South Africa's experience. As such, the authors propose that only minimal entry barriers are appropriate. While they set aside the problem of identifying which minimum barriers are necessary as an issue of 'calibration', they nonetheless suggest that what is required today in terms of education and training is too much. In addition, they suggest that the marketplace needs multiple levels of expertise from lawyers, which also justifies a lower level of education and training.

In "'I love my American job' – professional prestige in the Indian outsourcing industry and global consequences of an expanding legal profession", Swetha Ballakrishnen illustrates the changing meaning of legal work conducted by lawyers in India who participate in the "outsourcing industry". Her article reveals that the way Indian lawyers think and feel about their work and evaluate its worth has changed, even though the work itself has remained the same. Ballakrishnen analyzes markets of prestige, arguing that traditional status markers, which have to do with client differentiation, the type of knowledge and work sophistication, can no longer serve as indicators for the way Indian lawyers conceive of outsourced legal work. Instead, what matters are factors such as being part of an apparatus of international clients, enjoying Western work environments and having opportunities to meet foreign colleagues. These, in turn, impact the demand for such jobs in India and lawyers' willingness to see them as part of the opportunities available to legal professionals.

Conclusion

The papers in this issue provide a comparative view of current trends in law and lawyering and in this regard they surely reflect our times. We live and work in an era in which we continue to struggle with questions of justice, deeply entangled in a globalized market for legal education and legal services. Too Many Lawyers? Obviously a question hard to answer, but one that offers an opportunity to revisit old questions about what it means to be a lawyer and at the same time develop and frame new perspectives about the deep connection between lawyers and justice.

Acknowledgements

Many thanks to Justice Daphne Barak-Erez, a member of the original group of organizers of the Onati workshop, who was unable to participate because of her appointment to the Israeli Supreme Court; to Angela Melville and the Onati Institute for their support and encouragement; to Avrom Sherr, Eliza Boudier and the anonymous reviewers of this special issue for their support and helpful comments; and to the participants in the Onati workshop for engaging in fascinating and vigorous discussions.

Notes

[1] John J. Wickham, Are there too many lawyers? (1889) 13 *Virginia Law Journal* 879 (quoting David Dudley Field).

[2] In pre-state Israel, for example, there were those who complained of a 'flooding of the profession' already in 1922, when there were only a very few lawyers.

[3] See, e.g., Conference proceedings: are there too many lawyers? (1983) 6 *Canada–US Law Journal* 98–213; Catherine Rampell, The lawyer surplus, state by state, *The New York Times*, 27 June 2011. Available at: http://economix.blogs.nytimes.com/2011/06/27/the-lawyer-surplus-state-by-state/; Debra Cassens Weiss, Is legal profession shakeout long overdue? Ratio of lawyers to Americans is 1 to 257, *ABA Journal*, 19 April 2012. Available at: http://www.abajournal.com/news/article/is_legal_profession_shakeout_long_overdue_ratio_of_lawyers_to_americans_is_/; Adam Levitin, The legal employment market, student debt, and legal education reform, *Credit Slips*, 12 February 2013. Available at: http://www.creditslips.org/creditslips/2013/02/the-legal-employment-market-student-debt-and-legal-education-reform.html (posted 2/12/2013).

[4] R.H. Sander & E.D. Williams, Why are there so many lawyers? Perspectives on a turbulent market (1989) 14 *Law & Society Inquiry* 431.

[5] It is worth mentioning that there are those who point an accusatory finger at the law schools for training too many lawyers. See, e.g., Jerome C. Knowlton, Embarrassments to legal education (1892) 1 *Michigan Law Journal* 12; more recently, see Brian Z. Tamanaha, *Failing Law Schools* (Chicago, IL, University of Chicago Press, 2012).

[6] R.J. Gilson, How many lawyers does it take to change an economy? (1992) 17 *Law & Society Inquiry* 635; Stephen P. Magee, The optimum number of lawyers: a reply to Epp (1992) 17 *Law & Society Inquiry* 667.

[7] We should note that Israel serves as an extreme case-study in this respect, in that it is a leading country in its per capita proportion of lawyers: over the past decade, the number of lawyers in Israel has doubled. Today, Israel boasts a ratio of one lawyer per 163 residents (in Tel Aviv, this is even greater, with a ratio of one lawyer to every 33 residents!). Fifty-five percent of newly qualifying lawyers are graduates of the law colleges that were opened in the last decade or two. These figures are exceptional also from a global perspective, albeit reflecting (the continuation of) a global trend and raising common issues.

What *does* and *should* influence the number of lawyers?

RICHARD L. ABEL
UCLA Law School, Los Angeles, CA, USA

Before we can ask whether there are too many lawyers we must answer several preliminary questions: whom do we consider lawyers, and what does and should influence their number? The term 'lawyer', which English-speakers take for granted, has no obvious equivalent in many other languages. Civil law countries have the category of 'jurist', including everyone with a law degree; but a very large proportion of law graduates would not be recognized as lawyers in common law countries. Terms like 'avocet',[1] 'avvocato',[2] 'abogado'[3] or 'anwalt'[4] refer to lawyers with rights of audience in court – but this criterion would exclude jurists employed by corporations and civil servants, who are considered lawyers in common law countries. Notaries in civil law countries perform many of the functions of common law lawyers. Japan is famous for having few *bengoshi* compared with its population; but many of the functions of lawyers in other countries are performed by tax accountants, patent attorneys, and judicial and administrative scriveners in Japan.[5] Any discussion of numbers, therefore, must be framed in terms of function rather than title.

I. Controlling the production *of* producers

All professions seek to control entry; that is what differentiates them from other occupational categories.[6] At a moment like the present, when legal professions in many countries worry that their numbers are increasing in the face of great uncertainty about the future of the global economy, it is essential to review the ways in which lawyers have regulated their numbers in the past: "Those who cannot remember the past are condemned to repeat it".[7]

Numerus clausus

Some legal professions had a *numerus clausus*: a fixed number of practitioners. Entry was dependent on obtaining an existing place by purchase, inheritance or appointment. French *notaires* are an historical example.[8] The Netherlands only recently liberalized its notariat, allowing numbers to rise in response to demand.[9] Many occupational categories in the United States enjoyed similar protections through state licensing.[10] Some still do. In New York a seat on the Stock Exchange sold for $3.25 million in 2005, and a taxi medallion recently sold for $1 million. A Los Angeles liquor license also cost $1 million.[11] When license holders do not simply admit self-interest in restricting the numbers, they offer unconvincing rationales. True, limiting liquor licenses may reduce alcohol consumption, but there are more effective and efficient ways to do so. We can reject a *numerus clausus* for lawyers.

State monopolies

The state can directly control the number of lawyers by making them state employees. Sweden has a state monopoly on liquor sales and China a state monopoly on tobacco; many governments monopolize lotteries. There are historical examples of state monopolies of lawyers: procurators and counsel for state enterprises in communist regimes, prosecutors and judges in most countries. But few today would advocate that all privately practicing lawyers become state employees.

Ascribed characteristics

Larson argued that the professional project sought to control not only *how many* could enter in order to extract monopoly rents but also *who* could enter so as to enhance lawyers' collective status.[12] (These two goals obviously can reinforce each other.) Caste is a classic mechanism for differentiating status. At independence, India recognized more than a thousand castes: hereditary, endogamous social categories that enjoyed (or were degraded by) occupational monopolies. Although this is an extreme example, it is far from unique. *Kohanim* had an exclusive entitlement to act as a priest in the Temple; the roles of blacksmith, healer and diviner were restricted by lineage in much of Africa. Everywhere heritable kingship and aristocratic titles conferred political power and rights in land. Even when social closure was not legally mandated, families perpetuated membership in occupational categories through inheritance and marriage. Many small firms were and still are family enterprises of fathers and sons (now also mothers and daughters), brothers (now siblings), and spouses. Anthony Trollope vividly portrayed the role of kinship in the Anglican Church hierarchy.[13] No one today would urge that lawyers be a caste.

Professions historically enhanced their status (and income) by excluding stigmatized categories. Most legal professions barred women until well into the twentieth century on the ground that gender 'unsuited' them for the practice of law.[14] Slavery barred African Americans. Many countries admitted only citizens. Well into the twentieth century, American legal elites openly voiced anti-Semitism. In 1913, Harlan

Fiske Stone (then Dean of Columbia Law School and later Chief Justice of the US Supreme Court) wrote a letter deploring "the influx to the bar of greater numbers of the unfit", who "exhibit racial tendencies toward study by memorization" and display "a mind almost Oriental in its fidelity to the minutiae of the subject without regard to any controlling rule or reason".[15] Henry S. Drinker, celebrated for writing the first American legal ethics code, railed as chairman of the Philadelphia bar's grievance committee against those who, having come "up out of the gutter ... were merely following the methods their fathers had been using in selling shoe-strings and other merchandise ...". There had been many complaints against "Russian Jew boys" until the requirement that applicants to the bar have a preceptor (sponsor) excluded them.[16] Nazi Germany took the next step by expelling Jews (54% of the Berlin bar, 62% in Vienna) and even the tiny number of women lawyers.[17] But excluded categories eventually overcame the obstacles. Jews rose as a proportion of admissions to the New York City bar from 26% in 1900–1910 to 36% in 1911–1917, 40% in 1918–1923, 56% in 1923–1929, and an astonishing 80% in 1930–1934.[18] The enrolment of women in American law schools increased by 1,650% between 1967 and 1983; indeed, because the number of men law students did not grow after 1973, all the increase in law school enrolments – and hence the profession – is attributable to the entry of women.[19] Racial barriers were the last to be lowered; and all minorities except Asian-Americans remain underrepresented in law schools and the profession.[20] Today most legal professions find this history acutely embarrassing and seek to enhance their collective status by making their membership *more* not *less* representative of the society they serve.[21] Status criteria, therefore, cannot and should not limit numbers.

Formal education

Formal education is the hallmark of modern professions, invariably seen as definitional. The 1979 English Royal Commission on Legal Services listed mastery of "a specialized field of knowledge" requiring a "period of education and training" as one of "the five main features of a profession".[22] Structural functional sociology is equally emphatic.[23] But there is ample reason for skepticism. Manchu China used an elaborate system of examinations to staff its civil service.[24] The English civil service (and its colonial Indian counterpart) was long filled by Oxbridge graduates who had read classics. In neither case did the knowledge these recruits were forced to demonstrate bear any relationship to the professional tasks they ultimately performed.

The relationship between formal education and legal professions is historically and culturally specific. That connection is strongest in civil law countries, whose universities have had faculties of divinity, law and medicine for more than a millennium. But formal education did not become the dominant entry path for American lawyers until the early decades of the twentieth century. In England, that transformation took a half-century longer, partly because there were so few university places and partly because many law dons preferred the logical rigor of Roman law, dismissing their own law as too incoherent to be worth studying or teaching. (Law student enrolment in England rose from just over 3,000 in 1960–1961 to over 8,500 two decades later; enrolment in polytechnic law departments, first opened in 1965, rose to nearly 6,000 in 1981–1982; hence the aggregate total rose nearly 500%.)[25] Indeed, *no* formal education was required in the United States until the twentieth century. Emulating the success of the American Medical Association's 1910 Flexner Report in drastically reducing the number of medical students,[26] the American Bar Association waged a long, vigorous campaign – including annual publication of a map seeking to shame delinquent states by highlighting them in black – to persuade regulators to impose educational requirements: first a high school diploma, then a baccalaureate, and finally graduation from a three-year law school.[27] This drastically reduced the number of part-time students from 31,319 in 1928 to 11,865 in 1953, greatly curtailing entry by those from poorer families.[28] California still allows graduates of unaccredited law schools and those studying in a law office to take the bar exam; New York allows those completing one year of law school and three of law office study to take the bar (but few in either state succeed in entering by this route). Such efforts by accreditors have not gone unquestioned. The US Department of Justice forced the ABA to end its hostility toward proprietary (for-profit) law schools by warning of possible antitrust prosecution.

Even today there is enormous variation in legal educational requirements. Law is a graduate degree in the US, Canada, and increasingly Australia and Japan. In the rest of the world, however, it is a first degree, whose length varies from three years in the UK to often twice as long in the civil law world. England allows those who read other subjects for their baccalaureate to cram three years of undergraduate law study into a single post-graduate year. Some American universities let students compress the seven-year BA–JD into six. And now, just as American medical schools are shortening the MD from four years to three,[29] American law schools are contemplating shrinking the JD from three years to two.[30] Some argue that the arduous training of doctors could be cut by a third (from 14 post-secondary years to 10). Many American law schools give full credit for a semester-long externship (pocketing the tuition while offering little or no pedagogy); Northeastern University Law School alternates periods of formal education and externships during the last two years. And many American law schools allow students to combine a three-year JD with a two-year Master's degree (business administration, public policy, urban planning, public health or social work) in four years rather than five (just as several medical schools allow a compressed course for the MD–MPH). Law students constantly complain about the irrelevance of legal education, and their subsequent employers complain that law graduates lack essential knowledge and skills. Studies of Scottish solicitors and Chicago sole practitioners found that they made little use of the knowledge they acquired through formal legal education.[31] (That is hardly surprising: few English majors become authors, few political science majors become politicians.) All this argues strongly against any simple correlation between legal education and the knowledge essential to practice law. Formal educational credentials appear to perform other functions.[32] They demonstrate discipline, ambition and educability.[33] They function as a warrant for the perquisites of income and status lawyers enjoy; and they distribute law graduates to increasingly stratified positions within the legal profession.[34]

But regardless of their justification, formal educational requirements clearly do influence the number of lawyers.[35] The most extreme example of legal education functioning as supply control is Japan's Institute for Legal Training and Research, the sole means of becoming a *bengoshi*. The ILTR historically accepted only about 2% of university law graduates taking the entrance examination after cramming for two years or more (although this is being relaxed, as it is in Taiwan and Korea, which had similarly restrictive entry).[36] The ABA campaign cut the number of unaccredited law schools from 106 in 1935 to 17 in 1962 and the number of students in those schools from 31,013 in 1928 to 3,218 in 1961.[37] Growing enrolment at accredited schools – from 5,385 in 1928 to 38,894 in 1961 – meant that the overall number of students remained relatively constant – 36,398 in 1928 and 42,112 in 1961 – despite the fact that the population grew by half and GNP 20-fold during this period. Increasing pressure for entry to the limited number of places allowed law schools to become far more selective. Harvard admitted four out of five applicants in 1937–1938 and one out of two as late as 1960 but just over one out of 10 in 2012.[38] At the same time, attrition within law school declined drastically. A Harvard dean was said to have greeted each first-year class by warning: "look to your left, look to your right, one of you will not be here next year".[39] Indeed, Harvard flunked out a third of its entering class in 1937. As late as 1968 a third of American law students failed to graduate in three years. Now, however, virtually all do so (California's unaccredited law schools offering an instructive counter-example).[40] In many civil law countries, by contrast, graduation from secondary school guarantees a university place, and law is often the largest faculty, but many entrants fail to complete their degrees, change subjects or never qualify to practice.

Making law schools gatekeepers can have unpredictable consequences. Individual law schools have obvious incentives to expand in order to generate income and raise status. Suffolk Law School, founded in Boston in 1914 over Harvard's opposition, enrolled almost 4,000 students just 10 years later, making it the world's largest law school, a boast it proclaimed on a rooftop neon sign big enough to be seen from Harvard Square, five miles away.[41] More recently, driven by *US News* rankings (which give greatest weight to the median LSAT scores of entering students), American law schools have cut enrolments, often by eliminating evening programs (thereby curtailing access for the poor, minorities and women).[42] Law schools seek to attract applicants by falsifying data on the scholarships they offer students and the jobs and salaries of their graduates.[43] At the same time, in response to declining demand for lawyers, more than half cut the size of their entering classes and a quarter of the rest expected to do so in 2013.[44] The number of students taking the LSAT fell 16% from October 2011 to October 2012. Even state monopolies on legal education can be broken by new private institutions. Increasing numbers of foreign law graduates seek entry despite protectionist obstacles.[45] Law school tuition has risen much faster than the rate of inflation; but educational loans by government and private lenders have made it possible for students to pay those fees (whether or not they will ever be able to repay the loans).

Some commentators have urged law schools to assert a strong role in controlling the number of lawyers by reducing admissions and encouraging students who perform less well in their first year to drop out.[46] Some want separate tiers of law schools for the two hemispheres of the legal profession, asserting that lawyers representing ordinary individuals require less expertise than those serving business and the wealthy. But when Alfred Z. Reed proposed different accreditation standards more than 90 years ago, the ABA responded by commissioning an establishment figure, Elihu Root, to write a report reaffirming the profession's fictitious unity.[47] And Gary Bellow persuasively showed that the legal problems of the poor are just as challenging as those of rich corporations, if not more so.[48]

Those arguing that law schools should control the number of lawyers must answer some hard questions. What gives law schools the moral authority to make that decision? What evidence do they offer for the proposition that the education they provide is essential for every practitioner? How can they ensure that self-interest does not contaminate their actions? What criteria will they use to determine the 'right' number of lawyers? What data are required for that calculation; how will they collect those data, and how reliable are they? Should law schools act individually? If so, won't their different interests and calculations produce divergent actions (so that some expand as others contract)? If they seek to act collectively, what institutional framework should they use? Where will it get the coercive power necessary to overcome the collective action problem? How will it defend against antitrust challenges? Should law schools control entry (through admissions or tuition levels) or graduation (by dismissing a proportion of entering students)? How will law schools ensure that efforts to lower enrolment do not disproportionately affect applicants disadvantaged by race, ethnicity, religion, class or gender or intensify professional stratification? Law schools should not regulate entry until they can offer answers that satisfy the society lawyers are supposed to serve.

Examinations

Although we take it for granted that lawyers must pass examinations, those actually are fairly recent innovations in common law countries, dating from the nineteenth century. In 1856 the Treasurer of Lincoln's Inn opposed any examination for barristers: "I do not see the mischief of men being called to the Bar, who are after all incompetent, whether it is from want of means, or from idleness, or from incapacity, or anything else". Having risen to become Chief Baron a quarter of a century later, he demonstrated a perhaps unfortunate consistency by exempting 141 aspiring solicitors from the Law Society's examination (nearly a tenth of those passing).[49] Even today examinations are not universal. A few American jurisdictions allow graduates of in-state law schools to practice without any further test, although ABA hostility has cut the number of states granting this 'diploma privilege' from a high of 32 to just one or two. Although the profession usually sets the examination in common law countries, the state does so in the civil law world.

Examinations, like formal education, are justified as necessary to establish a floor of competence, but Weber long ago warned:

> When we hear from all sides the demand for an introduction of regular curricula and special examinations, the reason behind it is, of course, not a suddenly awaked 'thirst for education' but the desire for restricting the supply of these positions and their monopolization by the owners of educational certificates. Today the 'examination' is the universal means of this monopolization, and therefore examinations irresistibly advance.[50]

There are many reasons to be dubious about the legal profession's examinations. States granting the diploma privilege dispense with it. Some exams are too easy. The English Bar examination historically had a very high pass rate even though many took it just a few months after coming down from Oxbridge having read a subject other than law.[51] For-profit cram courses (often very expensive) successfully teach to the test. There has *never*, to my knowledge, been an attempt to validate the examinations, i.e. to study empirically: (1) whether scores correlate with competence in practice; (2) all those passing are minimally competent; and (3) those failing are incompetent. The examinations have a disproportionate impact on test takers disadvantaged by class, race or language.[52] And there is ample evidence that those setting the test manipulate the pass rate to influence the number qualifying – a particularly dubious practice when the profession is in charge. In 1923 the pass rate varied from 25% in Texas through 46% in New York to 100% in North Dakota.[53] In 1985 it varied between 57% in California to 90% in Ohio.[54] There is no reason to believe that these results correlated with the competence of test takers in those states. Nationwide, the proportion passing declined from 59% in 1927 to 38% in 1948, rose to 76% in 1973, and declined to 64% in 1984.[55] Again, it is inconceivable that competence fluctuated in these ways. Indeed, New York explicitly made the examination more difficult in response to the dot-com bust at the end of the 1990s.[56] England exhibits similar patterns. Pass rates for the English Bar Final (part 2) rose to a high of 87% in autumn 1929 (just before the Crash), only to fall to 50% the next year and remain that low or lower for decades (partly because of the growing number of Commonwealth students).[57] Pass rates for the Law Society's Final Examination averaged 75% in 1909–1915, rose to 87% in 1918–1930 (including an astonishing 97% in 1920) to make up for catastrophic losses suffered during World War I, then declined steadily during the Depression to 54% in 1939 and stayed low except for a brief surge to 69% and 71% in the two years immediately after World War II.[58] Examinations should be constantly revalidated to ensure that they perform their only legitimate function: excluding the unqualified.

Apprenticeship

Before aspiring professionals studied at university they qualified through apprenticeship, which everywhere survives in some form, if not as a *de jure* requirement. Historically, it was a major barrier. English solicitors had to pay a premium of £100–500 (sometimes more than a year's average income) and support themselves without wages for five years.[59] English barristers had to pay a premium of 200 guineas for a two-year pupilage (100 guineas for the one-year pupilage that was mandatory after 1959).[60] The willingness of masters to take apprentices determines the number who can enter. Because some lawyers found apprentices a useful form of exploited labor, legal professions sometimes capped the number per master.[61] But once again the profession's efforts to limit supply in order to reduce competition among lawyers cannot be justified. And apprenticeship allows free rein to the preferences (and biases) of masters, who typically choose entrants like themselves, often kin. The contribution of apprenticeship to lawyer competence is uncertain and, as far as I know, has never been tested empirically.[62] Articled clerks in England often complained of wasting their time performing routine tasks: photocopying documents, even making tea.[63] At the very least, advocates of apprenticeship must ensure that it is designed to optimize pedagogy, not the master's profit or convenience. And a profession that mandates apprenticeship after students have invested years in higher education should ensure places for all, allocated without discrimination. Hence any apprenticeship requirement should not limit entry.

Employment

Even where the state does not monopolize the practice of law, employment options can restrict entry. An English solicitor must work for three years as assistant to a fully qualified solicitor before practicing independently. English barristers traditionally had to find a tenancy in chambers, which in London were restricted to the Inns of Court. Because they could not be salaried or enter partnerships, they often earned little during the early years of practice, making survival difficult for those without family support. Although almost all American states allow lawyers to practice independently immediately after qualifying, only 6% of the Class of 2011 did so.[64] A salaried associateship of 5–10 years is the only way to become a partner in most American law firms. This more market-oriented limitation appropriately introduces the last influence on the number of lawyers.

Market influences

If every effort to control supply by the profession or the state (often under pressure from the profession) is suspect as motivated by self-interest – another example of George Bernard Shaw's "conspiracy against the laity"[65] – is the market a solution? Market advocates argue, correctly, that all entry barriers enable the profession to extract monopoly rents from clients. By contrast, allowing supply to increase in response to demand reduces the cost of services and increases access. Milton Friedman, founder of the Chicago school of neo-classical economics, argued that even when justified in terms of ensuring the profession's clients a minimum level of quality, entry barriers actually lower aggregate quality by denying any service to those who cannot afford the prices charged by qualified professionals.[66] We can see consumers making price–quality tradeoffs when they use cheaper gypsy cabs instead of London's more expensive black cabs, or cheaper car services rather than New York's more expensive yellow cabs. During the Thatcher government, Lord McKay, the Lord Chancellor, vigorously pursued a program of reducing restrictive practices in the legal profession.[67] The recent 'crisis' in the American legal profession – unemployed graduates, lower starting salaries, law firm layoffs and dissolutions, spiraling educational indebtedness, declining law school applications, possible law school collapses – has led many observers to advocate further liberalization of the market for lawyers' services.[68] Although law students, lawyers, law firms and law schools are suffering real hardship, this could be seen as an inescapable example of the creative destruction Schumpeter claimed was one of the great virtues of capitalism.[69]

Marx argued, however, that labor markets are unique because labor differs from other commodities.[70] True, there are numerous examples of occupations with few or no entry barriers: street peddlers and door-to-door and telephone sellers of goods or services, domestic and agricultural workers, gardeners, child and home health care providers, casual workers (construction now, longshoremen at an earlier time). But these are undesirable jobs, paying less than minimum wage (sometimes nothing), with no benefits or job security. They tend to be filled by people of color, women and immigrants (often illegal). 'Free' markets without unions or government regulation are bad for workers (although, of course, economists would reply that they offer more jobs).

Free markets also are bad for consumers. Although Friedman notoriously argued that patients should be allowed to 'choose' unqualified brain surgeons, I doubt he did so himself. Clients trading off the quality of legal services for lower prices confront acute problems of information asymmetry.[71] They find it difficult, often impossible, to evaluate quality *ex ante*. Even *ex post*, outcome is a highly imperfect surrogate measure of professional expertise, since it does not control for other variables, such as case difficulty, the adversary's resources or the judge assigned. One-shot consumers (who are the vast majority of individual clients) cannot rely on their own experience.[72] Restrictions on advertising (for instance, of success rates) make it harder to assess reputation. In the absence of other indices, consumers may wrongly view price as a reliable signal of quality.[73] A truly free market in lawyers would offer clients no protection. Nor would malpractice liability or professional discipline adequately guarantee quality. Both operate only after the damage is done. We know that all tort victims greatly underclaim;[74] I would expect this problem to be even greater for legal malpractice (as it is for medical malpractice).[75] Furthermore, such claims are very difficult to prove; clients may have to demonstrate they would have prevailed in litigation absent the malpractice.[76] Professional discipline overlooks most misconduct; and many of the few lawyers who are punished recidivate.[77]

Therefore we still need entry barriers, however imperfectly they ensure minimum quality. Whichever ones are imposed, supply periodically will over- and under-shoot demand. All labor markets are 'sticky' because participants have sunk costs: training, opportunities foregone, the intrinsic pleasure of exercising skills, residence and the effect of career moves on other family members. For all these reasons professional labor markets are particularly sticky.[78] Attrition from the legal profession is very low.[79] College graduates choosing careers make comparative judgments about costs and benefits. For years I would kid students that they were in law school because they wanted a middle-class life and could neither add nor stand the sight of blood.

My feeble joke usually provoked embarrassed laughter – which I took to signify agreement. But the judgments of law school entrants are made under uncertainty.[80] All such judgments contain systematic biases. Applicants 'know' that some large firms pay graduates $160,000 a year – and most are convinced they have a shot at that prize.[81] Even without those biases, applicants would have to rely on imperfect information. Who can predict the demand for lawyers over the next 50 years – the likely length of a career? Many factors may influence demand: business cycles, technological innovation, globalization and international trade, the rise and fall of nations, government regulation, rights consciousness, changes in substantive law (tax reform, no fault divorce, decriminalization of drugs), even how we respond to climate change or terrorism. We cannot predict these changes or their effect on the demand for lawyers. Even 'experts' do not agree. The dean of Case Western Reserve University Law School claimed in a *New York Times* op. ed. that the US Bureau of Labor Statistics predicted a 10% increase in lawyer jobs during the decade 2010–2020.[82] This provoked a lawyer to write a letter to the editor claiming that the BLS predicted only 73,600 new jobs, not nearly enough for the more than 400,000 who will graduate during that period (but the writer ignored retirements by the large baby boom cohort).[83] The present imbalance between supply and demand may just be a product of the above factors; but it also can offer a salutary occasion to re-examine all the entry barriers, retaining only those necessary to ensure minimum competence.

II. Controlling production *by* producers

Entry control allows – and invites – professions to restrict competition among entrants. (Until supply control is secured, those outside the profession can flout its rules with impunity.) One of the first and most important anti-competitive practices is market divisions. Although Abbott argues that these jurisdictional lines are justified in terms of knowledge warrants, those are no more (and often less) persuasive than the assertions of exclusive expertise professions advance to defend entry barriers.[84] In the 1920s and 1930s, the California State Bar negotiated jurisdictional lines with banks and trust and title companies, claims adjustors, realtors, accountants and debt collectors. It sought to exclude non-lawyers from practice in lay magistrate's courts and before administrative agencies and prohibit them from drafting wills or handling real estate transactions.[85] Unlike legal professions in other countries, only American lawyers claim the exclusive right to offer legal advice, a perquisite that cannot be explained by their superior expertise. Historically, categories of lawyers often emerged as adjuncts of particular courts in which they had exclusive rights to practice: examples include ecclesiastical and Admiralty courts and Chancery in nineteenth-century England and the Patent Trial and Appeal Board in the US today.[86] The divided profession in England illustrates the symbiotic nature of some market divisions (for which there are analogies in civil law countries). English solicitors historically enjoyed two monopolies: direct access to clients and conveyancing (transfer of real property). Independently practicing barristers could be retained only through a solicitor but had exclusive rights of audience in higher courts. As the more prestigious and better established branch, barristers devised additional restrictive practices. They had to belong to one of the eight circuits and could practice in others only if the client paid an additional fee to the barrister as well as a kite fee to a circuit member (both designed to discourage non-members from poaching).[87] Ten percent of barristers were Queen's Counsel (appointed by the Lord Chancellor), who could charge much more by virtue of that rank and had to be assisted by a 'junior' (chosen from the rest of the Bar) at two-thirds of the QC's fee.[88] Legal professions established minimum or fixed fees (and failed to observe or police maximum fees). They banned advertising and solicitation (which had been commonplace in some jurisdictions). Federal polities confined lawyers to practice in a single sub-unit (state or province) or required them to qualify separately in each. Countries placed high, sometimes insuperable, hurdles in the path of foreign lawyers seeking admission. Specialization was transformed from *de facto* to a certificate and ultimately an exclusive jurisdiction.

The erosion of supply control combined with the hegemony of market ideology has led to the decline of restrictive practices. In England, rights of audience have been extended to all lawyers, and building societies, banks and estate agents may do conveyancing.[89] Qualified lawyers find it easier to move across jurisdictions, and legal work is being outsourced to lawyers in other countries. Multinational partnerships proliferate in number and grow in size. Fee schedules have been abolished.[90] Paralegals have advanced multiple claims to lawyers' territory: uncontested divorce, workers compensation, immigration, patent, tax.[91] Unbundling disengages functions requiring lawyers from those that can be performed by clients or lay advisers.[92] Rules against advertising (if not soliciting) have been relaxed.[93] Companies like Nolo sell web-based documents and handbooks.[94] At *We the People* non-lawyers help clients fill out forms.[95] In England the Citizens Advice Bureau has been guiding people through the welfare state bureaucracy since World War II. Law firm expansion is accelerated by the possibility of raising capital from non-lawyers. Mammoth global accounting and management consulting firms challenge large law firms, aided by the relaxation of bans on multi-disciplinary partnerships. It would be extremely unfortunate if lawyers sought to reduce the competition engendered by their rising numbers by seeking to reclaim these restrictive practices or devise others.

III. Demand creation

As the ability of professions to control entry and enforce restrictive practices erodes, they turn to demand creation. This is not a new phenomenon: the division of labor between solicitors and barristers (forcing the client to retain two lawyers) and the two-counsel rule requiring a QC to be assisted by a junior (forcing the client to retain two barristers) date from the nineteenth century. English medical consultants (i.e. specialists) will see patients only on referral from a general practitioner. We have known for more than 60 years that the supply of hospital beds significantly influences 'demand' for hospitalization.[96] Critics have accused the English legal profession of engaging in "supplier induced demand".[97] A group of American doctors and a hospital recently paid a substantial amount to settle allegations that they performed unnecessary medical procedures: angioplasties at nearly four times the national average.[98] Critics blame greed for the rise (and regional differences) in the rate of Caesarean sections. The American insurance industry and large institutions that are regularly sued have waged a campaign for decades to convince the public that there is a 'tort litigation crisis' caused by too many lawyers filing frivolous lawsuits.[99] But critics have shown that most of the increase in litigation is attributable to businesses suing each other.

There are many reasons to celebrate those who mobilize the law. I have argued that the real tort crisis is too few claims, not too many.[100] In the US the representation of criminal accused increased dramatically when the Supreme Court held that the Sixth Amendment guaranteed a right to counsel.[101] The same happened for civil litigants as legal aid was expanded throughout the world in the decades following World War II.[102] Legal insurance, which long guaranteed individuals in Germany access to justice,[103] was expanded in England as a means of shifting the cost of representation from the state to the parties.[104] England embraced conditional fees – long anathematized as a practice of American 'cowboys' – for the same reason. The aggregation of individual clients through institutions like trade unions, associations of tenants and homeowners, and consumer cooperatives, as well as legal doctrines permitting class actions, can make small claims financially viable.[105] Lenders can finance litigation that otherwise would be too costly to bring.[106] The rise of alternative dispute resolution can reduce the cost of settling disputes.

IV. Conclusion

The moral panic over 'too many lawyers' resembles warnings of a 'tort litigation crisis'.[107] Social constructivist theory urges us to ask *who* is defining the social problem and *why* they are doing so. Temporary imbalances between supply and demand are a cost of every profession. Legal professions emerged and matured by aggressively restricting supply, thereby increasing the monopoly rents they were able to extract and produce rising – some would say excessive – lawyer incomes. Recent increases in the production of lawyers were the response. They may have overshot the mark. Certainly law school enrolments failed to respond quickly to the global recession. But rather than rush to impose 'solutions' that once again restrict the production of lawyers, we should reflect on the historical and comparative experience of supply control by lawyers. The legal profession exists to serve the public, not its own members. Entry barriers can be justified only if they are demonstrably necessary to ensure a minimum level of competence. Advocates of restrictive practices must show they are essential to protect clients against lawyer overreaching or misconduct. Efforts to expand access to justice should be applauded, not stigmatized.

Notes

[1] A. Boigeol, The French Bar: the difficulties of unifying a divided profession, in: R.L. Abel & P.S.C. Lewis (Eds) *Lawyers in Society, Vol. 2: The Civil Law World* (Berkeley, CA, University of California Press, 1988), ch. 7.

[2] V. Olgiati & V. Pocar, The Italian legal profession: an institutional dilemma, in: Abel & Lewis (Eds) (1988), *op. cit.*, ch. 9.
[3] V. Jene, The legal profession in Spain: an understudied but booming occupation, in: Abel & Lewis (Eds) (1988), *op. cit.*, ch. 10.
[4] E. Blankenburg & U. Schultz, German advocates: a highly regulated profession, in: Abel & Lewis (Eds) (1988), *op. cit.*, ch. 3.
[5] K. Rokumoto, The present state of Japanese practicing attorneys: on the way to full professionalization?, in Abel & Lewis (Eds) (1988), *op. cit.*, ch. 4.
[6] M.S. Larson, *The Rise of Professionalism: A Sociological Analysis* (Berkeley, CA, University of California Press, 1977); M. Weber, *The Theory of Social and Economic Organization* (New York, The Free Press, 1947), p. 142.
[7] G. Santayana, *Reason in Common Sense* (Dover Publishing, 1905).
[8] Boigeol, *op. cit.*, p. 260.
[9] K. Schuyt, The rise of lawyers in the Dutch welfare state, in: Abel & Lewis (Eds) (1988), *op. cit.*, ch. 5, p. 201; N. Kuijpers, J. Noially & B. Vollaard, *Liberalisation of the Dutch Notary Profession* (CPB Netherlands Bureau for Economic Policy Analysis, 2005).
[10] W. Gellhorn, *Individual Freedom and Governmental Restraint* (Baton Rouge, LA, Louisiana State University Press, 1956); W. Gellhorn, The abuse of occupational licensing (1976) 44 *University of Chicago Law Review* 6; M. Friedman, Freedom of contract and occupational licensing, 1890–1910: a legal and social study (1965) 53 *California Law Review* 487.
[11] D. Cumming, Why has the price of taxi medallions increased so dramatically? An analysis of the taxi medallion market (2009) 17 *The Park Place Economist* 12.
[12] Larson, *op. cit.*
[13] A. Trollope, *The Warden* (London, Longman, Brown, Green and Longmans, 1855); A. Trollope, *Barchester Towers* (London, Longman, Brown, Green and Longmans, 1857); A. Trollope, *Doctor Thorne* (London, Chapman & Hall, 1858); A. Trollope, *Framley Parsonage* (London, Smith, Elder & Co., 1861); A. Trollope, *The Small House at Allington* (London, Smith, Elder & Co., 1864); A. Trollope, *The Last Chronicle of Barset* (London, Smith, Elder & Co., 1867).
[14] C. Menkel-Meadow, Feminization of the legal profession: the comparative sociology of women lawyers, in R. Abel & P.S.C. Lewis (Eds) *Lawyers in Society, Vol. 3: Comparative Theories* (Berkeley, CA, University of California Press, 1989), ch. 5.
[15] Quoted in J.S. Auerbach, *Unequal Justice: Lawyers and Social Change in Modern America* (Oxford, Oxford University Press, 1976), p. 107.
[16] *Ibid.*, pp. 126–127.
[17] Blankenburg & Schultz, *op. cit.*, pp. 128–129; S. Ladwig-Winters, The role of Jewish lawyers in the development of law in Germany, and their subsequent destiny until 1945 (Autumn 1999) *Justice* 21 (journal of the International Association of Jewish Lawyers and Jurists); S. Beller, *Vienna and the Jews, 1867–1938: A Cultural History* (Cambridge, Cambridge University Press, 1991), p. 37.
[18] R.L. Abel, *American Lawyers* (New York, Oxford University Press, 1989), pp. 85–86 (hereafter AL).
[19] *Ibid.*, p. 91.
[20] *Ibid.*, pp. 99–108.
[21] R.L. Abel, *English Lawyers between Market and State: The Politics of Professionalism* (New York, Oxford University Press, 2003), ch. 4 (hereafter ELMS).
[22] Royal Commission on Legal Services, *I Final Report* 28, 30 (1979).
[23] T. Parsons, A sociologist looks at the legal profession, in: *Essays in Sociological Theory* (New York, The Free Press, 1964); T. Parsons, The professions and social structure, in: *Ibid.*; T. Parsons, Professions (1968) 12 *International Encyclopedia of Social Sciences* 536; A. Abbott, *The System of Professions: An Essay on the Division of Expert Labor* (Chicago, IL, University of Chicago Press, 1988).
[24] S. Van der Sprenkel, *Legal Institutions in Manchu China: A Sociological Analysis* (Oxford, Berg Publishers, 1962).

[25] R.L. Abel, *The Legal Profession in England and Wales* (Oxford, Basil Blackwell, 1988), p. 465, Table 3.2 (hereafter LPEW).

[26] I have argued that the AMA's success in restricting the supply of doctors explains the American invasion of Grenada in 1983. President Reagan justified it in significant part as necessary to rescue Americans who were in medical school there – because they could not obtain places in the US.

[27] Abel, AL, ch. 3.

[28] *Ibid.*, p. 254, Table 5.

[29] A. Hartocollis, NYU and other medical schools offer shorter course in training, for less tuition, *New York Times*, 23 December 2012.

[30] D.B. Rodriguez & S. Estreicher, Make law schools earn a third year, *New York Times*, 17 January 2013. For responses, see Letters to the Editor, *New York* Times, 25 January 2013.

[31] C. Campbell, Lawyers and their public (1976) 20 *Juridical Review* 34; J. Carlin, *Lawyers on Their Own: A Study of Individual Practitioners in Chicago* (New Brunswick, NJ, Rutgers University Press, 1962), pp. 41 n.2, 77.

[32] Cf. R. Collins, *The Credential Society* (New York, John Wiley, 1979).

[33] E. Mertz, *The Language of Law School: Learning to 'Think Like a Lawyer'* (New York, Oxford University Press, 2007).

[34] J. Heinz & E. Laumann, *Chicago Lawyers* (Evanston, IL, Northwestern University Press, 1994).

[35] Cf. E. Freidson, *Profession of Medicine* (Chicago, IL, University of Chicago Press, 1970).

[36] Rokumoto, *op. cit.*; S. Miyazawa, K-W. Chan & I. Lee, The reform of legal education in East Asia (2008) 4 *Annual Review of Law & Social Science.*

[37] Abel, AL, p. 254, Table 5.

[38] *Ibid.*, pp. 59–60.

[39] R.D. Kahlenberg, *Broken Contract: A Memoir of Harvard Law School* (New York, Hill & Wang, 1992).

[40] Abel, AL, pp. 61, 256, Table 7.

[41] R. Stevens, *Law School: Legal Education in America from the 1850s to the 1980s* (Chapel Hill, NC, The University of North Carolina Press, 1983), pp. 75, 80.

[42] M. Sauder & R. Lancaster, Do rankings matter? The effects of *US News & World Report* rankings on the admission process of law schools (2006) 40 *Law & Society Review* 105.

[43] D.C. Weiss, No fudging: revised standard bars law schools from publishing misleading consumer information, *ABA.com*, 6 August 2012); B. Trachtenberg, Law school marketing and legal ethics (forthcoming 2013) *Nebraska Law Review*; P. Campos, The crisis of the American law school (2012) 46 *Michigan Journal of Law Reform* 177.

[44] D.C. Weiss, About half of law schools surveyed have cut first-year enrollment, *ABA.com*, 19 January 2012.

[45] Medicine, as always, offers an illuminating comparison. See D. Blumenthal, New steam from an old cauldron – the physician-supply debate (2004) 350 *New England Journal of Medicine* 1780.

[46] B. Tamanaha, *Failing Law Schools* (Chicago, IL, The University of Chicago Press, 2012); R.N. Jonakait, The two hemispheres of legal education and the rise and fall of local law schools (2006/07) 51 *New York Law School Law Review* 862; but see Chambliss, It's not about us: beyond the job market critique of US law schools (forthcoming 2013).

[47] A.Z. Reed, *Training for the Public Profession of the Law* (New York, The Carnegie Foundation for the Advancement of Teaching, 1921); Abel, AL, p. 46.

[48] G. Bellow, Turning solutions into problems (1977) 34(4) *NLADA Briefcase.*

[49] D. Duman, *The English and Colonial Bars in the Nineteenth Century* (Croom Helm, 1983), p. 80.

[50] H.H. Gerth & C.W. Mills (Eds) *From Max Weber* (London, Routledge, 1964), pp. 241–242.

[51] Abel, LPEW, pp. 41–42.

[52] Abel, AL, p. 103; Abel, ELMS, ch. 4.

[53] Abel, AL, p. 267, Table 16.

[54] *Ibid.*, p. 270, Table 18.

[55] *Ibid.*, p. 269, Table 17.

[56] D.J. Merritt *et al.*, Raising the bar: a social science critique of recent increases to passing scores on the bar exam (2001) 69 *Cincinnati Law Review* 929.
[57] Abel, LPEW, pp. 42, 310–314, Table 1.1.
[58] *Ibid.*, pp. 396–401, Table 2.10.
[59] Abel, LPEW, p. 149.
[60] *Ibid.*, p. 53.
[61] A limit of two was established in eighteenth-century England. *Ibid.*, p. 152.
[62] S. Ogilvie, Guilds, efficiency, and social capital: evidence from German proto-industry (2004) 58 *Economic History Review* 286.
[63] Abel, LPEW, pp. 155–156.
[64] NALP, *Class of 2011 National Summary Report* (2012). Available at: www.NALP.org/NatSummChart_Classof2011.pdf.
[65] G.B. Shaw, *The Doctor's Dilemma* (New York, Brentano's, 1909) (first published 1906). Adam Smith was first and just as cynical (if less epigrammatic): "People of the same trade seldom meet together, even for merriment and diversion, but the conversation ends in a conspiracy against the public, or in some contrivance to raise prices". A. Smith, *An Inquiry into the Nature and Causes of the Wealth of Nations* (New York, Modern Library, 1937) (first published 1776).
[66] M. Friedman, *Capitalism and Freedom* (Chicago, IL, The University of Chicago Press, 1962); M. Friedman & S.S. Kuznets, *Income from Independent Professional Practice* (National Bureau of Economic Research, 1945).
[67] Abel, ELMS, ch. 2. For further developments, see D. Clementi, *Review of the Regulatory Framework for Legal Services in England and Wales: Final Report* (Office of the Legal Services Commissioner, 2004).
[68] D.J. Merritt & D.C. Merritt, *Unleashing Market Forces in Legal Education and the Legal Profession*, Moritz College of Law Public Law and Legal Theory Working Paper Series (2012); G.K. Hadfield, Legal barriers to innovation: the growing economic costs of professional control over corporate legal markets (2008) 60 *Stanford Law Review* 1689; C. Winston *et al.*, *First Thing We Do, Let's Deregulate All the Lawyers* (London, Penguin Press, 2011); M. Pagliero, What is the objective of professional licensing? Evidence from the US market for lawyers (2011) 29 *International Journal of Industrial Organization* 473; M. Pagliero, Licensing exam difficulty and entry salaries in the US market for lawyers (2010) 48 *British Journal of Industrial Relations* 726; L.E. Ribstein, The death of big law (2010) *Wisconsin Law Review* 749; G.B. Shepherd, Cartels and controls in legal training (2000) 45 *Antitrust Bulletin* 438.
[69] J.A. Schumpeter, *Capitalism, Socialism and Democracy* (New York, Harper & Bros., 1947) (first published 1942), pp. 82–85.
[70] K. Marx, *Capital* (Chicago, C.H. Kerr & Co., 1906) (first published in German in 1867), vol. 1, ch. 1.
[71] G. Akerlof, The market for lemons: quality uncertainty and the market mechanism (1970) 84 *Quarterly Journal of Economics* 488.
[72] M. Galanter, Why the 'haves' come out ahead: speculations on the limits of legal change (1974) 9 *Law & Society Review* 95. Despite the alleged litigiousness of Americans, a survey found that they had an average of just two encounters with lawyers in a lifetime. B.A. Curran, *The Legal Needs of the Public* (Washington, DC, ABA, 1977).
[73] While practicing in Los Angeles, Richard Nixon charged a client $25,000 for advising that it would be safe to invest in France as long as de Gaulle was in power – something easily learned from the newspapers. The ex-vice president justified his fee by explaining that it would allow the client to boast: "as my lawyer, Dick Nixon, said to me the other day ...". P. Hoffman, *Lions in the Street* (New York, Saturday Review Press, 1973), p. 100.
[74] D. Harris *et al.*, *Compensation and Support for Illness and Injury* (Oxford, Clarendon Press, 1984); D. Hensler *et al.*, *Costs and Compensation for Accidental Injury in the United States* (Santa Monica, CA, Rand Publishing, 1991).
[75] P.M. Danzon, *Medical Malpractice: Theory, Evidence, and Public Policy* (Cambridge, MA, Harvard University Press, 1985).
[76] *Wiley v. County of San Diego* [1998] 966 P.2d 983 (Cal.).

[77] R.L. Abel, *Lawyers in the Dock* (New York, Oxford University Press, 2008); R.L. Abel, *Lawyers on Trial* (New York, Oxford University Press, 2010).
[78] R.B. Freeman, Legal cobwebs: a recursive model of the market for lawyers (1975) 57 *Review of Economics & Statistics* 179.
[79] J. Heinz & E. Laumann, *Chicago Lawyers: The Social Structure of the Bar* (New York, Russell Sage Foundation, 1982), p. 208, Figure 6.6.
[80] D. Kahneman, P. Slovic & A. Tversky, *Judgment under Uncertainty* (Cambridge, Cambridge University Press, 1982); D. Kahneman, *Thinking Fast and Slow* (New York, Farrar, Strauss and Giroux, 2011).
[81] C. Caponecchia, It won't happen to me: an investigation of optimism bias in occupational health and safety (2010) 40 *Journal of Applied Social Psychology* 601; G. Preuss & M.D. Alicke, Everybody loves me: self-evaluations and metaperceptions of dating popularity (2009) 35 *Personality & Social Psychology Bulletin* 937.
[82] L.E. Mitchell, Law school is worth the money, *New York Times*, 28 November 2012.
[83] Elizabeth F. Brown, Letter to the Editor, *New York Times*, 3 December 2012.
[84] Abbott, *op. cit.*
[85] Abel, *Lawyers on Trial*, ch. 1.
[86] Abel, LPEW, pp. 35–36.
[87] *Ibid.* p. 97.
[88] *Ibid.*, pp. 98–100.
[89] Abel, ELMS, chs 5–6.
[90] *Goldfarb v. Virginia State Bar* [1975] 421 US 77 3.
[91] ABA Commission on Nonlawyer Practice, *Nonlawyer Activity in Law-Related Situations: A Report with Recommendations* (Washington, DC, ABA, 1995).
[92] F. Mosten, *Unbundling Legal Services* (Washington, DC, ABA, 2000).
[93] *Bates v. State Bar of Arizona* [1977] 433 US 350; *Ohralik v. Ohio State Bar Association* [1978] 436 US 447.
[94] See www.nolo.com.
[95] See www.wethepeopleusa.com.
[96] M. Shian & M.I. Roemer, Hospital costs related to the supply of beds (1959) 92(4) *Modern Hospital* 71.
[97] G. Bevan, Has there been supplier-induced demand for legal aid? (1996) 15 *Civil Justice Quarterly* 58; G. Bevan, T. Holland & M. Partington, *Organising Cost-Effective Access to Justice*, Social Market Foundation Memorandum No. 7 (1994).
[98] R. Abelson, US settles accusations that doctors overtreated, *New York Times*, 4 January 2013.
[99] E.g. W. Olson, *Schools for Misrule: Legal Academia and an Over-lawyered America* (New York, Encounter Books, 2011). For critiques, see M. Galanter, Reading the landscape of disputes: what we know and don't know (and think we know) about our allegedly contentious and litigious society (1983) 31 *UCLA Law Review* 4; Saks; M. McCann & W. Haltom, *Distorting the Law: Politics, Media, and the Litigation Crisis* (Chicago, IL, University of Chicago Press, 2004); R. Lewis & A. Morris, Tort law culture: image and reality (2012) 39 *Journal of Law & Society* 562.
[100] R.L. Abel, The real tort crisis – too *few* claims (1987) 48 *Ohio State Law Journal* 443.
[101] *Gideon v. Wainwright* [1963] 372 US 335; *Argersinger v. Hamlin* [1972] 407 US 25.
[102] R.L. Abel, Law without politics: legal aid under advanced capitalism (1985) 32 *UCLA Law Review* 474.
[103] Blankenburg & Schultz, *op. cit.*
[104] Abel, ELMS, ch. 8.
[105] Galanter (1974), *op. cit.*
[106] R.L. Abel, How the plaintiffs' bar bars plaintiffs (2006–2007) 51 *New York Law School Law Review* 345.
[107] S. Cohen, *Folk Devils and Moral Panics* (Boulder, CO, Paladin, 1973).

Too many lawyers? Or should lawyers be doing other things?

CARRIE JOAN MENKEL-MEADOW
University of California, Irvine, School of Law, USA

ABSTRACT *This paper from the Symposium/Conference at Onati on Too Many Lawyers? suggests that there are not too many lawyers, nor too much legal education. Instead we should think about what legal education is 'good' for (what should those with a legal education do?), including problem solving, dispute resolution and reallocation of legal services for those underserved. The paper looks at how other professions (business consulting and architecture) have reframed themselves for new conditions of work – with varying supply and demand changes in their relevant fields. The paper also discusses implications for legal education of a broader conception of what lawyers learn and do.*

I. The problem: are there too many lawyers?

A variety of social and economic developments in the last decade or so have resulted in claims, in many countries, that there are 'too many lawyers' and in many countries 'too many law students' (see, e.g., Kritzer, 2012) (who, at great financial or opportunity costs for their educations, may train and prepare for a very complex profession, without a certain prospect of obtaining professional work, as that work is conventionally defined). These claims assume that we can measure and know what an optimal number of lawyers is, that we have certain expectations about what lawyers do or should do, and that something should be done to appropriately allocate legal education, legal services and entry into (and practice of) the legal profession (see Morgan, 2010; Green, 2012). In my view, all of these claims are problematic. Is the question whether there are too many lawyers admitted to practice or, too much legal education being offered? Is this a market question (too many lawyers will drive down fees and make the profession less profitable for those already in it), make access too difficult (supply and demand issues) or waste too many social resources on the production of law degrees without sufficient economic and social benefit? Or, is this a social or moral question – do too many lawyers drain the economy, the polity and the social fabric by producing conflict, increased transaction costs and turmoil, rather than serving to benefit the larger society by mediating conflict,[1] serving as statesmen (Kronman, 1995) or problem solvers, or 'social glue', rather than social repellents or irritants?

In this essay, I suggest that there is not too much legal education nor too many lawyers, if the goals of a legal profession include solving human problems and producing both peace and justice, as 'valued-added' forms of social goods produced by having legal knowledge. Furthermore, new challenges of inequalities, inadequate or unbalanced resources should force us to realign, re-imagine and innovate new methods of legal services delivery, which in turn should require different ways of structuring the acquisition and practice of legal knowledge and legal education, as other professions have begun to do (Awan *et al.*, 2011).

How do we measure the optimal number of lawyers (Magee, 2010)?[2] It is common to look at per capita ratios of lawyers to populations. So we learn that Israel and the United States have among the highest ratio of lawyers to general population [1:163 (Barak-Erez *et al.*, 2011) and 1:265 (ABA, 2008), respectively] and South Africa has one of the lowest [1:2,273 (McQuoid-Mason, 2012)].[3] But we know much less about whether lawyers are actually meeting the legal needs of the populations they serve and/or whether lawyers are serving an optimally productive function in society. As recently described by sociologist Rebecca Sandefur (2012), there have been few thorough legal needs studies in the United States (and many other countries) since the initial outpouring of interest in access to justice and legal needs studies in the 1970s and 1980s, though Herbert Kritzer (2010) reports on a number of state-based legal needs studies in at least half of the United States in the last twenty-five years (see, e.g., Curran, 1977; Cappelletti & Garth, 1979; Meeker *et al.*, 1985; ABA, 1994; Meeker *et al.*, 2000; Rhode, 2004). What we know from those older studies and a few newer ones is that both poor and moderate income individuals are grossly underserved by lawyers for their 'basic' everyday legal needs, including denials or disputes about public benefits, family law matters, legal status issues (e.g. immigration), basic property transactions (leasing and purchasing housing, now foreclosures), tax issues, neighbor and interpersonal disputes, and employment matters. Recent studies suggest that poor and moderate income individuals most often seek other 'non-lawyers' to help them solve 'legal' problems (Sandefur, 2012). Though many argue the problem is the cost and affordability of legal services, others have noted that low and moderate income individuals have either learned to use other resources or don't understand or want legal professionals to take on their problems (Sandefur, 2012; Kritzer, 2010). My own early work in assessing when people of moderate means sought lawyers demonstrated that ordinary people did not want to conceive of themselves as having 'problems' (so when asked about a legal problem they had actually encountered and sought legal advice for, they could not remember or denied use of a lawyer in handling their problem) (Menkel-Meadow, 1981). For many, what we legal professionals might call a legal 'problem' (needing a will, buying a house, signing a lease, making a consumer complaint, getting a traffic ticket, having an 'issue' at work, in the family or at school), was characterized as either a normal, if annoying, part of life, or a transaction, not a 'legal dispute' requiring legal representation or even advice.

As other students of legal needs and the use of professional legal services have noted, legal problems are 'socially constructed', both by those having the problems and those who seek to solve them (Felstiner *et al.*, 1981; Menkel-Meadow, 1985a). And now we know, in addition to such factors as case type, class, region, religious group, possibly race and gender, etc., there is also national and cultural variation in when people decide to go to lawyers (especially when there is greater access to justice, through government-supported judicare, legal aid or other social welfare or subsidy systems) (Kritzer, 1991, 2008; Genn, 1999; Genn & Paterson, 2002). The provision of legal services to those of low income in the United States has, for decades, been well below governmental subsidies in other countries (see Curran, 1977; Cappelletti & Garth, 1979; Legal Services Corporation, 1980, 2009; Meeker *et al.*, 1985; ABA, 1994; Meeker *et al.*, 2000; Rhode, 2004; Kritzer, 2010) and in the last three decades whatever government support there has been, particularly through the Legal Services Corporation funding, has been greatly diminished as annual allocation of funds for legal services has been reduced in real dollars almost threefold (the current budget allocation is close to what it was in actual dollars in the early 1980s when I first did studies of allocation of legal services to the poor) (Cohen, 2013; Menkel-Meadow & Meadow, 1983; Menkel-Meadow, 1984a; see also Abel, 1985). The United States is not alone in decreasing governmental support for legal services for those who can't afford them; recent changes in British Legal Aid have greatly reduced allocations for civil justice, as most legal aid is allocated to criminal defense, and civil problems are increasingly being referred to other processes (e.g. mediation, as discussed more fully below) (Legal Aid Act, 1988; Whitehead, 2011; Legal Services Act, 2007; Brennan, 2012).

Thus, usage of lawyers to solve some 'legal' problems is a complex social phenomenon in which the variable availability of legal services and subsidies for legal aid may structure people's expectations of how and when they can use lawyers to solve their problems. Choosing to use non-lawyers may be a fully adaptive strategy if lawyers are not sufficiently available at a 'fair' cost or at a cost that justifies the expense [consistent with findings that the same 'legal problem' (e.g. house ownership) may be handled by lawyers or not, depending on the economic value of the problem itself] (Kritzer, 1991, 2008). Whether lawyers or non-lawyers perform better, worse or the same in handling a wide variety of matters, remains a contested empirical question, requiring constant study by type of matter, and over time, with both new simplification (electronic and form documents) and simultaneously, complexification (more regulation, more complex claims and entities) of legal matters (Kritzer, 1998; Menkel-Meadow, 2012).

At the organizational level, early predictions of an ever-expanding market for lawyer services in the creation of ever-increasing new private entities and increased governmental regulation (Sander & Williams, 1989) have met with current realities of technological change and the possible 'replacement' of lawyer work product by increasingly routinized computer forms and electronic documentation and communication (Susskind, 2008), as well as ever-increasing competition from non-lawyer providers of legal services and the economic recession in general, which some argue has reduced the scope and amount of legal work (Stevens, 2012; Kritzer, 1998; compare Menkel-Meadow, 1985b). The question of whether there are too many lawyers now transcends any one jurisdiction, as scholars and practitioners consider what the 'globalization' of legal services means for us all – more work for more (specialized) lawyers around the globe (Gardner, Morris *et al.*, 2002) or increased competition from lawyers who are able to cross borders to practice, even as cross-border licensing to legitimate such practice remains somewhat unresolved (Terry, 1998, 2008, 2010; Silver, 2005; Sokol, 2007).

Another part of the 'too many lawyers' argument has to do with allocation of what kinds of lawyers to what kinds of matters. Current complaints in the United States that there are too many lawyers are mostly made by those seeking to enter the profession (or those who have newly entered in the recent economic downturn). A series of articles in the popular media (Segal, 2011a, 2011b), and now a series of lawsuits against a number of law schools arguing that they have over-claimed and misrepresented employment possibilities for graduates (Anziska, 2012; Shear, 2012),[4] mostly have to do with the ratio of highly paid (large law firm) jobs to the numbers of students graduating from law school with large debt (often between $100,000 and $150,000) who seek those highly paid (formerly up to $160,000 per year) jobs. Ironically, in some markets, with low-tuition state schools and employment pipelines to smaller firms or government agencies, employment rates may actually be more robust (or at least not declining at the same rate as in some big city markets).

Whether there are, in fact, too many lawyers, may depend on location, type of practice and the externalities of 'other' factors. Are there too many lawyers in Nevada, Florida and California where the economic crisis has caused mass foreclosures? Would many homeowners benefit from lawyers to renegotiate (or mediate) their mortgages (Schneider & Fleury, 2011; State of Nevada Foreclosure Mediation Program, 2012)? How flexible are modern specialized lawyers in shifting from one form of practice (mergers and acquisitions in boom times) to another (bankruptcy in economic downturns), and from one 'sphere' (corporate and entity representation) to another (individual representation) (Heinz & Laumann, 1994)?[5] Unlike employment in less specialized fields, flexible movement from one sphere to another is not easy and is variable with both type of professional knowledge as well as professional licensing and credentialing requirements [as is the case with differences between most older professions – e.g. medicine, architecture, accounting and nursing, which require licensing, with newer professions such as engineering, computer techs and business consulting, which do not (McKenna, 2006)]. Law licensing and credentialing is even more complex as states, not the nation (in the United States), regulate entry and also vary as to whether they permit specialization certification (as does California in a number of specialties) or reciprocal bar entry from other states or countries. Thus, the claims about too many lawyers tend to conflate a number of more complex issues – are there too many law graduates or law-trained individuals for what is currently available to be 'lawyered' about, at rates that justify the investment in a legal education, or are lawyers misallocated both in what they want to do and what they might actually be helpful for if they could be allocated to work in a different way.[6] Must all those who receive a legal education work in the same kinds of 'legal' jobs?

Most of the relatively rapid increase in the number of law students and lawyers in the last few decades has been attributed to the diminished exclusivity of entry barriers [in most Western and some Eastern, e.g. China and Japan (Chan, 2012), countries] to legal education (if not to full certification and bar membership) and the dramatic increase in the number of women, and the slightly less dramatic rise of minority group representation in legal education and the legal profession (Menkel-Meadow, 1989a, 1995; Kritzer, 2012).[7] Thus, to this author (and others), it seems deeply ironic that claims are made that there are 'too many lawyers', just as the legal profession becomes more diverse. This is not unrelated to the claim that there is too much litigation and too many lawsuits, just at the same time as new causes of action and increased litigation over basic human, civil and economic rights have increased access to the legal system for those who were previously denied both access and substantive claims and legal relief (Galanter, 1983, 1992, 2004). And, as others have argued, these claims have been made before, the legal profession has always been in 'crisis' as defined by some groups who lament what lawyers do or who they serve or how much they can monopolize their relative markets (Garth, 2012; Gans, 2012). What is an 'optimal' number of lawyers and legal claims and who should be available to handle those claims?[8]

As I will discuss more fully below, new entrants to the bar, who may diversify the practice of law, not only demographically, but substantively (Menkel-Meadow, 1987), may actually provide an opportunity for reconceiving just what it is that lawyers can, or should, do. We already know the bar is stratified and segmented and that different kinds of lawyers are 'segregated' in different parts of the profession, whether willingly or not (the 'push–pull' effect) (Menkel-Meadow, 1989b; Seron, 1996;[9] Wilkins, 2001). That lawyers in different segments of the bar might perform different kinds of services is well known and commonplace to us now, but the move from a more generalized conception of what lawyers do to more specialized conceptions is an opportunity to re-examine just what legal knowledge is and how it might be most effectively used to solve people's problems.

It might be useful to separate consideration of whether there are too many lawyers from the issue of whether there are too many law students or too much legal education. The United States, Canada [and Japan (Riles with Uchida, 2009), Korea, China and in some schools, Australia] are among a few countries that treat legal education as a subject of graduate education. In most countries of the world, legal education is still a general, undergraduate or first degree, conceptualized as a good general education for a well-educated citizen who might enter any number of useful professions.[10] Will we soon be asking the question of whether there are too many college graduates (Steinberg, 2010)? Other (developing) countries may be having different experiences, with less work available for the highly educated as more physical or unskilled labor might still be necessary for manufacturing, infrastructural development or export businesses.[11] But, employment issues to one side, legal education may be a particularly useful (if properly structured) form of knowledge to impart to any educated citizen of the world, whether obtained in graduate or undergraduate education and there may be more 'uses' of that legal knowledge than conventional deployment in what is considered a 'legal' career. Here I will contrast the much larger legal profession to the smaller and newer profession of business consulting, and the older profession of architecture and planning to see how realignments and the creation of 'new' knowledge and forms of expertise can expand the uses of knowledge to facilitate dramatic social, physical and economic change. Legal education could play a useful role in not only advising on and solving more problems and social issues, but could also be important in just allocations of goods, services and more dignitary human issues in an ever-changing world of commerce and human interaction, as law students, like business, architecture, engineering and science students, learn how to 'innovate' within their fields (Henderson, 2012; Lehrer, 2012).

Thus, the question of whether there are too many lawyers depends greatly on who is asking the question – *existing lawyers* who may want to control the market and limit entry[12] (see, e.g., Abel, 1988, 1989, 2003; see also Larson, 1977), *new entrants or law students* who see the current reported ratio of jobs to law graduates as declining [in the US about 30,000 jobs/annually for about 45,000 new JDs each year (Greenbaum, 2010[13])], *current and potential clients* (consisting of a wide and divergent group of individuals and organizations), or the *larger society* or *scholars* who aim to assess whether lawyers are socially productive, and if so, what it is that they produce. Though many have argued that lawyers may actually impede innovation and growth of market activities (Sander & Williams, 1989; Hadfield, 2000, 2008), I suggest here that legal knowledge can and should be deployed to decrease the cost (both economic and human) of disputes and conflicts and can also be utilized for more efficient and better transaction and entity creation and management.[14] Thus, the question is not 'are there too many lawyers?', but what should lawyers productively do [with implications for how they should be educated, trained and 'allocated' to do good work (Gardner, Csikszentmihalhi *et al.*, 2002[15])]?

II. The solution? What if lawyers did other things?

To the extent that legal education is a combination of a general education in ways of thinking and analyzing problems (a little bit different in civil and common law countries) and more specialized knowledge (both in subject matter expertise and process expertise), a legal education might actually permit 'lawyers' to do a variety of tasks in society. I begin with some of the applications of legal knowledge I know from my own experience and study, and then turn to some other possible adaptations of legal knowledge for other use, and contrast this to how at least two other professions – business consulting and architecture – have adapted to changing economic conditions by diversifying, and reconstituting their services and markets. I conclude with some observations about how legal education might have to adapt for changing conceptions of what lawyers do.

As someone who began her own career as a poverty lawyer, seeking to deliver both individual justice to the underserved and to engage in social change (through law reform, litigation and through community organizing and organizational representation), it was not long before I saw the inefficacy of much social change litigation and adversarial advocacy. I will not here recount all of my personal history that led to a focus on changing the legal paradigm from one of litigation 'victory' to legal problem solving,[16] but these observations were not mine alone. Critiques of litigation in the United States began in the late 1970s and early 1980s from different sectors of the legal profession. As recounted, not uncontroversially, by many different sectors of the legal profession [Chief Justice Warren Burger of the United States Supreme Court (Burger, 1982), the consumer empowerment movement (Abel, 1982; Harrington, 1985), including deprofessionalization efforts (Schonholtz, 1985; Merry & Milner, 1993), scholars and practitioners seeking more creative and Pareto optimal solutions to complex problems (Raiffa, 1982; Fisher *et al.*, 2011) and more just or forgiving solutions to crime and victimization (Umbreit, 2000)], joined by those in economics, political science, game theory, business, labor and many other fields (Menkel-Meadow, 2000, 2009a),[17] arguments about both quantitative factors (too many cases clogging the system and making litigation too expensive and too time consuming) and qualitative factors (creating better solutions to problems), were used to suggest other ways for lawyers to work. From this critique the modern 'alternative' (now called 'appropriate') dispute resolution movement was born.[18] Even hard core social justice litigators, like Gary Bellow, were sometimes critical of the individual lawsuit (and litigation) as the best way to achieve social justice (Bellow, 1977). Cases might be won, including cases against governmental and private organizations and institutions, but adaptive officials or lawyers on the 'other side' would soon learn to circumvent legal rulings or change the rules themselves.

In the late 1970s and early 1980s, (some) consumer lawyers, family lawyers, employment and labor lawyers, commercial lawyers and, oddly enough, military and government lawyers began to focus on 'other' ways to use their legal skills. Labor law had always used mediation and arbitration as one form of dispute resolution (Menkel-Meadow, 2011a); family lawyers turned first to mediation, then to 'collaborative law' (Tesler, 2001); construction lawyers began to use 'partnering' agreements requiring pre-dispute meetings and mediation (Carr *et al.*, 1999); large-scale commercial lawyers moved toward more arbitration [especially in transnational disputes (Born, 2010)], then to mediation[19] and then to a series of hybrid processes, including mini-trials, med-arb and arb-med, summary jury trials and others (Menkel-Meadow *et al.*, 2011). The public sector followed with court-annexed ADR programs, including arbitration, mediation, early neutral evaluation and other hybrids, formally authorized and then sometimes required in both federal and state practice.[20] In the United States, the 'ADR' concept spread also to governmental decision making and policy formation, as trained facilitators managed complex rule and regulation drafting in 'negotiated rule-making' processes or 'reg-neg' (Harter, 1982) or what are now called 'consensus building processes' (Susskind *et al.*, 1999; but see Menkel-Meadow, 2011b). Even in the binary world of criminal justice (guilt/innocence; punishment or freedom) these new processes were harnessed to the reform seeking efforts of social workers, probation officers, creative judicial officials[21] and others who looked for 'restorative' justice to reintegrate offenders with their communities and to provide some restitution or emotional relief for victims (Menkel-Meadow, 2007a). This latter movement for restorative justice in criminal law also helped contribute both the theory and practice for the development of new processes and institutions in international law [including the new field of 'transitional justice' (Teitel, 2002) in post-conflict settings, both between and within countries].

These developments in the legal profession were accompanied by social theory considering such issues as democratic deliberation, public participation and policy decision making. Social theorists, such as Jürgen Habermas (1985), Stuart Hampshire (2000), Jon Elster (1995) and others, explored best and second-best processes for political decision making, with some (Hampshire) focused on adversarial, Anglo-American agonistic approaches, and others suggesting that other forms of process might be better or at least more 'robust' in arriving at good decisions, depending on the context and type of decision made (Elster, 1995; Menkel-Meadow, 2005b). Hampshire, in acknowledging that there is unlikely to be any universal agreement about the substantive good, suggested that human beings might agree on processes so that they could live together productively and make good decisions: "The skillful management of conflict is among the highest of human skills" (Hampshire, 2000, p. 35). Legal processes, including hearings, trials, negotiation, mediation and compromises, are seen as important in maintaining the social, political and, yes, moral health of societies with competing goals and diverse populations. This social theory has been harnessed to descriptions of different kinds of skills and processes that could be and have been used by lawyers, policy makers and others who craft solutions to legal, social and political problems.

The rapid movement to these new or reconfigured processes led to an outpouring of new skills training, initially conducted outside of the traditional law schools, offered to practitioners in a variety of continuing education (including within and by courts) or privately offered professional training programs. After a first generation of general skills training in mediation, arbitration and facilitation, the new field of 'dispute system design' was spawned around the development of the design of structured dispute resolution programs, both within institutions and in situations of iterated dispute or transaction management (Ury *et al.*, 1988; Feinberg, 2006; Menkel-Meadow, 2009b).[22] An even more specialized form of process expertise and institutional design in post-conflict dispute resolution has developed alongside this new 'profession' in international law (Stromseth *et al.*, 2006).

Efforts to document and report on the dimensions and market share of these new professions have been largely unsuccessful, in large part because so much dispute resolution (mediation, arbitration and hybrids) is conducted in the private sphere without any requirements for reporting to public agencies in the United States (Stipanowich, 2004).[23] Nevertheless we know that a vast number of cases filed in the American courts are settled through one of these processes, whether in the courts themselves (through mandatory settlement conferences, court-annexed mediation or arbitration programs) or through private processes.[24] We also know the use of these court-annexed and private processes is on the increase in the United Kingdom [Lord Woolf reforms in England and Wales (Lord Woolf, 1996; see also Goriely *et al.*, 2002)[25] and increased use in Scotland too], and now in Europe, as well, through the EU's Directive on Mediation (2008),[26] as well as in Australia (King *et al.*, 2009), Asia (Lee & Hwee, 2009) and South America

(Leathley, 2007). In the United States arbitration is now mandatory (and pre-emptive of litigation) in almost all consumer and employment disputes as pre-dispute assignment to arbitration is found in almost all contracts, and the practice has been sustained by the United States Supreme Court against virtually all constitutional and statutory challenges (Sternlight, 2002).[27] Most family courts (a matter of state, not federal law in the United States) require divorcing parents to attend mandatory mediation or conciliation programs.

As in the United States, there is much debate about whether mediation and other ADR processes really are being used successfully, whether there is lawyer resistance or client reluctance, or scholarly critique of the 'privatization of justice' (see, e.g., Genn, 2009), all while new laws, regulations, court pressures and the globalization of legal procedures push almost inexorably toward the increased use of these processes. One report in the United States projected that

> employment of arbitrators, mediators and conciliators is expected to grow faster than the average for all occupations through 2018. Many individuals and businesses try to avoid litigation, which can involve lengthy delays, high costs, unwanted publicity and ill will. Arbitration and other alternatives to litigation usually are faster, less expensive, and more conclusive, spurring demand for the services of arbitrators, mediators and conciliators. Demand will also continue to increase for arbitrators, mediators and conciliators because all jurisdictions now have some type of dispute resolution program. (BLS, 2010–2011)[28]

Within this 'newer' area of legal expertise there are at least ten new possible sites of work:

- court ADR (mediators, arbitrators, early neutral evaluators, court counselors and administrators);
- private mediation, arbitration and other forms of dispute resolution;
- mass claim management (at both decision-making and facilitative layers, as well as in more conventional representation and advocacy);
- drafting and management of contract-based mandatory dispute programs;
- community forms of ADR (mediation and community organizing and empowerment);
- internal organizational dispute resolution (ombuds and related processes in both governmental and private organizations);
- government policy formation in facilitated consensus-building procedures;
- international diplomacy in both public and private negotiations for treaties, trade agreements and private commercial dealings;
- participation in less adversarial criminal processes at both domestic and international levels (Victim–Offender Mediation, local peacekeeping, international tribunals and commissions); and
- a variety of 'preventative' dispute resolution processes:

  - such as construction partnership;
  - dispute system design; and

○ transactional mediation.

These 'newer' forms of dispute resolution lawyering work use both conventional litigation, dispute-based modalities of thinking and structuring work, but they also use different approaches – not just to 'win' a case for a client, but to effectuate the client's goals, through the recognition of needs and interests of others who work with one's clients, and in some cases, even the concept of 'client' is different than in the conventional legal paradigm. Non-partisan legal problem solving may not always involve conventional representation [remember the "lawyer for the situation" (Hazard, 1978)].[29] Lawyers as dispute resolution professionals or peacemakers may work within different conceptual mind-sets as well as in different work locations, e.g. NGO's (neither governmental nor profit-based work settings with very different programmatic and organizational goals).

New forms of ADR and dispute resolution practice are also located within the counseling parts of the legal profession. Dispute system designers (a now fancy name for what many lawyers have done for decades) advise clients with iterated disputes (both within their organizations, e.g. employment disputes and outside of their organizations with clients, vendors, suppliers, etc.) about how to develop internal dispute resolution programs or more recently 'preventative' processes and measures for workplace relations, ethics, communication and problem solving. Some governmental and private organizations use ombuds, mediator offices, peer counselors, hotlines, as well as more formal grievance processes to handle, prevent, manage and, when necessary, resolve such disputes. Lawyers and legal adjuncts provide education and training in conflict resolution and handling, both internally within organizations and more conventionally to clients as outside counsel.

International organizations, such as the UN, World Bank, IMF, International Red Cross and others, are often not subject to traditional national or international law (because of the unique legal status of international organizations), for resolution of both internal and external disputes and thus have created their own 'justice' systems.[30] These dispute systems may be motivated by other values than litigation vindication – preventative resolution or management to insure healthy workplaces, and efficient communication of systemic issues within the organization (Sturm & Gadlin, 2007), though these processes are not without their critics as well (Edelman *et al.*, 1993).

In order to design such processes, lawyers will have to expand their knowledge of legal concepts and processes beyond those more commonly taught in law schools to include problem-solving strategies, economics, organizational development and sociology, decision making, human resources management, psychology and a variety of other topics more often taught in business management or public policy programs. Goals of such organizations may be different depending on whether they are public, private, hybrid or international in scope and purpose. Clearly, there is no single paradigm of the lawyer's work that describes what this work entails.

At the international level, without any accurate accounting of which I am aware, dispute resolution in both its formal (the many new international tribunals which have been created in the last few decades[31]) and more informal fora [truth and reconciliation commissions, hybrid national courts for past atrocities, use of local indigenous processes such as *gacaca* in Rwanda (Bolocan, 2004)] have produced literally thousands of new legal jobs in an increasingly denationalized form of lawyering (Menkel-Meadow, 2011c). As William Twining has so eloquently argued, globalization of law can mean both 'transnational' legal systems or 'sub-national' or more local legal systems (Twining, 2009), leading to a greater complexity of legal pluralism, both in substantive law and processual law, all of which may require new kinds of 'lawyers' or legal professionals or 'translators' at many different layers of law and legal institutions.[32]

III. Implications for legal education

The key ideas in these new forms of 'lawyering' are that they operate with different concepts and modalities. While legal knowledge in the form of substantive legal knowledge, including laws, rights and regulations, as well as procedural knowledge, along with legal interpretation techniques and theories, are still important, this legal knowledge must be combined with a range of other substantive and processual forms of knowledge. Lawyers, until clinical education made some impact, have never been well trained in people management and communication skills though legal services are often personal services. Institutional design instruction has been very limited with now constitutionalized discussions of legal theory, jurisprudence and separation of powers, where those who work in the private sector might better be trained in organizational development, interpersonal relations and management strategies.

Decision making, problem solving and judgment, often implicit in the legal curriculum, must now be made more explicit, as they have been with a few new textbooks (Jackson *et al.*, 2010; Brest & Krieger, 2011) and teaching materials, and in some schools, with new courses.[33] Some diversification of law school types and teaching within law schools might be well advised for 'tracks' of emphasis to focus on different models of lawyering – public and private lawyering, dispute or litigation-based, problem solving, transactional, counseling, creative (start-ups, intellectual property, organizational design and form), social and community service, as well as others, to better reflect the diverse sites in which some legal knowledge might be of use.

A basic grounding (say one or two years) in basic legal knowledge (public and private law, legal reasoning, jurisprudence, legal history), legal ethics and legal skills (research, writing, communication, interviewing, counseling, planning, negotiation, drafting, etc.) might then lead to more specialized and interdisciplinary advanced work including business- or socially-based subjects (see, e.g., Menkel-Meadow, 1999, 2007b).[34] Or, Americans could move to a more generalized first degree in law (as is common in most parts of the world), with more specialized training and different subjects in graduate law programs [as is happening with the increasingly globalized and specialized LLM (Acello, 2012)].[35]

Law schools could choose either to integrate complex intellectual and substantive learning with skills needed for the practice of law (and those skills might vary depending on what kind of law practice[36]) or law schools might choose (like medical schools) to separate the foundational intellectual, conceptual and substantive study from the more practical 'applied' or clinical problem-solving skills in service to clients. Different schools might make different choices as some have already tried to do with shortened programs (Michigan and the University of Dayton's two-and-a-half-year programs, Southwestern's intensive two-year program) or longer programs (joint degree programs with business and policy schools or joint graduate programs in other substantive fields for those more inclined to academic or more substantively specialized work, e.g. science/technology and the law).

In legal education the debate about whether there is a 'core' all must study ('thinking like a lawyer' in private and public law subjects) or whether legal education can be segmented at earlier stages of study has been with us since law study first began at the University of Bologna centuries ago. The debate continues on many continents now as legal educators consider whether to diversify forms of legal education (digital, distance, 'transsystemic' or transnational, general, more specialized) or 'converge' on a more uniform American-graduate school model of legal education, which assumes a core course of study [in both method (Socratic and clinical) and substance (required courses at least in the first year)] for all who call themselves lawyers. While some continue to believe in the importance of the 'core' aspects of 'thinking' (or 'behaving') like a lawyer as a jurisprudential or 'law-jobs' (Llewellyn, 1930) matter, others are ready to concede that lawyers might be trained in a variety of different ways. Others might think that a general education might be particularly important where lawyers need the flexibility to 're-train' and move from one specialty to another over a life time of economic, technological and social change.

IV. Comparing legal work with other professions: entrepreneurship, new problem solving, and adaptations in professional practice

Here I briefly explore how two other professions, one newer profession (business consulting) and an older one (architecture), have or are beginning to adapt professional ideas, service delivery and forms of practice to changes in economics, demographics, legal environments and other social changes.

In a recent history of the development of the modern business consulting profession, Christopher McKenna describes the far more flexible and adaptive model of the 'new' business consultant with several different strands of expertise (McKenna, 2006). Like lawyers, business consultants are 'knowledge brokers'. Like lawyers, there is a tension in the profession of management consulting about whether to husband knowledge and skills loyally within a single institution (the law firm, the large company, the particular governmental agency, the advocacy organization or 'cause') or whether to build and trade on expertise by moving around and sharing 'accumulated' knowledge and best practices. With different rules about confidentiality, but perhaps stronger market incentives to compete and/or replicate what others do, business consultants in the twentieth century emerged from several different traditions – auditing, financial services, capital markets and investments, economic forecasting and advising, and computer technology (Arthur Andersen).

McKenna chronicles different conceptual goals of several different founders of the field including James McKinsey, Martin Bower, Edwin Booz, George

Armstrong, Thomas Watson and others, and illustrates their different adaptations to different regulatory conditions from the 1930s onwards (Glass-Steagall Banking Act of 1933; Securities Act of 1933 to Sarbanes-Oxley and more recent fluctuations in regulation and deregulation of market-based enterprises). Business consulting was originally born out of the separation of banking from investing and separation of the older accounting profession from internal business consulting, but as prescient entrepreneurs left big corporations to trade on their own knowledge of best practices, organizational design and decision strategies for diversification, mergers, acquisitions and divestment strategies, their accumulated knowledge and ability to move from one organization to another permitted an 'outside' consultancy practice to emerge.

While McKenna and other business historians note that the brokering of information by outsiders often resulted in a remarkable similarity in management strategies both across and within industries, organizational change was easier to design and implement with the advice of skilled outside experts. Thus, both legal developments (changes in the regulatory climate) and economic forces (and market incentives) have produced a greater flexibility and ability to change paradigms, concepts and practices. Of course, current critiques (including McKenna's) of management consulting is that there can be 'too quick' shifts of paradigms with bandwagon effects [Six Sigma (Pande & Holpp, 2001), Seven Habits (Covey, 1989), Corporate Excellence (Peters & Waterman, 1982)] that can produce such failures as Enron (Jeffrey Skilling was a 'master' at business consulting and 'out of the box thinking') and group think and corporate conformity. The Enron scandal brought a quick end to the Andersen firm which had so skillfully (pun absolutely intended) recombined business consulting with audit functions after the regulatory climate changed.

At the peak of the economic boom, lawyers actually feared competition from the consulting industry and attempted regulation of the most creative efforts to add legal consulting to the ever-expanding portfolio of multi-national business consulting firms which had begun to offer 'one stop shopping' for consulting services for the world's largest companies.[37] The current economic recession seems to have (temporarily) dampened that effort[38] but the adaptability of the business consulting industry is still instructive for the more troubled and slower-to-adapt legal profession. Specialization and difference of strategies actually helped to expand the market of business consultants as some, using their prior expertise (e.g. engineer Arthur Little), went 'deep' into consulting with one kind of industry; others (accountants) chose to accumulate more general knowledge and instead develop consulting themes around organizational structures, management protocols and investment strategies, including compliance consulting (which lawyers took up as a specialty after business consultants). A third strand of consulting focused on government contracting, leading to a whole segment of the profession anchored to 'the beltway bandits', consultants to federal agencies in Washington, DC (remarkably resilient, even in times of economic downturns). Indeed, it could be said that the business consulting profession 'invented' the public–private partnerships of the 1980s and 1990s as deregulation allowed combinations of organizations to take on many of the projects of the state, thereby assuring a relatively stable, if not growing source of business (Guttman & Wilner, 1976).[39] Other business consultants specialized in the non-profit (hospitals, NGOs, universities and religious, cultural, and charitable organizations) sector, with a variety of different 'tax-exempt' issues.

When the American market for business consulting seemed somewhat 'saturated' in the 1970s and 1980s, the 'profession' was exported to Europe and Asia (and American business schools saw a boom in foreign MBA students, demonstrating the symbiotic but ultimately complex, relationship between professional schools' need for tuition revenue and the danger of elimination of one market source for professional work).[40]

Thus, market conditions affected different industries differentially, but those in business consulting actually could profit from change in either direction. Though some suggest that lawyers can do the same (transfer from 'm and a' to bankruptcy and corporate reorganizations) there has been less evidence of this where large firms try to keep lawyers from all parts of the specialties in their ranks. Litigation patterns (and moves to cheaper in-house counsel from more expensive firm lawyers) seem to be highly correlated with economic cycles. As lawyers as corporate counselors, compliance monitors, tax advisers and now organizational and investment strategists (especially with that all powerful JD–MBA joint degree[41]) compete with management consultants (with complex internal ethical rules and discipline muddying the waters) it remains to be seen who will win the competition for new forms of complex corporate and organizational work, but my money is on the more flexible, adaptive and entrepreneurial business consultants.[42] In some countries (first Australia, now the UK) restrictions on non-lawyer investments in law firms have been lifted so that the 'market forces' of capital investments can be brought into law firms to finance and perhaps spur change. How much 'multi-disciplinary' practice will emerge remains unknown. Multi-national business models applied to lawyering have brought us the modern development of 'outsourcing' legal services to India, another form of business judgment that threatens American (but grows Indian) legal employment (Ballakrishnen, 2012).

Adapting to these developments in more specialized forms of business consulting, business schools have modified their curricula more often and more flexibly than law schools. Pioneering such innovations as shortened 'Executive MBA' degrees and courses held in international or field-specific locations, most business schools now offer courses of varied (not only semester, year or quarterly) schedules, cooperative work by students, co-taught courses, problem-oriented courses and even a 'case method' first used at Harvard Business School that attempts to make business education rigorous and practical decision-based at the same time. Business schools rarely 'require' as large a core curriculum as law (or medicine), recognizing that a 'business' discipline actually requires many different kinds of specialized expertise. Though some might attribute this to the lack of a core discipline, and others suggest that business education has never required a license or formal schooling, the better business schools have been good 'incubators' of both new ideas for business management and for creating social networks. Perhaps because business is by definition 'entrepreneurial', so has business education been more entrepreneurial or adaptive to change.

As another point of contrast, a new movement in the older profession of architecture has attempted to reframe the 'doing' of architecture by renaming the field as one of 'spatial agency' (Awan *et al.*, 2011; http://www.spatialagency.net). By reconceiving the purpose of designing the use of physical space to include redesign of old spaces, to encourage more collaboration between 'professional designers' and 'users' of space, to solve problems of density in new urbanization, increased demographic diversification of common users and relations of space to each other (habitation, food production and storage, childcare), and to work together to 'make policy, as well as stuff', a world-wide collaborative of architects and planners, working through a website to share ideas and projects, has attempted to reframe the work of its 'profession'. Having posted a number of actual projects and designs for new and old spaces and suggestions for physical space issues, the 'group' now seeks to document its work, through websites, books and shared projects to expand the conception of what it means to be an architect or planner. Though this very politicized reconception of a profession broadens the conception of what it means to be an architect, it also seeks some 'deprofessionalization' of its expertise (a move that lawyers know well from the 1960s/1970s de-legalization movement in the early days of consumer activism) to increase participation by those professionally trained and those with other skills and experiences, as well as end users of the physical space and designs – those who are 'socially embedded in the built (or non-built) environment'.

As the present economic recession has decreased new building (in some, but not all parts of the world), the need for redesign of old spaces to solve new physical, social and economic problems has increased the possibilities of 'new' forms of architecture and design solutions. In a discipline that does require some licensing and credentialing, as well as training and education, new institutions and forms of education and collaboration have been designed to foster this kind of 'collaborative' work in the design field.

Some of the younger generation of lawyers and recent graduates have begun some forms of new entrepreneurial activity to launch new sectors of legal or quasi-legal practice. There are the new 'social entrepreneurs' who offer legal services for start-ups, multi-national enterprises, new media and new 'micro-enterprises', hoping to combine profitable work with social good (Bornstein, 2007).

At the level of community lawyering for the underserved population, new ideas to create small new 'incubator' law firms loosely linked across the country with like-minded practitioners in different regions in contiguous specialties (e.g. immigration, family relations, criminal law, small business, social welfare, civil rights, consumer law, rights advocacy and community legal education) are emerging.[43] Some of the work to create and support new incubator community law practices is located within law schools (clinics, externships, mandated skills training) and others depend on fellowships from large law firms or other private sources or foundations, committed individuals and other institutions. The Open Society Institute in the United States, for example, has supported a wide variety of innovative lawyering projects, some focused on individual service with social change models and others focused on new forms of legal services delivery. If 'necessity is the mother of invention', in this case there are two potentially overlapping 'necessities' – service for the underserved desperately needing legal services and lawyers desperately seeking gainful and useful employment. Though others have suggested that older, now retired and very skilled lawyers might usefully serve the underserved (Galanter, 1999), there is little evidence that this has occurred or fully satisfied the needs of the underserved. But the 'old and in the way' might both train and facilitate entrance into the profession of the 'new with no place to go'.

Enterprising students and young lawyers seek training for themselves and new sets of clients to explore other ways to organize for legal and social benefits and to work together. NIMBY land disputes (not in my backyard) still exist and may be pursued through conventional lawsuits, but communities and profit-seekers also get together more often to explore shared interests of job creation, tax revenues, provision of social services and meeting of community needs through processes that are more collaborative (as in 'spatial agency' architecture) (Podziba, 2012). Mass disasters (Katrina, BP Spill, September 11) create needs for faster-than-the-legal-system can provide solutions and creative legal actors have been active in pursuing a variety of new ways to deal with those needs. 'New' lawyers have been instrumental in mediating all sorts of workplace reorganizations, including immigrant day labor sites and collaborative collective bargaining processes, in both union and non-union settings, especially in times of reduction in force recessions (Menkel-Meadow, 2011a) and organizational dispute resolution. Creation of new 'legal intelligence' and expert systems, such as the creation of legal computer programs, is not totally new in law but more interactive applications (as in case settlements, consumer dispute resolution, etc.) permit some computer-assisted legal information to be disseminated to solve both individual and group legal issues.

All of this requires new paradigms of legal thought and training, as well as practice, but by looking for new solutions to difficult social and legal problems in these troubled times, there may be opportunities for new sites of legal work. If architects are 'spatial agents', my colleague Sameer Ashar says lawyers should conceive of themselves as 'relational agents', or as we dispute resolution theorists like to call ourselves, 'social and legal relationship engineers' or 'process architects' (pick your own favorite comparative professional metaphor!).

V. Policy implications and some concluding thoughts

Here are some of my observations about the relationship of legal knowledge, legal paradigms and legal education to the question about whether we have too many lawyers. First, law study may be an entry 'portal' into a large number of other kinds of work – business, politics (either as a candidate or in the new profession of political consulting), policy work, government (non- or quasi-legal work), NGO advocacy in both legal and non-legal settings, community, labor or other interest group organizing work,[44] creative work (start-ups of many kinds, including scientific, educational, economic and entertainment), real estate work, education (teaching others about the law, whether lay people or other law students), deal making and social entrepreneurship, and peace work (whether legal mediation or non-legal international or domestic). With some knowledge of the law all of these jobs and others we cannot even imagine at the moment are likely to be performed with a better sense of justice, equity, logic and rule-based accountability.[45]

Second, if there are 'too' many or just 'many' lawyers, maybe some reallocation might actually provide for some better distribution of lawyers to those who are currently underserved. If the legal profession were subject to regular market forces, an oversupply of lawyers should lead to a lowering of price and to reallocation of services. How market efficient and sensitive the legal profession is continues to elude many of us, though judging from the radio advertising I am hearing in my community (the greater Los Angeles–Orange County area) there are price flexibility and new services (mortgage renegotiation) being offered to the general public. It is probably time for a new study of small firm practice and adjustments to the current economic climate in a variety of different legal markets. The economic recession may not just eliminate jobs, it might restructure them and shift them to other sectors.

Third, perhaps if 'too' many lawyers are trained in the same way there might be some competition or reconfiguration of how legal education is delivered. Though I am a bit of a skeptic on this front as a faculty member of a brand new law school that promised to be different and is rapidly conforming to a conventional American 'elite' and conformist model, some schools are offering more diversified legal education with the hope of making more 'practice-ready' lawyers or training lawyers to do different things. Perhaps it is time to return to the ill-fated Reed Report on legal education (Reed, 1921) and recognize that American legal education might be diversified, sectored and specialized (Tamanaha, 2012).

Fourth, some might use law study to change the way we think about the world – conventionally arguing for new or different laws, or, as has been my hope, to rethink law school as a school for social, political, economic and legal problem solving where, in the words of my 'other' law school (Georgetown), "law is the means, justice is the end".[46] Entrepreneurial (socially, legally and economically) new lawyers might just adapt, reconfigure and reconceive the work that lawyers do and see that there is more that people with legal education can do, not just for personal gain, but for the global society in which we live. With other ways to practice law (more conflict resolution, more diversity of the individual and organizational client base, with different forms of practice, and more sites and locations of legal issues, some policy-based, some law-making, some transactional, some dispute resolving), there should be both more and different work for those who call themselves lawyers. The question then might be, not 'are there too many lawyers?', but are lawyers being socially productive and what are they doing? There is no one 'right' way to practice law, as there most certainly is no one way to achieve social justice (Sen, 2009). If clients were asked what they wanted lawyers for would we have different answers to the question of whether there are too many lawyers and what they should do with their legal knowledge?

Acknowledgements

Thanks go to Sameer Ashar, Bryant Garth, Robert Meadow, Peter Reilly and Carole Silver for comments and suggestions on this paper and Michael DeShong for research assistance. Thanks also to Eyal Katvan, Carol Silver and Neta Ziv for organizing the conference on "Too Many Lawyers" at Onati and to the other conference participants for stimulating papers and discussions about these issues across many different legal systems and cultures.

Notes

[1] Alexis de Tocqueville's claim that lawyers in America (as the social 'aristocracy') mediated class conflict and conflict between the people and the government and served to ensure useful and productive management of conflict, while raising important issues of critique of the polity and its governance, through litigation and statesmanship (1835, Ch. XVI).

[2] For one view, Stephen P. Magee argues that lawyers are rent seekers and foster too many lawsuits and too much inefficient regulation, preventing more "positive facilitative effects" for a less regulated and litigated about economy.

[3] David McQuoid-Mason notes that these measures are all relative as South Africa's per capita ratio is much higher than other nations in Africa, e.g. Kenya where the ratio is 1:10,000.

[4] Although the lawsuit against New York Law School was recently dismissed (Lattman, 2012), other suits remain pending against such schools as Thomas Jefferson, University of San Francisco and Southwestern Law School (all of these in California).

[5] John Heinz and Edward Laumann have demonstrated two non-substitutionary 'hemispheres' of the bar – lawyers serving corporate interests and those serving individuals (Heinz & Laumann, 1994).

[6] Scholars have demonstrated that lawyers are 'stickily' allocated to their work by their own choices and market forces; lawyers who train to be (and are paid accordingly) sophisticated corporate lawyers who specialize in highly complex matters are not likely to be 'reallocated' to different tasks at different rates of pay – many would prefer to be under- or unemployed than shift work location, both for economic and status-based reasons (see, e.g., Hadfield, 2000).

[7] Other scholars have reported on the rapid influx into the profession in the United States of returning veterans, first from WWII and then from Viet Nam (see, e.g., Morgan, 2010).

[8] The addition of new substantive claims for consumer rights, anti-discrimination laws, human rights, social, political, economic, racial, gender and other forms of equality and equity were also accompanied by claims for greater diversification of the profession so that claimants might have lawyers who literally 'felt' and represented their 'pain' and experience.

[9] Carroll Seron found women more likely to be in solo or part-time, 'local' work.

[10] There might even be a new market for legal education in the United States for law training for those who specifically don't want to be lawyers – there are a few undergraduate programs in 'law and society' or criminology now – but one could imagine a graduate school of law study intended for those who do not want to 'practice' law but want to know about law to enter government, public policy, administration, journalism or business careers.

[11] I am personally skeptical of these claims. Almost any kind of work (regardless of how it is compensated), is better performed by those with education [ask your local waiter or barista (as opposed to barrister) if you are a middle-class well-educated person].

[12] This is Richard Abel's long-standing argument about "the professional project" as being one of market control.

[13] These are reported as 'pre-recession' (2008) figures. The ABA report of law school placement for 2011 by law school is even more dismal. My top-ranking law school (Georgetown) had a placement rate of just over 60% for its 2011 graduates. See ABA Report of 2011 Law Placement, available at: www.taxlawblog.com.

[14] For earlier arguments that lawyers can and should be efficient 'transaction cost engineers' and productive transaction managers, see for example Gilson (1984) and Gilson and Mnookin (1994, 1995), Mnookin *et al.* (2000) and Peppet (2004).

[15] Howard Gardner, Mihaly Csiksentmihali and William Damon (2002) compare the ethically integrated profession of genetics with the ethically questionable profession of modern journalism where profit and personal ego now dominate other professional goals of information gathering and dissemination. Consider where the legal profession belongs in this taxonomy.

[16] For the scholarly versions and skills imperatives of my early work, see Menkel-Meadow (1983, 1984b).

[17] In the cited articles, I provide fuller descriptions of both the legal concepts and contributions of non-legal scholars to the origins of the modern ADR movement.

[18] For a more complete recount of this history, see Menkel-Meadow (2005a).

[19] The Center for Public Resources, founded in 1979, became a think tank and promoter of ADR for use in commercial large-scale disputing and eventually created and managed not only new processes, but developed industry protocols for dispute resolution in a variety of different substantive businesses and fields, e.g. oil and gas, employment, franchising, construction, banking, health, etc.

[20] See, e.g., Civil Justice Reform Act (1990); Administrative Dispute Resolution Act (1990, 1996); and Alternative Dispute Resolution Act (1998).

[21] For example, Justice Judith Kaye, who, in New York, became a proponent of problem-solving courts designed to treat and help with the recovery of drug users, sex workers, and families in drug, vice and specialized family courts (see, e.g., Kaye, 1997; Berman & Feinblatt, 2005).

[22] Two new legal texts for law school teaching are now in development for this field, by Rogers, Bordone, Sander and McEwen (Wolters Kluwer, 2013) and by Bingham, Martinez and Smith (Oxford, forthcoming).

[23] Thomas Stipanowich sought to report on statistics and usage of mediation and arbitration processes in public settings (courts) and private settings (reporting on some limited data available from the American Arbitration Association and similar organizations, and reporting on some few studies of ADR usage in both settings). Like Professor Stipanowich, many of us in the ADR field have tried to get access to a variety of data sources on ADR usage. Over ten years ago I served on the Advisory Board of a major national research institution seeking to document the effects of the 'privatization' of the judiciary, as increasing numbers of judges left the bench for more lucrative private mediation and arbitration positions. JAMS (Judicial Mediation and Arbitration Services), one of the leading private ADR providers in the United States (originally founded by a retiring California state judge) refused to release any data on their case load, third party neutral fees, etc. claiming that what their clients most valued was 'private' dispute resolution. [In California, litigants can use 'rent-a-judges' who are former judges who may render (arbitral) decisions with the full force of law that even includes an appellate process, but promises privacy (see California Code of Civil Procedure §§638–645; see also Hadfield, 2004; Menkel-Meadow, 2010).]

[24] While one often hears that only 2% of all cases filed are actually tried, therefore over 90% of cases are settled in some fashion, we know that actually the settlement rate is much lower. Many cases (perhaps as much as another 20–30% of cases) are terminated in ways other than full adjudication (motions or summary judgments) or negotiated or mediated settlement (see Kritzer, 1986; Hadfield, 2004).

[25] New studies in the UK reveal that the Woolf reforms have actually 'front-loaded' and increased expenses in the early stages of civil litigation (Lord Justice Jackson, 2010).

[26] Some have opined that the use of mediation in mandatory settings might be a violation of Article 6 of the European Convention on Human Rights. See Jacqueline Nolan-Haley (2012) discussing *Halsey v. Milton Keynes General NHS Trust* (2004) (see also de Hoon & Verbeck, 2011).

[27] See most recently *AT&T Mobility v. Concepcion* (2011).

[28] The United States Bureau of Labor Statistics projected a 14% growth rate from 2008 to 2018 in the employment of arbitrators, mediators and conciliators.

[29] Geoffrey Hazard discusses Louis Brandeis' work in 'representation' of both creditors and debtors in bankruptcy.

[30] These international organizations increasingly employ individuals with multi-national legal education credentials and experience, as well as non-lawyers. This is an especially good employment site for those without national bar licensure.

[31] For example, International Criminal Court for Former Yugoslavia, Rwanda, International Criminal Court, the Dispute Settlement Body – Appellate of the World Trade Organization, the European Court of Justice, the European Court of Human Rights, the Inter-American Court of Human Rights, The Tribunal(s) of the Law of the Sea, not to mention the expansion of the private international arbitral tribunals which administer the private international civil justice system (the ICC, the LCIA, CIETAC, the Cairo Arbitration Tribunal, etc.) (Dezalay & Garth, 1996; see, e.g., also Ahdieh, 2004; Berman, 2007).

[32] With different kinds of legal educations, see e.g. Strauss (2006).

[33] For example, Harvard's first year Problem Solving Workshop, a prior Harvard course in Analytic Methods for Lawyers, involving instruction in statistics, accounting, asset valuation, economics, game theory and decision making.

[34] Edward Rubin, as a new Dean, sought, unsuccessfully, to have Vanderbilt Law School reconfigured with two tracks – one for public lawyers and the other for private-business market-based lawyers with virtually two different curricula.

[35] In the last few years I have taught specialized courses in International Dispute Resolution, Consensus Building, Conflict Resolution and Mediation, and Dispute System Design in law schools (some open to other kinds of students who are not lawyers) in Australia, Singapore, the UK, Israel, Switzerland, Central America, South America (Argentina, Paraguay and Brazil), China and Canada; this is not counting several programs run by American law schools or other sponsoring agencies abroad but which include many American students within their regular legal studies programs.

[36] Many American law schools now tout their ability to train 'practice-ready' graduates, but what kind of practice may actually remain stratified (elite schools to corporate law firms and public interest; local schools to small firms, prosecutor or government offices) or at least specialized. One strategy for legal education marketing in this time of economic uncertainty for lawyers is law schools explicitly advertising for specialized practice areas. Others proclaim the rigor and excellence of their general legal education.

[37] My law school devoted a large part of its annual retreat one year to discussing the impact of this growing 'multi-disciplinary practice' on the job market and the legal education of our students. At the same time, the American Bar Association scurried to make rules prohibiting some aspects of multi-disciplinary practice to prevent even more competition for lawyers by accountants and business consultants, just another stage in the professional monopolization project. In England some of these issues had appeared earlier in competition for conveyancing work and the slow removal of the distinction between barristers and solicitors for rights of audience in courts.

[38] And post-Enron legislation in the United States now formally restricts certain combinations of services under one roof.

[39] Called by some 'the shadow government'.

[40] Legal education may be going through a similar process as many law schools (especially the bigger and more prestigious ones, like Harvard and my Georgetown home) derive revenue from increasingly large foreign LLM classes, but which may diminish the need for American lawyers abroad or those doing multi-national work.

[41] One suggested solution to the 'are there too many lawyers' problem, of course, is to suggest more specialized education (law and engineering, law and business, law and planning) through joint or dual degrees or, as is emerging in countries where law is a first degree, more secondary legal degrees with greater specialization. I do not know of any studies yet documenting whether second or specialized degrees in fact enhance employment possibilities.

[42] Other readers of this paper have reminded me of the resiliency of lawyers to invent new forms of legal actions ('big' litigation for 'big' law firms, new causes of action for public interest and now human rights lawyers) and new partnerships, perhaps with business consultants and others, to continue to provide and expand legal services in new domains. Lawyers, like business consultants, have been highly adaptable to new market conditions, often creating their own new services and markets. And remember, of course, lawyers dominate many legislatures so their ability to create new laws and new employment remains strong.

[43] Such incubator ideas have emerged at CUNY (Community Resource Network, New York) and my own new (University of California, Irvine) law school (see, e.g., Boniwell & Rosenberg, 2012), as a consortium of law schools seeks to expand this network. One of my students is active in creating a national website called Just Leap (Justice Through Legal Entrepreneurship and Access to Partnering), which hopes to digitally link experienced lawyers with younger ones for mentoring, advising and collaboration on cases, focusing on sharing resources, knowledge, training and advice, with the hope of adding 'new blood' in groups of young lawyers to serve those who need access to legal services. Designers of the website hope to establish 'crowd-sourcing' forms of information sharing and partnerships with older lawyers and younger lawyers forming start-ups in their communities, not unlike some of the efforts in the Spatial Agency website. Thank you Edgar Aguilosocho for your groundbreaking work. Washington and Lee Law School in Virginia has begun an innovative program in which third-year students all serve in yearlong clinics, with mandated skills training to prepare students for practice, now called 'practice-ready' law graduates.

[44] Remember President Obama began as a community organizer in Chicago before he went to law school, worked as a civil rights lawyer and then ran for office.

[45] Note I said 'likely to be' not are .... Many lawyers and many with legal education do not necessarily perform their work admirably or with logic and justice, just because they have a legal education.

[46] Quotation on Law Library building, attributed to law student, but mostly likely derived from German legal jurisprudent, Rudolf von Jhering's Der Zweck im Recht (Law as the Means, 1913).

References

Abel, R (Ed.) (1982) *The Politics of Informal Justice, Vol. 1: The American Experience* (New York, Academic Press).

Abel, R. (1985) Law without politics: legal aid under advanced capitalism, *UCLA Law Review*, 32, pp. 474–642.

Abel, R. (1988) *The Legal Profession in England and Wales* (Oxford, Blackwell).

Abel, R. (1989) *American Lawyers* (New York, Oxford University Press).

Abel, R. (2003) *English Lawyers Between Market and State: The Politics of Professionalism* (Oxford, Oxford University Press).

Acello, R. (2012) The business of law: are LLM's losing?, *American Bar Association Journal*, April, pp. 28–29.

Ahdieh, R. (2004) Between dialogue and decree: international review of national courts, *New York University Law Review*, 79, pp. 2029–2163.

American Bar Association (ABA) (1994) *Legal Needs and Civil Justice: A Survey of Americans: Major Findings from the Comprehensive Legal Needs Study* (Consortium on Legal Services and the Public, ABA).

American Bar Association (ABA) (2008) *Data* (Bureau of Labor Statistics).

Anziska, D. (2012) *Law School Litigation*. Available at: http://www.anziskalaw.com, accessed 22 May 2012.

Awan, N., Schneider, T. & Till, J. (2011) *Spatial Agency: Other Ways of Doing Architecture* (London, Routledge Press).

Ballakrishnen, S. (2012) *I Love My American Job: Professional Prestige and the Western Halo Effect*, paper prepared for Oñati Workshop: Too Many Lawyers? Facts, Reasons, Consequences and Solutions, 19–20 April.

Barak-Erez, D., Katvan, E. & Rostain, T. (2011) Workshop Proposal: Too Many Lawyers? Fact, Reasons, Consequences and Solutions, Onati Institute for Socio-legal Studies.

Bellow, G. (1977) Turning solutions into problems: the legal aid experience, *NLADA Briefcase*, 34(4).

Berman, G. & Feinblatt, J. (2005) *Good Courts: The Case for Problem-Solving Justice* (New York, New Press).

Berman, P.S. (2007) Global legal pluralism, *Southern California Law Review*, 80, pp. 1155–1237.

Bolocan, M.G. (2004) Rwandan Gacaca: an experiment in transitional justice, *Journal of Dispute Resolution*, pp. 355–400.

Boniwell, J. & Rosenberg, E. (2012) *Closing the Justice Gap: Creating and Supporting Community Lawyers*, student paper.
Born, G. (2010) *International Arbitration: Cases and Materials* (New York, Aspen Publishers).
Bornstein, D. (2007) *How to Change the World: Social Entrepreneurs and the Power of New Ideas* (Oxford, Oxford University Press).
Brennan, D. (2012) The Legal Aid Bill will enable multinationals to exploit the poor, *The Guardian*, 26 March.
Brest, P. & Krieger, L. (2011) *Problem Solving, Decision Making, and Professional Judgment: A Guide for Lawyers and Policy Makers* (Oxford, Oxford University Press).
Bureau of Labor Statistics (2010–2011) *Occupation Outlook Handbook: Judges, Magistrates and Other Judicial Workers*. Available at: http://www.bls.gov/oco/ocos272.htm.
Burger, W. (1982) Isn't there a better way?, *American Bar Association Journal*, 68, pp. 274–277.
Cappelletti, M. & Garth, B. (1979) *Access to Justice* (Alphan aan den Rijn, Sijthoff and Noordhoff).
Carr, F. *et al.* (1999) *Partnering in Construction: A Practical Guide to Project Success* (Chicago, IL, ABA Publishing).
Chan, K.-W. (2012) *Who Controls the Size of the Legal Profession in Japan?*, paper prepared for Oñati Workshop: Too Many Lawyers? Facts, Reasons, Consequences and Solutions, 19–20 April.
Cohen, I.G. (2013) Rationing legal services, *Journal of Legal Analysis*, 5, p. 221.
Covey, S. (1989) *The Seven Habits of Highly Effective People* (New York, Free Press).
Curran, B. (1977) *The Legal Needs of the Public: The Final Report of a National Survey* (Chicago, IL, ABA).
Dezalay, Y. & Garth, B. (1996) *Dealing in Virtue: International Commercial Arbitration and the Construction of a Transnational Legal Order* (Chicago, IL, University of Chicago Press).
Edelman, L., Erlanger, H. & Lande, J. (1993) Internal dispute resolution: the transformation of civil rights in the workplace, *Law and Society Review*, 27, pp. 497–534.
Elster, J. (1995) Strategic uses of argument, in: K. Arrow *et al.* (Eds.) *Barriers to Conflict Resolution* (New York, W.W. Norton & Company), pp. 236–257.
Feinberg, K. (2006) *What Is Life Worth? The Unprecedented Effort to Compensate the Victims of 9/11* (Cambridge, MA, PublicAffairs).
Felstiner, W., Abel, R. & Sarat, A. (1981) The emergence and transformation of disputes: naming, blaming, claiming …, *Law & Society Review*, 15, pp. 631–654.
Fisher, R., Ury, W. & Patton, B. (2011) *Getting to YES: Negotiating Agreement Without Giving In*, 3rd ed. (New York, Penguin Books).
Galanter, M. (1983) Reading the landscape of disputes: what we know, don't know (and think we know) about our allegedly contentious and litigious society, *UCLA Law Review*, 31, pp. 4–71.
Galanter, M. (1992) Law abounding: legislation around the North Atlantic, *The Modern Law Review*, 55, pp. 1–43.
Galanter, M. (1999) Old and in the way: the coming demographic transformation of the legal profession and its implications for the provision of legal services, *Wisconsin Law Review*, pp. 1081–1117.
Galanter, M. (2004) The vanishing trial: an examination of trials and related matters in federal and state courts, *Journal of Empirical Legal Studies*, 1, pp. 459–570.
Gans, M. (2012) Not a new problem: how the state of the legal profession has been secretly in decline for quite some time. Abstract available at: http://ssrn.com/abstract=2173144.
Gardner, H., Csikszentmihalhi, M. & Damon, W. (2002) *Good Work: When Excellence and Ethics Meet* (Jackson, TN, Basic Books).
Gardner, H., Morris, T. & Anand, N. (2002) Your expertise: developing new practice recipes for success, in: L. Empson (Eds.) *Managing the Modern Law Firm: New Challenges, New Perspectives* (Oxford, Oxford University Press), pp. 64–90.
Garth, B. (2012) Crisis, crisis rhetoric, and competition in legal education: a sociological perspective on the (latest) crisis of the legal profession and legal education. Abstract available at: http://ssrn.com/abstract=2166441.
Genn, H. (1999) *Paths to Justice: What People Do and Think About Going to Law* (Oxford, Hart Publishing).
Genn, H. (2009) *Judging Civil Justice: The Hamlyn Lectures* (Cambridge, Cambridge University Press).

Genn, H. & Paterson, A. (2002) *Paths to Justice Scotland: What People in Scotland Do and Think About Going to Law* (Oxford, Hart Publishing).
Gilson, R. (1984) Value creation by business lawyers: legal skills and asset pricing, *Yale Law Review*, 94, pp. 239–313.
Gilson, R. & Mnookin, R. (1994) Disputing through agents: cooperation and conflict between lawyers in litigation, *Columbia Law Review*, 94, pp. 509–566.
Gilson, R. & Mnookin, R. (1995) Foreword: business lawyers and value creation for clients, *Oregon Law Review*, 74, pp. 1–14.
Goriely, T., Moorhead, R. & Abrams, P. (2002) *More Civil Justice? The Impact of the Woolf Reforms on Pre-action Behaviour* (London, Law Society).
Green, B. (2012) *The Flood of US Lawyers: Natural Fluctuation or Professional Climate Change?*, paper prepared for Oñati Workshop: Too Many Lawyers? Facts, Reasons, Consequences and Solutions, 19–20 April.
Greenbaum, M. (2010) No more room at the bench, *Los Angeles Times*, 8 January.
Guttman, D. & Wilner, B. (1976) *The Shadow Government: The Government's Multi-Billion Dollar Giveaway of Decision-Making Powers to Private Management Consultants, 'Experts', and Think Tanks* (New York, Pantheon Books).
Habermas, J. (1985) *The Theory of Communicative Action, Vol. 1: Reason and the Rationalization of Society* (Boston, MA, Beacon Press).
Hadfield, G. (2000) The price of law: how the market for lawyers distorts the justice system, *Michigan Law Review*, 98, pp. 953–1006.
Hadfield, G. (2004) Where have all the trials gone? Settlements, nontrial adjudications, and statistical artifacts in the changing disposition of federal civil cases, *Journal of Empirical Legal Studies*, 1, pp. 705–734.
Hadfield, G. (2008) Legal barriers to innovation: the growing economic costs of professional control over corporate legal markets, *Stanford Law Review*, 60, pp. 1689–1732.
Hampshire, S. (2000) *Justice Is Conflict* (Princeton, NJ, Princeton University Press).
Harrington, C. (1985) *Shadow Justice: The Ideology and Institutionalization of Alternatives to Court* (Westport, CT, Greenwood Press).
Harter, P. (1982) Negotiating regulations: a cure for malaise, *Georgetown Law Journal*, 71, pp. 1–118.
Hazard, G. (1978) *Ethics in the Practice of Law* (New Haven, CT, Yale University Press).
Heinz, J. & Laumann, E. (1994) *Chicago Lawyers: The Social Structure of the Bar*, 2nd ed. (Evanston, IL, Northwestern University Press).
Henderson, W.D. (2012) The inferiority complex of law schools, *The National Jurist*, 21, pp. 4–5.
Hoon, M. de & Verberk, S. (2011) *The New Judge: The Judge as Conflict Manager*, Tilberg University, TISCO Working Paper No. 002/2011.
Jackson, H. *et al.* (2010) *Analytical Methods for Lawyers*, 2nd ed. (New York, Foundation Press).
Kaye, J. (1997) Changing courts in changing times: the need for a fresh look at how courts are run, *Hastings Law Journal*, 48, pp. 851–866.
King, M. *et al.* (2009) *Non-Adversarial Justice* (Sydney, The Federation Press).
Kritzer, H. (1986) Adjudication to settlement: shading in the gray, *Judicature*, 70, pp. 161–165.
Kritzer, H. (1991) Context, context, context: a cross-problem, cross cultural comparison of compensation seeking behaviour, paper prepared for Law & Society conference, Amsterdam, June.
Kritzer, H. (1998) *Legal Advocacy: Lawyers and Non-Lawyers at Work* (Ann Arbor, MI, University of Michigan).
Kritzer, H. (2008) To lawyer or not to lawyer: is that the question?, *Journal of Empirical Legal Studies*, 5, pp. 875–906.
Kritzer, H. (2010) Examining the real demand for legal services, *Fordham Urban Law Journal*, 37, p. 255.
Kritzer, H. (2012) *It's the Law Schools Stupid! Explaining the Continuing Increase in the Number of Law Schools*, paper prepared for Oñati Workshop: Too Many Lawyers? Facts, Reasons, Consequences and Solutions, 19–20 April.
Kronman, A. (1995) *The Lost Lawyer: Failing Ideals of the Legal Profession* (Cambridge, MA, Belknap Press of Harvard University Press).

Larson, M. (1977) *The Rise of Professionalism: A Sociological Analysis* (Berkeley, CA, University of California Press).
Lattman, P. (2012) 9 Graduates lose case against New York Law School, *New York Times*, 22 March.
Leathley, C. (2007) *International Dispute Resolution in Latin America: An Institutional Overview* (Alphan aan den Rijn, Kluwer Law International).
Lee, J. & Hwee, T.H. (Eds) (2009) *An Asian Perspective on Mediation* (Singapore, Academy Publishing).
Legal Services Corporation (1980) *The Delivery Systems Study: A Report to the Congress and President of the United States* (Washington, DC, Legal Services Corporation).
Legal Services Corporation (2009) *Documenting the Justice Gap in America: The Current Unmet Civil Legal Needs of Low-Income Americans*, 2nd ed. (Washington, DC, Legal Services Corporation).
Lehrer, J. (2012) *Imagine: How Creativity Works* (Boston, MA, Houghton Mifflin Harcourt).
Llewellyn, K. (1930) *The Bramble Bush: On Our Law and Its Study* (Oxford, Oxford University Press).
Lord Justice Jackson (2010) *Review of Civil Litigation Costs: Final Report* (Norwich, The Stationery Office).
Lord Woolf (1996) *Access to Justice Final Report to the Lord Chancellor on the Civil Justice System in England and Wales* (Lord Chancellors Department, UK).
Magee, S.P. (2010) Lawyer capture of national congresses: the optimum number of lawyers and a radical proposal for legal change, in: F.H. Buckley (Eds.) *The American Illness: Essays on the Rule of Law* (New Haven, CT, Yale University Press), ch. 2.
McKenna, C. (2006) *The World's Newest Profession: Management Consulting in the Twentieth Century* (Cambridge, Cambridge University Press).
McQuoid-Mason, D. (2012) *Access to Justice in South Africa: Are There Enough Lawyers?*, paper prepared for Oñati Workshop: Too Many Lawyers? Facts, Reasons, Consequences and Solutions, 19–20 April.
Meeker, J., Dombrink, J. & Mallett, L. (2000) Access to justice for the poor and moderate income populations: issues for California Latinos, *The Justice Professional: A Critical Journal of Crime, Law and Society*, 13, p. 91.
Meeker, J., Dombrink, J. & Schumann, E. (1985) Legal needs of the poor: problems, priorities and attitudes, *Law & Policy*, 7, p. 225.
Menkel-Meadow, C. (1981) *The 59th Street Legal Clinic: Evaluation of an Experiment* (The Committee).
Menkel-Meadow, C. (1983) Legal negotiation: a study of strategies in search of theory, *American Bar Foundation Research Journal*, pp. 905–937.
Menkel-Meadow, C. (1984a) Legal aid in the United States: the professionalization and politicization of legal services in the 1980s, *Osgoode Hall Law Journal*, 22, pp. 29–67.
Menkel-Meadow, C. (1984b) Toward another view of legal negotiation: the structure of legal problem solving, *UCLA Law Review*, 31, pp. 754–842.
Menkel-Meadow, C. (1985a) The transformation of disputes by lawyers: what the dispute paradigm does and does not tell us, *Missouri Journal of Dispute Resolution*, 2, pp. 25–44.
Menkel-Meadow, C. (1985b) Nonprofessional advocacy: the 'paralegalization' of legal services for the poor, *Clearinghouse Review*, 19, pp. 403–411.
Menkel-Meadow, C. (1987) Excluded voices: new voices in the legal profession making new voices in the law, *University of Miami Law Review*, 42, pp. 29–53.
Menkel-Meadow, C. (1989a) The feminization of the legal profession: the comparative sociology of women lawyers, in: R. Abel & P. Lewis (Eds) *Lawyers in Society, Vol. 3: Comparative Theories* (Berkeley, CA, University of California Press).
Menkel-Meadow, C. (1989b) Exploring a research agenda of the feminization of the legal profession: theories of gender and social change, *Law & Social Inquiry*, 14, pp. 289–319.
Menkel-Meadow, C. (1995) The feminization of the legal profession: the comparative sociology of women lawyers, in: R. Abel & P. Lewis (Eds) *Lawyers in Society: An Overview* (Berkeley, CA, University of California Press).
Menkel-Meadow, C. (1999) Taking problem-solving pedagogy seriously: a response to the Attorney General, *Journal of Legal Education*, 49, pp. 14–21.
Menkel-Meadow, C. (2000) Mothers and fathers of invention: the intellectual founders of ADR, *Ohio State Journal of Dispute Resolution*, 16, pp. 1–37.

Menkel-Meadow, C. (2005a) Roots and inspirations: a brief history of the foundations of dispute resolution, in: M. Moffitt & R. Bordone (Eds) *The Handbook of Dispute Resolution* (San Francisco, CA, Jossey-Bass), pp. 13–31.

Menkel-Meadow, C. (2005b) The lawyer's role(s) in deliberative democracy, *Nevada Law Journal*, 5, pp. 347–369.

Menkel-Meadow, C. (2007a) Restorative justice: what is it and does it work?, *Annual Review of Law and Social Science*, 3(1), pp. 161–187.

Menkel-Meadow, C. (2007b) Taking law and _____ really seriously: before, during and after 'The Law', *Vanderbilt Law Review*, 60, pp. 555–595.

Menkel-Meadow, C. (2009a) Chronicling the complexification of negotiation theory and practice, *Negotiation Journal*, 25, pp. 415–429.

Menkel-Meadow, C. (2009b) Are there systemic issues in dispute system design? And what we should [not] do about it: lessons from international and domestic fronts, *Harvard Negotiation Law Review*, 14, pp. 195–231.

Menkel-Meadow, C. (2010) Dispute resolution, in: P. Cane & H. Kritzer (Eds) *The Oxford Handbook of Empirical Legal Research* (Oxford, Oxford University Press), pp. 596–624.

Menkel-Meadow, C. (2011a) The National Labor Relations Act's legacy: collective or individual dispute resolution or not?, *American Bar Association Journal of Labor and Employment Law*, 26, pp. 249–266.

Menkel-Meadow, C. (2011b) Scaling up deliberative democracy as dispute resolution in healthcare reform: a work in progress, *Law and Contemporary Problems*, 74(3), pp. 1–30.

Menkel-Meadow, C. (2011c) Why and how to study 'transnational' law, *University of California Irvine Law Review*, 1, pp. 97–128.

Menkel-Meadow, C. (2013) ADR: does it work? Measurement and other issues, *Harvard Negotiation Law Review*, forthcoming.

Menkel-Meadow, C. *et al.* (2011) *Dispute Resolution: Beyond the Adversarial Model*, 2nd ed. (New York, Aspen Publishers).

Menkel-Meadow, C. & Meadow, R. (1983) Resource allocation in legal services: individual attorney decisions in work priorities, *Law & Policy Quarterly*, 5, pp. 237–256.

Merry, S. & Milner, N. (Eds.) (1993) *The Possibility of Popular Justice: A Case Study of Community Mediation in the United States* (Ann Arbor, MI, University of Michigan Press).

Mnookin, R., Peppet, S. & Tulumello, A. (2000) *Beyond Winning: Negotiating to Create Value in Deals and Disputes* (Cambridge, MA, The Belknap Press of Harvard University Press).

Morgan, T. (2010) *The Vanishing American Lawyer* (Oxford, Oxford University Press).

Nolan-Haley, J. (2012) Is Europe headed down the primrose path with mandatory mediation?, *North Carolina Journal of International Law and Commercial Regulation*, 37, forthcoming.

Pande, P. & Holpp, L. (2001) *What is Six Sigma?* (New York, McGraw-Hill).

Peppet, S. (2004) Contract formation in imperfect markets: should we use mediators in deals, *Ohio State Journal of Dispute Resolution*, 19, pp. 283–367.

Peters, T. & Waterman, R. (1982) *In Search of Excellence: Lessons from America's Best Run Companies* (New York, Harper and Row).

Podziba, S. (2012) *Civic Fusion: Mediating Polarized Public Disputes* (Washington, DC, ABA Publishing).

Raiffa, H. (1982) *The Art and Science of Negotiation: How to Resolve Conflicts and Get the Best Out of Bargaining* (Cambridge, MA, Harvard University Press).

Reed, A. (1921) *Training for the Public Profession of the Law: Historical Development and Principal Contemporary Problems of Legal Education in the United States, with some Account of Conditions in England and Canada* (Ulan Press).

Rhode, D. (2004) *Access to Justice* (Oxford, Oxford University Press).

Riles, A. (2009) Reforming knowledge: a critique of the Japanese legal profession reforms (with Takashi Uchida), *Drexel Law Review*, 1, pp. 3–51.

Rogers, N., Bordone, R., Sander, F. & McEwen, C. (2013) *Designing Systems and Processes for Managing Disputes* (Fredercik, Md Wolters Kluwer).

Sandefur, R. (2012) Money isn't everything: moderate income households' use of lawyers' services, in: M. Trebilcock, A. Duggan & L. Sossin (Eds) *Middle Income Access to Justice* (Toronto, University of Toronto Press), ch. 7.

Sander, R. & Williams, E.D. (1989) Why are there so many lawyers? Perspectives on a turbulent market, *Law & Social Inquiry*, 14, pp. 431–480.

Schneider, A. & Fleury, N. (2011) There's no place like home: applying dispute systems design theory to create a foreclosure mediation system, *Nevada Law Journal*, 11, pp. 368–396.

Schonholtz, R. (1985) Neighborhood justice systems: work structure and guiding principles, *Mediation Quarterly*, 5, pp. 3–30.

Segal, D. (2011a) Law school economics: ka-ching!, *New York Times*, 16 July.

Segal, D. (2011b) What they don't teach law students: lawyering, *New York Times*, 19 November.

Sen, A. (2009) *The Idea of Justice* (Cambridge, MA, Harvard University Press).

Seron, C. (1996) *The Business of Practicing Law: The Work Lives of Solo and Small Firm Lawyers* (Philadelphia, PA, Temple University Press).

Shear, M. (2012) The case against law school, *New York Magazine*, 4 March.

Silver, C. (2005) Winners and losers in the globalization of legal services: situating the market for foreign lawyers, *Virginia Journal of International Law*, 45, pp. 897–934.

Sokol, D. (2007) Globalization of law firms: a survey of the literature and a research agenda for future study, *Indiana Journal of Global Legal Studies*, 14, pp. 5–28.

State of Nevada Foreclosure Mediation Program (2012) *About the Program*. Available at: http://foreclosure.nevadajudiciary.us/index.php/about-program, accessed 22 May 2012.

Steinberg, J. (2010) Plan B: skip college, *New York Times Week In Review*, 16 May. Available at: http://nytimes.com/2010/05/16/weekinreview/16steinpagewanted=all.

Sternlight, J. (2002) Is the US out on a limb? Comparing the US approach to mandatory consumer and employment arbitration to that of the rest of the world, *University of Miami Law Review*, 56, pp. 831–864.

Stevens, E.L. (2012) Will law school students have jobs after they graduate?, *Washington Post*, 31 October–1 November.

Stipanowich, T. (2004) ADR and the 'vanishing trial': the growth and impact of 'alternative dispute resolution', *Journal of Empirical Legal Studies*, 1, pp. 843–912.

Strauss, P. (2006) Transsystemia – are we approaching a new Langdellian moment? Is McGill leading the way?, *Journal of Legal Education*, 56, pp. 161–171.

Stromseth, J., Wippman, D. & Brooks, R. (2006) *Can Might Make Rights? Building the Rule of Law After Military Interventions* (Cambridge, Cambridge University Press).

Sturm, S. & Gadlin, H. (2007) Conflict resolution and systemic change, *Journal of Dispute Resolution*, pp. 1–63.

Susskind, L., McKearan, S. & Thomas-Larmer, J. (1999) *The Consensus Building Handbook: A Comprehensive Guide to Reaching Agreement* (Thousand Oaks, CA, Sage Publications).

Susskind, R. (2008) *The End of Lawyers? Rethinking the Nature of Legal Services*, 1st ed. (Oxford, Oxford University Press).

Tamanaha, B. (2012) *Failing Law Schools* (Chicago, IL, University of Chicago Press).

Teitel, R. (2002) *Transitional Justice* (Oxford, Oxford University Press).

Terry, L.S. (1998) A case study of the hybrid model for facilitating cross-border legal practice: the agreement between the American Bar Association and the Brussels Bars, *Fordham International Law Journal*, 21, pp. 1382–1499.

Terry, L.S. (2008) The legal world is flat: globalization and its effect on lawyers practicing in non-global law firms, *Northwestern Journal of International Law & Business*, 28, pp. 527–559.

Terry, L.S. (2010) From GATS to APEC: the impact of trade agreements on legal services, *Akron Law Review*, 43, pp. 875–984.

Tesler, P. (2001) *Collaborative Law: Achieving Effective Resolution in Divorce Without Litigation* (Chicago, IL, ABA Publishing).

Tocqueville, A. de (1835) *Democracy in America* (New York and London, Penguin Classic, 2003) (Issac Kramnick, ed; Gerald Bevan, translator).

Twining, W. (2009) *General Jurisprudence: Understanding Law from a Global Perspective* (Cambridge, Cambridge University Press).
Umbreit, M. (2000) *The Handbook of Victim Offender Mediation: An Essential Guide to Practice and Research* (San Francisco, CA, Jossey-Bass).
Ury, W., Brett, J. & Goldberg, S. (1988) *Getting Disputes Resolved: Designing Systems to Cut the Costs of Conflict* (San Francisco, CA, Jossey-Bass).
Whitehead, T. (2011) Ministers accused of pushing mediation to hide legal aid cuts, *The Telegraph,* 24 February.
Wilkins, D.B. (2001) Why global law firms should care about diversity: five lessons from the American experience, in: J. Drolshammer & M. Pfeifer (Eds) *The Internationalization of the Practice of Law* (Alphan aan den Rijn, Kluwer Law International), pp. 43–66.

Acts

Administrative Dispute Resolution Act of 1990 (US)
Alternative Dispute Resolution Act of 1990 (US)
California Code of Civil Procedure §§638–645 (US)
Civil Justice Reform Act of 1990 (US)
Council Directive 2008/52/EC of 22 May 2008 [on certain aspects of mediation in civil and commercial matters]
Legal Aid Act 1988 (UK)
Legal Services Act 2007 (UK)
Negotiated Rulemaking Act of 1990 (US)

Cases

AT&T Mobility v. Concepcion [2011] 131 S.Ct. 1740
Halsey v. Milton Keynes General NHS Trust [2004] 1 WLR at 3007

Unauthorized practice of law and the production of lawyers

NETA ZIV
Department of Law, Tel Aviv University, Ramat Aviv, Tel Aviv, Israel

ABSTRACT *Discussions regarding the 'flooding' of the legal profession have often focused on issues of jurisprudence and legal culture (how people resolve disputes), accessibility to legal education (growth in the number of law schools), social and cultural factors (the status of the profession) and structural barriers to professional entry (how difficult it is to become a lawyer). In this paper I discuss the increasing number of lawyers in Israel (now the highest per capita in developed countries) in reference to an additional factor: the most extensive rules regarding unauthorized practice of law, strictly guarded and enforced by the Israeli Bar Association. In Israeli society law has increasingly become an accepted forum for resolving private and public disputes. At the same time, any kind of activity entailing provision of legal advice, legal documentation or representation is restricted to lawyers only – thus entry into the profession becomes the only way to take part and become engaged in the field of legal services.*

I. Introduction

The literature attempting to explain the growing number of lawyers in modern societies has addressed the topic from different angles. Jurisprudential explanations connect people's increasing turn to law with the emergence of more lawyers to handle legal procedures. Accordingly, legal culture (especially litigiousness) directly bears on the number of lawyers a society produces; in a less legalized culture there would not be as much of a need for lawyers (Rhode, 1997–1998, pp. 993–994).

Others target expansion of legal education and the growing number of law schools as an important contributor to this phenomenon.[1] To be sure, the rising numbers of students who choose legal education in and of itself reflects changes in legal culture. However, there are external reasons – beyond general trends of 'legalization' – that may have led to the expansion in legal education. These include development of a market of law teachers who spur the demand for teaching institutions, changes in regulation relating to opening new law schools and legal education serving as a springboard for public service work. Under this view the excessive number of law school graduates infuses higher entry levels into the profession.

Another explanation points to structural barriers imposed by the state or bar associations upon entry into the profession as a central cause for lawyers' influx. The claim is that lax closure measures, which have traditionally limited entry into the legal profession (including bar exams and clerkship periods) have led to the 'flooding' of the legal profession (Larsen, 1977; Abel, 1988; Paterson, 2012, pp. 24–28).

Not surprisingly, many law societies adopt this reasoning. They constantly worry about professional overcrowding and attempt to tighten barriers to control entry. Restrictive measures, in turn, spur demand and lead to a circular cause–effect dynamic that fuels the process and keeps it thriving.

In this paper I discuss the growing number of lawyers in Israel – now the highest per capita in developed countries – in reference to an additional factor: the most extensive rules regarding *unauthorized practice of law*, strictly guarded and enforced by the Israeli Bar Association. To be sure, I recognize the impact of the aforesaid factors (legal culture, legal education, structural barriers and social status) upon this occurrence. Moreover, I believe there is no single or overriding explanation for the increase in the number of lawyers where this phenomenon takes place, Israel included. The purpose of this paper is to shed light on one factor – albeit a central one– to the discussion on the topic.

I claim that to understand why people become lawyers, we must inquire into the division of labor within the 'field of legal services'. Legal culture, in the sense of people's notion that they need professional assistance in certain circumstances, is a starting point for this discussion. We then must inquire how and from whom they can obtain these services. Regulation by way of *unauthorized practice of law* rules (hereinafter UPL) is central to this discussion. If law broadly defines exclusive activities and jurisdictions within which only lawyers may operate, and against trends of legalization, we can expect a steady increase in the number of people interested in entering the legal profession. The combination of a monopolized territory within which assistance from experts and professionals becomes essential, together with UPL rules restricting non-lawyers from providing services within this defined terrain, will evidently cause the number of entrants into the legal profession to rise.

I believe this process carries significant force in explaining the sharp rise in the number of lawyers in Israel. Israeli law restricts any kind of activity entailing the provision of legal advice, preparation of a legal document, as well as representation before designated administrative and all judicial and quasi-judicial tribunals, to lawyers only. The Israel Bar Association (IBA) vehemently enforces these rules: it initiates legal proceedings against 'intruders' who allegedly trespass into the restricted jurisdiction, as well as against lawyers who collaborate with them. The IBA is mostly concerned with commercial bodies that have entered the field, but since 2007 it has also targeted non-profit organizations that seek to provide legal services for fees (although usually at a lower rate than private firms) assisted by law students, volunteers and paralegals.

Thus, amidst a highly legalized culture, entry into the legal profession becomes the only way to take part in providing legal services. Hence UPL rules and practices can explain the constant increase in the number of lawyers in Israel to unprecedented comparable rates.

In this article I connect increasing trends of legalization and litigiousness in Israeli society and UPL normative arrangements, as enforced by the IBA. I analyze litigation initiated by the Israel Bar Association to enforce the UPL rules against 'trespassers' and inquire to what extent the services they offer posit a competition with lawyers. I then compare the UPL rules with similar regulatory arrangements in the health profession in Israel, and demonstrate that the medical field works under a completely different normative arrangement. I conclude with a note on competition between non-lawyers and lawyers, and a proposal to change the rules of UPL which I believe may decrease the demand to enter the legal profession.

II. More lawyers, more law

Since the 1990s, the Israeli legal profession has grown dramatically in size. Already in 2006 the number of lawyers per capita in Israel was among the highest in the world – one lawyer per 200 residents. From 1968 to 2005 the number of lawyers had increased by 1,552%, while the population grew by 246% (Barzilai, 2007, pp. 256–257). In 2012 there were over 50,000 registered lawyers in the country, bringing the ratio to one lawyer to 160 residents. Despite the proclaimed economic hardship of lawyers in small firms, the number of law students entering law schools continued to rise in the last decade. In 1996, 6,000 students began their law studies; in 2006, the number rose to 15,000.[2] The demand for legal education was met with more liberalized state policies on the supply side. Since 2005, Israel's Council for Higher Education has approved the opening of three private law schools in the northern and southern parts of the country, joining four research-based public law schools and five private colleges, altogether graduating over 2,000 law students per year.[3] In 2010, 13,000 out of the 16,000 law graduates studied in law colleges, and only 3,000 in universities.[4]

The growth in the number of law students and lawyers emerged as Israeli society became more 'legalized'. Since the mid-1980s, with the rise of an individualist ideology and market economy, 'rights discourse' has become salient, demonstrated by an increasing reliance on adjudication for resolving individual, social and political conflicts. The number of court cases in all categories and all courts has risen at a much higher pace than demographic growth (Barzilai, 2007, pp. 265–267). Barzilai claims that statistically "one in every six citizens in Israel has litigated a case in the courts" (Barzilai, 2007, pp. 265–266).[5] The legalization process has been twofold. First was the increasing turn to the Supreme Court to resolve public and social oriented disputes that beforehand remained in the political, communal or public sphere.[6] The second was the increasing turn to adjudication to resolve personal and commercial disputes. To be sure, much of this legalization process was itself led by jurists – judges and lawyers alike, who created a demand for lawyers' services and broadened the scope of judicial intervention. The point remains, nonetheless, that it is becoming hard to navigate the judicial or bureaucratic system without the assistance of an expert, namely, a lawyer.

However, as in many other countries, the increase in practicing lawyers has not guaranteed more equitable access to justice. Parker claims "[i]t is naive to expect the market in justice ever to be organized so efficiently that the majority will be able to afford the services they need" (Parker, 1999; see also Rhode, 2000, p. 118).[7] Evidence indicates that the legal needs of the poor in Israel are not met by the growing number of lawyers entering the profession.[8] Data from the Israel Court Administration shows that in 2007 78% of defendants were not represented by a lawyer in litigation. In debt collection proceedings, 95% of debtors were not represented (while only 6% of creditors appeared without a lawyer).[9]

This is a crucial point for our discussion. The combination of a highly legalized culture, expanding needs for professional assistance and barriers in the access to justice have spurred the development of non-lawyer activities seeking to fill this gap. Concerned with lawyer competition, the IBA has moved to harness UPL to halt the acclaimed threat to lawyers' monopoly in providing legal services.

III. Unauthorized practice of law in Israel – norms and policy

The expanding role of law in Israeli polity and society developed against broad restrictive unauthorized practice of law (UPL) rules, embodied in section 20 of the Israel Bar Association Act of 1961 (hereinafter section 20). This normative arrangement was adopted in 1961 (when there were less than 2,000 lawyers in Israel), and has not been amended since. To be sure, struggles to entrench lawyers' jurisdictional exclusivity are not unique to the Israeli legal profession; they vary according to the legal culture and beliefs about the nature of legal services in each society, the makeup of the legal profession and its relation to other institutions (Rhode, 1981; Abel, 2010; Auerbach, 1976; Halliday & Karpick, 1998).

Comparatively Israel's is one of the broadest arrangements both historically as well as currently (OECD, 2007, pp. 138–341). Israeli polity at the time of the IBA's enactment – under which lawyers were not considered part of the ruling elites and national ethos – generated the first arrangement, which situated the legal profession within the private sphere holding a strong monopoly; the lack of challenges to the bar's monopoly for over four decades enabled this arrangement to endure with no significant change (Ziv, 2003).

Section 20 sets the jurisdictional boundaries to lawyers' exclusive right of practice, confining the following activities to lawyers:[10]

(1) Representation of another person before any judicial or quasi-judicial tribunal.
(2) Representation of another person before designated administrative agencies.[11]
(3) Preparing documents of a legal nature on behalf of another person or negotiating towards preparation of such documents.
(4) Legal consultation and provision of a legal opinion.

Sections (1)–(2) restrict representation, and are bounded by the nature of the body at stake (judicial/quasi-judicial), or its inclusion in a closed list of administrative agencies.[12] Sections (3) and (4) are broad and vague: they apply to preparation of a 'document of a legal nature', providing 'legal advice' or a 'legal opinion'.

Clearly it is difficult to set the boundaries between a document that is legal in its 'nature' and one that is not: is a standard rental contract a document of this sort? What about a 'do-it-yourself divorce kit'? Similarly, the boundary between provision of legal information and legal opinion/advice is murky, and varies according to the circumstances. Is assisting a person to file a claim before a health insurance company considered provision of a legal opinion? Does preparation of a tax return fall within this definition?

Section 20 represents an essentialist methodology, assuming things are 'legal' or 'non-legal' based on the nature of the task and its inherent characteristics. However this is obviously not the case; what is considered legal in one place and time may not be so in another [see Rhode (1981) for comparison]. It is impossible to draw stable lines between what lawyers do and what other professionals do, as "[m]any individuals, including accountants, bankers, real estate brokers, insurance agents, and title and trust officers, cannot provide competent services without referring to legal concerns" (Rhode, 1990–1991).

Furthermore, these are not the important questions to ask if we care about access to justice and quality legal services. Nevertheless, section 20 channels the deliberations into inquiries of this sort, and situates the legal and public debate on the topic within an essentialist framework.

The Israel Bar Association has been enforcing UPL rules vigorously, to ensure that the expanding demand for legal assistance will remain within the exclusive jurisdiction of lawyers. For the most part, the bar grounded its arguments in altruistic reasoning: the need to protect clients and to ensure legal services of good quality. It claimed that lawyers are best suited to guarantee these objectives since they possess distinctive knowledge and expertise (acquired through formal education, clerkship and entry exams) and are bound by ethical rules, enforced by a formal disciplinary process.

However, as in other jurisdictional professional struggles, it is the vocational self-interest of lawyers that the bar actually seeks to protect.

The IBA committee overseeing UPL is named 'The Committee to Protect the Profession'.[13] It targets a variety of activities deemed as trespassing upon lawyers' jurisdiction: debt collection by companies that receive and redeem (cash) checks, bills and banknotes; provision of legal services by lawyers employed by non-profits; representation of commercial companies in small claims court by non-lawyers; representation of students in academic disciplinary hearings by law students; work conducted by patent writers; non-lawyer representation of holocaust survivors in quasi-judicial proceedings; non-lawyer advice in debt collection proceedings; tenders issued by public agencies inviting proposals to provide debt collection services; and tax calculation, under which lawyers and non-lawyers operate together.[14] In all these instances, the bar initiated inquiries on its own behalf, in addition to handling complaints from lawyers, judges and the public.

IV. Two pronged struggle: commercial companies and lawyers

The bar's most extensive efforts to counter UPL targeted companies that engaged in realizing entitlements, mainly in the area of medical, health and disability benefits. In the early 1990s several companies identified the potential market of claims for monetary compensation due to illness, disability, accidents and other injuries, against the state (The National Insurance Institute and other public agencies), as well as private insurance companies and sick funds.[15] Since the mid-1990s the IBA has initiated civil actions against numerous companies, asking the courts to prohibit them from carrying out activities that allegedly violated section 20. In most cases these proceedings were not based on complaints from dissatisfied clients, but on the bar's proactive initiative.

Following these proceedings most companies negotiated concessions with the bar, under which they agreed to limit their scope of activities to fit the boundaries of section 20; eventually many were driven out of the market. Two companies, however, decided to "fight all the way". As will be described below, Pitzuy Nimratz and The Center for Realization of Medical Rights continued to litigate the cases initiated by the IBA, and asked the court to interpret section 20 narrowly, in a way that would define its activities as falling within its boundaries.

Parallel to these proceedings, the bar realized it had to cope with a growing number of lawyers who discovered the advantages of this emerging field of market activity and cooperated with the companies. Some lawyers were employed by the companies; others set up referral agreements with them. Lawyers were needed for cases that required litigation or more complex legal proceedings. Not surprisingly, most of these lawyers were new entrants into the profession or those with lesser social capital and networks from which they could entice clients (Auerbach, 1976).

To tackle the problem from within, the bar utilized a disciplinary rule, enacted in 1998 for this purpose. Section 11B.(a) of the Israel Bar Association Rules (Professional Ethics) prohibits lawyers from providing services to clients referred to them by an entity which is not a law firm, if it is a for-profit body that advertises itself as providing legal services. Section 11B.(b) prohibits lawyers employed by entities other than law firms from providing legal assistance to anyone other than their employer, if the employer is a for-profit company and collects fees for the services it provides.[16] Disciplinary section 11B. was used, therefore, to deter lawyers from cooperating with commercial bodies operating in the vicinity of section 20. The bar hoped that by use of a two-pronged approach – civil action and disciplinary rules – it would succeed in eradicating the encroachment on its once exclusive jurisdiction.

However, the struggle for territorial exclusivity is an infinite endeavor; professions are constantly on guard for novel forms of threats to their jurisdictional turf, and at the same time need to police their members from cooperating with the perpetrators.

V. Medical rights and UPL litigation

Clearing the field

As mentioned above, at the first stage of the IBA's struggle against UPL, most companies terminated their operations or altered them significantly. The first company to challenge the IBA was Pitzuy Nimratz. Its main business was processing individual monetary claims against public and private agencies due to disability, illness or injury. It operated by way of filling forms on behalf of clients, writing letters to apply for compensation, assisting in filing claims before administrative agencies and appeals before quasi-judicial panels.[17] It employed doctors and other experts, and referred cases to lawyers when appropriate.

Since Pitzuy Nimratz did not concede to the bar's demands, the IBA filed a case before the Jerusalem District Court, requesting a temporary and a permanent injunction to prevent the company from overstepping the exclusive jurisdiction reserved for lawyers. As part of the proceedings the presiding judge ordered the company to notify its customers that the lawyers they are referred to may be violating Disciplinary Rule 11B.[18]

Pitzuy Nimratz thus challenged the validity of Rule 11B. in the Israeli Supreme Court.[19] Although the court acknowledged that the rule infringes upon a number of rights and interests (freedom of vocation of the company, the individual freedom to choose a lawyer and furthering access to justice), it affirmed the rule. The court accepted that Rule 11B. serves an appropriate objective – to prevent circumventing ethical rules that apply to lawyers (including prohibition of advertising as well as conflict of interests), and that the means purported to achieve this end are proportionate.[20]

Shortly after this decision, the Jerusalem District Court ruled in the civil case against Pitzuy Nimratz, in which the bar moved to curb its activities based on section 20. The court opened its decision with a caveat, alerting itself to the problematic nature of restrictive directives such as those included in section 20. It identified the existing arrangement as monopolistic, stating that although the IBA claimed to be furthering a public interest, it may well be that explicit altruistic reasoning disguises lawyers' self interest.[21]

Notwithstanding this caveat, the court accepted the suit in part, and rejected it in part. The decision appears to be a well intentioned, albeit hopeless attempt to draw the lines between what is permitted and what is prohibited under section 20, according to the type of task performed and its inherent characteristics. For example, the IBA argued that the decision over whether a claim is legal or not is in and of itself 'legal' in its nature, and that accordingly, Pitzuy Nimratz may not perform the initial screening and channeling of its caseload. The court rejected this claim as unreasonably broad and tautological. On the other hand it accepted the argument that addressing agencies on behalf of clients in a way that goes beyond describing 'the dry facts of the case' is prohibited, since it constitutes the drafting of a document of a legal nature or the provision of legal advice. Neither party appealed this decision.

Pitzuy Nimratz itself ceased to operate; however new commercial entities entered the field of 'medical rights' realization. The IBA continued its struggle against the principal new entrant to the field: *The Center for Realization of Medical Rights.*

Strengthening efforts to curtail UPL – The Center for Realization of Medical Rights

The Center for Realization of Medical Rights (CMR) was established in 2003.[22] It is the largest and most well-known company of this sort, very much due to an aggressive advertising and marketing campaign on street billboards, radio stations and other media.[23] Most of the company's clients are claimants of monetary allotments from The National Insurance Institute due to illness, injury or other physical or mental condition.[24] The rest are divided between claims against pension funds, The Ministry of Defense and the IDF (Israel Defense Forces).

CMR adopted a practice that attempts to work 'around' section 20, asserting they do not perform any activity reserved for lawyers only, and that they abide by the Pitzuy Nimratz ruling. Their work method consists of 'preparing the case' for clients who had been accepted for service following some initial screening process. The company works with a number of doctors who specialize in preparing 'expert opinion' in support of the claim. According to their director, CMR consultants are well trained, and have acquired distinctive and specialized expertise in the area of 'medical rights'.[25] The most crucial input for the client is the capability to conceptualize complaints and events the client portrays in lay terms into an actionable claim under the law: while the client says "my shoulder hurts", the consultant and then doctor conveys this information into a phrase such as: "I cannot lift my arm more than 45° (degrees) above my hip" – a condition which creates an entitlement. As part of the service, CMR puts together the clients' 'claim files'; it refers clients to specialist doctors who are familiar with the entitlement system and advise them which examinations to take (CMR pays for the medical opinion prepared by the doctor); it channels the claim to the appropriate administrative course; and it prepares all necessary documentation for review by the Medical Committee at the National Insurance Institute. CMR does not represent the client before the committee. If the claim is dismissed the client is not referred to a lawyer, and may choose for herself whether to appeal the decision.

According to the company's founder and CEO, 'the law' is not a resource reserved for lawyers exclusively; suggesting that CMR is doing the work of lawyers upsets her. Beyond the principle assertion that not everything legal is within the restricted domain of lawyers, she expresses a negative view about what lawyers do and how they do it, claiming that many do not know the field in-depth and are not interested or well organized enough to handle such claims (especially for small amounts); lawyers are contentious and escalate the controversy rather than finding a practical solution, and they have no personal or social skills to deal with people, who must expose private and sensitive personal details (a skill highly underscored in her enterprise). Moreover, she asserts that the services her company offers increase access to justice for people who otherwise would not have had any recourse to realize their rights.[26]

In 2007 The Israel Bar Association sued The Center for Medical Rights in the Jerusalem District Court, requesting an injunction to halt its activities (as well as monetary damages). The bar claimed that CMR's practice constitutes the unauthorized practice of law as it prepares cases to be considered by the National Insurance Medical Committees, represents clients before these committees, and refers clients to lawyers.[27]

The reasoning articulated by the IBA in the lawsuit was 'altruistic': lawyers are bound by a set of substantive norms aimed at protecting clients' interests. These include fiduciary and confidentiality duties, prohibition on conflicts of interest, solicitation, advertising and regulation of fees. In contrast, CMR is unregulated and acts under no constraints; hence clients remain unprotected.

In April 2012 the Jerusalem District Court accepted the IBA's suit and issued an injunction preventing CMR from engaging in a series of activities, which lie at the core of the company's operations. The injunction prohibited representing or arguing on behalf of clients before quasi-judicial bodies; preparing legal documents, including preparation of appeals on administrative rulings if they include any reference to law and judicial decisions; assisting clients with filling out forms if this entails any kind of wording beyond technical details; filing medical expert opinions (by doctors) attached to claim forms; providing legal opinions and legal advice; and approaching designated bodies with a request for compensation and damages (including the National Insurance Institute – NII).

In its ruling the court interpreted section 20 broadly, reiterating that its rationale is to protect the quality of service provided to clients, not the interests of lawyers. The court underscored the fact the employees within CMR receive no formal training, and that its activity is unregulated, in contrast to that of lawyers. CMR appealed the decision to the Israeli Supreme Court, which issued a stay on the lower court's orders pending resolution of the appeal.[28] A number of non-profit organizations asked to join the appeal as *amicus curiae*, in order to present before the court the broader aspects of the legal issue, in particular the implications of the ruling on non-profit organizations assisting in rights fulfillment, with or without lawyers.[29] The case is pending a decision.

Indeed, CMR operates in a regulatory void: there are no formal educational and training requirements, no licensing or official oversight, no ethical rules that govern its employees, although they are exposed to clients' personal and sensitive information. Given the lack of any regulatory framework, quality of service depends on voluntary measures adopted by companies. The only recourse available for clients is private litigation, which is not a common venue clients utilize.[30] A search in Israeli legal databases reveals that between 2005 and 2011 CMR was involved in nine legal disputes: in four of them CMR was the plaintiff (sued for payment against services) and in five it was a defendant (in suits claiming overpayment or other monetary disputes). Although there may have been other cases in which the parties reached a compromise without court intervention, it seems that the number of cases in which clients had sued CMR is quite low.

Indeed, the lack of regulation is an issue for concern. As Rhode has suggested, the need for regulation increases when the service at stake is in a vital area of life, when lay oversight of market failure is difficult to obtain, and when the topic is highly complex and requires standardized skills and training (Rhode, 1981). It seems that statutory or administrative oversight of enterprises like CMR is a preferable arrangement. However, this debate is not taking place in Israel at present, since the dispute has been channeled solely to the boundaries of UPL, rather than examining an alternative apparatus.[31]

VI. Competition with law firms?

The IBA heralded the District Court's decision in the CMR case, calling it "a dramatic victory".[32] It appealed to the public to prefer lawyers over CMR, underscoring the court's contention that the Israel Bar Association's objective is to protect the public, rather than lawyers. Nonetheless, it is hard to escape the notion that the motives underlying the bar are, in fact, mixed, and that this project is motivated at least partially to curb competition.[33] To what extent do CMR and other companies comprise a competitive threat to lawyers? It is hard to verify this point, but numerous indicators illustrate that some competition does exist.

Despite limitations on lawyers' advertisement, an Internet search reveals there are a number of law firms that handle monetary claims against the National Insurance Institute (together with damages claims against public and private authorities and medical negligence suits). Some have adopted the term 'medical rights realization' in their professional profile.[34] These are mostly small firms, and it is unlikely that they can serve mass claimants as CMR does, with its 100 consultants and medical experts. One of these law firms warns prospective clients of commercial companies that provide 'medical rights realization' services. It spells out anecdotal cases in which clients were harmed by such companies, explains lawyers' advantages (for example, the ability to provide legal representation), and cites judicial decisions stating the companies are in violation of section 20. Moreover, following the CMR ruling, the IBA announced it was establishing a lawyer referral database for clients with 'medical rights cases', and held two conferences on the topic to discuss its legal success.[35]

Whether competition is real or imagined, the fact remains that the IBA believes lawyers are harmed by CMR and similar companies. It is not clear, however, whether the public is harmed by this competition. Data shows that there has been a constant increase in the number of claims filed before the NII in the area of disability allowances of various sorts (general disability, work-related disability, allowance for a disabled child, etc). In 2000 there were about 130,000 claims for disability allowance, while in 2005 the number increased to around 170,000 and in 2010 to more than 200,000.[36] Despite governmental measures to tighten eligibility criteria for disability entitlement in 2004, the rates of entitlement for disability allowance continued to rise (although at a slower pace).[37] The NII has reported that over the last decade there has been a continuing increase in the number of people recognized as eligible for disability allowance, which exceeds population growth. For example, in 2010 the disability eligibility rate increased by 3.7%, while the population grew by 1.7%.[38]

The NII explains this finding as related to changes in substantive eligibility criteria rather than to greater accessibility to realizing entitlement; however this explanation can be contested. It may well be that better access to 'medical rights' may have partially contributed to this situation, and that the entrance of commercial companies into the field of medical rights had an impact on the public potential to realize entitlements of this sort.

VII. Health profession – a proliferated regulatory regime

In contrast to the regulatory and practical arrangement of legal services, the medical profession in Israel illustrates an alternative regime under which doctors operate alongside semi- (or sub-) professions.[39]

Medical services can be discussed comparatively despite inherent differences from law in the principles underlying allocation. Health services have, for the most part, been considered a public resource, and many medical professionals (doctors, nurses, lab technicians) are employed in public institutions. The Israeli medical profession underwent significant changes in its locus – it shifted from the private to the public sphere between 1948 and 1963, and again in 1991 with the enactment of the National Health Insurance Act (Filc, 2009). In contrast, law has always been considered a resource allocated according to private principles – as most lawyers work in private law firms.

Notwithstanding, the question of unauthorized practice (in this case, of medicine) is common to both professions, historically and at present. The dynamics of the division of labor between nurses and doctors, doctors and podiatrists, doctors and homeopathic healers, psychiatrists and psychologists, to mention a few, all reflect what Abbott labels the "diagnosis, inference and treatment" trilogy, i.e. the struggle for exclusive jurisdiction based on the group's acclaimed unique knowledge (Abbott, 1988, pp. 40–52). Similarly to lawyers, doctors too have fought against the encroachment on their professional turf by groups within the medical profession as well as from the outside (Abbott, 1988, pp. 71–72).

The starting point of the Israeli law governing the work of doctors incorporates explicit and quite broad instructions about unauthorized practice. Section 1 of The Doctors' Ordinance (hereinafter Ordinance) broadly defines the activities within the 'medical vocation' ('Isuk berefua'), reserved for doctors only, if conducted towards the ill or injured. These include examining, diagnosing, curing, issuing prescriptions, supervising in situations of pregnancy and birth, or providing other services which are usually provided by a doctor, including acupuncture healing.[40] Section 3 of the Ordinance prohibits any person who is not a doctor to work in the medical vocation as defined above, excluding dentists, pharmacologists, midwives, nurses (or anyone else providing nursing activities), as well as podiatrists and surgical podiatrists.[41] Section 5 reserves the right to use the title 'doctor', 'surgeon' or 'acting in the medical vocation' to doctors only; section 6 prohibits doctors from employing non-doctors to perform activities defined within the 'medical vocation'. However, section 7 permits doctors to employ, under their supervision, nurses, paramedics and other aides, as long as they do not perform medical tasks – including care, supervision or surgery of a patient – if these entail the use of discretion or of a professional skill of a doctor. In addition, section 8 bars a person that conducted an act reserved for doctors only from suing (in court) for fees to be awarded for his work.[42]

This legal framework is very restrictive, and is structured similarly to the IBA Act, including a broad definition of the terms 'medical vocation', 'examining' and 'curing' patients. It prohibits the use of a title without authorization, and restricts collecting fees for unauthorized practice.

Notwithstanding, there is a critical difference between them, which opens up the possibility for non-doctors to provide medical services. Section 59 of the Ordinance authorizes the Ministry of Health to define exemptions and exceptions to the Ordinance in relation, among other things, to exclusive practice.[43]

Exemptions may be applied to nurses or aides, who can be authorized to 'diagnose' and 'cure' patients, as designated by the state official; and to medical students, dentists and foreign doctors. Nurses (and authorized aides) may be permitted – by the state official and by way of administrative regulations – to carry out designated activities under the conditions set forth by the regulations.[44] In accordance with the regulations prescribing these 'designated activities', a director of a hospital or a clinic may permit the nurse or aide to conduct them, an authorization which may be extended, in specific regulations set forth by the state, to performing these tasks at the patient's home.[45] Section 59A. includes a general authorization (to be stipulated in regulations) for the performance of acupuncture, under the supervision of a licensed doctor.

Based on this general authorization the Minister of Health issued detailed regulations prescribing activities that can be performed by a group of non-doctor professionals. The Doctors' Regulations [Capacity to Perform Exceptional Activities (2001)] lays out, in minute detail, those medical measures which can be carried out by nurses and other aides, providing they have the necessary qualifications to do so.

The regulations distinguish between two types of nurses ('authorized nurse' and 'practical nurse'), and assign particular permitted tasks to each. For every set of tasks there are specific conditions which must be satisfied for the nurse to be allowed to carry them out. Measures include the removal of an arterial line during birth, defibrillation in intensive care units for cardiac arrhythmias, intravenous insertions for oncology patients, adjustment of respiratory equipment during emergency situations, insertion of morphine for terminal patients and of radioactive substance for epilepsy monitoring – to mention a few measures indicated in the regulation.

For each measure specific training preconditions are set, as well as supervisory requirements. The regulations specify which measures can be carried out at the patient's home and which must be done in a doctor's presence.[46] They differentiate between types of nurses according to their level of prior education and training.

The regulations continue to define a number of 'aides', which are also permitted to perform specific medical tasks. Paramedics, lab technicians, x-ray machine technicians, heart–lung machine operators, blood donation takers, physiotherapists – are all allowed to perform measures which are no doubt 'medical' in their nature. They include the adjustment of a cardiac pacemaker, operation of a plasma machine, connecting and disconnecting a heart–lung machine, suction of respiratory system – to mention a few such tasks, each according to the training and expertise of the medical aid.

The Ordinance, although laying down exclusive jurisdictional boundaries, incorporates a mechanism enabling sub-professions to perform medical work with patients. The arrangement defines a specific task, designates it to a particular professional, and requires ample training and, at times, supervision.

In addition to the arrangements included in the Doctors' Ordinance, in 2008 *The Regulation of the Medical Professions Act* was enacted. This law regulates the work of a number of professions that provide treatment alongside the traditional medical profession: speech therapists, physiotherapists, occupational therapists, dietitians, clinical criminologists, podiatrists and surgical podiatrists, and chiropractors.[47] The law sets out requirements for receiving a professional certificate (education, practical training, exams), creates an advisory board, establishes ethical standards and disciplinary processes and – of course – sets exclusive practice rules accordingly.

Hence regarding the medical profession – a classic, traditional profession similar to law – the field of medical services has evolved. To be sure, doctors have always worried about competition – from curing and healing professionals of a non-Western tradition (acupuncturists and other Eastern/Chinese doctors), from professionals who specialize in a narrow field (podiatrists, chiropractors), from developmental and rehabilitative professionals (speech and occupational therapists), and of course from the sub-professions of the traditional medical profession (nurses, paramedics, technicians).

Indeed, doctors did not give in easily to attempts to encroach upon their turf, but have been steered to some type of territorial truce with other professionals in the healing and curing 'business'. In Israel it is the state – rather than the professional association – that defines the division of responsibilities and authorization to practice medicine and it has led to the current arrangement described above.

This process can be characterized as social openness, rather than social closure. The proliferation of medical knowledge and practice to new professions, and the redrawing of boundaries between traditional doctors and the new professionals, strengthen their unique, perhaps elevated, status. This is particularly so towards the professionals regulated in the Doctors' Ordinance (nurses, x-ray technicians), whose roles are strictly defined and fixed, while doctors maintain a residual authority to continue and control the field. Whether this arrangement was imposed upon doctors against their will or accepted by way of concession, the current state of affairs is that the medicine and health field is open to more than one profession. To practice medicine and be part of the practicum of peoples' treatment and cure, one does not have to become a doctor. There is a choice to become a nurse, a paramedic, a physiotherapist or to learn how to operate a heart–lung, an ultrasound or an x-ray machine. The questions asked in this context are not if the nurse is performing 'a medical act', but whether she has the qualifications to do so; not if the radiology technician is using a 'medical device', but whether he has been trained to do so. Making sure these questions are answered in a satisfactory manner will protect the public interest in qualitative health services more than a continued struggle to keep the turf under the exclusive jurisdiction of doctors. As for the numbers, there are not 'too many doctors' in Israel; on the contrary. In 2009 the State Comptroller published a report describing the serious lack of doctors in the country.[48]

A similar regulatory approach needs to be adopted in the area of legal services, where entry into the field of legal services immediately encounters the profession's gatekeepers, armed with UPL laws as their primary weapon. No wonder, therefore, that so many people opt to become lawyers.

VIII. UPL and the number of lawyers in Israel

What conclusions can we draw from UPL about the number of lawyers in Israel? It is possible only to speculate about this question, based on the following considerations.

(1) *Competition*: at the margins of UPL a new practice has evolved in the last decade: thousands of people a year are being served by non-lawyers in realizing their entitlements in the area of disability, injury and illness. Many of them would probably not have had access to lawyers. This practice challenged the conception that rights are only the business of lawyers – a position vehemently rejected by the IBA. The bar sees this development as harsh competition with the profession, especially as the growing number of lawyers has made it difficult for lawyers to find sufficient work.
(2) *Excluding areas of practice from section 20 (by legislative amendment)*: it is possible to amend the law and define designated areas of practice that would be removed from the definition of UPL and from the exclusive jurisdiction of lawyers, albeit with a tradeoff. In exchange, legislation would impose conditions to ensure quality control and oversight of the new service providers, who would begin the process of 'professionalization'. Medical rights are but one area in which this change could take place; others are employment law, real estate transactions, family and estate law.
(3) *Market expansion*: if UPL rules are relaxed, additional providers could choose to enter the newly regulated area of practice. A development of this sort would in all likelihood expand supply, as well as entice clients to seek service within a competitive regulated market. The new service providers could work laterally, alongside lawyers, or horizontally, under their supervision (similar to the doctor–nurse arrangement).
(4) *Creating new professions, reducing the number of lawyers*: narrowing UPL rules could open up new possibilities for the development of expertise and specialization. It would probably dissuade potential law school candidates from entering the full 'lawyer-track', and divert them into choosing a sub- or semi-legal profession in its stead.

It is not coincidental that Israel has both the highest numbers of lawyers per capita, but also very broad UPL rules. Although UPL may not be the only reason for this occurrence (or even the main one), it very likely impacts the flooding of the profession. UPL creates a bottleneck that directs any person interested in providing legal services or legal assistance to the full track of becoming a lawyer. Despite the growing number of lawyers in Israel, data do not indicate better and more equal access to justice. In this paper I have argued that relaxing UPL rules, in tandem with proper regulation, may in all likelihood increase competition and improve access to justice. The case of medical rights illustrates the difficulties of the IBA (similar to other professional organizations) to forgo its exclusive monopoly over the field of legal services.

It may well be that the changes proposed in this paper will work to lawyers' advantage. Similar to doctors, who have situated themselves at the top of the medical 'professional chain', acquiescing to the new professions by way of subordination, lawyers too could distinguish themselves from other legal providers, by building expertise and accepting subordinate new providers. This could lead to a decline in the number of lawyers in Israel, but to the rise of new legal professions, benefitting both the public and the profession, and making law more accessible to all.

Notes

[1] See, in this issue, Levin and Alkoby (2012), Zer-Gutmann (2012), Silver (2012), Katvan (2012) ....

[2] Israel Council for Higher Education, Students in institutions of higher education by level of degree, type of institution and field of study, Table 10. Available at: http://www.che.org.il/download/files/table10.xls, accessed 29 January 2009; Israel Council for Higher Education, Students in institutions of higher education by level of degree and field of study 1996, 2001, 2004–05, Table 9. Available at: http://www.che.org.il/download/files/table_9_3203.xls, accessed 29 January 2009.

[3] The new colleges are the Haifa Law College, the Zefat Law College in the Galilee, and the Sapir Law College in Sderot. See also Eyal Katvan (2012, this issue).

[4] Council for Higher Education, 2010, Table 10. Available at: http://che.org.il/?page_id=6802, accessed 26 June 2012.

[5] According to Barzilai, "[l]itigation in circuit courts has grown by 2265 per cent, in district courts it has increased by 4843 per cent, and in the High Court of Justice (HCJ) by 667 per cent. In all categories of the judiciary, litigation has increased more rapidly than the pace of demographic growth".

[6] The legacy of this development is associated with Chief Justice Aharon Barak and has drawn much controversy (Sapir, 2008; Rabin & Shany, 2003–2004, pp. 2–3).

[7] Parker (1999) provides information on discrepancies between increased market competition for legal services and availability of lawyers, depending on the type of service and clients.

[8] There is no official research on the legal needs in Israel. Information on the availability of legal services to the poor, however, illustrates a growing want in this area. See Shai (2004), noting the rise in people requesting state legal assistance as well as assistance from non-governmental organizations between 2001 and 2003. See also Knesset (2004), discussing the immense unmet legal needs which are not addressed by the state, the bar and civil society.

[9] Data provided by Deputy Court Administration Director, Judge A. Gilon, in a letter dated 1 March 2009 to attorney Ela Alon from Tel Aviv University Program 'Law in the Service of the Community' (on file with author). Data about debt collection can be accessed at: http://www.knesset.gov.il/committees/heb/material/data/H17-05-2011_11-58-01_reshut87b2010.pdf.

[10] The Israel Bar Association Act of 1961, 5721–1961, section 20.

[11] These include: The Debts Execution Registrar; The Land Registration Registrar; The Companies Registrar; The Partnership Registrar; The Patent and Trademark Registrar; The Copyright Registrar; and The Income Tax, Land Tax and Inheritance Tax Officers.

[12] Courts have ruled that the list mentioned in section 20(2) is closed; see, for example, Civ.A.4405/02 *The Israel Bar Association v. Ravivo Takdin-34,* 12(02)(2) [2002] (Decision rendered 13 November 2005).

[13] See, for example, The Israel Bar Association, *Annual Activity Report 2009*, pp. 122–124; The Israel Bar Association, *Annual Activity Report 2010*, pp. 136–138; The Israel Bar Association, *Annual Activity Report 2011*, pp. 154–156.

[14] The Israel Bar Association, *Annual Activity Report 2011*, at pp. 136–137.

[15] On the development of this trend see: Ziv (2008, pp. 454–456).

[16] Section 11B. of The Israel Bar Rules (Professional Ethics), 1986.

[17] The exact activities of the company were never fully portrayed or contested, as the parties agreed on the facts that would constitute the basis of the legal ruling.

[18] This is a rather irregular decision. The civil courts do not have jurisdiction against lawyers, and disciplinary Rule 11B. governs lawyers only. Nevertheless, the court ordered Pitzuy Nimratz to notify its customers that the lawyers may be in violation of the disciplinary rule [Civ. Req. 423/02 (Civil Claim 4033/02 *The Israel Bar Association v. Pitzuy Nimratz Ltd*), decision rendered 10 April 2002). This decision was confirmed by the Supreme Court (Civ. Ap. Req. 4196/02 *Pitzuy Nimratz v. The Israel Bar Association*, decision rendered 4 July 2002, Justice A. Grunis).

[19] H.C. 9596/02 *Pitsiy Nimratz v. The Israel Bar Association* et al. PD 58(5) 792 [2004].

[20] The decision did not impose a heavy burden upon the Israeli bar association to demonstrate that there is no alternative to restricting lawyers from cooperating with commercial entities. In this sense the court did not take up a critical stance in scrutinizing the legitimacy of the restriction.

[21] Civil Claim 4033/02 (Jerusalem District Court) *The Israel Bar Association v. Pitzuy Nimratz Ltd*, decision rendered 13 November 2005.

[22] Based on an interview with CMR's CEO (Livnat Poran), (March 2012), on information published on CMR's website and on a review of litigation by and against the company in the last five years (see http://www.medical-rights.co.il/).

[23] A similar enterprise is Zchuti – The Experts for Realization of Medical Rights. Interviews with Zchuti management were conducted in April 2012 by the author. See http://www.zhuti.co.il/landing_page.asp?Id=47263232371&gclid=CPyVmvzag68CFcgntAoddFoR4A.

[24] A public body which operates as Israel's central social security institution, responsible for most welfare and other social assistance programs.

[25] Training is conducted in-house and depends on internal policies.

[26] According to the company's website they adhere to the following principles: the rights of every citizen to know how to assert one's rights; fiduciary towards the client and assistance vis-à-vis institutions (without legal counsel); direct professional work, accurate and targeted towards relevant authorities; full transparency towards the client; client participation throughout the process in all information, estimates and evaluations (see http://www.zhuti.co.il/about.asp?id=9).

[27] C.A. 9270/07 (Jerusalem District Court), *The Israel Bar Association v. The Center for Medical Rights*, decision rendered 4 April 2012. The claim was made under section 20 as well as section 386 of the National Insurance Act, which restricts representation before the National Insurance to a lawyer, a CPA, a close friend, a representative of a workers' union or employers' union, or any other person who had received authorization or permission to do so.

[28] C.A. 4223/12 *The Center for Realization of Medical Rights v. The Israel Bar Association*. The stay on the district court's decision was issued by Justice E. Arbel (CM 3522/12).

[29] Nine organizations providing legal assistance directly or facilitate access to justice. Amici are represented by the author.

[30] It is not possible to ascertain whether the low number of claims is a result of high client satisfaction or due to barriers to litigation.

[31] In the UK, for example, The Legal Services Act of 2007 abolished almost all exclusive arrangements reserved for solicitors, to be replaced by a regulatory arrangement of other legal professions in designated areas of practice. See, for example, Flood (2008).

[32] Israel Bar Association: "In a dramatic victory (in the case of) the bar association against Livnat Poran the court decided: a well founded fear of public harm", (4 April 2012). Available at: http://www.israelbar.org.il/article_inner.asp?pgId=128475&catId=6.

[33] In a personal message following the ruling the head of IBA, attorney Doron Barzilai, stated: "We will not be deterred, we will continue the struggle against professional trespassers, we will continue to preserve our livelihood ..." (IBA website, 4 April 2012, http://www.israelbar.org.il/article_inner.asp?pgId=128503&catId=3082).

[34] See, for example, http://www.barac.co.il/ (Meir & Daniel Barak); http://www.davidsaar.co.il/newlanding3/tviot_bituah.htm?gclid=COaN7am-jq8CFcgw3wodU2Edww (law firm of Dr David Saar, who states that the law firm's staff includes a doctor and an 'economist'); http://www.ashkenazi-law.co.il/100740/ (Tsafrir Ashkenazi Law Firm); http://www.herzog-lawyers.com/ (Zvi Herzog Law office); www.law-shalev.co.il/ (Arik Shalev, law firm for 'Medical Rights Realization'); http://www.bechar.co.il/profile.html (Bechar law offices); http://www.navot.co.il/ (Barak Nevot law firm); http://www.abclaw.co.il/site/detail/detail/detailDetail.asp?detail_id=2842631 (Amir Bitton law firm).

[35] See, IBA announcement, 12 May 2012: "For the first time: establishment of lawyer database to refer medical rights cases". Available at: http://www.israelbar.org.il/article_inner.asp?pgId=130629&catId=3082.

[36] Table taken from interview with outgoing director of NII, Esther Domincini, can be found at http://www.themarker.com/career/1.1672800 (see Arlozorov, 2012).

[37] See Knesset Research and Information Center Letter to MK Haim, 2 November 2010 – 'Disability Allowance in Israel'. According to information provided by the NII in 1998, 3.7% of the population was entitled to disability allowance, and in 2009, 4.7%. The growth rate has decreased (from 4.5–

6.4% to 2.6–4.5%), (pp. 3–4). The threshold for entitlement was increased from a 40% to a 60% requirement of medical/functional limitation (at p. 4).

[38] National Insurance Institute, *Annual Report 2010 – Disability Allowance*, p. 2. Available at: http://www.btl.gov.il/Publications/Skira_shnatit/2010/Documents/nechut.pdf.

[39] On semi-professions see Ezioni (1969).

[40] Doctors' Ordinance [1987], section 1.

[41] Doctors' Ordinance [1987], section 3.

[42] A similar provision is included in The Israel Bar Association Act (section 98), however it is worded as a prohibition imposed upon a court from hearing a fee claim if it is based on an activity restricted to lawyers only.

[43] Doctors' Ordinance, section 59 & 59A.

[44] Doctors' Ordinance, section 59(a)(1) & 59(b).

[45] Doctors' Ordinance, section 59(b) & 59(b1.).

[46] The Doctors' Regulations (Capacity to Execute Exceptional Measures) 2001 Regulations 6122, 23 August 2001.

[47] The Regulation of the Medical Professions Act of 2008, Sefer Hukim 2172, 30 July 2008, p. 720.

[48] State Comptroller, Report 59B., 2009 Medical and Nursing Human Resources, pp. 355–389. Available at: http://www.mevaker.gov.il/serve/contentTree.asp?bookid=545&id=0&contentid=10196&parentcid=undefined&bctype=10195&sw=1280&hw=954.

References

Abbott, A. (1988) *The System of Professions – An Essay on the Division of Expert Labour* (Chicago, IL, University of Chicago Press).

Abel, R.L. (1988) *The Legal Profession in England and Wales* (Oxford, Basil Blackwell).

Abel, R.L. (2010) *Lawyers on Trial* (New York, Oxford University Press).

Arlozorov, M. (2012) In Israel many are spoiled I don't understand why people hate the NII, *The Marker*, 27 March.

Auerbach, J.S. (1976) *Unequal Justice, Lawyers and Social Change in Modern America* (Oxford, Oxford University Press).

Barzilai, G. (2007) The ambivalent language of lawyers in Israel: liberal politic,s economic liberalism, silence and dissent, in: T.C. Halliday *et al.* (Ed.) *Fighting for Political Freedom: Comparative Studies of the Legal Complex and Political Liberalism* (Portland, OR, Hart Publishing), pp. 247, 256–257.

Ezioni, A. (1969) *Semi Professions and their Organization: Teachers, Nurses, Social Workers* (New York, The Free Press).

Filc, D. (2009) *Circles of Exclusion: The Politics of Health Care in Israel (The Culture and Politics of Health Care Work)* (New York, Cornell University Press).

Flood, J. (2008) Will there be a fallout from Clementi? The global repercussions for the legal profession after the UL Legal Services Act of 2007, The Jean Monnet/Robert Schuman Paper Series.

Halliday, T.C. & Karpick, L. (1998) *Lawyers and the Rise of Western Political Liberalism* (Oxford, Oxford University Press).

Katvan, E. (2012) The 'overcrowding the profession' argument and the professional melting pot, *International Journal of the Legal Profession*, 19(2–3), pp. 301–319, this issue.

Knesset (2004) *Committee of Public Complaints, Protocol of Proceedings: Public Inquiries of People with Legal Needs who Cannot Afford to Purchase Legal Services*, 17 March. Available at: http://www.knesset.gov.il/protocols/data/html/zibur/2004-03-17.html.

Larsen, M.S. (1977) *The Rise of Professionalism: A Sociological Analysis* (Berkeley, CA, University of California Press).

Levin, A. & Alkoby, A. (2012) Is access to the profession access to justice? Lessons from Canada, *International Journal of the Legal Profession*, 19(2–3), pp. 283–299, this issue.

OECD (2007) *Policy Roundtables, Competitive Restrictions in Legal Professions* (Paris, OECD).

Parker, C. (1999) *Just Lawyers: Regulation and Access to Justice* (Oxford, Oxford University Press).

Paterson, A. (2012) *Lawyers and the Public Good. Democracy in Action?* (Cambridge, Cambridge University Press).
Rabin, Y. & Shany, Y. (2003–2004) The Israeli unfinished constitutional revolution: had the time come for protecting economic and social rights, *Israel Law Review*, 37(3), pp. 2–3.
Rhode, D.L. (1981) Policing the professional monopoly: a constitutional and empirical analysis of unauthorized practice prohibitions, *Stanford Law Review*, 34, p. 1.
Rhode, D.L. (1990–1991) The delivery of legal services by non-lawyers, *Georgetown Journal of Legal Ethics*, 4, p. 209.
Rhode, D.L. (1997–1998) Too much law, too little justice; too much rhetoric, too little reform, *Georgetown Journal of Legal Ethics*, 11, p. 989.
Rhode, D.L. (2000) *In the Interests of Justice: Reforming the Legal Profession* (Oxford, Oxford University Press).
Sapir, G. (2008) *The Israeli Constitutional Revolution – How Did it Happen?*, Bar Ilan University Publishing Law, Working Paper No. 08-02. Available at: http://papers.ssrn.com/sol3/papers.cfm?abstract_id=1082230#.
Shai, Y. (2004) *Bodies Providing Free Legal Services to People with Limited Means* (The Knesset Research & Information Center, Background Paper for Discussion).
Silver, C. (2012) Coping with the consequences of 'too many lawyers': securing the place of international graduate law students, *International Journal of the Legal Profession*, 19(2–3), pp. 227–245, this issue.
Zer-Gutman, L. (2012) Effects of the acceleration in the number of lawyers in Israel, *International Journal of the Legal Profession*, 19(2–3), pp. 247–263, this issue.
Ziv, N. (2003) Combining professionalism, nation building and public service: the professional project of the Israeli bar, 1928–2002, *Fordham Law Review*, LXXI(4), p. 1621.
Ziv, N. (2008) Who moved my gown? On the unauthorized practice of law in Israel, *Bar Ilan Law Studies*, 24, p. 439.

The flood of US lawyers: natural fluctuation or professional climate change?

BRUCE A. GREEN
Fordham University School of Law, New York, USA

ABSTRACT *This paper considers how US courts, which regulate the US legal profession, should respond to the perceived excess of lawyers (i.e. to the lack of adequate employment opportunities for lawyers). It begins by summarizing the courts' regulatory role. It then situates the contemporary flood-of-lawyers problem in the unavailability of well-paid legal work, not in the absence of a need for lawyers' services: many people need lawyers, but they cannot afford them. Next, the paper explores whether the problem is simply a product of natural economic fluctuation which will be solved naturally, particularly if potential law school applicants become better informed, and suggests that the problem is at least in part an artificial product of professional regulation. Finally, the paper explores possible regulatory solutions, concluding with the possibility of eliminating lawyers who perform adequate but lowest-quality work. It concludes that using regulatory means of lowering the tide of lawyers is not viable.*

Many believe that there are too many US lawyers, by which they mean that US lawyers are competing for too few paying clients and too few jobs that require or utilize a law license (Dolin, 2007; Greenbaum, 2010; Tamanaha, 2012). Some unemployed lawyers recently sued the US law schools from which they graduated, blaming the 'nationwide glut' of lawyers on law schools' expansion of admissions while legal employment opportunities decreased (Shaer, 2012). Other possible causes of the perceived overabundance of lawyers include that too many college graduates are attending law school for lack of better career alternatives, out of idealized expectations about their career prospects, or lured by the easy availability of federal loans for tuition (Podgers, 2011; Tamanaha, 2012), and that economic stagnation, technology, and global competition (including outsourcing) have reduced the need for US lawyers among clients who can afford legal services (Henderson & Zahorsky, 2011). Whatever the causes, this situation raises a regulatory question: If there is a flood of US lawyers, can and should courts do anything through their oversight of lawyer licensing and discipline to stem the tide? This paper explores this question, concluding with an examination of what most would see as a 'modest proposal'[1]: that US courts respond to the excess of lawyers by de-licensing the least capable ones.

Background: regulation of the US bar – quality and quantity

Unlike in many other countries, regulation of the bar in the United States is principally in the hands of state judiciaries. State courts have authority to admit new applicants to practice law, establish standards of professional conduct, and discipline or disbar lawyers who engage in professional misconduct or cease to be competent. Most state courts delegate significant aspects of these responsibilities to professional staff or to volunteer lawyers.

The most expensive entry requirements for admission to the US bar are an undergraduate degree and a law degree. Although a handful of states still hold out the possibility of 'reading for the bar,' virtually no applicants take advantage of this alternative (Sloan, 2011a). And while law schools may admit applicants without an undergraduate degree, this rarely occurs. Most state judiciaries require graduation from an American Bar Association (ABA)-accredited law school, thereby leaving it to the ABA to determine the length of law school (generally, 3 years for full-time students) and the curricular and other requirements. The cost of a legal education has burgeoned in the past few decades; although the causes are disputed, among those cited have been pressures to provide clinical training, smaller classes, more individualized education, and other expensive forms of curricular and noncurricular assistance in response to accreditation requirements, competition for rankings, and complaints from law firms and clients that law students are inadequately prepared for practice (ABA, 2012b; Bourne, 2012; Tamanaha, 2012; US Government Accountability Office, 2009).

After graduating from law school, applicants are required to pass a written bar examination, for which law school typically does not completely prepare them. Bar examinations are administered semiannually. Most states administer standardized written tests generated by the National Conference of Bar Examiners based on federal or nationally consistent law. The tests mainly assess knowledge of the substantive and procedural law and the ability to apply the law to factual scenarios. Some states attempt to test certain lawyering skills as well. Applicants generally devote weeks of study to the examination, purchase a bar review course or written study materials, and pay an examination fee; however, these expenditures of time and money ordinarily pale in comparison to the length and cost of a formal undergraduate and legal education.[2] Most law graduates who sit for the bar examination receive a qualifying score (National Conference of Bar Examiners, 2012) and are then licensed to practice law, but a significant minority of each state's applicants fail the examination, in which case they may retake it at a later time.

Over time, the gap has grown between the abilities of newly admitted lawyers and the necessary skills and knowledge to practice law. But the assumption that graduates' ill-preparedness is attributable to the deficiency of legal education seems doubtful. The expansion of legal writing, simulation and clinical courses, while running up the cost of a legal education, probably makes graduates better prepared than in the past. The gap nevertheless has expanded because law has become more complex and highly specialized over time (Morgan, 2010) and because there is a lower tolerance for learning at clients' expense.[3]

Once admitted to practice, lawyers have no significant regulatory requirements to maintain their licenses other than to refrain from professional misconduct. States have no postgraduate apprenticeship or articling requirement for new lawyers.[4] Most states require lawyers to pay periodic licensing fees and take a modest number of hours of Continuing Legal Education courses of unproven utility (Grigg, 1998). No state requires lawyers to demonstrate continued competence or proficiency in their areas of concentration as a condition of retaining a law license. As far as I know, no state has ever seriously considered adopting a certification or relicensing requirement.

A law license provides relatively exclusive authority to perform the full array of legal work. The legal profession's monopoly is given legal effect by laws forbidding the "unauthorized practice of law" (UPL; ABA, 2012a). These laws generally prohibit nonlawyers from representing clients in court, giving clients legal advice, or drafting legal documents for clients. A law license in the United States is a general license to hold oneself out as a lawyer and to perform virtually any or all of the work reserved to lawyers. The profession is not formally divided into particular areas of practice, and lawyers may practice in multiple areas or move freely between different practice areas and settings. Although some professional organizations certify lawyers as specialists in certain areas of law, state courts do not require such certifications as a condition of practicing in particularly complex areas. Lawyers are expected, as a matter of self-restraint and the professional duty of competence, to refrain from offering services that they are unequipped to provide. New lawyers may perform relatively simply legal tasks and/or work under supervision or in collaboration with more experienced lawyers while obtaining on-the-job training necessary to perform more demanding work.

In theory, and subject to constitutional or other legal restrictions on their authority, the US regulatory process affords courts various opportunities to regulate the size of the bar directly or indirectly. Most directly, courts or the admissions authorities to whom they delegate responsibility might keep numbers down by restricting entry to the profession or by delicensing some number of admitted lawyers. Indirectly, they may limit the number of lawyers by establishing more difficult or expensive eligibility or licensing requirements – e.g. a requirement of even lengthier and more expensive legal education as a prerequisite for admission, or high licensing fees or other onerous requirements to retain a license.

Since the late nineteenth century, the requirements for US law practice have evolved, but never expressly with an eye toward limiting the number of lawyers (Jarvis, 1996). The express aim of the court-supervised admission and regulatory processes has been to maintain the quality of the bar, not the quantity of practitioners. Of course, the legal profession's entry requirements in a given jurisdiction have an impact, to a greater or lesser degree, on the extent of the profession's monopoly (Abel, 1996). In the United States, the attorney admissions requirements coupled with UPL provisions have the effect of limiting the size of the legal profession. But courts have never acknowledged that a purpose of admissions requirements is to maintain the economic viability of law practice by maintaining an artificial limit on the bar's size, and the steadily increasing number of lawyers indicates that this is not a substantial unacknowledged motivation.

Even if by happenstance, however, regulatory requirements and market forces do establish increasingly significant barriers to entering the legal profession and maintaining a law practice. In the early twentieth century, the legal profession in the United States was viewed as a vehicle for social mobility for lower-income individuals because entry was relatively inexpensive and little capital was required to establish a law practice (Auerbach, 1976). Today, however, it is questionable whether law will remain an affordable path to social mobility other than for those admitted to top-tier law schools or who receive scholarships to attend law school (Segal, 2011b). In 2012, many students borrow more than $100,000 to attend private law schools (Tamanaha, 2012). If a student performs reasonably well at one of the most prestigious law schools or exceptionally well at a lower-ranked one, he or she will likely be able to enter a mid-size or large law firm, earn a starting salary in excess of $100,000, and pay down student loans while gaining useful experience and contacts. If not, starting salaries (or fees from clients if an entrepreneurial graduate strikes out on his or her own in a solo or small firm practice) may be too low to make loan repayments feasible. Despite efforts to make the legal profession more accessible, the result may be to make the pool of applicants increasingly less diverse.

Is there a flood of lawyers?

Are there too many lawyers in the United States? The answer depends on what one means by the question. In the mid- to late-nineteenth century, the complaint might have been that there was a flood of incompetent and unethical lawyers because of the ease of entry (MacCrate Report, 1992). That is the complaint that prompted the establishment of the ABA and state bars beginning in the 1870s. The establishment of higher barriers to entry in the early twentieth century, while reducing competition, did not guarantee lawyers a livelihood, however. In the 1930s, at least until the New Deal era, even top graduates of top law schools had difficulty landing employment in the law.[5]

At a more recent point in history, the complaint about the excess of lawyers reflected a perception not that there was too little available legal work but that there was too much. That we appeared to have so many more lawyers per capita in the United States than in other industrialized countries was said to be symptomatic of an over-regulated, overly litigious society.[6,7] The complaint about the flood of lawyers became a trope of opponents of environmental, safety, and business regulation and proponents of tort reform, among others. However, the charge that the legal profession is overpopulated has become less prominent in the rhetoric of those who complain that laws and lawsuits are bad for business.[8]

Since the recent economic downturn, lawyers and law students in the United States have taken up the charge, albeit with a different meaning. Their complaint is that there is not enough legal work to justify the number of lawyers (Segal, 2011b).

At first, one might be skeptical, given the common understanding that there are significant unmet legal needs. The legal profession presumes that those with legal problems are best served by obtaining legal assistance, because it is difficult for individuals to navigate the law and legal processes on their own. Most low- and middle-income individuals with legal problems, such as tenants in eviction proceedings, individuals seeking divorces, and applicants for government benefits, are unrepresented (Rhode, 2000, 2005). This might suggest that there are not too many lawyers but too few.

A trio of scholars – Clifford Wilson, Robert Crandall, and Vikram Maheshri – recently made this argument (Winston & Crandall, 2011, pp. 82–94). Their proposed solution to the unmet need for legal assistance is not to reduce the professional ranks but to deregulate entry into the legal profession in order to swell the ranks. Eliminating or liberalizing UPL restrictions would allow individuals to provide legal services without the necessity of an expensive, three-year legal education. For less expensively trained legal professionals, representing low-income individuals would presumably be economically viable. Increased competition would, thus, expand access to legal services. Other countries offer models for licensing and regulating paralegals or other categories of legal professionals to perform law-related work, including certain legal work that US lawyers now monopolize, but for which quicker, inexpensive legal training will suffice. However, the organized bar in the US has traditionally defended both the idea of a unified profession and the professional monopoly (Green, 2009; MacCrate Report, 1992).

Implicit in the idea of deregulating the admission process is recognition that, under the current regulatory regime, which demands that lawyers be highly educated, laws of supply and demand will not reduce legal fees enough to make lawyers more broadly accessible to lower- and middle-income individuals.[9] Legal services are not a commodity that a seller has an economic incentive to unload at the lowest price. Lawyers' stock in trade is their time, and if they cannot use their time profitably enough by rendering legal assistance, they will use their time in business or some other pursuit. The obvious ways to make legal services more accessible to low- and middle-income clients, other than by subsidizing them, is to lower the educational barriers to entry and open professional practice to individuals who cannot use their time more profitably. This would seem to be at odds, however, with courts' regulatory objectives, particularly if one assumes that the extensiveness of legal training reflects the complexity of law practice.

The contemporary flood-of-lawyers complaint, then, is not that there are too few clients but that there are too few *well-paying* clients and *well-paying* legal positions to support the number of highly qualified lawyers produced by US law schools under the current lengthy and expensive licensing processes. At least for new lawyers, complaints about the number of lawyers are implicit complaints about the cost of becoming a lawyer: If one could become a lawyer without the costs of tuition, living expenses, and deferred earnings, and without having to repay debt incurred by many young lawyers to finance seven years of higher education, more lawyers could afford to serve the low- and middle-income client population and, in any event, fewer would have cause to complain about the scarcity of career and employment opportunities in the law.[10]

As so understood, the complaint that there are too many US lawyers seems undeniable. If there were doubt, testimony would be offered by the many recent US law school graduates who cannot find full-time legal positions or who cannot find any entry-level positions in the legal field,[11] by the many unemployed mid-level lawyers who cannot find new positions, and by solo and small-firm private practitioners struggling to keep their heads above water.

Natural fluctuation?

One might be tempted to view the flood of lawyers as a product of natural fluctuation that will eventually be resolved naturally: Sometimes there will be too many lawyers for available legal work, sometimes too few, and the market will eventually take care of the problem (Sander & Williams, 1989). The need for lawyers will vary at any given time based on various factors, including the level of economic activity, the nature and extent of regulation, and the availability of alternatives to lawyers such as the use of paralegals or technology (ABA, 1973). That seems to be the lesson of the post-World War II decades, during which the number of US lawyers and law schools increased explosively, despite occasional 'market gluts' during temporary economic downturns (MacCrate Report, 1992; Bickerton, 2003).

That is evidently the organized bar's assumption in reaction to claims, including legal claims, by recent law school graduates who assert that they were induced to attend law school by misleadingly rosy projections about the availability of well-paying jobs (Shaer, 2012; Segal, 2012). Instead of promoting regulatory solutions, such as higher barriers to entry into the legal profession (which might well incur the opposition of antitrust authorities in any event), the bar has promoted market solutions. It has called on law schools and other institutions of the legal profession to provide more, and more accurate, information, to enable the market to work more efficiently (Tamanaha, 2012). Presumably, the expectation is that college graduates will then make better informed choices about whether to attend law school in pursuit of a legal career, and more will make the economically intelligent choice not to seek entry into the legal profession, thereby gradually bringing the number of lawyers seeking paying work into alignment with the number of clients seeking to retain lawyers.

One might question, however, whether the flood of lawyers is primarily a problem of inefficient markets and asymmetrical information that can be solved by greater candor. The theory is not necessarily supported by recent experience: Since the most recent economic downturn, there has been abundant, accessible information in the popular and professional press about the scarcity of legal employment prospects, but interest in attending law school, although sharply diminishing, has remained high (Segal, 2012). This may be explained, for example, by the unrealism or wishfulness of college graduates or the absence of alternative employment. Either way, it does not ensure a natural thinning of ranks.

Moreover, the flood of lawyers is at least in significant part a creature of lawyer regulation. There is nothing free about either the market for law licenses or the market for legal services. As previously discussed, both are heavily regulated. Those needing legal services are limited to hiring lawyers or representing themselves. The requirements of undergraduate and graduate education along with bar passage make lawyers expensive. The regulatory premise is that consumers of legal services lack the necessary sophistication and information to distinguish between competent and incompetent legal practitioners, and, therefore, for the protection of the public, the licensing and disciplinary processes and the UPL laws must limit the pool of legal practitioners to those who are competent to practice.

When there seemed to be a high demand for paid legal services, universities and entrepreneurs decided to establish law schools that exploited the lawyer monopoly created by courts as regulators.[12] Once a university opens a law school, it is unlikely to close it, even if the quality of the applicant pool decreases. Having fixed costs, law schools have a disincentive to reduce the size of their entering classes too drastically, although many have begun enrolling smaller classes. As potential consumers of legal education become savvier and the number of applications drops, law schools may enroll less capable applicants in order to meet their costs.

An alternative market-driven answer is that competition among lawyers for limited numbers of clients and positions is good, or at least tolerable, because clients and employers will retain the best lawyers and the least competent will be forced to leave law practice for other labor. The problem with this theory is that, from the legal profession's perspective, clients (and especially unsophisticated ones) cannot effectively distinguish good lawyers from bad ones (Wilkins, 1992). That is both because clients lack the specialized knowledge adequately to judge the quality of lawyers work and because client confidentiality obligations preclude lawyers from giving prospective clients enough information on which to make effective assessments. Were it otherwise, courts would not perceive a need to protect the public by denying admission to applicants who, based on a bar examination, appear to lack the requisite competence to practice law. Just as clients cannot distinguish the incompetent from the competent, they cannot distinguish the mediocre from the proficient. The flood of lawyers may trigger an unseemly competition over clients but not necessarily generate the benefits to clients that are already expected to accrue from wider choice.

Regulatory responses: stemming the tide

Upstream solutions

If courts perceive that there are too many lawyers and that the public is poorly served as a result, they can reduce the number of lawyers in any of several ways. The most obvious possibility would be to raise the floodgates at the point of entry by admitting fewer applicants to the bar. This may happen naturally if the passing grade on the bar examination is kept steady in absolute terms, so that as much proficiency on the part of applicants is demanded now as several years ago. If the size and quality of the law-school applicant pool drops as more college graduates perceive a law degree to be a bad investment, graduates might be expected to perform less well than their predecessors (Segal, 2012). But there are no guarantees that test-taking ability will decline relative to the quality of the applicant pool. Law schools may respond to the problem by placing more emphasis on preparing its students for the bar examination, thereby enabling graduates who are less well prepared for actual practice to perform as well as their predecessors on the exam.

An alternative for courts and bar examiners under their aegis is to require higher bar exam scores in relative terms. Artificially reducing the percentage of admitted lawyers in this way can be justified by the need to preserve the quality of the bar. At least in theory, licensing a steady number and percentage of law-school graduates annually, even if admitted law students' credentials decrease, would diminish the quality of the bar, thereby undermining the core regulatory objective of preserving professional competence. The question can be framed not as whether to reduce the number of admitted lawyers in order to reduce competition among lawyers for the sake of lawyers' economic wellbeing, but whether to reduce the number of admitted lawyers in order to protect the public from incompetent ones.

One problem with this approach is that it requires acknowledging the inadequacy of the bar examination and a presumption that, even if applicants are performing as well as predecessors admitted to the bar in the past, they are still less qualified as demonstrated by LSATs and college grade point averages. Besides being unsubstantiated, the presumption would call the legitimacy of the bar admission process into question.

A related problem is that the bar examination is, at best, just a rough measure of aptitude. It is not a test of whether graduates can already practice law; many who pass are incapable of doing so. Nor is the exam a proven or absolute predictor of one's future ability to become competent in one's future area of legal practice. Therefore, it seems unfair and arbitrary to deny admission to those who may score lower than others on an examination but seem to be sufficiently capable in absolute terms to embark on a legal career, and especially unfair given the time and expense of a legal education. The exam focuses primarily on legal knowledge and analytic and writing abilities, but law practice requires many other capabilities (Maguire Shultz & Zedeck, 2009).[13] Those who score lower on the bar exam may have capabilities that the exam does not test and might go on to become better and more successful lawyers. Or they may limit themselves to areas of practice that draw on their capabilities and that others are uninterested in pursuing. The public might be better served by having a larger number of graduates compete rather than limiting the number of new lawyers in a manner that may not correspond to ultimate ability to practice proficiently in one's chosen area.[14]

One can anticipate other objections. As it is, bar examinations are subject to varied and frequent criticism.[15] If bar passage rates became significantly lower, law schools would object because a legal education would become an even riskier and less attractive option; paradoxically, the result would be to further discourage qualified applicants. Lowering the bar passage rate might also turn out to affect minorities and low-income applicants disproportionately, thereby further thwarting efforts to diversify the legal profession and to provide opportunities for social mobility.[16] As

Robert McKay noted thirty years ago, a time when applicants' qualifications were improving, limiting the growth of the legal profession by reducing the bar passage rate seems unlikely and undesirable "in a free society in which the legal profession has traditionally insisted upon open access to the profession for all qualified applicants" (McKay, 1984, pp. 45–46).

In any event, it seems unlikely that courts could reduce the number of newly admitted lawyers enough to make a noticeable impact on the level of competition for legal work. Certainly, the impact would not be noticeable broadly across the profession, but would be concentrated in the area of entry-level employment. Admitting fewer lawyers would do nothing for mid-level and senior lawyers competing for too few clients or employment opportunities.

An alternative is for courts (themselves or through the ABA) to erect barriers even further upstream, that is, by establishing more onerous requirements for admission to, or graduation from, law school.[17] California offers one model in its regulation of non-ABA-accredited in-state law schools. Students in these schools are required to pass a standardized examination midway through law school in order to continue to graduation and sit for the ordinary bar examination (Jarvis, 1996). Courts could conceivably reduce the number of new lawyers by requiring all law students to pass such an examination at an intermediate point. Arguably, such a requirement would be a more humane alternative in one respect: it would reduce the number of students who pay for a full three years of law school before being denied admission. But it would also prejudice law schools that would have to forgo tuition, increase the anxiety of a legal education, and eliminate some students who were poor test-takers but potentially excellent lawyers.

Downstream solution

The less obvious, but perhaps theoretically most attractive, alternative, is to erect barriers downstream – that is, to remove the licenses from the least capable practicing lawyers by requiring periodic re-certification and denying it to those who perform their work least well. This alternative is attractive in theory because it eliminates the need to make distinctions among individuals who have never practiced law based on an examination that does not perfectly predict whether one will later become a good lawyer. Instead, a re-certification requirement would focus on whether one is in fact a good lawyer.[18]

Lawyers might be providing below average services for any number of reasons. Some never developed the skills and knowledge to perform legal work well. Some engage in particular legal work for which they lack the requisite skills and knowledge. Some are fully capable of good work but are unmotivated, distracted or over-committed. Some were once capable but have failed to keep up with changes in the law or in modes of practice. From the public's perspective, it may not matter why a lawyer is rendering mediocre or poor work. If it is possible for courts to identify the least capable lawyers, and there are more lawyers than work to support them, the public would presumably be served by delicensing those who perform most poorly, thereby protecting clients who are themselves incapable of making reliable qualitative distinctions among lawyers.

Among the advantages to this approach is that it could be directed at lawyers in all practice settings, not just those seeking entry-level positions. And if courts were aggressive enough, they could entirely eliminate the perceived glut of lawyers, thereby ensuring the economic viability of legal careers for those better lawyers who remained. It might be argued that courts should not be in the business of regulating competition among lawyers, but this could be characterized as an incidental byproduct of efforts to maintain the quality of the bar.

The periodic re-certification of lawyers would not be a professional anomaly (Barnard, 2001). Doctors in certain specialties or subspecialties must be periodically re-certified.[19] Some boards require doctors to demonstrate improvement and professional growth not just maintenance of their professional skills. Commercial airline pilots must also demonstrate their ability periodically. Every six months, some pilots must complete a flight with an Federal Aviation Administration (FAA)-certified test rider who is specifically trained to evaluate a pilot's capabilities and ensure that their knowledge of the flight systems is current.

Models for evaluating practitioners already exist in the legal profession. For example, in New York City, membership on a panel of the Legal Referral Service requires a demonstration of experience and capability in one's area of practice. Applicants are interviewed by lawyers who work in the same area and applicants' written work is reviewed. Later, clients who are referred to a panelist are surveyed, and client complaints are investigated. If complaints are found to be justified, panel members can be removed. Other models exist with regard to lawyers seeking judgeships (and similarly in respect of sitting judges seeking new appointments). Selection and nominating committees and bar associations in various jurisdictions evaluate whether individuals are qualified to serve as judges typically based upon interviews of the candidates and of others familiar with their work and reviews of their work product.

Most likely, a proposal that, to raise the general quality of the US bar, a percentage of US lawyers should be required to surrender their law licenses, even though they are performing within the professional standard of competence, would be regarded as facetious. The bar would dismiss such a requirement without serious consideration on the grounds that it is at once anti-competitive and unfair to consumers who have an interest in choice and, at the same time, unfair to lawyers who have a stake in continuing to pursue their chosen careers.

Even if one agreed that a re-certification requirement made sense in theory, there would be convincing practical objections based on the difficulty and cost of devising fair and reliable methods for ascertaining the quality of lawyers' work. Lawyers' work varies enormously. No written test or battery of written tests could reliably gauge the actual quality of their work. It would be necessary for someone actually to examine lawyers' work. Reviewing written work would not be enough, since much of a lawyer's work may consist of counseling, negotiating, oral advocacy or other unwritten work. It would be necessary for examiners to observe lawyers at work for an extended period of time in order to obtain a sufficient basis for evaluation. The observations would encroach on attorney–client relationships and confidentiality, however.[20] In addition, because law practice varies so greatly from lawyer to lawyer, an examiner would probably have to work in the same field as the lawyer to be capable of assessing the work that he or she observed. It might prove difficult to find examiners in all areas of practice whose ability to assess a particular lawyer's work is credible. Even some acknowledged masters might be viewed as politically or culturally biased or as incapable of evaluating competitors impartially and objectively.[21] In the end, even the best evaluations may be imperfect. For example, generally indifferent lawyers may be more careful when they know they are being observed. There are more than a million US lawyers. Periodically examining them would be a huge and costly endeavor, even if enough lawyers with the requisite experience, integrity, objectivity and evaluative ability could be found to examine them all. From the perspective of maintaining professional competence, few would be convinced that the benefits justify the cost.

Moreover, objections based on unfairness to lawyers and consumers have some legitimacy. Most lawyers would consider the re-certification process burdensome (although it might provide a beneficial learning opportunity and an incentive to keep one's skills and knowledge current). Lawyers who lost their livelihoods (or worried about the possibility) would perceive the re-certification requirement to be harsh and unfair. These lawyers would not necessarily be providing incompetent or neglectful services in absolute terms. The incompetent are presumably removed via the ordinary disciplinary process following client complaints. Rather, the lawyers who lost their livelihood – after having invested substantial time and money into pursuing the legal profession – might be individuals who were competent but simply below average. Arguably, having invested their lives in the law, below-average lawyers should be allowed to continue. It might also be argued that clients should have the option of retaining lawyers whose performance is in some respects below average, because the lawyers may be valued in other respects: for example, they may inspire confidence, provide comfort, or have particular knowledge of the client or the client's work.

Conclusion

The perceived flood of US lawyers is, in part, a product of the regulatory process, which makes law practice attractive and lucrative for some by excluding nonlawyers and demanding high qualifications. But it seems unlikely that courts will employ regulatory measures to reverse the tide. The more effective a measure would seem to be, the more implausible or impractical it will seem; and theoretically the most effective, a re-certification requirement which would raise the level of professional practice while stemming the tide of lawyers, seems the least viable. That may say something about the US legal profession and its regulatory process. Although professional regulation has been a source of pride for the legal profession for more than a century, its emphasis has been on eliminating unethical and dangerous lawyers, not on enhancing the quality of practice. This is not necessarily to say, however, that the profession is indifferent to quality and to whether and how lawyers develop after they are admitted to practice. It may simply be that the US legal profession has sufficient, if not absolute, confidence in natural economic forces to address both the quality and the quantity of lawyers.

Notes

[1] This would be perceived as a 'modest proposal' at least in the sense in which the term was used by Swift (1729), when he proposed satirically that poor Irish families reduce their burdens by selling their children as food for the well-to-do English.

[2] Bar examinations have been criticized on multiple grounds, including that they disadvantage those who cannot afford a bar review course and that they place a premium on memorization (Jarvis, 1996).

[3] Legal academia in the United States is a lightning rod for dissatisfaction, and many of the complaints are unsubstantiated if not contradictory. For example, the assertion that US law schools should do a better job of preparing students to practice immediately upon being licensed is at odds with complaints about the cost of legal education and, especially, the suggestion that to control cost, law school should be reduced from three years to two (Segal, 2011a).

[4] Delaware requires five months of supervised law practice, which may be undertaken while in law school (Del. Sup. Ct. Rules, R. 52(a)(8)). Vermont requires three months of supervised law practice, which, likewise, may be undertaken while in law school (Vt. Sup. Ct. Rules of Admission, § 6(i)2).

[5] The autobiography of Lawrence Walsh, a future federal judge who struggled academically at Columbia Law School, discussed the difficulty of finding legal employment in the early 1930s, even for his classmates who were editors of the law review (Walsh, 2003).

[6] In 2004, Japan reportedly had one lawyer for every 6,305 people, while the United States had one lawyer for every 186 people (Nakazato *et al.*, 2006).

[7] Twenty years ago, Chief Justice Warren E. Burger observed that "our society is drowning in litigation" and that the "view that there are too many lawyers is widely held by other intelligent laymen, as well as by many leaders of the bar" (Cross, 1992). "Many [California lawyers polled in 1992] agreed that the rising tide of lawsuits stems directly from the growth of the legal profession, whose membership has more than tripled in the past four decades. Nearly half of the poll's respondents favor limiting the number of new lawyers admitted to the bar" (Editorial, 1992).

[8] Another occasional criticism is that the legal profession draws talented individuals away from areas of greater social good such as medicine and engineering (Cross, 1992).

[9] It is also questionable whether the overabundance of lawyers will have a substantial impact on legal fees at the high end, given the highly specialized nature of corporate law practice (Hadfield, 2000).

[10] The increasing difficulty for many US law graduates of recouping the cost of higher education through a career in law practice is now well recognized (Segal, 2011b).

[11] Many law graduates cannot find legal employment and many others "are relegated to jobs as temporary, part-time or contract lawyers, or other work unworthy of their degrees" (Harper, 2011).

[12] This was allegedly motivated in part by the role of "[l]aw schools [as] profit centers, paying overhead and subsidizing programs far from the world of the 1Ls" (Press, 2011).

[13] This is somewhat less true than it was before most states adopted the Multistate Performance Test, which is produced by the National Conference of Bar Examiners to measure certain fundamental lawyering skills. Because this is a written test, however, it is limited in the number of skills it can measure and its capacity to measure those skills.

[14] Lowering the bar passage rate would also seem to be unfair to lower-performing graduates who, though perhaps uncompetitive for legal employment, could pursue other career opportunities more effectively with a law license than merely with a law degree. The law license has often been regarded as a professional credential of significant value even for those who do not intend to, or cannot, achieve a career in the law. It seems harsh to deny bar admission to individuals who seem to have the capacity to become competent lawyers, based on the highly fallible prediction that they will be less capable than others, when the market might steer them away from legal employment in any event.

[15] The bar examination has been said to overemphasize memorization, and therefore not adequately measure one's qualifications to practice law. Curcio (2002, p. 363) criticizes the bar exam as "over-inclusive, allowing those with a very narrow range of skills to obtain a law license ... [and] under-inclusive by testing a very narrow range of skills in a way that is unrelated to the practice of law."

[16] As it is now, many believe that the admissions process disadvantages minorities (Sloan 2011b; Adams 2008).

[17] Amar and Ayres (2011) have suggested that, alternatively, law schools could offer low-performing students incentives to drop out.

[18] An alternative, but less sweeping, approach would be for disciplinary agencies to review the quality of lawyers' work generally when questions of competence are raised in an individual case. At present, disciplinary authorities do not consider whether a lawyer's neglect or negligence is generally symptomatic of inferior work. "The enforcement of competence in disciplinary cases has looked for proof of incompetence only to individual instances of charged neglect. Courts do not permit disciplinary agencies to engage in general appraisals of the qualifications of an admitted lawyer to practice law. As a result, only relatively blatant cases of incompetence are selected for disciplinary prosecution, and they often appear in isolation from the rest of the lawyer's practice, which may also be infected with incompetence, but of an unreported or milder variety" (Wolfram, 1986, pp. 190–191).

[19] Although doctors do not need to be recertified to maintain their medical licenses, many do need to be re-certified to maintain their status as board accredited. Although passage rates are high for both initial certification and re-certification, the examinations provide an incentive for lawyers to continue training and demonstrate professional growth and development (Federation of State Medical Boards, 2012).

[20] The profession puts a premium on lawyer–client confidentiality. Clients might be reluctant to share information or communicate with their lawyers if they knew the work was being reviewed.

[21] Many areas of legal practice are very difficult to judge objectively. There are no set criteria as to what makes a good lawyer. This means that there is substantial room for bias to creep into an evaluation. Practicing lawyers evaluating their competitors are particularly likely to be perceived as biased. Especially in challenging economic times, lawyers would have a perceived interest in limiting the possible competition in their field.

References

Abel, R.L. (1996) England and Wales: a comparison of the professional projects of barristers and solicitors, in: R. Label & P.S.C. Lewis (Eds) *Lawyers in Society an Overview* (Berkeley, CA, University of California Press), pp. 39–92.

Adams, E.A. (2008) ABA approves bar pass standards for accreditation, *American Bar Association Journal*, 11 February. Available at: http://www.abajournal.com/news/article/aba_approves_bar_pass_standards/, accessed 23 February 2013.

Amar, A.R. & Ayres, I. (2011) Paying law students to quit law school, *Slate*, 18 November. Available at: http://www.slate.com/articles/news_and_politics/jurisprudence/2011/11/law_schools_should_pay_students_to_quit_.html, accessed 26 June 2012.

American Bar Association (1973) *Report of the ABA Special Committee on Professional Utilization* (Chicago, American Bar Association).

American Bar Association (2012a) *ABA Model Rules of Professional Conduct, Rule 5.5*, Available at: http://www.americanbar.org/groups/professional_responsibility/publications/model_rules_of_professional_conduct/rule_5_5_unauthorized_practice_of_law_multijurisdictional_practice_of_law.html, accessed 26 June 2012.

American Bar Association (2012b) *Frequently Asked Questions: Frequently Asked Questions- Accreditation Process*, Available at: http://www.americanbar.org/groups/legal_education/resources/frequently_asked_questions.html, accessed 16 March 2012.

Auerbach, J.S. (1976) *Unequal Justice: Lawyers and Social Change in Modern America* (New York, Oxford University Press).
Barnard, J.W. (2001) Renewable bar admission: a template for making "professionalism" real, *Journal of the Legal Profession*, 25, pp. 1–73.
Bickerton, B.A. (2003) The sky is falling law firm layoffs in a bad economy, *Boston Bar Journal*, 47(1), pp. 19–20.
Bourne, R.W. (2012) The coming crash in legal education: how we got here, and where we go now, *Creighton Law Review*, 45, pp. 651–697.
Cross, F.B. (1992) The first thing we do, let's kill all the economists: an empirical evaluation of the effect of lawyers on the United States economy and political system, *Texas Law Review*, 7(645).
Curcio, A. (2002) A better bar: why and how the existing bar exam should change, *Nebraska Law Review*, 81, pp. 363–423.
Dolin, J.M. (2007) Opportunity lost: how law school disappoints law students, the public, and the legal profession, *California Western Law Review*, 44, pp. 219–255.
Editorial (1992) Score one for Dan Quayle: too many lawyers, suits, *Deseret News*, 21 July.
Federation of State Medical Boards (2012) For the public. Available at: http://fsmb.org/ua.html, accessed 20 July 2012.
Green, B.A. (2009) ABA ethics reform from 'MDP' to '20/20': some cautionary reflections, *Journal of the Professional Lawyer*, 2009, pp. 1–12.
Greenbaum, M. (2010) No more room at the bench, *Los Angeles Times*, 8 January.
Grigg, L. (1998) The Mandatory Continuing Legal Education (MCLE) debate: is it improving lawyer competence or just busy work?, *Bringham Young Law Review*, 12, pp. 417–434.
Hadfield, G.J. (2000) The price of law: how the market for lawyers distorts the justice system, *Michigan Law Review*, 98, pp. 953–1006.
Harper, S.J. (2011) Suffering in silence; as unhappy as the respondents to our midlevel survey sound, their plight could be worse. Just ask some of their fellow law school graduates, *American Lawyer*, 82, published online by Lexis, document ID: 1202511938585.
Henderson, W.D. & Zahorsky, R.M. (2011) Paradigm shift, *American Bar Association Journal*, 97, pp. 40–47.
Jarvis, R.M. (1996) An anecdotal history of the bar exam, *Georgetown Journal of Legal Ethics*, 9, pp. 359–412.
MacCrate Report (1992) *Legal Education and Professional Development: An Educational Continuum*, (American Bar Association, Section on Legal Education and Admissions to the Bar), p. 104.
Maguire Shultz, M. & Zedeck, S. (2009) Final Report – Identification, Development and Validation of Predictors for Successful Lawyering, Available at: http://ssrn.com/abstract=1353554, accessed 21 February 2013.
McKay, R.B. (1984) The future of professional independence, *The Lawyer's Professional Independence: Present Threats/Future Challenges*, (Chicago, American Bar Association), pp. 39–52.
Morgan, T.D. (2010) *The Vanishing American Lawyer* (New York, Oxford University Press).
Nakazato, M., Ramseyer, J.M. & Rasmusen, E.B. (2006) The Industrial Organization of the Japanese Bar: Levels and Determinants of Attorney Income, *Center for Law, Econonomics and Business*, Working Paper No. 559, 2006.
National Conference of Bar Examiners (2012) *Bar Examination and Admission Statistics*, Available at: http://www.ncbex.org/publications/statistics/, accessed 1 December 2012.
Podgers, J. (2011) The state of the union: the nation's lawyer population continues to grow – barley, *American Bar Association Journal*, 97(7), p. 58.
Press, A. (2011) The law school troubles; it's been another dreadful year for the public image of law schools, *American Lawyer*, September, 126, published online by Lexis, document ID: 1202511941503.
Rhode, D.L. (2000) *In the Interests of Justice: Reforming the Legal Profession* (New York, Oxford University Press).
Rhode, D.L. (2005) *Pro Bono in Principle and Practice: Public Service and the Professions* (Stanford, Stanford University Press).

Sander, R.N. & Williams, E.D. (1989) Why are there so many lawyers? Perspectives on a turbulent market, *Law & Social Inquiry*, 12(3), pp. 431–479.

Segal, D. (2011a) What they don't teach law students: lawyering, *New York Times*, 19 November. Available at: http://www.nytimes.com/2011/11/20/business/after-law-school-associates-learn-to-be-lawyers.html?pagewanted=all, accessed 20 June 2012.

Segal, D. (2011b) Law school economics: ka-ching!, *New York Times*, 16 July. Available at: http://www.nytimes.com/2011/07/17/business/law-school-economics-job-market-weakens-tuition-rises.html?scp=1&sq=law%20school, accessed 20 June 2012.

Segal, D. (2011c) Is law school a losing game?, *New York Times*, 8 January. Available at: http://www.nytimes.com/2011/01/09/business/09law.html?pagewanted=all, accessed 20 June 2012.

Segal, D. (2012) For 2nd year, a sharp drop in law school entrance tests, *New York Times*, 19 March. Available at: http://www.nytimes.com/2012/03/20/business/for-lsat-sharp-drop-in-popularity-for-second-year.html, accessed 20 June 2012.

Shaer, M. (2012) The case(s) against law school, *New York Magazine*, 4 March. Available at: http://nymag.com/news/features/law-schools-2012-3/, accessed 20 July 2012.

Sloan, K. (2011a) Law school? Who needs it? "Reading the law" remains an option, but carries its own challenges, *National Law Journal*, 5 December.

Sloan, K. (2011b) ABA faces diversity dilemma with proposed change to law school standards, *lawjobs.-com*, 22 July. Available at: http://www.law.com/jsp/article.jsp?id=1202504348774&slreturn=1, accessed 20 June 2012.

Tamanaha, B.Z. (2012) *Failing Law Schools* (Chicago, University of Chicago Press).

US Government Accountability Office (2009) *Higher Education: Issues Related to Law School Cost and Access* (US, USGAO).

Walsh, L.E. (2003) *The Gift of Insecurity: A Lawyer's Life* (Chicago, American Bar Association).

Wilkins, D.B. (1992) Who should regulate lawyers?, *Harvard Law Review*, 105, pp. 801–873.

Winston, C.M. & Crandall, R.W. (2011) *First Thing We Do, Let's Deregulate All the Lawyers* (Washington, DC, Brookings Institute Press).

Wolfram, C.W. (1986) *Modern Legal Ethics* (St. Paul, MN West Publishing).

It's the law schools stupid! Explaining the continuing increase in the number of lawyers

Herbert M. Kritzer
University of Minnesota Law School, Minneapolis, USA

Abstract *Many countries around the world have experienced sharp increases in the number of legal professionals over the last 40–50 years. In this paper, I focus on the role of the gatekeepers, which in most countries today are the institutions that provide education and training for those hoping to enter the profession. I argue that while the profession may have an incentive to control the 'production of producers', the educational institutions do not share this incentive. While this argument has been made previously, in this paper I seek to draw out the implications of the institutional incentives, both with regard to how the institutions operate to supply education and training, and with regard to the impact on the demand for the education and training the institutions provide. The discussion considers developments in a range of both common law and civil law countries.*

Introduction

How are we to understand the phenomenal growth in the number of legal professionals in many countries around the world over the last 50 years? Is it simply that the demand for the services that legal professionals provide has increased as economies and populations have grown? That undoubtedly explains some growth. Does it reflect broader societal changes toward a profession-oriented, post-industrial society (Bell, 1973)? That undoubtedly explains some of the growth. Is it a result of the feminist movement that has opened legal education and legal practice to women who had previously been largely excluded from the profession? Again, that is a piece of the puzzle. The argument of this article is that a crucial element is the interests of the educational institutions that train future lawyers.

In common law countries the gatekeeper to the legal profession was, until sometime in the twentieth century, the profession itself. This gatekeeping was accomplished largely through apprenticeship, which was either formally or informally necessary to become a licensed practitioner. As described by Richard Abel the apprenticeship often involved forgoing some or all income which provided a further barrier to entry (Abel, 1988, pp. 35–62, 139–164). While outside the US apprenticeship has survived to some degree in forms such as traineeships, pupilages and articles, by the mid- to late-twentieth century universities had largely become the primary training ground for those seeking to enter the profession (Abel, 1986, pp. 10–11; 1988, pp. 270–281). Importantly, while the profession has an incentive to 'control the production of producers', the universities generally have no such incentive. Given the shift in control from the profession to the educational establishment, those educational institutions have played a central role in the continuing growth in the number of law graduates and lawyers.

Universities are driven by a variety of incentives, two of which are revenue and prestige. These two incentives will tend to work in opposite directions: the former tends to push for greater numbers while the latter pushes for restriction in numbers. However, in an educational system with a strong pre-existing prestige ranking, institutions lower down in the hierarchy will be driven more by the revenue incentive, often turning away only those who are manifestly unprepared, if even those. The institutions concerned about prestige will focus on a combination of qualifications and selectivity, allowing enrollments to increase only as long as the desired balance can be maintained. Some very prestigious schools, such as Harvard, can attract large numbers of very highly qualified applicants and have high enrollments, while other schools toward the bottom in prestige may have large enrollments because they are at best minimally selective in their admissions policies.

The educational institutions represent the supply side of the production of producers. However, that is only half of the equation. The other half is the demand side: students seeking legal education. Students can have a range of motivations: potential income, social status, the prospect of interesting and satisfying work, and/or service to a community or an ideology (Chen, 2012, p. 1185; Lentz & Laband, 1995, p. 181). The decision over whether to seek a legal education will depend on the strength of those motivations, the perceived likelihood of succeeding with regard to the motivation, and the costs of obtaining the education.

In the sections that follow I will consider both the supply side and the demand side of the legal education/training equation. With regard to the supply side, I will focus largely on what has changed over the last 30–50 years, and the factors that might account for these changes. With regard to the demand side, I consider the issues confronting potential law students as they consider their motivations, prospects for achieving those motivations, and the costs of obtaining the necessary education and training.

The supply side

The law school and law student explosion

In 1963, in the United States, there were 135 ABA-accredited law schools enrolling 46,666 students in JD (or LLB) programs; that year a total of 9,638 degrees were awarded by these programs. By the 2011–2012 academic year there were 201

ABA-accredited schools and JD enrollment had more than tripled to 146,288; the prior year 44,495 JD degrees were awarded. Thus, enrollment grew by about 100,000 and the number of ABA-accredited schools by 66. Moreover, the average JD enrollment at an ABA-accredited law school more than doubled, from 345 to 729. About two-thirds of the 100,000 additional students reflected growth in the number of women pursuing JDs, from only 1,739 in 1963–1964 to 68,262 in 2009–2010; the number of men pursuing JDs grew by 74 percent over this period from 44,927 to 78,026.[1] There was a surge in the number of law schools as the baby-boom generation arrived with the number of schools increasing by an average of two per year from 1965 through to 1980; in the last 30 years, there has been an average of about one school added each year.

Figures on enrollments in other countries are harder to find, but there is reasonably good information on the growth in the number of schools with law programs. Richard Abel reports that, prior to World War II, 12 English universities offered academic programs of legal education; by 1980–1981, this number had grown to 49 including 24 programs in what were then called polytechnics (Abel, 1986, p. 10); in 1986–1987 there were something over 4,000 law graduates (Kibble, 1989, p. 135). The archived website of the now defunct UK Council on Legal Education (UKCLE) shows 75 law programs in England and Wales, plus one English-law program in Scotland and both of the law faculties in Northern Ireland that offer English law degrees. A UKCLE 2001 report noted that at that time there were about 10,000 law graduates each year, about 45 percent of whom were entering the legal profession;[2] some portion of these graduates were from Scotland and Northern Ireland, but the figure suggests that the number had probably doubled over the prior 15 years.

In 1960 there were six university law schools in Australia (Weisbrot, 1989, p. 85). This had doubled to 12 in 1987, and has since grown to 31 (Prior, 2008, pp. 14–15). By 2008, Australia had 28,000 students studying law.[3] At that time there were a total of 40,000 lawyers in Australia (Prior, 2008, pp. 14–15).

Compared to England, and Australia, the provision of legal education in Canada has been relatively stable since the late 1980s (through to at least 2002). The number of law graduates in Canada was steady during that period at about 3,500 per year, 2,500 of whom were "called to the bar" (Brusegard, 2004, p. 5). From 1980 through to 2010 no new law schools opened in Canada (Levin & Alkoby, 2012, ms. p. 1). For a period of 22 years from 1976 to 1998 the number of first-year law students in common law programs remained steady at about 2,000 (Cohen, 1998). However, at least in Ontario, there has been some growth since 1997, with the number of entering students growing by about 40 percent. What explains this relative stability compared to other common law countries is unclear.

Germany is a country where universities have long played a major role in preparing legal professionals (Korioth, 2006, p. 86).[4] In modern Germany preparation for legal practice begins with a university education concluding with a first state examination, which is then followed by practical training; a second state examination follows the completion of the period of practical training. The university stage is essentially open to all-comers meeting the requirements for entrance into a university; while students might be turned away from their first-choice schools, all are guaranteed a place at one university or another, and studies are free of charge (Korioth, 2006, p. 90). The result is large numbers of students studying law: 100,000 across 43 law faculties circa 2003 (Korioth, 2006, p. 89),[5] which is an average of 2,325 per law faculty; the largest law faculty enrolls about 4,000 students (Korioth, 2006, p. 91). The typical student takes the first examination after about five years; about 50 percent of those who begin law studies ultimately pass the first state examination.[6] Circa 2003, something over 10,000 per year ultimately pass the second state examination (Korioth, 2006, p. 89). The number of students starting law studies increased from under 10,000 per year prior to 1983 to something of the order of 20,000 per year by the early 1990s, a figure that has remained relatively stable.

There were only nine law departments in Japanese universities before World War II. By 2005 there were 93 law departments with about 45,000 students starting (undergraduate) law studies each year (Yoshida, 2006, p. 209). As I discuss below, very few of the eventual graduates of these programs went on to become fully qualified lawyers (*bengoshi*) because of limits imposed on the number who could pass the National Bar Examination required for entry into the Legal Training and Research Institute (LTRI);[7] only LTRI graduates are qualified to appear as advocates in court, although many other law graduates perform a range of tasks commonly done by lawyers in the US (Saegusa, 2009, pp. 371–372). The system was changed in 2004 with the creation of post-graduate legal education in Japan; 74 new law schools were created to provide this education. The expectation was that a substantial portion of graduates of these programs – possibly 50 percent (Saegusa, 2009, p. 393) or possibly even 70–80 percent (Foote, 2013, ms. p. 4) – would pass the National Bar examination and enter the LTRI for a 12-month course of study. However, the pass rate on the new exam, which started out at close to 50 percent, was under 25 percent for 2011. Several of the new law schools which had very low pass rates have announced plans to close or merge after current students complete their JDs. It does appear that the low pass rate has served to discourage potential students from applying to one of the new JD programs; the number of applicants has declined from 73,000 in the first year the schools were in operation to 18,446 in 2012 (Foote 2013, ms. p. 5).[8]

Clark (2012, p. 337) provides data on the increase in the number of law students from 1970 to 2009 for several additional civil law countries: from 59,000 to 216,000 in Italy; from 21,000 to 112,000 in Spain (actually down from 160,000 in 1990). In contrast, the growth in France has been minimal, from 158,000 to 170,000. Clark also shows the growth in the numbers studying law in several Latin American countries, where the increases have been as high as a factor of 10 or more (Clark, 2012, pp. 340–342).

None of the figures discussed above adjust for population. Figure 1 shows the number of law students per 10,000 population for 1960, 1970 and one year in the period 2008–2010 (except for Venezuela and Columbia which are for 2000). The figure suggests several points. First, the growth in the US and Canada has been modest over the last 50 years. Second, for the remaining countries, there have been very significant increases over the last 50-year period. Third, the per capita

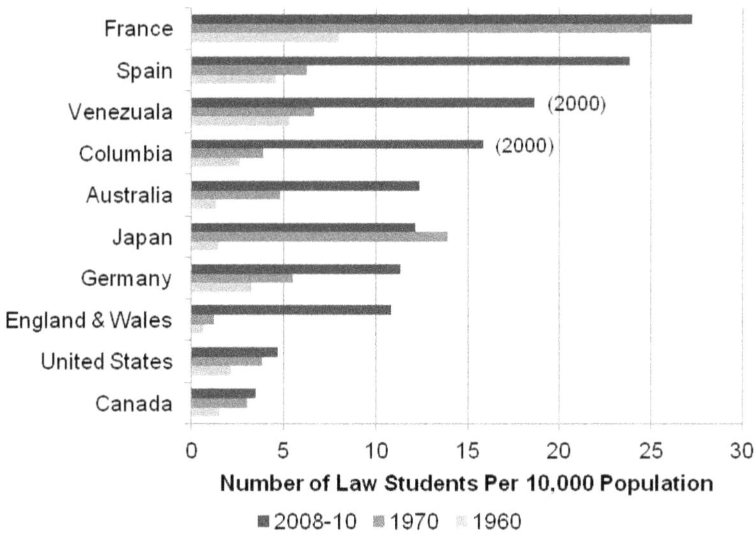

Figure 1. *Comparing per capita enrollment in legal studies*

enrollment in legal education circa 2010 varies sharply, and the United States stands near the bottom among the countries compared; only Canada is actually lower. Ideally, one might want to use a subset of the population as a base of comparison (e.g. 18–30 year olds); however, that information is not readily available for many of the countries being compared.

Explaining the increased supply of legal education

Some of the increased number of places for students to study law reflect demand driven by demographics. Two factors that stand out are the number of persons of the right age to start such studies (i.e. the post-war baby boom) and the opening of educational and professional opportunities to women. Some of the increased numbers reflect nation-specific developments such as the unification of Germany. Some of the increased numbers reflect deliberate decisions by governments to widen the scope of educational opportunity; this occurred in both Australia and Germany. Moustafa (2010, pp. 613–618) tells a different kind of story about the sharp increase in the number of students studying law in Egypt that began around 1960. According to his analysis, admissions were opened up both to make the universities less elitist and to downgrade the prestige of the legal profession whose members were antagonistic toward the Nasser regime. The best students who once might have entered the law faculty were drawn to other faculties such as economics and political science that would lead to secure careers in government service. Moreover, the standards for admission to law faculties fell, resulting in large numbers of students; this in turn led to large numbers entering the legal profession which increased competition and pushed down incomes.

While demand is a major factor in decisions about supply, one must consider other factors. Central here is finance. In most countries, the bulk of the cost of higher education, including legal education, has been state-funded. In Great

Britain, until 1998, universities charged no tuition and students could receive modest maintenance grants to cover living expenses; while tuition increased substantially in Britain after it was introduced, university education continued to be highly subsidized at least through 2011. Effective September 2012, tuition rose to as much as £9,000 per year and a system of government loans to students replaced most of the remaining direct government subsidy with repayment set at 9 percent of income exceeding £21,000 per year for 30 years after which any remaining debt is forgiven (Hutton, 2012). In Germany, education at public universities continues to be tuition-free in most *Lander*. Canadian universities do charge tuition, but it continues to be modest in comparison to the cost of providing education; for example, the average tuition for law students in 2010–2011 was $4,633. All but four of the universities in Australia are public; while tuition typically is of the order of $8,000–$10,000 per year, this reflects a significant governmental subsidy and Australian students can receive loans that are paid off after graduation based on formulas based on the graduate's income.

While education in most of the other countries considered above is largely delivered by public universities, in both Japan and the United States private universities play a major role. In Japan, 70 percent of students attend private universities. Both public and private universities charge substantial tuition. For private universities in 2006, tuition averaged about $13,000 with public universities at about $8,000.[9]

In the US, the split between public and private is the reverse of Japan, with 73 percent of students attending public universities; only 16 percent attend private, nonprofit colleges and universities. At the undergraduate level, public education in the US continues to be subsidized; average tuition for public four-year colleges and universities is about $7,300 compared to $27,293 for private institutions.[10] While in the US the public subsidy for university education has generally been declining over the last 30 years, in recent years the decline for public law schools has been especially sharp; in a small number of states the subsidy for law students has all but disappeared, essentially privatizing the school (see Fischer, 2010).[11] The average tuition and fees at public law schools for students who are residents of the state funding the institution has risen from $2,006 in 1985 to $18,472 in 2009 (medians from $1,792 to $16,546). For students who are not residents, the average published tuition at public institutions has increased from $4,724 to $30,413. This puts the nonresident tuition fairly close to the tuition charged by private law schools, which in 2009 averaged $35,743 (up from $7,526 in 1985).[12]

What about factors related to the interests of the educational institutions? Compared to many other types of professional-level training provided through universities, legal education as it has been done through the twentieth century is relatively inexpensive. It requires relatively minimal facilities beyond lecture halls and libraries (Segal, 2011a).[13] It can be delivered to large numbers of students, and the number of students can be increased in ways that are disproportionate to increased costs of providing that education. The facilities faculty need for their own research and writing are relatively modest compared to other disciplines of comparable prestige. Law schools have the potential of being a profit center – a "cash cow" (Bourne, 2012, p. 686; Tamanaha, 2012, p. 127) – for a university. In the words of one observer, "It is one of the academy's open secrets: law schools toss off so much cash they are sometimes required to hand over as much as 30 percent of their revenue to universities, to subsidize less profitable fields" (Segal, 2011b). This is by no means unique to the United States. One possible explanation for the increase in both the number and size of law faculties in England is that the revenue per student more than covers the cost of educating the additional students, and the surplus can be redirected to subsidize more costly areas of instruction or contribute disproportionately toward central institutional costs.

A second factor related to institutional interests is that having a law faculty or law school adds a measure of prestige for an institution. Why, for example, did the University of St. Thomas in Minnesota decide it needed to have a law school? No one suggested that there was a shortage of places for law students in Minnesota. The university's explanation was that it was creating a different kind of law school; according to the school's mission state, one that places an emphasis on values reflecting a dedication "to integrating faith and reason in the search for truth through a focus on morality and social justice". The university had received some significant gifts to fund the startup costs for the school, but arguably the larger goal was to increase the institution's prestige regionally if not nationally. Several years after the law school was started, St. Thomas flirted with creating a medical school, which would have further established its bona fides as a major institution, but quickly abandoned that plan almost certainly due, at least in part, to the much greater costs involved in starting a medical school compared to a law school.

As noted above, there has been a sharp increase in the number of law faculties in England in the last 25 years. An important development in the history of English higher education was the rebranding of more than 60 polytechnics and other institutions as universities under the terms of the Further and Higher Education Act 1992. Many of these new universities proceeded to establish degree-granting law faculties, and the motivation to do so was probably a combination of the revenue over and above costs that might be produced and a view that a true university should have a law faculty.

As discussed previously, Japan has recently changed educational requirements for those hoping to become *bengoshi*. As part of the change, planners anticipated that perhaps 20 schools would create post-graduate JD programs (Maxeiner, 2003, p. 10). The relevant authorities chose not to impose any specific limit and to recognize any program that met a set of minimum requirements, resulting in 74 new schools being created, almost all of which were located at universities with existing undergraduate law programs. Despite the fact that many of these universities had relatively few students who had passed the LTRI admissions exam, there was clearly a felt need to create new programs. This may have partly reflected a view that having a JD program was important in order to maintain an existing undergraduate program (Maxeiner, 2003, p. 11). However, it is also likely that universities believed having a JD program was important for the public's perception of the institutions, or the faculty who taught in the existing undergraduate programs saw having a JD program as important for their own status within the academy. Some would probably argue that the most important factor was prestige. In post-war Japan, the undergraduate law faculties have been one of the most prestigious undergraduate faculties. Failing to create a JD program could put the prestige that had accrued as a result of having an undergraduate law faculty at risk. A fear of loss of prestige would create tremendous pressure to create a JD program.

One final consideration that explains the creation of at least some private law schools and one or more public programs in the US is an institution's sense of mission. That is, the university starts a law school with the goal of turning out lawyers who will bring a particular perspective or approach to their future practices. As noted above, the University of St. Thomas expressed its reason for starting a law school in terms of a sense of mission. Most other law schools that would fall in this category are affiliated with religious movements or perspectives (Ave Maria Law School, Regents University Law School, Liberty University School of Law). The law school that was created in 1983 at the City University of New York had as its goal producing public interest lawyers and the school still describes itself as the "premier public interest law school in the country". It may be the case that one or more private law schools in other countries were also established as expressions of a particular religious or political perspective.

One important development over the last 25 years is that the relative cost of starting a law school has declined. As noted above, the infrastructure that was in the past needed to create and maintain a law school was lecture halls and a library. For a new law school, the capital required to create a library that met accreditation standards, in terms of both the physical space and the collection, was quite large. Today, a new law school can rely upon electronic resources for much of what students need for their studies, which students can access remotely, further reducing the physical space that is needed. Law schools need to have librarians to assist students and faculty, subscriptions to online materials, and the infrastructure to access those materials in the form of wireless networks, but all of this is significantly different from the infrastructure needed a quarter of a century ago.

The demand side

Choosing to study law

One puzzle is the continued strong interest in studying law even in the face of evidence that likelihood of success in pursuing law as a career is either small or declining. The extreme example has long been Japan where the barriers to becoming a fully qualified legal professional, a *bengoshi*, have been formidable. The undergraduate faculties of law in Japan have long drawn many times the number of students who would ever win a place at the Legal Training Institute – through the 1980s only 2–3 percent of those taking the exam (Yoshida, 2006, p. 211). As discussed above, in 2004 Japan introduced post-graduate law schools. In 2011 those schools admitted 3,150 students, down from a peak of 5,800 in 2006 soon after the new law schools had started (Foote, 2013, ms. p. 5); but even with this more selective system, the pass rate of the new National Bar Examination has been running around 25 percent (Foote, 2013, ms. p. 40). The drop in numbers of potential students seeking places in the JD programs probably reflects the reality that the bar exam has continued to be a major hurdle that blocks the majority from gaining entrance to the LTRI.

The major attractions of a career in law include the potential financial rewards, satisfying work and the opportunity to help people (Lentz & Laband, 1995, p. 181). A 1995 survey of first-semester law students at a range of schools asked them to rate the importance of each of seven goals as possible motivating factors in the decision to enter law school; 96 percent rated "developing a satisfying career" as important or very important, with 86 percent and 78 percent giving one of those ratings to "desire for eventual financial security" and "helping individuals", respectively.[14] How the importance of these goals may have been affected by developments since 2008 is unclear.

Law constitutes one of the occupations which carry a significant potential of prestige and substantial financial rewards. Other professional occupations such as medicine, accounting or engineering offer the potential of these same things. However, law offers something these other fields generally lack: no apparent need to feel comfortable with mathematics, something that a significant proportion of people lack. Anyone who has tried to introduce statistical or mathematical information in the typical American law school class has undoubtedly observed the glazing over of eyes among most of the students in the room. Of course, for some students this is not an issue: those coming from an undergraduate degree in economics or accounting, or who had studied science or engineering. In countries such as England or Australia where law is a first degree, the response of students to such material may be even less enthusiastic.

Financing legal education

Central to the continued demand for legal education has been the combination of subsidy and the availability of financing (i.e. student loans). Generally, governments which provide the subsidy and the financing or protections to financial institutions making student loans have to date not been willing to impose limits which would impact demand. As noted previously, direct government subsidies to public law schools in the US have been declining in recent years, and this has shifted a greater portion of law school revenue to student loans. Moreover, as also noted previously, the rise in tuition at both public and private law schools in the US has been relentless, and has been sustained by students taking on an increasing amount of debt (Tamanaha, 2012, pp. 109–111). The average debt of graduates in 2008–2009 was $100,002 for those graduating from private law schools and $66,045 for those graduating from public law schools (Bourne, 2012, p. 672). These figures represent more than a 40 percent increase over the debt of those graduating in 2001–2002. For 2011 graduates, the corresponding figures are $125,000 and $75,700 (Weiss, 2012), which would put the increase over the decade at more than 50 percent.

The clear question is how long this can continue, particularly in light of the continuing effects of the economic crisis of 2007–2008 which heavily impacted the job market for law graduates. One article spoke of the "law school bubble" (Henderson & Zahorsky, 2012) and another of "the coming crash in legal education" (Bourne, 2012); both argued that the current system in the US is not sustainable under current economic conditions. The unknown is whether students will become less willing to take on substantial debt ($100,000–$200,000) given the uncertainties over job prospects (see the next section) or if government will become less willing to provide the loan guarantees and subsidies. Importantly, Tamanaha (2012, pp. 154–155) has shown that the dependence on government loans (or government-guaranteed loans) is greatest for students who attend law schools where students have the least probability of being able to pay back those loans. Similarly, the average debt tends to be highest for graduates of those same schools (Tamanaha, 2012, pp. 110–111, 122–124). Tamanaha has suggested that the government should cap government student loans for each law school, end any government guarantee for private loans and make private loans dischargeable in bankruptcy. The net effect of such changes would be to make the providers of private loans much more cautious and attentive to the likelihood of the loans being repaid. Law schools would be forced to rationalize the size of their programs, to reduce costs, and to design programs that produce graduates who can repay the loans they receive. Tamanaha also raises the possibility of applying to law schools the rule now applied to for-profit colleges, whereby an institution loses its eligibility to receive funds from federal loans if a high proportion of graduates are unable to repay those loans.

As noted above, the number of students applying to Japan's new JD program has declined, leading to a parallel decline in enrollments in those programs. A decline may be starting in American law schools; as shown in Figure 2,[15] the most recent three years have seen a sharp fall in the numbers taking the Law School Admissions Test (LSAT), from 171,500 in 2009–10 to 112,515 in 2012–13. The numbers applying to law school have declined (14 percent from 2010–2011 to 2011–2012), and the

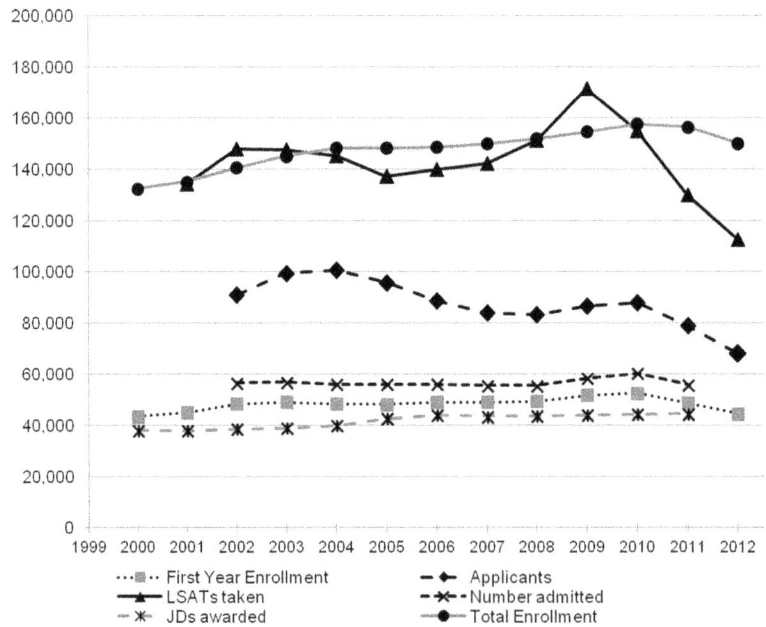

Figure 2. *Trends related to American law schools*

2011–2012 and 2012–2013 academic years saw drops of 7 percent and 9 percent, respectively, in the number of entering JD students.[16] However, as the figure also shows, there has been a pattern of decline in applicants since at least 2000. Most likely the declines are not spread evenly across law schools, but rather are more concentrated in the lower ranked schools.

The importance of money provided through loans as the source of revenue for American law schools should not be underestimated. Almost 90 percent of law students borrow to finance at least part of their legal education (Bourne, 2012, p. 672), totaling at least $3.7 billion in 2010 (Henderson & Zahorsky, 2012, p. 32); this is over $25,000 per student pursuing a JD. If one takes the mean published tuition of private law schools as the best estimate of the mean cost of legal education, money from loans constitutes well over 70 percent of law schools' revenue after taking into account the discounting enjoyed by half or more of students at most schools (Bourne, 2012, p. 667).[17] There are at least some law schools where tuition revenue is virtually 100 percent dependent on loans students obtain from the federal government. A sharp change in the amount of loan funds coming to the law schools would have a major impact. Funds could also become scarce if repayments drop, which in turn reduces the replenishment of funds available for future loans (Henderson & Zahorsky, 2012, p. 32).

In England, because of the government subsidy for legal education, the debt burden appears to have been considerably less than in the US. Still, only 20 percent of pupil barristers in 2009–2010 reported having no educational debt; over half had debts of at least £10,000 and 6 percent owed more than £40,000 (*Solicitors Journal*, 2012). For trainee solicitors, the pattern (as of 2009) does not differ a great deal: 18 percent had no debt, 55 percent had debts of at least £10,000 and 35 percent had debts of more than £15,000 (Baksi, 2010). This will all change with the new regime that started in September 2012 under which students borrow from the government and then repay based on income over a 30-year period. How this will impact the number of students pursuing a legal education and ultimately the number seeking to enter the profession is not knowable, at least for several years.

It is likely that the debt issue is important in Japan, although I could find no published discussions (in English) of debt as a factor in legal education in Japan. Based on correspondence with legal academics in Japan there does not appear to be any government subsidies or loan guarantees for students pursuing the new JD degree; students rely primarily on support from their families. One would surmise that debt issues would loom fairly large in the Japanese context.

Changing prospects for a career in law

Not everyone who seeks a degree in law, whether an American-style post-graduate JD degree or the more common first degree, seeks to obtain employment that requires a law degree. We have no data on what proportion of entering students have no interest in a career as a qualified lawyer. One regularly hears that a legal education is a good background for many careers other than law, and while this is true, it is also true of any area of study that instills strong analytical skills. While the drop in total law school enrollment for 2011–2012 was less than 1 percent, for the 2012-2013 academic year total enrollment dropped slightly over 4 percent.

Nor is everyone completing formal training able to successfully pass required exams, or obtain a training contract, or find a job working as a legal professional. In the US, the best estimate is that 10 percent of those who attempt the bar exam never succeed in passing, and hence are unable to pursue a career as a lawyer (Yakowitz, 2010, p. 3). Data from 20 years ago show that about a quarter of law graduates were at that time not working as lawyers, with a quarter of those not in the workforce; most of the rest were working in non-law occupations, many in top or midlevel management positions (Baker & Jorgensen, 2000, p. 16). Presumably some portion were those who had been unsuccessful in their efforts to pass the bar exam, with others either having never sought to enter practice and having abandoned, at least temporarily, the profession either due to personal circumstances (e.g. family responsibilities) or after having failed in their efforts to make a go as a legal practitioner. More recently, the number of graduates of American law schools who are able to find employment as a lawyer has decreased, and the problem is inversely related to the ranking of the law school from which one obtains a degree (Tamanaha, 2012, pp. 114–118).

Analyses from the After-the-JD study show that the most dissatisfied among US law graduates in the first years of practice tend to be drawn from graduates of top level law schools, particularly graduates who come from upper middle class families (see Dinovitzer & Garth, 2007). A large proportion of these graduates have positions as associates in large law firms with salaries at or approaching the high end of what new JDs can hope to earn. However, this group finds the work itself, both the substance and the time demands, unsatisfying. That is, while they may have both the income and prestige they probably sought, they do not have the autonomy or interesting assignments they expected. The study finds that the most satisfied may be among those whose ambitions were modest, who attended a third or fourth tier law school, and for whom the status of even a lower level of practice without high income represents a step up from their other career opportunities. Importantly this study is following lawyers who completed law school in 2001; given the combination of the sharp rise in the debt burden of law school graduates and the reduced job prospects of many graduates, recent graduates of those lower ranked schools may face a particularly harsh job market while carrying a heavy debt burden (see Tamanaha, 2012, pp. 110, 118).

The economic downturn has created difficulties for American law graduates regardless of what kind of career a graduate might have hoped to pursue. Law firms both large and small (and medium) have reduced hiring (Bourne, 2012, pp. 657–659); firms have shed both associates and partners. The large corporate law firms may change their hiring strategies to focus on a smaller number of schools as 'suppliers' (see Furlong, 2012). Jobs in government service or public interest have declined as government has shed employees and funds for public interest groups have declined. While American law schools continue to turn out about 45,000 new JDs each year, projections suggest that the job market will produce only about 25,000 openings per year for those graduates through to 2018 (Tamanaha, 2012, p. 139). The result is that finding a job after graduation is now a challenge for a much larger proportion of law graduates, and will continue to be a challenge, at least until a significant number of baby boomers now in practice choose to retire. The amount that has now been written about this issue (see, for example, Koppel, 2011; Lowrey, 2010; Segal, 2011a; Sloan, 2010) has likely sensitized many potential law students to the difficulties they may face and this *may* account for the declines in LSAT-takers, law school applicants and entering JD students. However, while most commentators seem to be pessimistic (but see Mitchell, 2012), only time will tell whether either the worsened job prospects of law graduates or the apparent decline in interest in attending law school represents more than temporary phenomena.

What about other countries? As discussed above, demand for the JD programs in Japan has clearly dropped as it has become evident that the prospects of success on the new bar exam continue to be dim, even if they are not anywhere near as dim as was the case under the old system. In Ontario (the only province of Canada for which I have been able to find data for more than a few years), the number of applicants has, with the exception of one year, risen steadily over the last decade.[18] The last year has seen some discussion of an 'articling crisis' which refers to the problem of a small portion (12 percent in 2011) of law graduates being unable to secure 10-month positions as articled clerks which is a requirement to qualify for practice (Gray, 2011); in part this probably reflects that the number seeking such positions increased 25 percent between 2006 and 2010 (McKiernan, 2011). In England it has long been the case that a significant number of those completing the legal practice course (LPC), which is the one-year post-LLB course required for those hoping to enter practice as solicitors, have encountered difficulties in securing traineeship positions; those difficulties appear to be increasing. In part this reflects that there are many more places in the LPC (14,482) and many more students enrolled in the course (9,337 in 2010) than there are available training contracts (5,809 in 2010). Moreover, the government cut funding that provided positions for 750 traineeships for potential legal aid solicitors (Rose, 2010). It is important to note that the hunt for training contracts does not end if one is not secured the first year; this means that the number actually seeking such contracts is considerably greater than the number successfully completing the LPC each year (Nair, 2011). On the barristers' side of the profession, the number of pupilages declined by about 20 percent between 2007–2008 and 2010–2011 (*Solicitors Journal*, 2012).

Conclusion

How will law schools and law students respond to the potential financial challenges and the changing career prospects that either have developed or appear to be on the horizon? Will many of those who hoped to study law turn to other pursuits in light of growth in the cost of legal education and the dimmed prospect of a lucrative career? If applications to law schools continue to drop, will law schools seek to maintain their current level of enrollments or adjust their size and budgets to reflect the changed market for the education they deliver? Will alternative methods of delivering legal education at a lower cost, thus imposing lower burdens and risks on students, become an important factor (see Tamanaha, 2012, pp. 172–177)? What, if any, impact will any of these changes, should they occur, have on the number of lawyers offering their services to the public?

The current momentum, both in terms of demand and supply, may be difficult to slow. There are too many interests that have a stake in the system as it now exists. While one might expect major changes in demand, one could also speculate that the types of persons who choose to pursue legal education are less sensitive to the risks than the average student might be. In his recent book, *Thinking, Fast and Slow*, Daniel Kahneman (2011, pp. 256–258) describes what he labels "entrepreneurial delusion" by which he means the "optimistic temperament" possessed by many entrepreneurs who grossly overestimate the likelihood that their new businesses will be successful given that about two-thirds of new small businesses in the US fail within the first five years. It may be that those who choose to pursue law degrees suffer from what Tamanaha labeled "optimism bias", which one might label "career delusions": they know that a significant number of law graduates encounter trouble in launching a professional career, but they believe they are different. Tamanaha describes this "optimism bias" as follows (2012, pp. 143–144):

> Law students are high achievers, accustomed to doing well with effort. They assume that this reliable path to past success will pay off again without fully realizing – until they sit in the class and look around – that everyone else in the room is just as smart and hard working. Only after arrival do the long odds of success sink in – and then it is too late.

This is reinforced by

> independent surveys that find that most law students would enroll even if they knew that only a tiny number of them would wind up with six-figure salaries. Nearly all of them, it seems, are convinced that they're going to win the ring toss at this carnival and bring home the stuffed bear. (Segal, 2011a)

One study of students entering American law schools found that 99 percent predicted they would be in the top half of their class, and about a third predicted they would be in the top 10 percent (Sander & Bambauer, 2012, p. 901). Students who are unwilling to ask about the chances of success because they believe they are sure to succeed are unlikely to choose not to pursue a legal education. While growth of the legal profession may slow, optimism bias means that the growth in the number of lawyers is likely to continue in the absence of externally imposed controls.

Countries such as Japan and Korea, that have long had rigid controls, may be allowing some growth in the number of fully qualified lawyers, but that growth in terms of absolute numbers is modest and there is no indication that it will be anything but modest even when there has been much discussion about the need for significant growth. Where such controls have not existed it is likely to be politically difficult to impose them. For example, in the 1990s the Law Society in England sought to freeze the number of positions available in the legal practice course (LPC) in order to deal with the bottleneck that would-be solicitors faced in obtaining training contracts; however, it backed down when providers of the LPC threatened legal action over the anti-competitive impact of any such limits (Rose, 2010). In other words, the economic interest of the providers of legal education trumped the interest of the professional body.

Acknowledgements

This paper was prepared for presentation at the workshop on "Too Many Lawyers? Facts, Reasons, Consequences and Solutions", International Institute for the Sociology of Law, Õnati, Spain, 19–20 April 2012. My thanks go to Masayuki Murayama, Daniel Foote, Avrom Sherr and Hazel Genn for sharing with me their insights regarding developments in their own countries. Thanks also to David Clark for sharing with me, what was at the time, a forthcoming chapter comparing legal education around the world, and to Richard Sander for sharing with me the data from the 1995 National Study of Student Performance in the First Year of Law School.

Notes

[1] All of these statistics are from the website of the ABA Section on Legal Education and Admission to the Bar.
[2] See http://www.ukcle.ac.uk/students/directory/, last accessed 10 February 2012.
[3] See http://www.alsa.net.au/about-alsa.
[4] See Clark (2012) for a discussion of the development of legal training and education in civil law countries.
[5] The number had peaked at 112,756 in 1997, and was down to 92,577 in 2010.
[6] This is based on Korioth's observations that about 20 percent (or more) "change their subject or leave the university before taking the First State Examination" (p. 90), 10–20 percent "fail an intermediate examination" (p. 95, n54), and 30 percent "who take the first state examination fail to pass" (p. 96).
[7] For many years, only 500 exam takers per year passed; by 2005 the number passing each year had been increased to 1,500 (Yoshida, 2006, p. 211).
[8] South Korea has had a system very similar to Japan's (see Kim, 2006), and is making a similar shift to post-graduate legal training as preparation for the national bar exam with one important difference: the number of post-graduate law schools and the number of students in those schools will be strictly limited (Ahn, 2006, p. 236).
[9] See http://www.japan-press.co.jp/2006/2499/education.html, last accessed 20 February 2012.
[10] See http://chronicle.com/article/Costs-at-4-Year-Private/128201/, last accessed 20 February 2012.
[11] There is also a phenomenon of formerly private law schools becoming affiliated with state universities, but remaining private; examples are the former Detroit College of Law which is now affiliated with Michigan State, Franklin Pierce with the University of New Hampshire and the Dickinson Law School with Pennsylvania State University.
[12] These figures are from http://www.americanbar.org/content/dam/aba/migrated/legaled/statistics/charts/stats_5.authcheckdam.pdf; see also Tamanaha (2012, pp. 107–108).
[13] A significant emphasis on clinical training would change this calculus in a major way.
[14] Author's computations based on data from the 1995 National Study of Student Performance in the First Year of Law School conducted by Richard Sander, Kris Knaplund and Kit Winter.
[15] The sources for the data shown in Figure 1 are the Law School Admissions Council (http://www.lsac.org/LSACResources/default.asp) and the ABA Section on Legal Education and Admission to the Bar (http://www.americanbar.org/groups/legal_education/resources/statistics.html).
[16] The drop in total law school enrollment for 2011–2012 was less than 1 percent, probably reflecting the increasing number of LLM students that American law schools are admitting (largely as a means

of generating revenue); figures for total enrollment for 2012–2013 are not available as this article is being written.

[17] My figure of 70 percent ignores the fact that not all of the money loaned is paid to the law schools; some is used to cover living expenses.

[18] See http://www.ouac.on.ca/statistics/law-school-application-statistics/.

References

Abel, R.L. (1986) The decline of professionalism, *Modern Law Review*, 49, pp. 1–41.

Abel, R.L. (1988) *The Legal Profession in England and Wales* (Oxford, Basil Blackwell).

Ahn, K.W. (2006) Law reform in Korea and the agenda of 'graduate law school', *Wisconsin International Law Journal*, 24(1), pp. 223–242.

Baker, J.G. & Jorgensen, B.K. (2000) Leaving the law: occupational and career mobility of law school graduates, *Journal of Legal Education*, 50(1), pp. 16–34.

Baksi, C. (2010) Trainee solicitors fact debts of more than £10,000, *Law Society Gazette*. Available at: http://www.lawgazette.co.uk/news/trainee-solicitors-face-debts-more-10000.

Bell, D. (1973) *The Coming of Post-Industrial Society: A Venture in Social Forecasting* (New York, Basic Books).

Bourne, R.W. (2012) The coming crash in legal education: how we got here, and where we go now, *Creighton Law Review*, 45(4), pp. 651–697.

Brusegard, D. (2004) *The Implications of Demographic Change in the Legal Profession* (Ottawa, Canadian Bar Association). Available at: http://www.cba.org/cba/futures/pdf/demographics_feb04.pdf.

Chen, J. (2012) A degree of practical wisdom: the ratio of educational debt to income as a basic measurement of law school graduates' economic viability, *William Mitchell Law Review*, 38(3), pp. 1185–1208.

Clark, D.S. (2012) Legal education, in: D.S. Clark (Ed.) *Comparative Law and Society* (Cheltenham, UK, Edward Elgar Publishing).

Cohen, D.S. (1998) How many lawyers and law students? The supply of lawyers in Canada, *BarTalk*. Available at: http://www.cba.org/bc/bartalk_95_00/08_98/guest_cohen.aspx.

Dinovitzer, R. & Garth, B.G. (2007) Lawyer satisfaction in the process of structuring legal careers, *Law & Society Review*, 41, pp. 1–50.

Fischer, H. (2010) *ASU's Law School Moves to Privatize*. Available at: http://www.azcentral.com/business/abg/articles/2010/11/04/20101104abg-lawschools1104.html.

Foote, D.H. (2013) The trials and tribulations of Japan's legal education reforms, *Hastings International and Comparative Law Review*, 36, forthcoming.

Furlong, J. (2012) Why are you recruiting?, *JDSUPRA Law News*. Available at: http://www.jdsupra.com/post/documentViewer.aspx?fid=d6f42bb1-04e1-459c-8277-d12ce18508c8.

Gray, J. (2011) Law profession faces an 'articling crisis', *Globe and Mail*, 2 November. Available at: http://www.theglobeandmail.com/report-on-business/industry-news/the-law-page/law-profession-faces-an-articling-crisis/article2221786/.

Henderson, W.D. & Zahorsky, R.M. (2012) The law school bubble, *ABA Journal*, 98(1), pp. 30–35.

Hutton, W. (2012) How will £9,000 tuition fees affect students? We'll be finding out, *Guardian*, 27 January. Available at: http://www.guardian.co.uk/commentisfree/2012/jan/27/how-will-tuition-fees-affect-students.

Kahneman, D. (2011) *Thinking, Fast and Slow* (New York, Farrar, Straus and Giroux).

Kibble, N. (1989) Access to legal education and the legal professions in England, in: R. Dhavan, N. Kibble & W. Twining (Eds) *Access to Legal Education and the Legal Profession* (London, Butterworths).

Kim, C.R. (2006) The national bar examination in Korea, *Wisconsin International Law Journal*, 24(1), pp. 243–260.

Koppel, N. (2011) Law school loses its allure as jobs at firms are scarce, *Wall Street Journal (Online)*, 16 March.

Korioth, S. (2006) Legal education in Germany today, *Wisconsin International Law Journal*, 24(1), pp. 85–107.

Lentz, B.E. & Laband, D.N. (1995) *Sex Discrimination in the Legal Profession* (Westport, CT, Quorum Books).
Levin, A. & Alkoby, A. (2012) Is access to the profession access to justice? Lessons from Canada, *International Journal of the Legal Profession*, 19(2–3), pp. 283–299, this issue.
Lowrey, A. (2010) How law school went from being a sure thing to a bum deal, *Washington Post*, 31 October.
Maxeiner, J.R. (2003) *The New Japanese Law Schools* (Kansas City, MO, University of Missouri Kansas City). Available at: http://law.bepress.com/cgi/viewcontent.cgi?article=1183&context=expresso.
McKiernan, M. (2011) Articling crisis set to grow: stats show jobless candidates double as law schools expand, *Law Times*, 6 June. Available at: http://www.lawtimesnews.com/201106068480/Headline-News/Articling-crisis-set-to-grow.
Mitchell, L.E. (2012) Law school is worth the money, *New York Times*, 28 November.
Moustafa, T. (2010) The Islamist trend in Egyptian law, *Politics and Religion*, 3(3), pp. 610–630.
Nair, K. (2011) The hunt for the legal training contract: advice for law graduates, *Guardian Careers Blog*.
Prior, L. (2008) *The Pinstriped Prison* (Sydney, Macmillan Australia).
Rose, N. (2010) Legal training system failing law students, *Guardian*. Available at: http://www.guardian.co.uk/law/2010/jul/13/legal-training-law-students.
Saegusa, M. (2009) Why the Japanese law school system was established: co-optation as a defensive tactic in the face of global pressures, *Law & Social Inquiry*, 34(2), pp. 365–398.
Sander, R. & Bambauer, J. (2012) The secret of my success: how status, eliteness, and school performance shape legal careers, *Journal of Empirical Legal Studies*, 9(4), pp. 893–930.
Segal, D. (2011a) Is law school a losing game?, *New York Times*, 9 January. Available at: http://www.nytimes.com/2011/01/09/business/09law.html?pagewanted=all.
Segal, D. (2011b) Law school economics: k-ching, *New York Times*, 16 July.
Sloan, K. (2010) What are they thinking? Law school applications are increasing despite dark career prospects, *National Law Journal*, 12 July, p. 1.
Solicitors Journal (2012) Further drop in pupilages, 24 January, p. 5.
Tamanaha, B.Z. (2012) *Failing Law Schools* (Chicago, IL, University of Chicago Press).
Weisbrot, D. (1989) Access to legal education in Australia, in: R. Dhavan, N. Kibble & W. Twining (Eds) *Access to Legal Education and the Legal Profession* (London, Butterworths).
Weiss, D.C. (2012) Average debt of private law school grads is $125k; it's highest at these five schools, *ABA Journal*. Available at: http://www.abajournal.com/news/article/average_debt_load_of_private_law_grads_is_125k_these_five_schools_lead_to_m.
Yakowitz, J. (2010) Marooned: an empirical investigation of law school graduates who fail the bar exam, *Journal of Legal Education*, 60(1), pp. 3–40.
Yoshida, K. (2006) Legal education reforms in Japan: background, rationale, and the goals to be achieved, *Wisconsin International Law Journal*, 24(1), pp. 209–222.

Coping with the consequences of 'too many lawyers': securing the place of international graduate law students

CAROLE SILVER[*,**]
*Indiana University Maurer School of Law, Bloomington, Indiana, USA
**Law School Survey of Student Engagement, USA

ABSTRACT *This article considers the role of international graduate law students as potentially contributing to the 'solution' of the economic challenges facing US law schools. It suggests that intense competition for international graduate students from law schools within and outside of the United States creates challenges for US schools interested in maintaining and developing their international student populations. Understanding what international students want will help schools succeed in this competition. Satisfying those desires may require schools to allow globalization to infiltrate their structures, activities and traditional approaches to educating lawyers.*

1. Introduction

The concern that there are 'too many lawyers' has some currency in the United States today. Regardless of the position taken in the debate about what the number of lawyers should be, however, US law schools are experiencing the effects of the *perception* that there are too many lawyers. In 2011 and 2012, fewer individuals sat for the law school entrance exam than in earlier years (LSAC, 2012b), and the number of applicants declined substantially in each of the last two years (LSAC, 2012a). It appears that the combination of job market concerns and what Bryant Garth (2013) describes as the "rhetoric of crisis" have contributed to the perception that the market for law graduates is overly saturated. Commentators on legal education predict that these forces will cause law schools to close, faculty hiring to slow and their salaries to decrease (Chemerinsky, 2010; Leiter, 2012).

Just as businesses look for growth opportunities when they perceive market saturation (Shane, 1996; Menkel-Meadow, 2012), law schools also may look for new populations of prospective students; specifically, they may look overseas (Hansen,

2012). In the mid-1990s, a dip in US law school enrollment coincided with the development of graduate programs for international law graduates[1] that have become important elements of the financial structure of many schools. The growth of these graduate programs has brought schools at least three benefits: (i) a new source of tuition income that is (ii) de-linked from the complication of *US News*, and (iii) a basis for the schools to claim some connection to the forces of globalization that have assumed importance in light of increased cross-border activities of law firms and their clients, and the receding barriers imposed by national trade regulations (Silver, 2011). At the same time, a global market for law students challenges efforts by any single regulator to control the supply of lawyers (Steele, 2012).

Unlike in the mid-1990s, today US law schools face significant competition for international students, particularly from other English-speaking common law (ESCL) countries (Macready & Tucker, 2011, p. 3). Competition for internationally mobile students cuts across discipline, and the United States – while still the leading destination – has not maintained its share of this market (OECD, 2010). In order to secure the position of the United States as a leading receiving country for international law students, and perhaps even to increase the proportion of international students who choose the United States as the site of their overseas legal studies, US law schools must consider and respond to the reasons international students pursue international legal education. Doing so, however, will press schools to revisit the current approach that educates international and domestic students largely in isolation from one another, and which diminishes the potential influence of globalization. Instead, as US law schools vie for international students, they also must come to terms with their willingness to allow globalization to infiltrate their structures, activities and mission.

To address these challenges, this article draws on an empirical study of international law students to provide insight into their goals and experiences. The study gathered information from students who earned an LL.M. or similar one-year postgraduate law degree in 1996, 1998 or 2000 from one of eleven US law schools, which were selected to provide a diverse group of law schools with regard to regional location and reputation (as reflected in their *US News* rank).[2] Graduates were surveyed about their backgrounds and motivations for enrolling in a US law school, their careers before and after studying in the United States, and their experiences in the United States. Responses to the survey were received from 360 graduates living in 55 countries (and representing 68 birth countries); follow-up interviews were conducted with 66 of the survey respondents.[3] To supplement these data, I interviewed other lawyers involved in international practice to learn more about the market for international law graduates and the role occupied by US legal education.[4]

The article begins in section 2 by describing the current conditions that provide context for interpreting the significance of the presence of international law students. Section 3 draws on survey and interview data that explore what international students want from their overseas legal education. It considers why US law schools have been a valuable resource for international students despite the apparent disconnection between US legal education and expertise in home country law, on one hand, and the failure of US law schools to satisfy certain goals of the students regarding their overseas legal studies, on the other. Section 4 identifies salient issues for US law schools to address in order to maintain – and perhaps grow – their market share for educating international law graduates. The conclusion suggests issues that may take precedence going forward.

2. Setting the scene: challenges for US law schools

The news is filled with stories of the challenges plaguing law schools, their students and recent graduates. More American Bar Association (ABA)-accredited law schools are producing more law graduates, and law school tuition also has increased, but because of the sluggish economy and a decrease in high-end corporate transactions, the job market cannot accommodate more new lawyers and higher wages (Hylton, 2012).

Between 2000 and 2009, the number of US lawyers grew by more than 15% (ABA, 2011) while the rate of growth for the US population as a whole was below 10% (Mackun & Wilson, 2011). Expansion of the lawyer population during this period corresponds to the creation of new law schools and growth in the number of students at existing schools. Over the same period, law students have paid more to become lawyers, and have enjoyed ready access to borrowed funds to finance their studies. Problems in the job market for new graduates combine with these forces and have contributed to declining interest in law school, leading to fewer applicants (Kritzer, 2012).

To make up for this shortfall, US law schools increasingly may rely on alternatives to the traditional pool of students pursuing the juris doctor degree (JD) and look to international students as part of the solution. International student mobility – both in law and generally in higher education – has more than quadrupled over the last 30 years according to the OECD, and has "accelerated during the past 13 years, mirroring the globalisation of economies and societies" (OECD, 2010, p. 313).

> The number of foreign tertiary students enrolled worldwide has increased by 85 percent since the year 2000. However, ... the percentage of tertiary students leaving their home countries to study has remained stable, at about 2 percent, since 1999. Overall, the recent rise in student mobility has simply kept pace with the worldwide growth in tertiary enrollment over the same period. (Macready & Tucker, 2011, p. 10).

The United States is one of the primary receiving countries for international students. In 2008, "[t]he United States received the most (in absolute terms) with almost 19% of all foreign students worldwide, followed by the United Kingdom (10%), Germany (7%), France (7%) and Australia (7%)" (OECD, 2010, p. 314).

US law schools have benefitted from the developing global market in higher education. Beginning in the mid-1990s, they began courting international law graduates who wanted to practice law and were interested in studying the same subjects pursued by US JD students.[5] The similarity of curricular interests between this new wave of international law graduates and their JD students enabled schools to capitalize on existing resources by directing the international students into empty seats in ongoing courses (Tamanaha, 2012, pp. 64–65; Silver, 2006). More recently, there has been some increase in international JD enrollment, too, particularly among students from certain countries, including China (Silver, 2011).

Generally, graduate programs for international students were developed on the basis of being entirely student-funded with regard to tuition; that is, international students either paid tuition from personal resources or brought funding from their home country or employer. The survey of international law graduates described above confirms this financial bargain (Table 1). Approximately 40% of respondents reported relying exclusively on personal or family savings to finance their US law studies, and fewer than 2% were supported exclusively by their US law school. This presents a stark contrast to the funding of JD students by the same law schools (Tamanaha, 2012, pp. 99–100). Nor is the United States alone in this approach; generally, international graduate students pay full fare, while domestic students are supported by government subsidies and university scholarships (Thornton, 2012; Woodward, 2012).[6] Even this, however, is not stable: as law schools increasingly vie for a nationally diverse group of graduate students, they are more likely to use student funding as a means of competition, while the financing of tuition for domestic JD students is under significant stress (Kritzer, 2012).

Developing a pool of international applicants for a graduate program has served as an attractive strategy for law schools. Generating revenue through international graduate student enrollment offers the potential to avoid cost-cutting strategies that might offer relief from the financial pressures on law schools by diverting funds from JD programs, which likely would generate negative consequences with regard to competition and ranking.[7] This approach is not unique to law schools (Simon, 2012; Marklein, 2011).

While interest in revenue from mostly self-funded international students is shared across education levels, the role of rankings makes international students even more valuable to US law schools than they are elsewhere. International law students overwhelmingly enroll in degree programs other than the primary law degree offered in the host country, whether in the United States or elsewhere. By avoiding the JD, the credentials of most international students are 'off the books' for *US News* purposes (Silver, 2011).

Table 1. *Methods of financing US legal education for international graduate law students*

	Exclusive method of financing (%)	Contributed to financing (but not exclusive)(%)
Personal or family savings	40.2	69.7
Scholarship from US law school or university	1.9	15.6
External scholarship (employer or other funding organization)	15.8	35.8
Other financing method	6.4	14.4

Note: Percentages not intended to add to 100%.

US graduate programs for international lawyers have grown substantially since the mid-1990s, both in number of schools offering such programs and number of students enrolled (Silver, 2006; Tamanaha, 2012, p. 64). This reflects a general growth in non-JD program enrollment; according to the ABA (2012), "ABA-approved law schools reported a 39 percent increase in enrollment in non-J.D. programs from 2005 to 2012 and a 52 percent increase from 2000 to 2012". Determining the proportion of growth due to international student enrollment is difficult because available records are incomplete, but a rough proxy is the number of bar test-takers whose legal education was earned outside of the United States. According to the National Conference of Bar Examiners, in 1996, at the beginning of the period of growth of graduate US law school programs for international law graduates, 2.2% (1,589 individuals) of the individuals who sat for a US bar exam earned their legal education outside of the United States; by 2011, 7.1% (5,620 individuals) of all bar exam test-takers earned their legal education outside of the United States (NCBE, 1996, 2011).

Despite this growth, international graduate students comprised only 3.16% of the size of the JD population in 2005, the most recent year for which ABA statistics are available;[8] this is a somewhat smaller proportion than the approximately 4.5% of all 2005 bar exam test-takers who earned their legal education outside of the United States (NCBE, 2005),[9] and only slightly lower than the proportion of international students enrolled at all levels in US colleges and universities for the same period, when international students accounted for 4% of enrolled students (Healey, 2008).[10] More recently, in 2008, international students accounted for only 3.4% of college and university students in the United States, compared with the substantially larger proportion of enrollment they occupied in three other ESCL countries: 14.7% in the United Kingdom, 20.6% in Australia and 12.9% in New Zealand (OECD, 2010, Table C2.1). There is, thus, much room for growth in international student enrollment in US colleges, universities and law schools.

The financial contribution of international students generally in higher education is significant. "[I]nternational students contribute more than $21 billion to the US economy, through their expenditures on tuition and living expenses, according to the US Department of Commerce. Higher education is among the United States' top service sector exports" (IIE, 2011). They constitute an important element of funding for higher education elsewhere, too (Australian Bureau of Statistics, 2011). For US law schools, the tuition generated by graduate programs for international law graduates is free from certain of the burdens related to JD programs; notably, ABA oversight does not require parity among student opportunities for those in different degree programs, because accreditation and approval is limited to JD programs. In addition, for the bulk of international students who enroll in degree programs other than the JD, their admission does not trigger *US News* consequences.

Many US law schools have taken advantage of these conditions by limiting their investment in international student programs so that each tuition dollar from an international graduate program student is likely to yield a higher proportion of net income compared with that generated by JD tuition. For example, staffing of student services for international graduate and JD programs often differs.[11] Investment in faculty also may take a different approach. It is rare for schools to add to their tenure-track faculty (the most highly-compensated faculty group) because of growing demand from international students. In part, this relates to the practice of placing international students into vacant seats in courses whose primary audience is the JD population. But in addition, many schools use less expensive non-tenure track faculty to teach international students in courses catering to their interests in particular subjects, whether a core course – such as contracts – that is offered only for international students or a specialized course – for example on anti-corruption measures – that is particularly appealing to international students because of their experience working as lawyers.[12] This is not an assessment of the quality of teaching or mentorship by faculty who occupy non-tenure track positions; rather it simply identifies the ways in which schools have pursued growing numbers of international students without making investments that otherwise would be required to accommodate a larger student population. These strategies mean that international students have the potential to make a significant contribution toward solving the financial woes of law schools.

Limiting their investments carry increased risks for US law schools, however, because of expanding efforts from legal educators in other ESCL countries to recruit the same pool of international law graduates. Overseas competitors often charge lower tuition compared to the United States, although rates for international students may be higher than rates for domestic students in such countries (Woodward, 2012). In addition, schools in Australia, New Zealand, England and elsewhere may be more conveniently located to students' home countries – particularly for China and India, important sending countries – and may provide students with a more diverse international student experience because of greater national diversity at the university level, where law departments outside of the United States often are situated.

US law schools historically have had two crucial advantages in the competition for international students. First, studying law in the United States has provided international students with the promise of insight into US law, lawyers and law firms, which has been important in large part because of their role in the global economy. Whether working for or with US clients, lawyers or law firms, knowing how US lawyers are trained – and having an opportunity to become acquainted with US lawyers and law students – has held great value. Second, earning an LL.M. or similar one-year post-JD degree in the United States can qualify international students to gain a US law license by passing a state bar exam. This translates into a signal of legitimacy with regard to working in an international setting where US law may be relevant (Silver, 2011). While these attributes have enabled US law schools to compete successfully for international students in the past, each presents challenges going forward.

Overall, law schools may seek to rely on international students to balance the financial consequences related to decreasing JD applicants, changes in access to student loans and the challenging job market, among other factors. But it may be unrealistic to rely on international students' continuing and stable interest without also considering how their presence might change US legal education for all involved. That is, a one-way influence pressing out from US legal education and onto international students may have been the framework schools used in the past, when the competing alternatives available to international students were not as attractive. Today, neither bar qualification nor the lessons about US lawyers are reliably unique or deliverable, making it risky for law schools to stake their future financial security on them. If the goal is for an international population to serve as a long-term and central element of US legal education, it would benefit schools to consider what is necessary to satisfy international students and how this will change the educational experience of JDs, as well.[13]

3. Gaining insight: motivations and goals of international graduate law students

Understanding why international law graduates find US law schools attractive is central to schools maintaining their position as primary receivers of international students. Generally, students pursue international higher education for a variety of reasons, including gaining access to what is otherwise unobtainable at home (Reichman & Sterling, 2002, n. 59). Science students may study abroad in order to work in well-equipped labs unavailable in their home countries (Millard, 2005). Other students may find the international aspect of their experience most important. This may be related to learning to contextualize home country experiences (Rizvi, 2007, p. 5), to gaining access to an elite institution when that is otherwise unavailable at home (Brooks & Waters, 2009, pp. 1091–1092) or to the opportunity to develop skills such as English-language ability. The specific reasons for pursuing international study depend as much on home country as on the characteristics and interests of an individual student (Sayad, 2004). As Ronit Dinovitzer and John Hagan (2006, p. 121) explained, "the worth of a particular form of symbolic capital is based on its recognition as valuable in local settings".

These themes are echoed by the survey responses of international graduate law students. Many described their goal as the acquisition of elite status that otherwise was inaccessible at home. For example, one LL.M. graduate from Latin America explained his expectation that the LL.M. would signal social and professional capital by representing that

> your social skills are good because you came to the States all alone. You did this by your own, you just spent a lot of money, so that talks very good things about you. You know, that you are self-sufficient.... Self-motivated.... First of all, you had the money so you come from a family that can pay this. So, you have social skills; ... you might have contacts when you go back. So, there's a lot of things that ... really count at the time of hiring somebody. ... [Y]ou talk good English and they need people who talk in English because they have clients..., US and British, ... European that speak in English because it is a universal language. So they need a lot of people like you after the masters. (#67)

In order to unpack these factors, the survey asked international graduates about their motivations for enrolling in their US law schools. Table 2 sets out the responses, showing both the proportion of respondents who indicated that a particular factor was among their motivations (center column) and the proportion who indicated it was the most important motivation (right-hand column).

Table 2. *Motivations of international law graduates for pursuing US graduate legal studies*

Motivation	% respondents indicating this was important	% respondents indicating this was the most important reason for pursuing their US legal studies
Expansion of professional opportunities in home country	82	51
Interest in a particular area of law	54	19
Desire to improve English skills	51	6
Career advancement	39	14
Desire to live in the USA.	39	6
Influence of colleagues/friends who had earned an LL.M.	29	0.6
Path to job in the USA	29	7
Family considerations	21	3
Necessity for US bar exam	16	4

Note: Percentages not intended to add to 100%.

The ways in which US legal studies affect career opportunities are shaped by the professional hierarchies and opportunities for competition in each home country (Dinovitzer & Hagan, 2006; Silver, 2011), but certain common themes are reflected in Table 2 and in interviews. For example, according to LL.M. graduates and hiring partners at elite foreign and US-based firms, US legal education signals an understanding of the common law system and the acquisition of English language skills that are highly valued in many countries. According to one international graduate,

> 70% of clients are US-based companies. The better deals involve international parties. If you want to be on these deals, you must be able to speak, read, write in English as if it's your own language – almost mandatory. Most law firms require knowledge of English before hiring in a job as a lawyer. (#89)

Another graduate explained,

> I wanted to have . . . US clients and the only way I could do it was . . . studying . . . US law and talking good English. If not, you know, I wasn't able to do it. (#67)[14]

Even for lawyers whose clients are not US-based, however, US legal education offers benefits.[15] Familiarity with the common law system, for example, and with the ways in which US lawyers approach basic notions such as drafting contracts, provides confidence and credibility to international law graduates when they interact with US, British and other common law lawyers on transactions and in disputes.[16]

International law students also are motivated to acquire what might be described as technical knowledge and skills. English fluency is one example, and slightly more than half of the survey respondents indicated improving English as a motivating factor. Exposure to US law and legal theory also was a significant motivation. One graduate described his interest in learning US securities regulation: "When I studied law – I did my first state exam in '95 – there was no such thing in Germany as capital markets law or securities regulation. I mean insider dealing, for example, was not illegal" (#13). Others were more interested in exposure to theoretical approaches that were absent from their home country legal education, such as law and economics. The particular subject of interest may reflect the current legal debates and high stakes for corporate clients, and over the course of the survey years from 1996 to 2000, students shifted towards intellectual property[17] – a trend that now surely reflects the norm.

Generally, while the motivating factors listed in Table 2 were quite consistently ranked by respondents regardless of their home country, slight regional differences were present. The importance of the LL.M. as a means for expanding opportunities at home was not limited by where 'home' was located. But slightly more of the respondents born in Asian-Pacific countries and in Latin America, compared with respondents from other birth regions, indicated that their interest in a particular area of law motivated their decision to pursue the LL.M. At the same time, slightly fewer of the respondents born in Asian-Pacific countries considered living in the United States a motivation for pursuing US legal studies, compared with respondents born in the Latin America region and in Europe (including both EU and non-EU countries).

The motivating factors identified in Table 2 are not exclusive of one another and may interact in various ways. For example, while bar eligibility was cited by the smallest group of respondents, its influence is felt as an element of expanding professional opportunities, too. These and other factors were present in the explanation of one LL.M. graduate:

> In Korea, [the] LL.M. value is first, [an] American license – bar exam. [The] LL.M. is a process to get [a] license. Second value is prestige of [the] law school; it convinces clients of credibility. They say, "Oh, you graduated from [school's name], you can have this business." [The] third value of LL.M. is English improvement. Really, English is more important, but credential of license is important. (#81)

A second graduate explained that "having a master's degree in the United States allow[s] you to have more room to jump and to look for a higher kind of meaning. If you want to achieve, you have to [have] a different perspective. Not only from your side, but from the other people['s] side." (#84) In law school, then, the goals of international students are related to substantive and professional lessons. And while the law school experience is what begins the journey for international law students, it does not define the scope of the experience many hope to achieve (Silver, 2012). Instead, they aim for the gestalt of the US legal education experience, including participation in the social as well as academic life of the school (#11), passing the bar, and working in a law-related job in the United States (Silver, 2010). These social and experiential elements facilitate international students becoming "comfortable at working across national boundaries and cosmopolitan in lifestyle and outlook" (Brooks & Waters, 2009, p. 1087), and they are pivotal to imbuing the experience with its value as a mechanism for expanding professional opportunities at home. As one graduate from the EU explained, "people will look even more differently to you if you've had an American law firm experience. They think you know more than they know or people will ... kind of value you more" (#85).[18] That is, these additional experiences are elements of expanding professional opportunities at home.

Achieving comfort in a multinational setting is one of the most significant gains available from studying overseas, whether in law or another discipline, and stems from exposure to a nationally diverse peer group. This can facilitate learning how to navigate multi-nationality with regard to substantive law, styles of working and communicating, and differences in approaches to lawyering and learning. One can conceive of this as being akin to acquiring a global legal literacy (Silver, 2009b).

For most international law students, simply enrolling in a US law school graduate program promises exposure to certain experiences central to global legal literacy. They must interact with US culture, in English, by virtue of being physically present in school in the United States. Moreover, their international graduate program classmates may provide a nationally diverse cohort, which itself is an important part of the US law school experience. It was explained nicely by one US LL.M. graduate:

> I came here [to the US LL.M. program] hoping to meet people from different countries, different cultures, and it did open my mind. Literally, the first day I felt like I had been hit with an axe in my head and it opened ... I had traveled very little when I was younger, so I didn't know much of the world and I hadn't met anyone from Asia or, I don't know, different countries in Europe, Eastern Europe, Africa, so it was a new and very intense experience. (#75)

Today, however, it is difficult for many US law schools to attract this sort of national diversity in their graduate programs. Several factors explain this change, including the development of the EU's Erasmus program (Lonbay, 2012), which may result in decreased interest in the United States on the part of students from EU countries. Competition from other ESCL countries also challenges US schools' success in enrolling a nationally diverse group. One hiring partner explained that he considers legal education in most ESCL schools as essentially fungible (Silver, 2011, p. 29). This means that students may consider factors such as cost and the opportunity for relationships as more significant in deciding on the location for overseas studies.

Apart from the national diversity represented by international classmates, international students expect to gain an understanding of US law students and to learn alongside them. It is US immersion and context they desire, and while this is a logical expectation, it has proven difficult for schools to deliver.[19] International students generally report that it is difficult to establish relationships with US JD students. According to one graduate, "The only class in which I interacted with JD students was negotiations. This is one of the sad things about the program. I met lots of LL.M.s from many countries, but not enough JDs" (#92). Another graduate explained that

"LL.M.s stuck together. I was the only native English-speaker. But I had more in common with LL.M.s than with the JDs. None of the JDs became my friend. Americans are friendly, but they don't want to be your friend generally" (#80). In fact, it is relatively common for international students to report failing to become well-acquainted with any JD student. One interviewee reported that she interacted with "hardly any" JDs (#91). Occasionally, international students find that a personal – often romantic – relationship with a single JD student serves as their bridge to integration and immersion (#78); others connect through sports activities in which JDs also participate (#51). Aside from these sorts of coincidental meetings, however, interaction tends to be limited.

To master global legal literacy in the US context, international students must become part of an integrated international community that includes US students. They must have opportunities for interaction to allow for non-formal learning[20] and the acquisition of tacit knowledge (OECD, 2012; Eraut, 2000). However, as illustrated by the graduates' comments, above, simply enrolling in a US law school does not guarantee an international student either "meaningful interaction [with US law students] or the development of valuable intercultural communication skills and international perspectives" (Leask, 2009, p. 206).

Formal classroom experiences also present difficulties. US law faculty are unsure whether to treat international students similarly to JDs, ignore them entirely, look to them for comments on their home country law, or all or none of the above. Norms on these issues are scarce both within and across US law schools, and faculty attitudes range from considering international students an impediment to their teaching to appreciating their contribution to a diverse student experience. Students respond, sometimes in ways that do not further their learning. One graduate described a common experience:

> Some professors … don't call on LL.M.s in class. LL.M.s know this, and some do not prepare for these classes. But I did continue to prepare. Still, I felt that this unwillingness to call on LL.M.s affects our status with regard to the JD students. So I resented this practice. Also, it denied me the experience of being called on, one of the basic common experiences of US law school. (#84)[21]

The uncertainty of faculty is perhaps matched by the diversity of learning styles that international students bring to the United States. Differences in what Hofstede (1980) described as "power distance" affect the ways in which students may approach participation in a typically interactive law school classroom (Kingston & Forland, 2008, pp. 205–206). But as Kingston and Forland (2008, pp. 207–208) note, learning styles are not static; as international students become comfortable, their approaches may change.

Nearly all of the interviewed international graduates reported enjoying, and found invigorating, both the formal aspects of their education in the United States and their interactions with other international graduate students. As one graduate explained, "For me, one of … probably the best aspects was the fellow international students. … And that was probably the single best element of that LL.M." (#74). But the absence of meaningful interaction with American students is a frustratingly persistent complaint. The same respondent commented that, with regard to interactions with American JDs, there was

> more of a division..., very, very limited involvement with the US students. Far less than anybody in the LL.M. wanted, everyone in the LL.M. expected to be making far more American friends, and everybody sort of, the consensus was that was very difficult to do and that wasn't happening. (#74)

While this lack of interaction between international and domestic students is neither a uniquely American problem nor limited to the law school context (Woodward, 2012), it goes directly to one of the two reasons international students choose the United States over other ESCL countries for their legal studies: the opportunity to learn about and with future US lawyers. Law schools cannot control the relative position of US law, firms and lawyers in the global economy, but they do have power over the experiences of international students that occur within their walls. The nature of their interactions and integration into their schools is likely to be a key factor in the increasingly competitive market for international law students. If law schools are to rely more heavily on international students as a salvation for their current financial problems, this is a challenge that must be addressed.

4. Shifting positions:[22] from marginal to mainstream

To ensure continued competitiveness in the market for international graduate students, US law schools must capitalize on their advantages and respond to the interests outlined above. This involves providing an educational framework that enables meaningful interaction with an internationally diverse peer group, including US JD students, and one that offers exposure to practice experiences, too. Each of these has implications for the policies of US law schools; in the following discussion, my aim is to highlight the issues and suggest possible factors to consider rather than resolve the dilemmas.

What is unique about US legal education is part of what attracts international students. The Socratic method, for example, memorialized by John Jay Osborn's Professor Kingsfield, has contributed to the understanding of US legal education for domestic and international students. Implicit in this is the interaction between students and faculty and among students. International students, no less than domestic JDs, want access to this sort of interaction.

To extend this experience to international students, however, may change the classroom dynamic. The implicit assumption inherent in the current approach of US law schools that there is a one-way influence from the school to the international student must shift. As Leask (2009, p. 218) describes, it is necessary to "move away from deficit models of engagement". By including international students in the classroom conversation, faculty send a message that affirms the importance of the diversity they embody.

Integrating international and domestic students presents challenges in terms of language ability,[23] learning styles, differences in the risks and rewards of law school academic activities, and in legal expertise. Differences in degree programs often are the justification for keeping the two groups separate. Many schools focus on social interaction, using mentorship programs, for example, that pair international and JD students to establish a relationship between members of the two groups.[24] But to learn to work together, integration in the classroom is key. Evidence suggests that academic integration will help international students acclimate to their new environments more efficiently (Rienties *et al.*, 2011).

US law faculty may balk at the notion that they deliberately reorient their teaching to facilitate interaction between international and domestic students. Faculty correctly may claim inexperience in promoting collaboration between even US JD students (LSSSE, 2012, p. 13); expecting them to advance intercultural and interdegree program integration may ask too much. Some will question whether intentional integration must permeate the curriculum or can be left to particular courses. The experience of the LL.M. student who described his negotiations class as the sole site of interaction with JD students was common among my LL.M. interviewees, both in its transformative effect and as the sole example of such an experience.

If the proposition that forms the basis of this article is correct – that international students will become an even more significant mainstay of US legal education – then learning to teach to this new reality is a central task. Moving ahead, law schools might offer support for faculty, to help them "adapt their teaching to an international, culturally diverse ... environment rather than expecting learners to adapt to a monocultural, inflexible environment" (Leask, 2009, p. 212).

International students also seek US practice experiences, which increase their ability to use US legal education as a means for expanding opportunities at home. The current job market for new law graduates renders this particularly difficult, which in turn increases the attractiveness of experiential education during school. Certain law schools embed an externship in their programs for international students.[25] Others, however, may worry that offering clinic seats to international graduate students limits JDs' opportunities. Regulation also may play a role here, often to the detriment of international students. Externships may raise similar concerns about competition.

Bar eligibility is another continuing challenge. Most states prohibit international students from taking a bar exam after a single year of law school in the United States (NCBE & ABA, 2012, chart 4). Law schools have been reluctant to engage bar regulators in discussion on this issue, but, as noted earlier, bar eligibility is an enormous advantage of US law schools because several commercially important jurisdictions recognize eligibility based on the combination of home country education and one year of study in the United States. While other ESCL countries generally follow the UK system of "degree, vocational learning, training contract – [which] impedes the route to qualification rather than open it up" (Flood, 2012), change may be near: England, at least, is considering a new structure to facilitate international students' qualification. Such a change likely would reduce interest in US legal education on the part of international students.

One can imagine US law schools using these considerations as mechanisms of competition for international applicants. But schools have varying assets to draw on in satisfying the interests of international students. Some provide the 'great American campus experience', others are more focused on a substantive area or on experiential opportunities. There is some strength in maintaining sufficient flexibility so that US law schools can champion a common message: that US legal education – as opposed to that offered in another ESCL country – represents the gold standard.

5. Conclusion

International student mobility is a significant trend as well as big business. US law schools have benefitted from the presence of international students, who have flocked to special graduate programs designed specifically for them. But the market for international students is subject to increased competition at a time when US law schools are likely to feel more urgency to maintain or even increase the number of international applicants.

Until now, US law schools have spent little effort considering how to serve their international students. Rather, they offered them the opportunity to experience US law school as it has been delivered to domestic students in the JD program. In part, this may be exactly what international students seek – the classic US law school experience including the hallmark Socratic method. But in accepting this offer, international students have both conceded their marginality and foregone some of the more captivating experiential course offerings. Of course, this may suit the purposes of certain international students, but marginalization is unlikely to garner loyalty in a competitive market. Whether international students would find US law schools more attractive if their experiences were on a par with those of domestic JDs is a question that schools must grapple with as they vie for position in a global market for law students.

One of the lessons of the survey data presented here is that the market for international students is fueled by difference. The financial bargain is different for domestic and international students in the United States and elsewhere. Concern about an oversupply of law graduates is less acute with regard to international students in part because of the assumption that they will have different career paths than domestic students, returning home to pursue home country opportunities. This assumption may be unwarranted, but it highlights the ways in which law schools conceive of their international and domestic students as separate cohorts. Moreover, to the extent that international legal education provides an outlet for certain students to pursue a status unavailable at home, it may also contribute to the oversupply of lawyers outside of the US.

Going forward, international students may well want what their JD peers are after. To continue attracting international students, schools may be pressed to address the justifications upon which different treatment has been based. Investments of time and money are significant and, while perhaps proportionate when considering home country education and training, may not be persuasive that comparable treatment is justified. Moreover, to give international and domestic students equivalent experiences may require a shift in the teaching methods now used. This may benefit domestic students in much the same ways as it would provide new insight to international students, but US students who have not taken an affirmative act in recognition of globalization may reject its salience (Silver, 2013b).

As law schools consider whether to rely even more heavily on their international students, they also must address their competitiveness vis-à-vis legal education in comparable jurisdictions. Will the favor of the marketplace be won by the schools that most directly address the interests of international students, offering an equivalent – if not identical – experience to that enjoyed by domestic students? And if so, how will US law schools respond to these demands and maintain their unique identities? These are the dilemmas of globalization faced by myriad firms already. Now it is the law schools' turn.

Acknowledgements

Many thanks to Elizabeth Chambliss, Bruce Green, Eyal Katvan and John O'Hare for helpful comments; to the participants in the workshop on 'Too Many Lawyers? Facts, Reasons, Consequences and Solutions' for discussion of the larger context in which the paper evolved; to the International Institute for the Sociology of Law for support; and to Brendan Smith, Kyle Doherty-Peters, Kasie Gorosh and Matthew Antonini for research assistance. Certain of the research that forms the basis for this paper was supported by a grant from the Law School Admission Council (LSAC). The opinions and conclusions contained in this paper are those of the author and do not necessarily reflect the position or policy of LSAC. See Silver (2013a) for an expanded discussion of the issues raised here.

Notes

[1] 'International law graduate' is used here to describe individuals whose first degree in law is earned outside of the United States. 'International graduate student' and 'international law student' (used interchangeably) refer to international law graduates who enroll in a US law school post-JD degree program, such as an LL.M., M.C.L. or S.J.D.

[2] For additional information about the project, see Silver (2009a).

[3] Interviews are cited by a number to protect the identity of interviewees. All but two interviews of survey respondents were conducted in person; two were telephone interviews. Interviews were open ended, lasting generally between 60 and 90 minutes.

[4] I leave to others the job of considering the implications of whether there are too many lawyers – and particularly too many new law graduates – on lawyers' roles in satisfying unmet legal needs (Sandefur & Smyth, 2011; Addressing the justice gap, 2011; Menkel-Meadow, 2012).

[5] While space limitations prevent me from delving into the history of international graduate students in US law schools, see Silver (2002, 2006, 2009a, 2011, 2012) and Hupper (2008).

[6] See also Healey (2008, p. 345), noting that, with regard to universities in the United Kingdom, Australia and New Zealand, "universities under financial strain ... were allowed to charge full cost tuition fees to foreign students long before governments faced the political watershed of allowing universities to charge partial fees for domestic students".

[7] Healey (2008, p. 346) comments on a similar framework with regard to international student populations in Australia, Canada, New Zealand, the United Kingdom and the United States (denominated 'MESDC'): "the internationalization of MESDC universities was ... a response to (arguably dysfunctional) government policy, which saw foreign tuition income as a way to shore

up university finances without having to face the political challenge of deregulating domestic tuition fees."

[8] Figures were derived from data provided by the ABA Section of Legal Education and Admissions to the Bar, and ABA (2011).

[9] 2005 is the most current year of data available from the ABA relating to graduate student enrollment. For JD student enrollment, see ABA Section of Legal Education and Admissions to the Bar, statistics, available at: http://www.americanbar.org/groups/legal_education/resources/statistics.html.

[10] Compare with IIE (2011), reporting that international students accounted for only 3.2% of all enrollment in the United States in 2005–2006.

[11] See Silver (2013a) for a thorough discussion.

[12] See Georgetown Law Center's course, Anti-Corruption Laws and Enforcement Mechanisms – An International Approach, available at http://www.law.georgetown.edu/curriculum/tab_courses.cfm?Status=Course&Detail=1070, taught by adjunct professor Barbara Fredericks.

[13] I take up the issue of how the presence of international students may benefit JDs by offering opportunities to learn to work in a global environment separately in Silver (2013b).

[14] See Marginson (2008, p. 308): noting "four aspects of US hegemony: research concentration and knowledge flows, the global role of English, and American universities as people attractors and as exemplars of ideal practice."

[15] Interview #90: "Most of the clients we deal with are foreign clients and very often we have to deal with their legal counsel."

[16] See, for example, interview #11: "The biggest asset of an LL.M. is really that you get outside of your country, get involved in the foreign country, because it's long enough you learn about the people. As a lawyer you do pick up enough about the legal system to understand how they think, and if you end up practicing law, or if you end up in an international job like manager and you deal with Americans, you have a leg up on the people who haven't done this LL.M., in dealing with them, because you just know how they think, you know how they were brought up. I mean, you don't know it, but you have a much better feeling for it."

[17] Note, however, that the small number of respondents identifying intellectual property or any other topic as related to their motivation for studying in a US LL.M. program limits the significance of this finding.

[18] See also Mazlish & Morss (2005), suggesting four models of global elites. In addition, for some, the level of compensation paid to US lawyers has been an attraction, although the post-2008 job market may limit such opportunities.

[19] US schools are not alone in this regard (Woodward, 2012).

[20] Non-formal learning has been described by the OECD as an "intermediate concept" that may be "organised and can have learning objectives.... [It] may occur at the initiative of the individual but also happens as a by-product of more organised activities, whether or not the activities themselves have learning objectives" (OECD, 2012). See also Eraut (2000).

[21] Certain of the challenges described in the text might not characterize the experience of international JD students.

[22] See generally Wisker (2012), describing universities that assume their international students will come to learn and then return home as a 'colonial hangover' model.

[23] See de Figueiredo & Mauri (2012), describing the absence of language fluency as an asset in teaching about global interaction.

[24] See Silver (2013b) regarding the low impact of these programs.

[25] See Pacific McGeorge School of Law, http://www.mcgeorge.edu/Academic_Programs/LLM_and_JSD_Programs/LLM_in_Transnational_Business_Practice.htm.

References

ABA (2011) American Bar Association *Total National Lawyer Counts 1878–2011*. Available at: http://www.americanbar.org/content/dam/aba/migrated/marketresearch/PublicDocuments/total_national_lawyer_counts_1878_2011.xls, accessed 17 February 2013.

ABA (2012) American Bar Association legal education section reports preliminary data on non-JD enrollment growth, 2000–2012, 21 December. Available at: http://www.abanow.org/2012/12/aba-legal-education-section-reports-preliminary-data-on-non-j-d-enrollment-growth-2000-2012/, accessed 17 February 2013.

Addressing the justice gap: the poor need representation and thousands of law school graduates need work (2011) *New Yark Times*, 24 August, p. A22. Available at: http://www.nytimes.com/2011/08/24/opinion/addressing-the-justice-gap.html, accessed 17 February 2013.

Australian Bureau of Statistics (2011) 4102.0 – *Australian Social Trends*, 16 December 2011. Available at: http://www.abs.gov.au/ausstats/abs@.nsf/Lookup/4102.0Main+Features20Dec+2011#introduction, accessed 17 February 2013.

Brooks, R. & Waters, J. (2009) A second chance at 'success': UK students and global circuits of higher education, *Sociology*, 43(6), pp. 1085–1102.

Chemerinsky, E. (2010) Invest in higher education, *Los Angeles Times*, 27 December. Available at: http://articles.latimes.com/2010/dec/27/opinion/la-oe-chemerinsky-uc-tuition-20101221, accessed 17 February 2013.

Dinovitzer, R. & Hagan, J. (2006) Lawyers on the move: the consequences of mobility for legal careers, *International Journal of the Legal Profession*, 13(2), pp. 119–135.

Eraut, M. (2000) Non-formal learning and tacit knowledge in professional work, *British Journal of Educational Psychology*, 70(1), pp. 113–136.

de Figueiredo, J.N. & Mauri, A. (2012) Developing international managerial skills through the cross-cultural assignment: experiential learning by matching US-based and international students, *Journal of Management Education*, early online publication, 24 February, doi: 10.1177/1052562912437335.

Flood, J. (2012) What is fitness for purpose?, *Blog – Random Academic Thoughts (RATs)*, 29 February. Available at: http://www.johnflood.com/blog/2012/02/what-is-fitness-for-purpose/, accessed 17 February 2013.

Garth, B.G. (2013) Crisis rhetoric, crisis, and competition: a sociological examination of the (latest) crisis of the legal profession and legal education, *Stanford Law & Policy Review*, in press.

Hansen, M. (2012) Enrollment in non-JD programs at US law schools is up, figures show, *ABA Journal*, 21 December. Available at: http://www.abajournal.com/news/article/enrollment_up_in_non-j.d._programs_at_u.s._law_schools_figures_show/, accessed 17 February 2013.

Healey, N. (2008) Is higher education in really 'internationalising'?, *Higher Education*, 55(3), pp. 333–355.

Hofstede, G. (1980) *Culture's Consequences: International Differences in Work-related Values* (Beverly Hills, CA, Sage).

Hupper, G. (2008) The academic doctorate in law: a vehicle for legal transplants?, *Journal of Legal Education*, 58(3), pp. 413–453.

Hylton, J. (2012) Looking at the increase in the number of law schools and law students, 1950–2010, *Marquette University Law School Faculty Blog*, 25 July. Available at: http://law.marquette.edu/facultyblog/2012/07/25/looking-at-the-increase-in-the-number-of-law-schools-and-law-students-1950-2010/, accessed 17 February 2013.

IIE (2011) Institute of International Education Open Doors 2011: international student enrollment increased by 5 percent in 2010/11, led by strong increase in students from China, IIE Press Release, 14 November. Available at: http://www.iie.org/Who-We-Are/News-and-Events/Press-Center/Press-Releases/2011/2011-11-14-Open-Doors-International-Students, accessed 17 February 2013.

Kingston, E. & Forland, H. (2008) Bridging the gap in expectations between international students and academic staff, *Journal of Studies in International Education*, 12(2), pp. 204–221.

Kritzer, H. (2012) It's the law schools stupid! Explaining the continuing increase in the number of lawyers, *International Journal of the Legal Profession*, 19(2–3), pp. 209–225, this issue.

Leask, B. (2009) Using formal and informal curricula to improve interactions between home and international students, *Journal of Studies in International Education*, 13(2), pp. 205–221.

Leiter, B. (2012) A prediction about the law teaching job market for 2012–13, 1 August. Available at: http://leiterlawschool.typepad.com/leiter/2012/08/a-prediction-about-the-law-teaching-job-market-for-2012-13.html, accessed 17 February 2013.

Lonbay, J. (2012) The changing regulatory environment affecting the education and training of Europe's lawyers, *Journal of Legal Education*, 61(3), pp. 479–485.

LSAC (2012a) Law School Admission Council Current volume – three-year summary, *LSAC Resources: Data*. Available at: http://www.lsac.org/LSACResources/Data/three-year-volume.asp, accessed 12 March 2012.

LSAC (2012b) Law School Admission Council LSATS administered, *LSAC Resources: Data*. Available at: http://www.lsac.org/LSACResources/Data/lsats-administered.asp, accessed 12 March 2012.

LSSSE (2012) *Law School Survey of Student Engagement 2012 Annual Survey Results*. Available at: http://lssse.iub.edu/order_ar.cfm, accessed 17 February 2013.

Mackun, P. & Wilson, S. (2011) Population distribution and change: 2000 to 2010, 2010 Census Briefs, *US Census Bureau*, March. Available at: http://www.census.gov/prod/cen2010/briefs/c2010br-01.pdf, accessed 17 February 2013.

Macready, C. & Tucker, C. (2011) *Who Goes Where and Why?* (New York, Institute of International Education).

Marginson, S. (2008) Global field and global imagining: Bourdieu and worldwide higher education, *British Journal of Sociology of Education*, 29(3), pp. 303–315.

Marklein, M.B. (2011) US colleges push efforts to draw foreign students, *USA Today*, 22 June, p. 1A.

Mazlish, B. & Morss, E. (2005) A global elite?, in: A.D. Chandler & B. Mazlish (Eds) *Leviathans: Multinational Corporations and the New Global History* (Cambridge, Cambridge University Press), pp. 167–186.

Menkel-Meadow, C. (2012) Too many lawyers? Or should lawyers be doing other things?, *International Journal of the Legal Profession*, 19(2–3), pp. 147–173, this issue.

Millard, D. (2005) The impact of clustering on scientific mobility, *Innovation*, 18(3), pp. 343–359.

NCBE (1996) National Conference of Bar Examiners persons taking and passing by source of legal education, *National Conference of Bar Examiners 1996 Statistics*. Available at: http://www.ncbex.org/assets/media_files/Bar-Examiner/articles/1997/660297_statistics1996.pdf, accessed 17 February 2013.

NCBE (2005) National Conference of Bar Examiners persons taking and passing the 2005 bar examination by source of legal education, *National Conference of Bar Examiners 2005 Statistics*. Available at: http://www.ncbex.org/assets/media_files/Statistics/2005_Statistics.pdf, accessed 17 February 2013.

NCBE (2011) National Conference of Bar Examiners persons taking and passing the 2011 bar examination by source of legal education, *National Conference of Bar Examiners 2011 Statistics*. Available at: http://www.ncbex.org/assets/media_files/Statistics/2011Statistics.pdf, accessed 17 February 2013.

NCBE & ABA (2012) *National Conference of Bar Examiners and ABA Section of Legal Education and Admissions to the Bar Comprehensive Guide to Bar Admission Requirements*. Available at: http://www.ncbex.org/assets/media_files/Comp-Guide/CompGuide.pdf, accessed 17 February 2013.

OECD (2010) *Education at a Glance OECD Indicators*, 2010. Available at: http://www.uis.unesco.org/Education/Documents/45926093.pdf, accessed 17 February 2013.

OECD (2012) Recognition of non-formal and informal learning – home, *Directorate for Education*. Available at: file:///C:/Users/Carole%20Silver/Dropbox/onati%20april%202011/informal%20and%20nonformal%20learning%20oecd%200,3746,en_2649_39263238_37136921_1_1_1_1,00.html, accessed 17 February 2013.

Reichman, N. & Sterling, J. (2002) Recasting the brass ring: deconstructing and reconstructing workplace opportunities for women lawyers, *Capital University Law Review*, 29(4), pp. 923–977.

Rienties, B., Beausaert, S., Grohnert, T., Niemantsverdriet, S. & Kommers, P. (2011) Understanding academic performance of international students: the role of ethnicity, academic and social integration, *Higher Education*, early online publication, 24 July, doi: 10.1007/s10734-011-9468-1.

Rizvi, F. (2007) Paper presented at the 21st Century Curriculum: Taking Bearings. Curriculum Corporation 14th Annual Conference, Sydney. Available at http://www.curriculum.edu.au/verve/_resources/Rizvi_Teaching_Global_Interconnectivity_v.1.pdf, accessed 17 February 2013.

Sandefur, R. & Smyth, A. (2011) *Access Across America: First Report of the Civil Justice Infrastructure Mapping Project, Chicago, American Bar Foundation*. Available at: http://www.americanbarfoundation.org/uploads/cms/documents/access_across_america_first_report_of_the_civil_justice_infrastructure_mapping_project.pdf, accessed 17 February 2013.

Sayad, A. (2004) *The Suffering of the Immigrant*, David Macey (Trans.) (Cambridge, Polity Press).
Shane, S. (1996) Why franchise companies expand overseas, *Journal of Business Venturing*, 11(2), pp. 73–88.
Silver, C. (2002) The case of the foreign lawyer: internationalizing the US legal profession, *Fordham Journal of International Law*, 25(5), pp. 1039–1084.
Silver, C. (2006) Internationalizing US legal education: a report on the education of transnational lawyers, *Cardozo Journal of International & Comparative Law*, 14(1), pp. 143–175.
Silver, C. (2009a) *Agents of Globalization in Law: Phase 1*, LSAC Grants Report 09-01, March. Available at: http://www.lsac.org/lsacresources/Research/GR/pdf/GR-09-01.pdf, accessed 17 February 2013.
Silver, C. (2009b) Educating lawyers for the global economy: national challenges, *Kyung Hee University Law Review*, 44(3), pp. 419–455.
Silver, C. (2011) The variable value of US legal education in the global legal services market, *Georgetown Journal of Legal Ethics*, 24(1), pp. 1–57.
Silver, C. (2012) States side story: career paths of international LL.M. students, or 'I like to be in America', *Fordham Law Review*, 80(6), pp. 2383–2439.
Silver, C. (2013a) Holding onto 'too many lawyers': bringing international graduate students to the front of the class, *Onati Socio-Legal Series*. Available at: http://papers.ssrn.com/sol3/papers.cfm?abstract_id=2200169, accessed 17 February 2013.
Silver, C. (2013b) Getting real about globalization and legal education: potential and perspectives for the US, *Stanford Law & Policy Review*, in press.
Simon, S. (2012) Insight: public schools sell empty classroom seats abroad, *Reuters*, 8 March. Available at: http://www.reuters.com/assets/print?aid=USBRE8270A120120308, accessed 17 February 2013.
Steele, J. (2012) Can New York regulate the elite law schools?, *Legal Ethics Forum*, 15 October. Available at: http://www.legalethicsforum.com/blog/2012/10/can-new-york-regulate-the-elite-law-schools.html.
Tamanaha, B. (2012) *Failing Law Schools* (Chicago, University of Chicago Press), accessed 17 February 2013.
Thornton, M. (2012) The new knowledge economy and the transformation of the law discipline, *International Journal of the Legal Profession*, 19(2–3), pp. 265–281, this issue.
Wisker, G (Ed.) (2000) *Good Practice Working with International Students* (Birmingham, UK, SEDA).
Woodward, S. (2012) From foreign students, hardly a ringing endorsement for Australia, *Chronicle*, 6 August. Available at: http://chronicle.com/article/Australia-Loses-Its-Luster-as/133371/, accessed 17 February 2013.

Effects of the acceleration in the number of lawyers in Israel

LIMOR ZER-GUTMAN
Department of Law, COMAS, Rishon Lazion, Israel

ABSTRACT *The legal profession in Israel has undergone many significant changes in response to the dramatic increase in the number of lawyers that, although emerging in 1995, still continues. The article reveals and discusses these changes which were first expressed within the profession itself. A separate section deals with the effects on legal practice. Some effects on legal practice are more difficult to ascribe exclusively to the dramatic rise in the number of lawyers; they should be attributed to other factors. Still, the rise in the number of lawyers remains very meaningful. Another section discusses the influence exerted by the increase in the number of lawyers on ethical behavior and disciplinary courts. Such an influence was found to be weak or still inchoate.*

1. Introduction

The debate in Israel over the rise in the number of lawyers and its effect on the profession, the legal services market and society in general has historical roots as old as the profession's practice in Israel (Katvan, 2012). The debate intensified in late 1990 with the establishment of private law schools (Efron, 2011) that, by 1995, had led to a dramatic increase in the number of lawyers joining the ranks of the Israel Bar Association, a trend that has continued and since strengthened.

Professional training for lawyers in Israel requires about 4.5 years, with 3–3.5 years dedicated to earning a bachelor of law (LL.B.) degree, followed by a compulsory one-year internship. After completing an internship, candidates are required to take the Bar examination. All those who pass are accepted as members of the Israel Bar; membership is mandatory and represents a preliminary condition for practicing law in Israel. In this article I focus on lawyers, not students. Hence, regarding every element touching upon the dramatic rise in the number of lawyers in Israel and its effects, 1995 represents a watershed year.

In the past two decades, this trend has dominated debate regarding the profession. Despite the debate's complexity and duration, an in-depth and empirically grounded examination of the effects of the dramatic rise in the number of lawyers on the profession, its judicial practices and the ethical behavior of its members has yet to be conducted. The debate itself has been influenced by numerous contentions, opinions and positions regarding the range of these influences, but the purpose of this article is to objectively and empirically examine, wherever possible, the past and continuing influence of this explosion in Israel.

While the effects of growth continue to emerge, one outcome is the disruption of the professions' hegemony over its own constituency, achieved through the accelerated acceptance to the Bar of minority groups and residents of the periphery. Some, like the veteran professionals cited by Katvan (2012), might view this as a negative change whereas others, including myself, welcome this effect because it demonstrates that the profession has come to better reflect Israel's heterogeneous society.

In the article, Section 2 describes the unnatural and highly dramatic growth in the number of lawyers in Israel since 1995. Section 3 deals with the various effects of growth on the profession itself. Section 4 addresses the ways in which growth has influenced legal practice and Section 5 discusses the most intriguing effect for me, as a lecturer and researcher of legal ethics: the effect of this phenomenon on lawyers' ethical behavior and on disciplinary law. It is beyond the scope of this article to consider the effect of this phenomenon on Israeli society. I will conclude in Section 6.

2. The growth of the number of lawyers in Israel

The number of people practicing the profession of law began to swell considerably in the mid-1990s, leading to a doubling in the number of lawyers each decade since. Promoting this growth was the opening of non-university law schools (also called law colleges), which enabled the sharp increase in the number of law students eligible for and admitted to the Bar after 4.5 years of study and internship. The numerical data shown in the following table and figures illustrate this development.

Table 1 shows the number of law graduates admitted to the Israeli Bar each year since 1948 (the establishment of the State of Israel), ending in 2011 (data obtained by the author from the records of the Israel Bar Association). The table indicates a sharp rise in the number of graduates admitted to the Bar in 1995, which was the year when students from the first class of LL.B. graduates from non-university institutions were certified. It indicates that the average number of law graduates annually admitted to the Israeli Bar between1948 and 1994 stood at 337, while the average number of lawyers annually admitted since 1995 (the watershed year) soared to 2,583 by 2011. This represents a record increase of 7,670% in the annual average number of lawyers admitted to the Bar between the two periods.

The acute rise in the number of lawyers in Israel between 1990 and 2011 is shown in Figure 1 (Central Bureau of Statistics, 2011). Figure 1 begins with the data for 1980, when 7,254 lawyers were registered in Israel, and then jumps to 1990, when that number grew to 10,697, in order to compare the increase between these two

Table1. *Law graduates admitted to the Israeli Bar, 1948–2011*

Year	Number admitted	Year	Number admitted	Year	Number admitted	Year	Number admitted
1948	142	1964	168	1980	349	1996	1,894
1949	35	1965	247	1981	368	1997	2,131
1950	47	1966	240	1982	341	1998	1,922
1951	150	1967	265	1983	370	1999	2,176
1952	115	1968	271	1984	458	2000	2,591
1953	222	1969	302	1985	477	2001	2,779
1954	265	1970	374	1986	538	2002	2,625
1955	324	1971	352	1987	523	2003	2,496
1956	234	1972	353	1988	539	2004	2,271
1957	188	1973	413	1989	493	2005	2,793
1958	182	1974	387	1990	510	2006	2,770
1959	138	1975	367	1991	569	2007	2,784
1960	238	1976	406	1992	550	2008	3,167
1961	165	1977	459	1993	678	2009	3,217
1962	221	1978	394	1994	803	2010	3,472
1963	203	1979	394	1995	1,842	2011	2,979

decades with the sharp rise in the following two decades. The figure missing from the graph is the number of lawyers registered in 1995, when 14,480 graduates of new law schools entered the profession. Within one decade, 1990–2000, the number of lawyers doubled, from 10,697 to 23,127. This trend continued into the next decade, so that by 2010, the total number of lawyers admitted to the Bar reached 46,515. In the last two decades, the profession grew almost five-fold. The Israel Bar anticipates that this trend will continue, with the number of lawyers expected to reach about 80,000 by 2021 (*Orech HaDin*, 2010).

Figure 2 shows the results of a comparison between the rate of growth in the number of lawyers and that of Israel's population per capita. The rate of growth in the number of lawyers was significantly greater than the rate of growth in the overall population [data for the years up to 2005 from Barzilai (2007); data for the

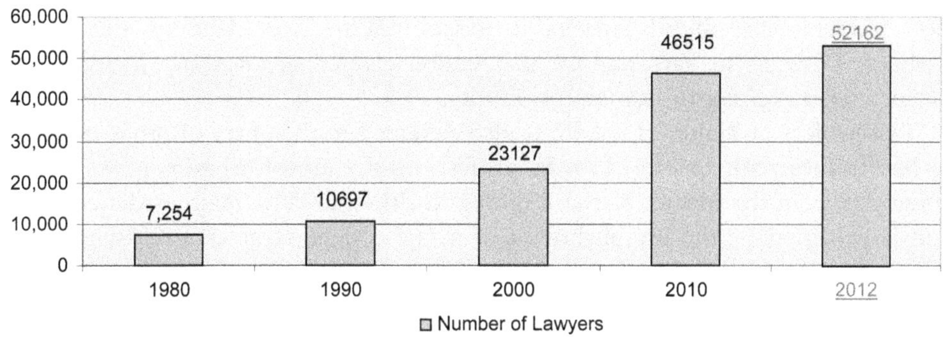

Figure 1. *Growth in the number of lawyers in Israel, 1980–2011*

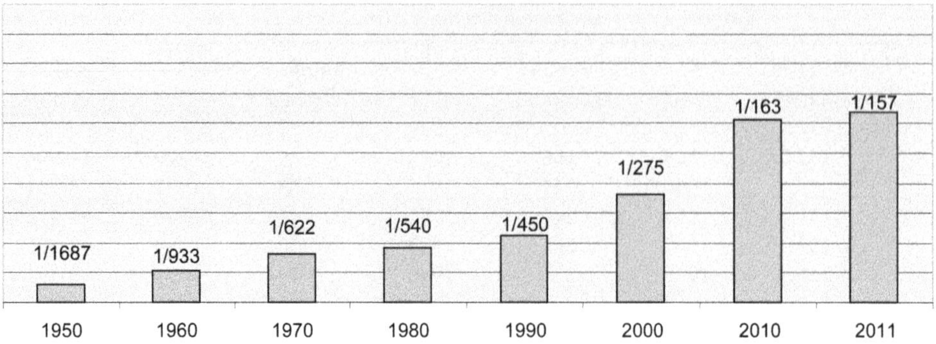

Figure 2. *Number of lawyers per capita, Israel, 1950–2011*

years 2006–2011 obtained from the Central Bureau of Statistics]. Since 2000, Israel has had the highest number of lawyers per capita of any country, with a sizeable gap separating it from the next on the list) Spain is second, than Lichtenstein, Greece, Island, the US and Italy, based on 2005 data) (Barzilai, 2007).

3. Changes in the legal profession

The growth in the number of lawyers, described in the previous section, transformed the profession's composition and structure (Ziv, 2010) to the point where the 'face of the legal profession' mirrored, perhaps for the first time, the face of Israeli society. The Arab minority, for example, which accounts for approximately 18% of Israeli society (Central Bureau of Statistics, 2010), had been counted among the profession's ranks since the establishment of the State in 1948, but in small numbers that did not proportionately reflect their presence in the population. While the Israel Bar Association does not collect data regarding members' ethnicity in its files, two important factors indicate that the overall growth in the lawyer population includes an increase in Arab lawyers. Since the opening of law colleges, there has been a sharp rise in the number of Arab students among all law students, and the majority of all students complete their studies to become lawyers (Katvan, 2012; Zaltzberger, 2009). In addition, the increase in the number of Arab lawyers led the Bar to create a new district, the Northern District, that includes around 2,500 lawyers (5% of all lawyers in Israel). With two elections held in the Northern District so far, almost the entire elected leadership, including the District's head, belong to the Arab minority.

The profession's altered terrain is also reflected in the entry of other minorities that had not formerly belonged to the profession: the ultra-Orthodox as well as new immigrants from the former Soviet Union and Ethiopia. The main evidence for this trend is provided by the establishment of a law college targeted exclusively at the ultra-Orthodox and by the continued opening of special tracks designated for the ultra-Orthodox within another law college (Shalev, 2011). The Dean of Ono Academic College reports that many Ethiopian and ultra-Orthodox students study in Ono Academic College's law school (Levi-Weinrib, 2010).

The profession has also become more diverse due to the large increase in the number of lawyers living and working in the periphery. Two decades ago it was almost impossible to find lawyers in towns located in Israel's southern and northern periphery. Today, in contrast, the presence of lawyers and law firms is quite substantial, particularly in comparison to the size of the local population. For example, in 2010 there were 346 lawyers in Ashkelon, a southern city, whereas in the 1990s there were only 70 lawyers practicing: the lawyer population grew at a rate of approximately 500%, while the city's general population grew by 30%.

Eyal Katvan (2012) describes the differences between law students in the universities and the colleges. He explains that these differences rest on their group affiliations, as described above (minorities and the residents of the periphery), with minorities tending to study law in the colleges rather than the universities. Katvan and I are thus describing the same phenomenon – the creation of a heterogeneous profession.

When examining changes in the legal profession, the number of women lawyers is always of interest. In Israel the main rise in the number of women lawyers occurred between the 1970s and 1980s; during the 1970s, women lawyers represented only 13.4% of all accredited lawyers, but by the 1980s, their numbers had reached 35%; by the 1990s, women represented 40% of all lawyers, a percentage that rose in 2010 to 43% (Elias & Shitrai, 1998). Because this trend began prior to the high rise in the total number of lawyers, we are unable to associate it with the increase in the total population of lawyers, although the entry of women may have contributed to its acceleration.

An additional important change in the profession pertains to its 'rejuvenation', with the majority of lawyers currently practicing in Israel being relatively young. In 2010, 60% of the lawyers listed with the Israel Bar were aged below 40 and only 10% over 61.[1] For the sake of comparison, consider that in 1970, 40% of all lawyers were below the age of 40 and 21% were over 60 (Yogev, 1971). We can see that the rate of lawyers in the below-40 group grew from 20% in 1971 to 40% in 2010 – meaning the profession has undergone 'rejuvenation'. Figure 3 shows the distribution, by age, for the years 1971 and 2010. We should note that between these two periods, the Israel Bar conducted no research and published no data on the basis of which we might forecast the age distribution of lawyers in the coming years. Hence, we are unable to ascertain with any certainty exactly when the decline in age began.

A further change in the profession which occurred at the same time as the high rise in the number of lawyers is the increasing educational level, expressed in the growing number of lawyers awarded an MA degree. In Israel, a BA in law (LL.B.) is sufficient for accreditation as a lawyer. Hence, those studying for an MA degree have already been certified. Before the high rise in the number of lawyers, a first degree in law was sufficient to find a job so only a few studied for a second degree. I believe that when the market of lawyers became full, certified lawyers continued their education for two reasons. First, they were possibly unable to find a job in the legal profession. Second, they found a job but believed that a second degree in law might improve their prospects. The rising number of lawyers studying for an MA degree implies an increase in the educational level of practicing lawyers. Figure 4

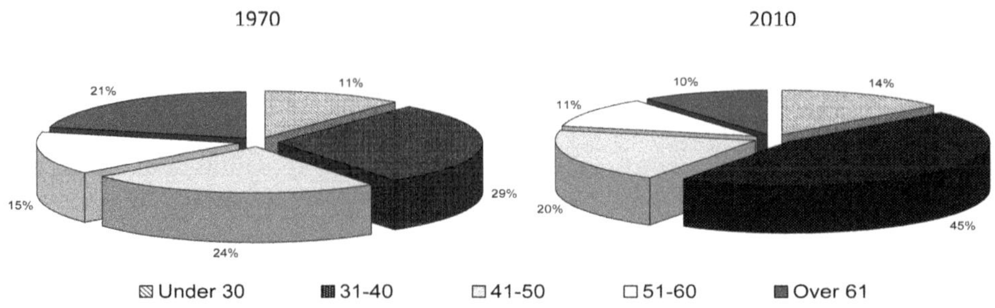

Figure 3. *Distribution of lawyers by age groups, 1970–2010*

provides data demonstrating the dramatic rise in the number of students studying for a university MA in law (called LL.M.) between the years 1979 and 2010. We can see from the figure that beginning in 1995 (the watershed year), the number of students enrolled in LL.M. programs accelerated. In that year, there were 395 LL.M. candidates whereas in 2010 the number had sprung to 2,380 candidates. However, the actual number of lawyers studying for an LL.M. degree is just a bit greater than that noted in the figure because the data shown relate only to those studying in the public universities. As of 2004, LL.M. programs have also been available in some of the law colleges not covered by the figure. According to the only report discovered, 135 students were enrolled in law college LL.M. programs (The National Council for Higher Education, 2010). Thus we can conclude that there were a total of 2,515 LL.M. students for that year, indicating an increase of 640% over a 15-year period. This growth is especially impressive when compared with the rise in the number of lawyers during those years, which increased by 300% (from 14,480 lawyers in 1995 to 46,515 lawyers in 2010). It should likewise be noted here that the universities

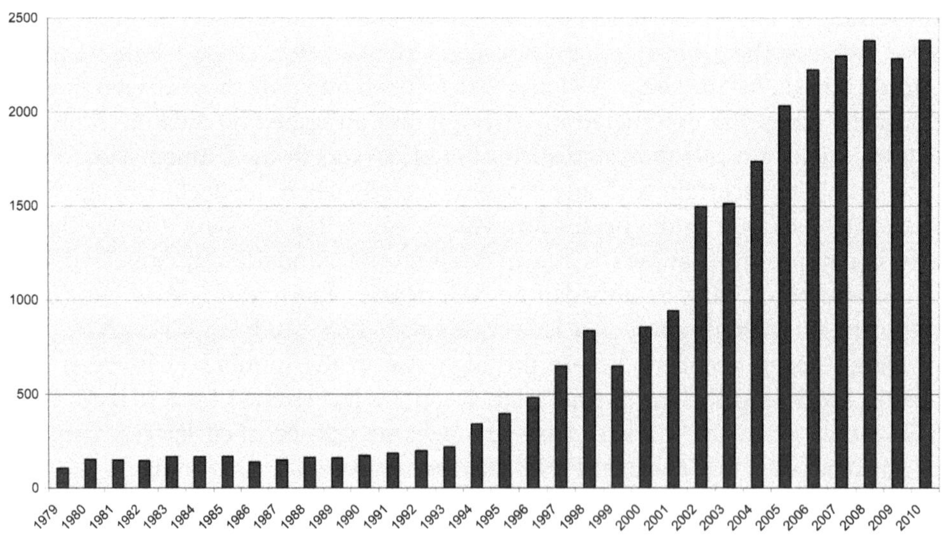

Figure 4. *Growth in the number of university LL.M. students, 1979–2010*

especially benefited from that increase and even encouraged it by opening special MA programs targeted at accredited lawyers. This change in policy apparently resulted from identification of the potential existing among law college graduates for students interested in upgrading their qualifications by means of a university-awarded LL.M.

Another effect of the acceleration in the number of lawyers in Israel is an increase in the number of lawyers leaving the legal profession. As one may expect, the oversupply of lawyers leads to a rise in the number of lawyers leaving the profession. The sole existing objective measure of the rate of professional exit is the category of non-practicing lawyers, who are exempt from Israeli Bar Association compulsory membership dues because of their limited status. Figure 5 shows a slight decline in the proportion of the bar represented by non-active members during the period from 1971 to 2011 (Barzilai, 2007; Israel Bar Association, 2010; *Orech Hadin*, 2011; Meltz, 2001; Yogev, 1971).

But Figure 5 tells only part of the story regarding exit. The Bar's compulsory membership dues are quite low, and likely do not exert a strong influence on the decision to exit the profession. Lawyers not actively practicing but interested in maintaining the option of doing so in connection with some issues or to present themselves as lawyers may continue paying their dues and thus continue to be listed as active paying lawyers (consider, for instance, the author of this article). A 2009 survey conducted by the Bar's Haifa District indicated that about 35% of the lawyers interviewed did not practice law even though they were listed as active paying members in the Bar's databank (*Dlatayim Ptuhot*, 2009). At the same time, the Israeli Bar Association estimated that in 2000 about a third of Israel's licensed lawyers did not work as lawyers (Ronen, 2000). It may well be that within that 30%, a considerable number never had any intention of practicing law but wished to study law because of its instrumental benefit to their current profession (e.g. accountants and firm managers). Exit therefore does not describe their relationship to the profession. In the absence of data

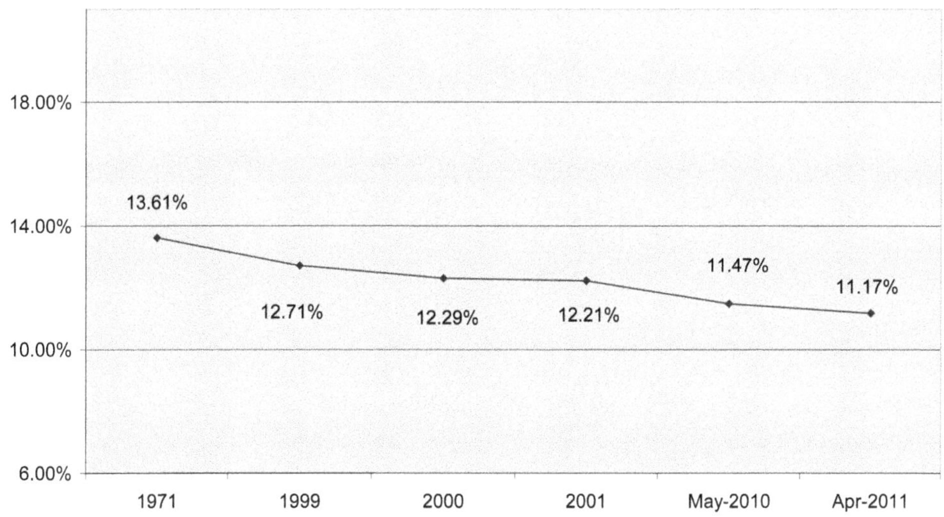

Figure 5. *Percentage of limited (non-active paying) members*

regarding the scope of the phenomenon, and given the fact that they were licensed lawyers, we nonetheless treat the entire 30% as having left the profession. Overall, the rate of lawyers exiting the profession is estimated at 30% of all lawyers.

Additional support for the high number of lawyers exiting the profession is the number of lawyers seeking a second career. For more than a decade, employment agencies have been reporting large numbers of lawyers seeking assistance in obtaining positions that do not involve the practice of law (Meltz, 2001; Muallem, 1999). These data resemble the results obtained by several surveys conducted among lawyers indicating that about half the interviewees (45% from one survey and 57% in another survey) reported dissatisfaction with their decision to become lawyers and indicated that they would choose another profession were they able to repeat the process (Roeh, 2011; Roth, 2009).

This estimated 30% exit rate of all lawyers is important when compared to the confirmed figure of 10% exit rate in 1971 (Yogev, 1971). One conclusion is that a meaningful increase in the exit rate during the interim between the two periods apparently did materialize. We may suggest that various factors contributed to the rise over the years although the surge in the number of lawyers, which greatly expanded supply and thus intensified the competition that negatively influenced lawyers' income, was a main factor motivating the trend.

This section has described the effects that the growth in the number of lawyers has had on the legal profession. The next section will describe the effects it has had on legal practice, effects that were as dramatic as those on the legal profession.

4. Changes in legal practice

One of the interesting questions emerging from this debate is whether the increase in the number of lawyers correlates with a rise in litigation in Israel's courts. Figure 6

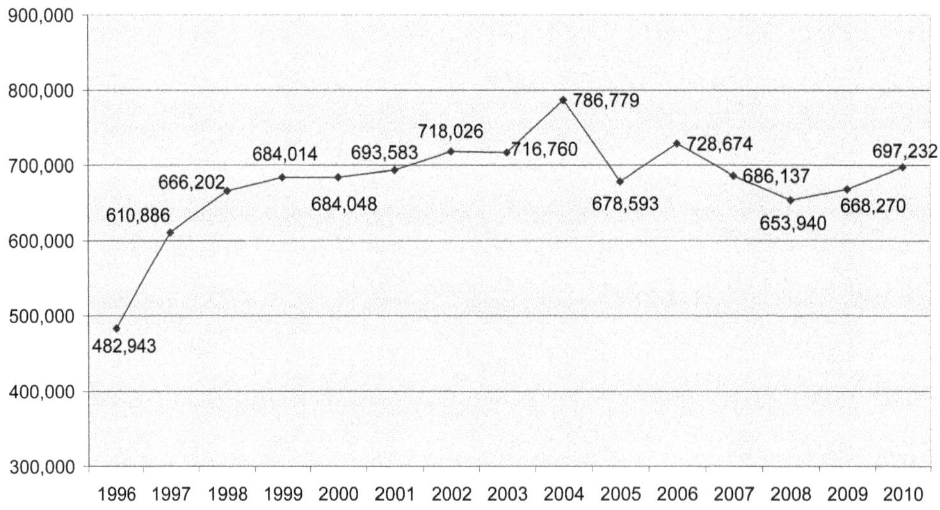

Figure 6. *Number of new files opened in the judiciary, 1996–2010*

shows the number of new files opened annually in Israel's judicial system between 1996 and 2010 (the data refer to the Labor Court, Family Court, but not the Supreme Court). We can observe a surge in the number of cases filed beginning in 1996, one year after the watershed, which reached its peak in 2004. This was followed by a moderate decline in the number of new filings that nonetheless remained approximately at the 1996 level, which suggests the significance of the witnessed increase (Ziv, 2010).

Additional factors also contributed to the rise in litigation, including the growth in Israel's population and especially the increased litigiousness that began to mark Israeli society, with almost every conflict finding its way to the courts (Mautner, 2008; Ziv, 2012).

The same period witnessed growth in lawyers pursuing public sector jobs, too, which suggests a relationship to the increasing number of lawyers. Prior to 1995, several sectors of the profession, including public administration, suffered from a noticeable shortage of lawyers. At the time, the market for new lawyers offered a wide range of opportunities; public administration often was a last choice for new graduates because of its inability to compete with the private sector in terms of salaries. The shortage was so severe that numerous positions in the public sector, including judges, remained empty because qualified lawyers could not be attracted to take these jobs. Some administrative offices dealt with the shortage by compromising in hiring decisions. For example, in the wake of the acute scarcity of lawyers employed by the District Attorney's Office, criminal cases were often filed in the Magistrate's Court by police officers, who were not educated as lawyers (Zamir, 2011).

Beginning in 1995, there is a gradual cessation of reports regarding shortages of lawyers and judges in the public administration. Signs of the change include, for example, the filing of criminal cases solely by lawyers, who took newly created positions in the police force. Lawyers now consider employment in the public sector to be highly desirable, with only in-house corporate counsel a position of greater preference for employment (Maanit, 2010).

Increased specialization also occurred during this period. Nearly 500 new legal specializations and sub-specializations were created in the legal market in order to attract attention and offer clients added value in a market saturated with lawyers (Zalmenovitch, 2011d). This was not, however, the sole impetus for the creation of new specializations. Consider, for example, the area of class action suits. Beginning in the middle of the first decade of 2000, we observe a notable rise in the scope of class action suits,[1] driven mainly by revisions in the Class Action Law, passed in 2006. However, when considering the fact that the new law itself did not alter the situation before the revisions in the law with respect to the implementation of class action suits (Klement, 2007), the rise in the number of lawyers remains a highly meaningful factor (Sharbit, 2005). A similar growth in the number of professional negligence suits filed against lawyers also suggests a meaningful correlation with the rapid increase in the lawyer population. Until about a decade ago, lawyers were rarely willing to file such a suit or represent the plaintiffs. Today, numerous such suits have been initiated and law offices even identify themselves as specializing in the representation of plaintiffs in such cases (Dubrowsky, 2010).

The trend toward multi-specialization of the legal professions is also evidenced by the development of a group of lawyers specializing in public interest lawyering. Public interest lawyering began to burgeon in Israel in the early 1980s, for reasons unrelated to the dramatic rise in the number of lawyers (Ziv, 2008). However, since the accelerated growth in the number of lawyers led to the expansion of the number of lawyers practicing in numerous areas, so it also enabled the growth in public interest lawyers. If at the start of this trajectory we could count the number of public interest lawyers on the fingers of one hand (Ziv, 2008), these lawyers currently number in the hundreds.

One of the fundamental principles associated with a market economy is that during surpluses in supply, prices drop. The legal services market, which has been unable to avoid the effects of this principle, has thus witnessed a decline in lawyers' fees (Zalmenovitch, 2011a). It is important to note that despite the decline in fees, evidence indicates that the legal needs of the poor in Israel are not met and access to justice has not improved (Ziv, 2012).

The decline in fees is especially prominent in small and medium-sized firms serving small households. Such firms generally deal with apartment and home sales, damage claims and family law. These areas are inundated with lawyers, which has sharply forced down fees, a trend already observable two decades ago. Moreover, a sizable gap in the fees charged between small and large firms differentiates small from large firms, with the latter often charging twice as much for the same work (Zalmenovitch, 2011b). Again, in the area of corporation law, which represents 13% of all industry hours invested, the larger and boutique firms are able to charge very high fees in contrast to the small firms that, due to the competition, are forced to provide their services at lower rates (Zalmenovitch, 2011b). These gaps are reflected in the finding that 16% of private sector lawyers receive 50% of all the income from fees collected in the market, with the other 50% of income divided among the remaining 84% (Zalmenovitch, 2011c).

The differences in fees between small and large firms are also reflected in the respective salaries paid. Two lawyers who completed their education at the same law school can find themselves earning significantly different salaries, with the gap escalating over time due to the fact that one was hired by a large commercial firm located in Tel Aviv whereas the other was hired by a small office primarily representing households, located in the periphery.

If the gap in their salaries can reach about 80% at the beginning of their legal careers, at the end of 10 years (assuming that both advanced in the same type of firm), that same gap will be in the hundreds of percent (Zalmenovitch, 2010). These gaps obviously reflect the differences in profitability between the two types of firm, small versus large. A further manifestation of these differences is the respective growth rate, with large firms showing rapid growth for over a decade.

In the early 2000s, law offices in Israel began to be publicly ranked according to various criteria. For the purposes of the current research, the most relevant criterion is firm size, which I use to demonstrate the dramatic rise in the number of lawyers during the period in question while focusing on the major firms.

In 2012, the top-10 list of Israeli law firms was closed by a firm having 100 lawyers. However, in 2000, not one firm among the top 10 firms was of that size.

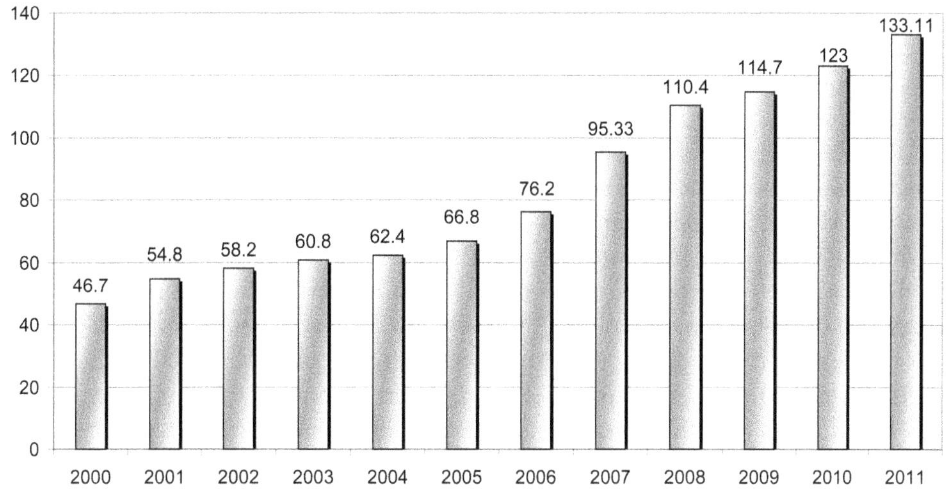

Figure 7. *The average size of the top 10 law firms, 2000–2012*

The firm ranked first in that year had 75 lawyers, with a firm of 100 lawyers not appearing until 2006, when it was ranked in first place. A comparison between the two tail ends of this period shows that a firm whose size ensured first place in 2000 (75 lawyers) ranked only thirteenth in 2012, with first place occupied by a firm having 184 lawyers. Additionally, in 2003, the last place on the list of 100 top-ranking firms was occupied by a firm having only 10 lawyers, while in 2012 such a firm would be found between the 162nd and 180th place, indicating that law firm growth has affected the entire market and not just the largest firms (data from Dun and Bradstreet).

Figure 7 shows the average size of the 10 largest law firms during the period 2000–2012. We can find some indication of the sharpness of the increase by comparing average firm size in 2000 (47 lawyers) to average firm size in 2012 (133 lawyers), which gives us an increase of 283%. This analysis obviously does not exclude the impact of other factors contributing to the dramatic rise demonstrated by Figure 7, especially the growth in business activity, the entry of international commercial companies, the intensification of privatization, as well as globalization. However, the rise in the number of lawyers enabled the impressive expansion of law offices throughout the market. Hence, it should be added to the factors contributing to the growth in the size of law firms.

5. Ethical behavior and the disciplinary system

The fascinating question addressed in this section is whether the growth in the number of lawyers has influenced lawyers' ethical behavior and the disciplinary system. The disciplinary system in Israel is unusual in comparison to parallel systems throughout the world because it is fully autonomous and under the almost exclusive control of the Israeli Bar Association, in which membership is compulsory.

Disciplinary law is comprised of two stages or levels. The first stage, investigation of a complaint, is conducted by regional and national ethics committees. These committees, composed solely of lawyers, review all grievances and decide which will be shelved and which will be transformed into a disciplinary complaint that will continue on to the next stage. In the second stage, the complaint is handled in one of the disciplinary courts located within each Bar's district, where all the sitting judges are also practicing lawyers (Zer-Gutman, 2010).

The question of greatest interest to me is whether a 'race to the bottom' in ethical behavior has begun in response to the profusion of lawyers. That is, has the surplus of lawyers and the accompanying need to compete for every client initiated a rise in unethical behavior among lawyers? An objective indicator of this race to the bottom would be a rise in the total number of complaints against lawyers presented to the ethics committees (the first stage of the disciplinary system) as well as a rise in the number of charges presented (the second stage of the system). Surprisingly, however, as shown in Figure 8, the total number of complaints submitted has not dramatically changed, with the numbers remaining fairly constant.

Figure 8 presents data obtained from the Tel Aviv District ethics committee, the district covering 70% of Israel's lawyers. This district began to collect data only in 2002; hence, the figure's curve begins in that year. As we can see there is considerable fluctuation in the number of inquiries made, the majority of which pertain to complaints against lawyers, with a good number representing queries directed by lawyers to the committee, which then directs them in their actions. In contrast to this fluctuation, it is astounding to observe that the number of complaints against lawyers has been fairly stable throughout the years. And so, despite the explosion in the number of lawyers in the district, a trend that has continued even after 2002, no change in the number of lawyers subjected to disciplinary proceedings has materialized. These data do not capture every dispute involving lawyers' services, however.

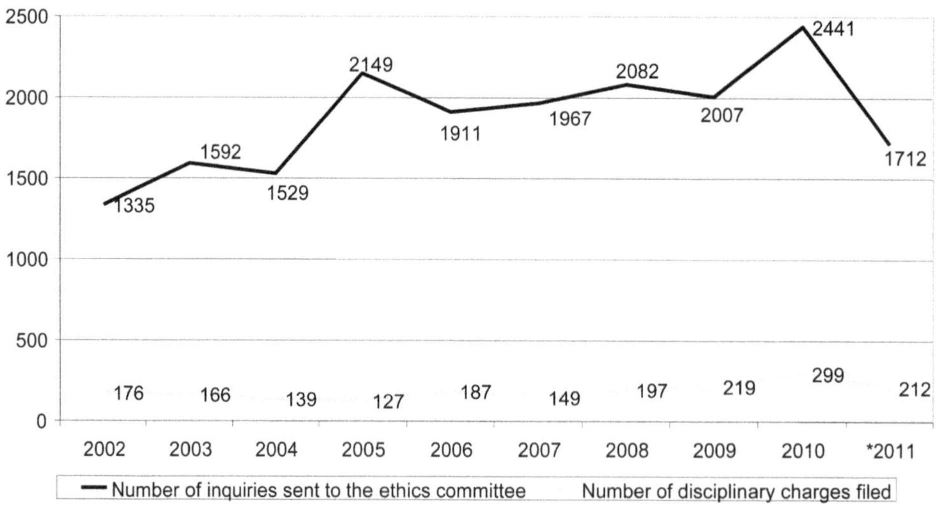

Figure 8. *Trends in inquires and disciplinary charges, Tel-Aviv district disciplinary system, 2002–2011*

Cases challenging such services also may be filed in court (on the basis of malpractice) and, as noted earlier, this has been a growing area of practice. Additionally, without additional resources for the ethics disciplinary authorities, it may be impossible to expand the number of cases in which charges are filed. A final possible explanation is a growing gap between the expectations of clients (resulting in more complaints) and the standards of the Bar disciplinary authorities (resulting in a stable number of charges filed). Another explanation why there is no change in the number of complaints might be that since 30% of lawyers are not practicing law (see Section 3) the change should be minimal, as it appears to be in Figure 8.

When considering ethical behavior, we might expect the severe competition to most influence young lawyers who have yet to establish themselves. This expectation, when coupled with the common contention regarding the decline in the quality of law college graduates (those certified after 1995) (Zarchin, 2011; Zaltzberger, 2010), might lead us to conclude that despite the consistent level of lawyers charged (as we have seen), most of those facing disciplinary charges will be lawyers with less than 15 years of practice (i.e. those certified after 1995). Yet, an empirical examination conducted in two of the main databanks maintained by the disciplinary system indicates otherwise, specifically, that the rate of disciplinary transgressions in the respective period is higher among veteran lawyers having at least 15 years of practice. The research thus shows that young lawyers commit relatively fewer disciplinary transgressions than their proportion among the entire population of lawyers might predict.

The first of these databanks contains all the case files of charges brought before the Tel Aviv District disciplinary court (Israel's largest district with respect to the number of lawyers) from 2008 until the third quarter of 2010. The files were examined for the seniority of the respective lawyer on the day the proceedings against him or her were initiated.

The second database contains details on all the lawyers suspended or disbarred after conviction by the disciplinary court, effective late 2010. This is the sole registry of convictions open to the public because the law obligates publication of the name of every lawyer either suspended or disbarred. It includes the name of the lawyer, his or

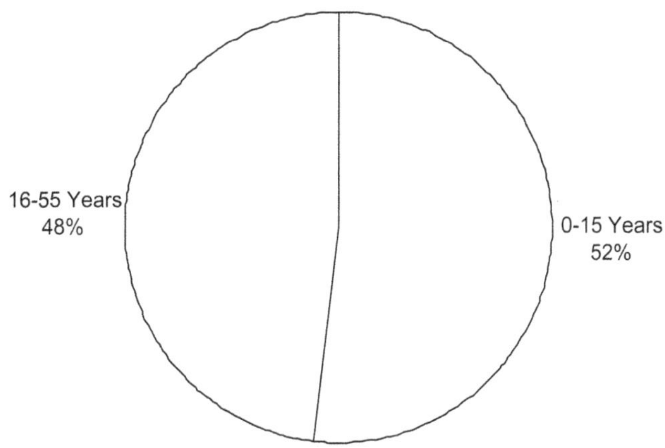

Figure 9. *Division of disciplinary charges according to the lawyer's years of practice (2008–2010)*

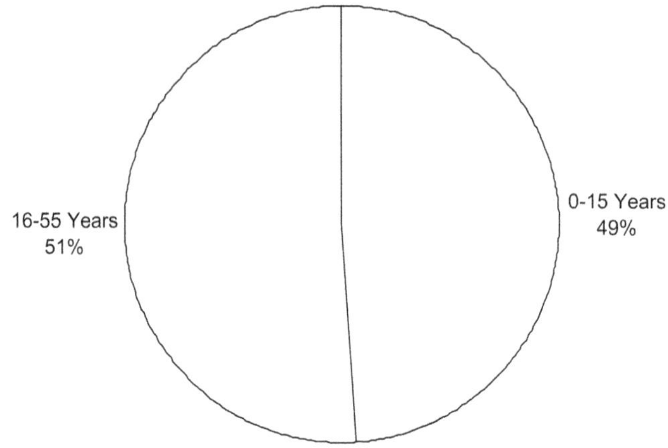

Figure 10. *Division of disciplinary punishments of suspension and disbarment according to the lawyer's years of practice*

her license number and date of the onset of sanctions, whether suspension or disbarment. Again, I checked the seniority of each lawyer who was suspended or disbarred as listed in the second databank.

Figure 9, based on the first databank, shows that lawyers having up to 15 years of practice, despite their representing 78% of all lawyers, are responsible for 52% of the disciplinary charges brought before the Tel Aviv District Disciplinary Court during 2008–2010. Even more amazing is the second half of the equation, according to which lawyers having more than 16 years of practice represent 22% of all lawyers yet are responsible for 48% of the disciplinary charges in that district, more than double their proportion in the total population of lawyers.

Figure 10, based on the second databank that contains details on all the lawyers suspended or disbarred after conviction by the disciplinary court, effective late 2010, presents similar data. We can see that lawyers having up to 15 years of practice account for 49% of all sanctions of suspension or disbarment. In contrast, lawyers having at least 16 years of practice account for 51% of disbarments or suspensions, despite their being only 22% of the lawyer population overall.

Together, these findings indicate that the increase in the number of new law graduates does not correlate with a rise in disciplinary charges. Lawyers who joined the Bar beginning in 1995 committed fewer offenses than what might have been expected given their proportion of the total population of lawyers. Moreover, common opinion attributing inferior behavior to younger lawyers is mistaken. It is surprisingly the veteran lawyers, who tend to complain about the participation of younger lawyers in the race to the ethical bottom, who have already reached that bottom.

6. Conclusion

This article has shown that the legal profession in Israel has undergone many significant changes in response to the dramatic increase in the number of lawyers that began in 1995 and still continues today. These changes were first expressed within the profession itself, which became more heterogeneous as it absorbed increasing numbers of minorities, new immigrants and residents of the periphery, groups previously unable to gain admission into university law schools. Women's entry into the profession, a trend that began before 1995, has likewise intensified, so that women currently comprise 43% of all lawyers. Another influence that can be credited to the increase in the number of lawyers is the rising educational level, with steadily mounting numbers of lawyers earning an MA since 1996. Another internal phenomenon, one quite predictable in saturated markets, is exit from the profession. In this regard, a surprising change is that while only 10% of the population of lawyers changed their profession in the past, the figure currently stands at 30%.

Contrary to the stated influences on the profession itself, some effects on legal practice are more difficult to ascribe exclusively to the dramatic rise in the number of lawyers; they should be attributed to other factors. Still, the rise in the number of lawyers remains meaningful, especially with respect to the broadening scope of litigation as well as the sharp rise in law firm size, particularly among Israel's largest firms. In addition, the decline in fees and the creation of new specializations and sub-specializations can be attributed almost entirely to the saturated market and intensifying competition between lawyers.

The influence exerted by the increase in the number of lawyers on ethical behavior and disciplinary courts was found to be weak or still inchoate. Contrary to accepted opinion, lawyers who joined the Bar after 1995 are less liable to commit disciplinary offenses, implying that some assumed ethical inferiority as well as competitive battles for clients have yet to demonstrate any influence in this area. As the data have surprisingly shown, veteran lawyers are more likely to commit disciplinary infractions, at almost twice the rate expected from their proportion in the total population of lawyers.

Acknowledgement

The author thanks Eyal Moise for excellent research assistance.

Note

[1] The registry of class action suits conducted in the courts on the basis of article 28, the Class Action Law (2006), see: http://elyon1.court.gov.il/heb/tovanot_yezugiyot/list.htm.

References

Barzilai, G. (2007) The ambivalent language of lawyers in Israel: liberal politics, economic liberalism, silence and dissent, in: T. C. Halliday *et al.* (Ed.) *Fighting for Political Freedom: Comparative Studies of the Legal Complex and Political Liberalism* (Portland, ORS, Hart Publishing), pp. 247, 250–251, 256–257.

Central Bureau of Statistics (2010) *Statistical Annual of Israel, 2010* (Jerusalem, Central Bureau of Statistics).

Central Bureau of Statistics (2011) *Statistical Annual of Israel, 2011* (Jerusalem, Central Bureau of Statistics).
Dlatayim Ptuhot (2009) Lawyers turning to the law, *Dlatayim Ptuhot*, February–March, p. 10 (in Hebrew).
Dubrowsky, L. (2010) The lawyers trap, *Yediot Aharonot* (daily newspaper) 12 May, (in Hebrew).
Efron, Y. (2011) What is the future of legal education in Israel?, *Alei Mishpat*, 8(45), pp. 58–61 (in Hebrew).
Elias, N. & Shitrai, M. (1998) *Women Lawyers Worth Less: Patterns of Segregation and Inequality in the Legal Profession in Israel*, Discussion Paper, Golda Meir Institute for Social Labor and Research Tel-Aviv University.
Israel Bar Association (2010) *The National Index of Lawyers: Towards the 10th Annual Conference, Eilat.*
Katvan, A. (2012) The 'overcrowding the profession' argument and the professional melting pot, *International Journal of the Legal Profession*, 19(2–3), pp. 301–319, this issue.
Klement, A. (2007) Guidelines to the interpretation of the Class Action Law, *HaPraklit*, 49, p. 131 (in Hebrew).
Levi-Weinrib, E. (2010) Who are the lawyers dedicating their time to pro bono representation?, *Globes*, 7 June (in Hebrew).
Maanit, C. (2010) Survey: only 2% of lawyers are interested in remaining in their current positions, *Globes* (daily newspaper), 2 September (in Hebrew).
Mautner, M. (2008) *Law and the Culture of Israel at the Threshold of the Twenty-First Century* (Tel Aviv, Tel Aviv University Press and Am-Oved) (in Hebrew).
Meltz, J. (2001) Off the record, *Globes* (daily newspaper), 4 October (in Hebrew).
Muallem, M. (1999) Have gown but no job, *Haaretz* (daily newspaper), 25 June (in Hebrew).
Orech HaDin (2010) Jubilee Issue, 10, p. 20 (in Hebrew).
Roeh, A. (2011) A *Calcalist* exclusive: 45% of lawyers would not repeat their choice of the profession, *Calcalist* (daily newspaper), 5 September (in Hebrew).
Ronen, M. (2000) Signing in at the employment bar, *Yediot Aharonot* (daily newspaper), 7 March (in Hebrew).
Roth, N. (2009) 57% of lawyers are unhappy with their profession; 80% would not recommend it to their children) *Haaretz* (daily newspaper), 23 March (in Hebrew).
Shalev, G. (2011) Interview with Prof. Gabriela Shalev, President, The Ono Academic College, and the current dean of the college's School of Law, *Orech HaDin*, 13, p. 63 (in Hebrew).
Sharbit, N. (2005) Lawyers are making careers on the backs of the banks, *Globes* (daily newspaper), 20 June (in Hebrew).
The National Council for Higher Education (2010) *Report prior to the opening of the 2010/2011 academic year* page 8. (A copy, in Hebrew is available with the author.)
Yogev, Z. (1971) *Survey, The Population of Lawyers in Israel, 1970/71* (Israel Bar Association), pp. 1–2, 47 (in Hebrew).
Zalmenovitch, D. (2010) The legal labor market and stresses on the assessment and employment of lawyers, p. 2 (July). Available at: http://www.glawbal.com/upload/2011%20Summary%20-%20GLa11L(1).pdf.
Zalmenovitch, D. (2011a) Distribution of specialization and billing income in the legal sector, p. 4. Available at: http://www.glawbal.com/upload/Practices%202011(1).pdf (in Hebrew).
Zalmenovitch, D. (2011b) Commodification and comparisons of legal fees – May 2011. Available at: http://www.glawbal.com/upload/Products%202011(1).pdf (in Hebrew).
Zalmenovitch, D. (2011c) The legal sector in the US and Israel, summary for 2011, pp. 8, 19. Available at: http://www.glawbal.com/upload/2011%20Summary%20-%20GLawBAL(1).pdf (in Hebrew).
Zalmenovitch, D. (2011d) Division of practice area and paid legal fees, pp. 1, 6. Available at: http://www.glawbal.com/upload/Practices%202011(1).pdf (in Hebrew).
Zaltzberger, E. (2009) The legal profession in Israel is currently facing its greatest crisis, *Globes* (daily newspaper), 9 January (in Hebrew).
Zaltzberger, E. (2010) The law colleges have contributed nothing to the level of academic educational, *The Marker* (daily newspaper), 21 October (in Hebrew).
Zamir, I. (2011) Israel's supply of lawyers, *Orech HaDin*, 11, pp. 22–23 (in Hebrew).

Zarchin, T. (2011) University deans: the level of the colleges is inferior, *Haaraetz,* 22 July (in Hebrew).
Zer-Gutman, Z. (2010) Reform of the lawyers' disciplinary system: were the deficiencies corrected?, *HaMishpat Law Review*, 15, p. 27 (in Hebrew).
Zer-Gutman, L. (2013) Anatomy of a Struggle: The Israel Bar Association and the legal clinics, *HaMishpat Law Review*, 17, p. 59 (in Hebrew).
Ziv, N. (2008) Lawyering in the name of social change in Israel: a forecast after two decades of activity, *Ma'asei Mishpat,* January, pp. 19, 26–28 (in Hebrew).
Ziv, N. (2010) Regulation of Israeli lawyers: from professional autonomy to multi-institutional regulation, *HaMishpat Law Review*, 15, pp. 159 173–174 & fn. 49 (in Hebrew).
Ziv, N. (2012) Unauthorized practice of law and the production of lawyers, *International Journal of the Legal Profession*, 19(2–3), pp. 175–192, this issue.

The new knowledge economy and the transformation of the law discipline

MARGARET THORNTON
Australian National University, Canberra, Australia

ABSTRACT *This article addresses the dramatic increase in the number of law students in Australia over the past two decades. It is argued that the transformation of legal education is attributable to the neoliberal turn, the embrace of the new knowledge economy, the adoption of a user-pays philosophy, the low costs associated with offering law courses and consumer demand. While the profession might mutter that there are 'too many lawyers', it has done little to inhibit the explosion in numbers. Indeed, the profession itself has been transformed as a result of neoliberalism and the acceptance of competition policy. What is perhaps most distinctive about the Australian experience is that less than half of all law graduates go into legal practice, while the other half is readily absorbed into government, the corporate sector, the not-for-profit sector and a host of other occupations. Furthermore, while legal practice has been a dynamic site of growth, the expansion has been largely concentrated in metropolitan centres. In fact, the evidence suggests that there may not be enough lawyers to service rural, regional and remote areas.*

Introduction: the neoliberal turn

Neoliberalism as the dominant political philosophy of the contemporary world has contributed to the dramatic reshaping of both legal education and the legal profession. The market as the leitmotif of neoliberalism has permeated every nook and cranny of society, a phenomenon that is percipiently captured by Roberts' (1998) phrase, "the market metanarrative". The privileging of profit-making and promotion of the self has eviscerated if not erased altogether a commitment to the public good and social justice. A rapacious form of capitalism is associated with the nineteenth century (Polanyi, 2001) but its 'second coming' (Comaroff & Comaroff, 2001) associated with the latter part of the twentieth century shows no sign of abating despite the global financial crisis (GFC) of 2009 and the subsequent European debt crisis.

Neoliberalism is not only an economic theory but also a means of constituting a radically different configuration of cultural politics (Giroux, 2004). The privatisation of the public sector and evisceration of the common good are notable manifestations of neoliberalism. The privatisation of public goods is pithily referred to by Marcos (cited in Coronil, 2001) as the 'striptease' of the state. Instead of a modicum of distributive justice being effected by the state according to the social liberal norm, the market is now expected to be the primary arbiter of the good. Perhaps the most dramatic example of the striptease of the state is that of higher education. Disinvestment in higher education has been typical of the West in recent years at the same time that there has been pressure to raise graduation rates to make nation-states more competitive on the world stage. Greater emphasis has been placed on knowledge as the basis of the economy (OECD, 1996; Jacob & Hellström, 2000). Indeed, Lyotard (1984) famously observed that knowledge had replaced land in the struggle between nation-states. As it might be posited that lawyers are the paradigmatic new knowledge workers – "the *par excellence* institutional inventors for their clients" (Cain, 1994, p. 31) – the idea of producing more law graduates would seem to conform with the embrace of the new knowledge economy.

I would therefore suggest that the dramatic increase in the number of Australian law graduates has been a by-product of the neoliberal turn and the decision to move away from agriculture and manufacturing as the basis of the economy. 'Too many lawyers' is an oft-repeated refrain,[1] but it is really only with an economic downturn that cries of over-saturation become vociferous. In Australia, the refrain has been heard occasionally (McInnis & Marginson, 1994, p. 28), but nothing has come of it. Despite the proliferation of law schools and law graduates, there is an exceptionally low rate of unemployment for law graduates. The unemployment rate for lawyers in 2006 (the last Census year analysed) was only 2% compared with the overall rate for Australia of 4.7% (Daly 2011, p. 6). Using a cross-sectional analysis of the Census data, Daly (2011, pp. 16–17) shows that investment in a law degree is still very profitable, thereby challenging the contention that there is an excess of law graduates.

What is more, a national report found in 2009 that there are insufficient lawyers to service rural, regional and remote (RRR) areas (McDougall & Mortensen, 2011, Mundy, 2008), a shortage that is likely to become pronounced with the retirement of the present generation (McDougall & Mortensen, 2011). It is also notable that the focus of the RRR discourse tends to be on 'access to justice' (Rice, 2011), a phrase that is singularly absent from the discourse of profit maximisation associated with the corporate law firms in metropolitan areas.

Both legal education and legal practice have been transformed by the neoliberal turn. While numerosity is not the whole story, it is a striking indicator of change. It also mirrors trends elsewhere. In approximately 25 years, the number of law schools in Australia has increased from 12 to 32, and there are more waiting in the wings. In 1986, there were 28,291 law graduates, which is the equivalent of the total number of students studying law today (ALSA, 2012). There were 87,858 graduates in 2006, which would equate to about 130,000 today. The graduate figure compares with 23,179 legal professionals, or practising lawyers, in 1986 and

62,806 today (McGowan, 2012). While the number of law graduates is outstripping the demand for legal professionals, the number of legal professionals grew by 80% between the Census years of 1991 and 2006 compared with 64% for the number of law graduates (Daly, 2011, p. 9). There is a growing demand for corporate lawyers, a point on which I shall elaborate, as well as for specialists in new knowledge areas such as intellectual property. The ratio of legal practitioners in Australia is approximately one practitioner for every 364 people.[2]

What is nevertheless significant about this statistical snapshot is that less than half of all law graduates go into traditional legal practice, that is, practice in private firms. Instead, they pursue careers in government, the courts, the corporate sector, community legal centres, the not-for-profit sector and a host of other alternatives. Economic growth also enables the ready absorption of law graduates into industries such as accountancy, banking and finance (Daly, 2011, p. 8). Law graduates employed as managers, advisors or policy analysts are unlikely to appear in the official statistics for legal practitioners if their employment does not require a current practising certificate.[3] Precise statistics are therefore hard to gauge, especially as increasing numbers are employed overseas.[4]

Figures on diversity in the profession are also difficult to track. For example, some law schools have conducted special programs for Indigenous students for several decades, but not more than a handful graduate each year. Law societies, such as the Law Institute of Victoria have developed programs to encourage the employment of Indigenous law clerks and the briefing of Indigenous lawyers. Victoria also has an Indigenous Law Students and Lawyers Association to support its members.[5]

In addition to concern regarding the ageing and replacement of RRR lawyers, there is disquiet regarding younger lawyers. Generation X (born between 1965 and 1979) is said to favour quality of life over career and salary, while Generation Y (born between 1981 and 1995) is said to be more concerned with money and promotion of the self than the work-oriented baby boomers (born between 1945 and 1965). While the profile of the profession is becoming younger, it is predicted that Generation Y will change employers frequently during their lifespan and experience several career changes (Patterson, 2006; Chanen, 2006), a factor that contributes to the increasing volatility associated with the profession.

The most dramatic demographic change in the legal profession is its feminisation. Reflecting the international trend (Schultz, 2003), women now comprise between approximately 65 and 70% of all law students. The conjunction of sex plus age is therefore pronounced. The 2006 Census showed that, while women comprised 41.6% of legal practitioners, they constituted 65% of those under 30 (Daly, 2011, p. 7). The more senior positions associated with autonomy and independence nevertheless remain masculinised, despite the hope that it would be 'just a matter of time' before gender equity in the profession was attained (Thornton & Bagust, 2007, p. 811). Whereas 54.7% of female lawyers were classified as employees in the 2006 Census, only 16.6% were classified as non-employees (that is, principals or partners in law firms; Campbell *et al.*, 2008, p. 8). The feminisation thesis must therefore be qualified, for it applies only to the employed or managed base of the organisational pyramid, not to professional practice as a whole.

Neoliberalism is not excited by the question of whether there are too many lawyers or whether women and minority groups are equitably represented; such questions are left for the supposedly invisible hand of the market to decide. I consider how the growth in law schools emerged and how a dynamic legal professional market has been able to absorb the new graduates with little more than some *sotto voce* muttering that there may be 'too many lawyers'.

The education revolution

In 1988, all Australian colleges of advanced education (CAEs) were declared by government fiat to be universities overnight.[6] Despite this radical move, there was not a commensurate increase in government funding. Influenced by Hayek (1960, 1976) and Friedman & Friedman (1962, 1980), the gurus of neoliberalism, higher education began to be viewed as a commodity rather than a public good. The new philosophy was implemented with the transition from free higher education to a system of user pays, which profoundly affected what was taught and how it was taught (Thornton, 2012).

In a partially deregulated environment that allowed universities to choose what courses they offered (apart from medicine), vice-chancellors in the new universities (the News) favoured law as they believed it could be offered cheaply – "under a gum tree" – as an inquiry into Australian higher education in the 1960s expressed it (Martin Report, 1964, p. 57). That is, it was thought that the teaching of law required no more than a handful of teachers and a few law books, as opposed to the expensive infrastructure required for science and medicine. The News were also attracted by the idea of offering a prestigious professional program to well-credentialed students in order to augment their status vis-à-vis established universities (the Olds), as well as the prospect of attracting discretionary income in an increasingly competitive environment. Their ambitions were boosted by the virtually unstoppable demand for law places in a flourishing economy.

Despite initial resistance, public opposition to the re-introduction of fees was cleverly assuaged by, first, euphemistically referring to them as a 'contribution' (the Higher Education Contribution Scheme; HECS);[7] second, the initial contribution was set at a modest AU$1,800.00 per annum across all courses, which allayed concerns about equity; third, and this was the *pièce de résistance*, HECS did not have to be paid up-front but was repayable only when a graduate earned a specified minimum salary.[8]

However, once fees are accepted as the norm, it is only a matter of time before they insidiously begin to be ratcheted up, as can be seen in the case of the United Kingdom (Browne Report, 2010). Also, the Hayekian philosophy that law students expecting to receive high salaries should pay more for their tuition than, say, science or humanities students, began to take hold and differential rates were introduced.[9] As a result, law schools everywhere began to increase their enrolments – in the Olds as well as the News. More students initially resulted in more staff, but deficits could be met only by taking in more students. In this way, an endless spiral was set in motion. The explosion in numbers soon led to the adoption of cheaper forms of pedagogy – large lectures and exams rather than small-group teaching, continuous assessment and research essays. Block teaching or 'intensives' offered over a few days and online delivery became widespread, but less money did not inhibit expansion. On the contrary, cheap and 'efficient' forms of pedagogy in conjunction with the relentless demand encouraged more universities to establish law schools. If a university allocated only a portion of the income per law student (HECS plus the government contribution) to its law school, a central 'tax' could be levied to subsidise the research-intensive parts of the university and to spend money on marketing to attract top students.

Once a law degree had been approved by a university and the relevant admitting authority, it was not subject to further review; there was no overseeing body seriously looking at the resourcing of law schools or the way the number of lawyers was creeping up. A quasi-independent advisory body at the national level, the Commonwealth Tertiary Education Commission (CTEC), had been in existence until the time of the Dawkins reforms but was disbanded soon afterwards. Shortly before its demise, the CTEC had completed a comprehensive report on Australian law schools (Pearce Report, 1987) which suggested (*inter alia*) that there was then no need for another Australian law school (Pearce Report, 1987, vol. 3, p. 998). The Dawkins reforms and the embrace of competition policy, which I discuss below, induced a convenient amnesia regarding the recommendations. National bodies that might have been expected to speak out, such as the Committee (then Council) of Australian Law Deans (CALD), were hesitant about adopting an overtly critical stance towards government policy in view of their diverse constituencies and dependence on government funding. Careful planning did not accord with the market metanarrative, which favoured flexibility and adaptability according to the vectors of supply and demand at any given moment.

To establish a professional law program, a university needed no more than the approval of the relevant admitting body and the support of the local law society. Arguments in terms of distinctiveness, such as a regional or suburban location, a focus on distance education or a particular specialisation, together with an acceptable basic curriculum, were sufficient to secure approval. The proposal might make passing reference to resources but the admitting authorities did not regard this as their responsibility. Hence, a high degree of variation in resourcing emerged. A set of (non-mandatory) standards for Australian law schools was adopted by CALD only in 2009 (CALD, 2009). There is nevertheless a compulsory curricular element that is common across all Australian law schools – a cluster of 11 subjects colloquially known as the 'Priestley Eleven'[10] – designed to facilitate reciprocal admission rights between jurisdictions.

One element of difference that has emerged is the increasing popularity of the Juris Doctor (JD) in lieu of the LLB as the basic legal qualification.[11] As a graduate entry course, the JD was allegedly introduced to circumvent the government prohibition on charging domestic undergraduate students full fees (Cooper *et al.*, 2011, pp. 45–46), as there is no cap for graduate courses. It was also hoped that the JD would appeal to international students as there is no cap on the fees they might be charged either. The experience of the JD has nevertheless been chequered with undergraduate, postgraduate and hybrid incarnations (Cooper *et al.*, 2011). I interpolate here that while the LLB is a bachelor degree in Australia, it is commonly undertaken jointly with another bachelor degree, such as arts or commerce, over five years or so.

The emergence of the Australian Qualifications Framework (AQF) in 2011 has led to the questioning of inconsistencies in degree programs. As the JD purports to be offered at Masters level, the regulatory agency, Tertiary Education Quality and Standards Agency (TEQSA) has made it clear that it will require more of law schools than the laissez-faire approach favoured to date. The JD falls under the Masters Degree (Extended) category of the AQF, the outcomes of which are specified as "specialised knowledge and skills for research and/or professional practice and/or further learning" (AQF Council, 2011, pp. 17–18). It is notable that the requirement for a JD to include a "significant proportion of practice-related learning" comports with the more applied focus favoured by law firms. This could entrench the idea that the proper destination for law graduates is employment in traditional legal practice rather than the wide array of occupations that is presently the case. I now consider how competition policy has augmented this orientation.

Transforming legal practice

Competition policy

The impact of neoliberalism on legal practice has been profound. Competition became an official plank of Australian government policy as a result of the Hilmer Report in 1993. It advocated the restructuring of the economy, designating the regulatory role of the state to be one primarily concerned with facilitating the market in ways deemed beneficial to consumers.[12] This policy welcomed new entrants to the market but their success or failure would be determined by supply and demand mediated by efficiency and cost. Competition policy was to have wide-ranging ramifications for the delivery of services of all kinds, including higher education and legal services. While some lawyers were initially lukewarm about accepting competition policy, it was soon officially adopted as a goal by legal professional associations (Parker, 1997, p. 43).

So significant has been the effect of competition policy on the legal profession it has been suggested that the practice of law is no longer a profession with an elevated status, but an occupation (Weisbrot, 2002, p. 28). This is because competition policy has caused the profession to lose its traditional monopoly over certain areas of practice, such as conveyancing, which have been opened up to specialist providers. Competition policy also means that the provision of legal services is no longer subject to regulation according to professional legal norms alone but to regulation and scrutiny by the Australian Consumer and Competition Commission (ACCC). The acceptance of competition also led to the demise of many of the restrictive and anti-competitive practices of the past (Baxt, 1995; Farmer, 1994).

Competition policy has also given rise to some very significant changes in the structuring of law firms and has placed Australia to the fore in terms of innovation. These developments include the creation of multi-disciplinary practices (MDPs), the incorporation of legal practices (ILPs) and listing on the stock exchange. MDPs involve lawyers forming a one-stop shop that includes experts with various complementary skills, but lawyers have not been automatically accepted as the dominant partners in MDPs. They have tended to be add-ons to multinational accounting firms, such as PricewaterhouseCoopers, which are well advanced in terms of global organisation as knowledge corporations (Weisbrot, 2002, p. 33). Perhaps, for this reason, the take-up rate for MDPs has been lower than anticipated.

By contrast, the incorporation of solicitors' firms and other businesses providing legal support services has proven to be very popular. In 2008, over 20% of Australian legal service businesses were incorporated (ABS, 2009); more than 1,000 of these ILPs are in New South Wales, which was the first jurisdiction to allow incorporation in 2001 (Mark & Gordon, 2009). Incorporation is regarded as a sophisticated advance on the partnership model for, in addition to the benefit of limited liability, it provides taxation set-offs and flexibility in constitutional arrangements, capital financing and the management and distribution of profits, including the way employees are rewarded. Each ILP is required to have at least one legal practitioner director. Incorporation has had particular appeal for small single-jurisdiction firms rather than multi-jurisdiction firms, as all jurisdictions were not initially in favour (Mark & Gordon 2009, p. 511; Parker, 2010, pp. 97–98).

Incorporation paved the way for other business structures and, in 2007, Slater and Gordon became the first law firm in the world to be listed on the stock exchange (Mark & Gordon, 2009, p. 515).[13] The initiative reveals perhaps more clearly than any other the extent to which legal practice has been imbued with the spirit of competition, which threatens to leave professionalism languishing in the rear. Shareholders, after all, are primarily investors interested in maximising the return on their investment. Following Australia, the United Kingdom moved to deregulate legal practice,[14] and it is notable that Slater and Gordon was one of the first firms to apply to list in London (Whealing, 2012a).

The culture of competition that shapes the routine business practices of corporate clients inevitably affects lawyer–client relationships, particularly when financial constraints begin to bite. Almost every day there are reports of new initiatives designed to cut costs and maximise profits, many emerging from technological innovations in e-space (Mark *et al.*, 2012), while others build on the initiatives devised to promote competition, such as franchising (Mark & Gordon, 2009, p. 517) and the funding of civil litigation by commercial entities for profit (Cashman, 2012; Moran, 2012). The use of cheap foreign jurisdictions to provide routine legal services has been around for a while but there is concern that increased usage could deleteriously impact on the hiring of Australian law graduates (Firmspy, 2011). Savvy law graduates, however, have their eye on the ball and will be looking to the international arena as a source of new opportunities.

The lure of the global

References to globalisation have become trite but its centrality to contemporary lawyering cannot be ignored. The British Empire spearheaded the nexus between capitalism and globalisation in the nineteenth century, which was so successful that global capitalism itself arguably became the new notion of empire (Hardt & Negri, 2000). In this imperial paradigm, nation-states have been rendered marginal as capital has become uncontrollable. Paralleling the flows of capital are human flows comprising asylum seekers, guest workers and opportunistic jobseekers. The one-way movement from developing to developed countries points to a brain drain with its negative social ramifications, which are accorded short shrift by global capitalism.

The globalisation of higher education represents a striking manifestation of the thesis as higher education has become a major export earner for Australia. The high uncapped fees international students can be charged renders tertiary education markets extremely attractive. The federal nature of higher education policy together with the support of the Department of Foreign Affairs and Trade (DFAT) and the International Legal Services Advisory Council (ILSAC) have boosted Australia's ability to export higher education, especially to Asia. As a result, the higher education 'industry' quickly became the third highest export earner. Australia now has the largest proportion of international students of any OECD country (OECD, 2011). However, global markets are risky. Factors such as the GFC, which has increased competition between nation-states for students together with currency fluctuations, economic growth in key source markets, including the huge investment by China in higher education, have severely affected enrolments, underscoring the fragility and volatility of higher education markets (Deloitte Access Economics, 2011). In 2012, it was reported that export earnings in Australia from the sector had dropped from AU$18.5 billion to AU$15.8 billion in a year, with further falls anticipated (Trounson, 2012, p. 23).

The nation-state sits in the neoliberal driver's seat and acts as the market's key facilitator. In addition to supporting the higher education 'industry', the Australian government assists in the export of legal services to developing countries. The Law Council of Australia has also sought improved access for Australian lawyers to the US foreign legal services market, such as through the 'Fly-in, fly-out' (FIFO) program. Australian lawyers are also part of the migratory flow of human capital as they head for New York, London or Hong Kong, the major financial hubs of the world, in order to secure 'fabulous compensation' because their services have worldwide markets (Storper, 2001, p. 97).

Globalisation entails not only an exodus of lawyers from Australia but also lawyers from elsewhere coming to Australia. ILSAC encourages the opening up of Australian markets to foreign lawyers even though they are precluded from practising Australian Law. The restriction could well be lifted, especially as foreign lawyers are also being encouraged to immigrate to Australia, unequivocally putting paid to any suggestion that there might be 'too many lawyers'. This is graphically illustrated by a recruitment drive conducted by the President of the Law Council of Australia in Northern Ireland in 2011, designed to encourage young Irish lawyers to come to

Australia to help fill the demand for RRR practitioners (Law Council of Australia, 2011).

The internationalisation of the Australian economy was a plank of the Keating Government's competition policy 20 years ago (Keating, 1992, p. 9), which we now see being applied to law with such enthusiasm. As a sometime European-oriented country located in the Asia-Pacific, Australia possesses a significant international sensibility (Weisbrot, 2002, p. 32). In addition to the willingness of the legal profession to innovate and adapt, as seen by incorporation and listing on the stock exchange, a new breed of global lawyer is being groomed to sustain the arrangements for these capital flows.

While the Australian legal profession is only now contemplating a national legal profession (McClelland, 2011), a move that mainly serves the interests of the large multi-jurisdictional firms, the new incarnation of empire has also encouraged the large corporate firms to internationalise and establish offices all over the world (McGregor, 2012). Allens, the second Australian firm to open in Ulaanbaatar, the Mongolian capital, did so to assist Rio Tinto, one of its biggest clients, in a project described as "the world's largest undeveloped copper and gold mine" (Whealing, 2012b). Thus, just as multinational corporations flit from place to place to pursue new opportunities, their lawyers are now likely to be not far behind. Young graduates are thrilled at the prospect of an exotic placement for a few years.

The late twentieth century was marked by moves towards very large national law firms through takeovers and mergers in the pursuit of profit maximisation, a pattern that is being replicated at the global level in the twenty-first century.[15] The financial rewards are commensurably greater and they have clearly taken a leaf out of the books of their multinational clients as they become players on the global stage. First of all, their size is daunting. Ashurst has almost 1,000 lawyers in Australia, with another 1,200 globally (Merritt, 2012a); second, there is the question of the profit pool, given that Ashurst has a turnover of US$1 billion and the firm could be doing business in 10 or 15 different currencies; third, there is the issue of heightened competition between associate lawyers as they vie for partnerships and other rewards.

While global firms receive a disproportionate amount of attention, smaller and medium-sized firms may benefit from international mergers, as they are able to pick up practice groups or partners in areas that the global firms wish to discard (Dean & Collings, 2012). It is apparent, however, that the beneficiaries would be restricted to firms in the main metropolitan financial hubs rather than RRR firms. It would therefore seem that global legal practice, while contributing to the diversity and volatility of graduate destinations is also contributing to the increasing metro-centrism of Australian law firms.

Preparing graduates for what?

The message of neoliberalism is one that values applied knowledge over theoretical or doctrinal knowledge – 'know how' over 'know what'. This has profoundly affected what is taught in the legal academy and how it is taught (Thornton, 2012). Critical and theoretical knowledge of all kinds has been contracted in favour of vocationalism, which is shaped by the idea that traditional legal practice is the natural destination of the law student. The impetus in favour of the applied was accentuated by a constellation of factors associated with the proliferation of new law schools following the Dawkins reforms of 1988. These factors included the transmutation of students into customers so that they became more concerned with credentialism than education and the pedagogical effects of massification, particularly online delivery.

The problem with the applied or practice-ready orientation of legal education is that it fails to take cognisance of the fact that at least 50% of law graduates do not pursue careers in legal practice. Even prior to the Dawkins reforms 25 years ago, the Pearce Report recognised that the law degree was replacing Arts as the generalist degree of choice. A graduate survey conducted by the Pearce Committee in the mid-1980s revealed that no more than 56% of all graduates were then employed in private legal practice (Pearce Report, 1987, vol. 2, p. 534). While this statistic legitimised the importance of teaching law as a liberal degree, which was endorsed by the Pearce Report, the commitment to a liberal legal education was relatively short-lived. Social, contextual, theoretical and interdisciplinary approaches were soon under threat with the neoliberal turn and the focus once again on the production of practice-ready graduates. The diffuse nature of alternative career destinations means that there is no unified voice comparable to that of law societies, the powerful corporate law lobby or the legal profession more generally to speak with authority regarding the desirable knowledge or skills to be included in a generalist law degree.

A period of practical legal training (PLT) on completion of a law degree has been a requirement for admission in lieu of articles in most Australian States since the 1970s,[16] but increased competition in the legal labour market has stepped up the pressure on law schools to groom graduates to be practice-ready even before they embark on a PLT program. Participation in a clinical program, which gives students a taste of practice, usually from a social justice perspective, is an option in some law schools but clinics are expensive and open only to a few in a mass system. In deference to the dominance of the legal profession, the inculcation of practical skills throughout the curriculum is single-mindedly directed towards preparing graduates for traditional legal practice, a scenario I have suggested that has been disrupted by the impact of competition policy and globalisation.

However, the imperative in favour of practice does not emanate from the profession alone. As the post-Dawkins law schools were anxious to assure law firms that their students were competitive with graduates of the established law schools, the incorporation of practice-oriented skills into the law curriculum was seen by the new law schools as a way of endowing their graduates with an edge in the market. A number of law schools, such as Newcastle (NSW), Flinders and Bond Universities, made a point of integrating skills subjects formally into their LLB curricula. Even law schools with an established reputation for providing a liberal legal education, such as La Trobe, jettisoned this orientation in favour of an applied focus (Thornton, 2006). The pressure to include more applied knowledge frequently came from students anxious about their future, although this is not always the case.[17]

Predicated on the assumption that law graduates will necessarily gravitate towards legal practice, the apparent disjuncture between a liberal law school curriculum and legal practice continues to be questioned by practitioners and their supporters. David Weisbrot, a former President of the Australian Law Reform Commission, drawing on the recommendations of a major report of the Commission (ALRC, 2000), is strongly of the view that law schools should focus on what lawyers actually do, thereby justifying the acquisition of professional skills such as professional responsibility and the ability to communicate with clients (ALRC, 2000, pp. 36–39). Weisbrot's view is echoed by recent commentators from the United States. A scathing attack on law schools and their scholarship appeared in the *New York Times* towards the end of 2011, which voiced the anger of both corporate law firms and their clients about what is seen as an expensive legal education that ignores the realities of practice (Segal, 2011). The concern is that law firms, or, more accurately, their corporate clients, have to pay for the practical training of graduates while being billed at top charge-out rates. This opinion piece epitomises the widening gap between the study of law as an academic discipline and legal practice as a technocratic and business-oriented activity. The question of US law graduates pursuing careers other than legal practice would seem to be accorded short shrift by the literature.

Criticisms of this kind revive the ancient academic/practice conflict, especially the question of whether a law school owes its primary loyalty to the dispassionate values of the university or to a profession in which the presuppositions of practice are accepted without question. Unsurprisingly, corporate clients are disgruntled about paying top dollars for work carried out by a new recruit undergoing basic training. The correlative question is whether this training should be the responsibility of law students who are paying high tuition fees, even when they do not propose to go into legal practice. Large corporate clients of US law firms are beginning to view new attorneys as 'worthless' (Cunningham, 2011), which could result in even greater emphasis being placed on the inclusion of practical skills in the law degree at the expense of critique. In light of the domination of the market, it has recently been argued that the desirable skills should not be restricted to advocacy, communication, negotiation and the preparation of documents, but should also include business and marketing (Dilloff, 2011, p. 357).

Despite the increasing diversity in Australian law graduate destinations, corporate law firms are still regarded as the elite area of legal practice because of their wealth and prestige. Their status and the way they are able to seduce law schools with financial support and law students with summer clerkships, high salaries and attractive conditions enables them to perpetuate the prevailing hierarchy of graduate destinations – with themselves at the apex – and to influence the law curriculum to a disproportionate degree. Billable hours, comparatively little autonomy over work (Nelson, 1997, p. 73; Macfarlane, 2008, p. 61), the relentless long hours culture, and disapproval of maternity leave and flexible work (despite the rhetoric; Wald, 2010; Thornton & Bagust, 2007), as well as the sloughing off of a concern with social justice are all played down.[18] The pressure on law schools to produce practice-ready graduates has insidiously increased as competition in the market has given rise to ever larger and more specialised corporate firms at the national and, now, the international level.

A 2010 survey by Graduate Careers Australia revealed that only 43.7% of graduates started work in law firms (a drop from 49.1% five years earlier) (Guthrie, 2012; Berkovic, 2011). As mentioned, there has been a considerable increase in the number of lawyers over all, but the percentage of graduates going into alternative legal careers, particularly as in-house counsel in the corporate sector, has also increased markedly. The 2010 survey revealed that 20.1% of law graduates entered industry and commerce (12.4% of whom joined the business and financial sector), 24.5% went into government, 3.9% into education and 2.7% into the not-for-profit sector. While there is undoubtedly a knowledge overlap between legal practice and in-house lawyering, it is apparent that most law graduates do not go into corporate law firms. As well as providing training for public life and good citizenship, a law degree prepares graduates for a wider variety of careers than is the case with most other disciplines. The appeal of the law degree is nevertheless at least partially dependent on its retaining a liberal character, which the deans of some Australian law schools have acknowledged.

It is notable that, despite the impact of global markets on both higher education and the legal profession, globalisation has exerted relatively little impact on the core law curriculum to date. Law deans, however, have begun to stress the need for the inclusion of a global dimension. Professor Gillian Triggs, former Dean of Sydney Law School, for example, has stressed that a narrow focus on legal practice does not accord with the internationalisation of legal services (Firmspy, 2011). While many law schools offer optional subjects in international, transnational, global and comparative law, surprisingly few mandate the inclusion of an international component in their degree requirements. Globalisation is not specified by the Priestley Eleven and the concept has been slow to enter the consciousness of the admitting authorities, which still evince a nineteenth-century doctrinal mindset. One would think that the pressure on law schools to produce practice-ready graduates would have exerted a change of heart in light of current developments, albeit that the admitting authorities tend to be dominated by judges who preside over domestic courts.

Conclusion

Despite the exponential increase in the number of law graduates in Australia, the refrain that there are 'too many lawyers' does not seem to apply – provided that one interprets the term 'lawyer' broadly. Since the Dawkins reforms of 1988, the economy has expanded exponentially and is continuing to expand, increasing not only the demand for legal services but the demand for new knowledge workers with generic legal skills who are able to contribute productively to society in multifarious ways.

Although the proportion of law graduates becoming lawyers in private practice is declining, despite the profession's growth and increasing diversity, a law degree equips graduates for the burgeoning demands of government, private corporations, the not-for-profit sector, the United Nations, journalism and a host of other careers. The preponderance of these careers is law-related, though this is not always the case. Despite the reality, increasingly powerful corporate law firms, especially those with global reach, are exerting pressure on law schools, both consciously and unconsciously, to produce practice-ready graduates to serve their particular needs, an aim that is becoming more and more difficult to satisfy in light of the increasing complexity of corporate legal practice.

The challenge for law schools is to devise a law curriculum appropriate for productive legal workers and well-rounded global citizens alike and to resist the temptation to produce narrow technocrats. Rather than devising ways to maximise the profits of already wealthy multinational corporations, might not the creative abilities of the most talented law graduates be deployed elsewhere? Recognition of the need for social justice for all, which includes those who live in RRR areas, Indigenous people and others for whom capitalism and its benefits are elusive, is an important message for law students to appreciate. An exclusive focus on preparing practice-ready graduates for corporate law firms primarily concerned with capital accumulation not only impoverishes the discipline of law but society more generally.

Acknowledgements

Versions of this paper were presented at a workshop entitled 'Too Many Lawyers? Facts, Reasons, Consequences and Solutions', at the International Institute for the Sociology of Law, in Oñati, Spain, on 19–20 April 2012, and at the Legal Profession Group Meeting of the International Sociological Association, in Bonn, on 1–4 July 2012. Thanks to Eyal Katvan, Carole Silver and Neta Ziv for organising the former and to Ulrike Schultz for the latter. Thanks also to Helen McGowan for reading the text and the Australian Research Council for financial assistance (DP120104785).

Notes

[1] Pietro Calamandrei, an Italian lawyer and politician, wrote an article with that title in 1921 (Carmignani & Giacomelli, 2009, p. 2).

[2] The population of Australia in 2012 was 23 million.

[3] Approximately 5,011 were admitted to practice by Australian Supreme Courts in 2011 (McGowan, 2012, Table 3).

[4] For example, a graduate survey from the University of Sydney revealed that 11 per cent had taken positions overseas within four to six months of completion of their final year of study (Sydney University Careers Centre, 2012).

[5] The association is called Tarwirri. Available at: http://tarwirri.com.au/index.php/about/(Tarwirri, 2012).

[6] The reforms are colloquially known as the 'Dawkins reforms' after the Hon. John Dawkins, the minister who introduced them (Dawkins, 1988).

[7] This government scheme is now known as the Higher Education Loan Program (HELP) but continues to be commonly referred to by its original acronym of HECS.

[8] In 2011/2012, this was AU$47,195 (this is just below the median starting salary for law graduates of AU$50,000; Daly, 2011, p. 15). The income-contingent scheme has been emulated in the United Kingdom and elsewhere.

[9] A domestic law student's contribution for a 2012 Commonwealth supported place (based on a HELP loan) is AU$9,425 per annum or 84% of the allocation paid to the university. This means that only 16% of the nominal cost of educating a law student comes from the state. This compares with 22% for a science place and 52% for a humanities place (Norton, 2012, p. 50).

[10] After Priestley J who chaired the Law Admissions Consultative Committee in 1992. The 11 common subjects are criminal law, tort law, contract law, land and property law, equity and trust law, administrative law, constitutional law, civil procedure, evidence, company law, and legal ethics.

[11] Melbourne Law School was the first Australian law school to make the JD its sole law degree satisfying the requirement for admission to practice (Larcombe & Malkin, 2011). The University of Western Australia has since emulated what has come to be known as the 'Melbourne Model'.

[12] Competition policy was incorporated into the *Competition Policy Reform Act 1995* (Cth).

[13] Integrated Legal Holdings, listed in 2007, which operates a number of firms under the one business structure, is the only other Australian firm to have gone down the listing path to date (Parker, 2010).

[14] *Legal Services Act 2007* (UK) came into operation in 2011.

[15] In the Asia-Pacific region, Mallesons Stephen Jacques has entered a 'Swiss-style verein' with prominent mainland Chinese firm King & Wood, to become King & Wood Mallesons; Blake Dawson Waldron has adopted the name of its international alliance partner, Ashurst; and Freehills has negotiated a linkage with global giant Herbert Smith (Merritt, 2012b, p. 33).

[16] PLT courses vary in length but are usually of no more than six months' duration and are delivered via a variety of sandwich, placement and online modes. They may also enable students to work in simulated law firms.

[17] There is little unanimity among law students as to what constitutes the most desirable destination upon graduation. Two surveys of law students at the Australian National University in 2010 revealed that approximately 35% wanted to be lawyers, 30% wanted to work in international organisations, 10% in government and 20% definitely did not want to be lawyers (Boag *et al.*, 2010, pp. 6–7).

[18] Corporate lawyers are also likely to be less happy than in-house, public interest lawyers and academics (Kelk *et al.*, 2009; cf. Levit & Linder, 2010; Cantrell *et al.*, 2007, p. 65).

References

ABS (Australian Bureau of Statistics) (2009) *Legal Services. Australia 2007–08.* Cat. No. 8667.0 (Canberra, Australian Bureau of Statistics). Available at: http://www.abs.gov.au/AUSSTATS/abs@.nsf/Lookup/8667.0Main+Features12007-08?OpenDocument, accessed 14 May 2012.

ALRC (Australian Law Reform Commission) (2000) *Managing Justice: A Review of the Federal Civil Justice System*, Report No 89 (Sydney, Australian Law Reform Commission). Available at: http://www.alrc.gov.au/sites/default/files/pdfs/publications/ALRC89.pdf, accessed 14 May 2012.

ALSA (Australian Law Students Association) (2012) *About ALSA.* Available at: http://www.alsa.net.au/about-alsa, accessed 12 May 2012.

AQF Council (Australian Qualifications Framework Council) (2011) *Australian Qualifications Framework* (Adelaide, South Australia, Australian Qualifications Framework Council for the Ministerial Council for Tertiary Education and Employment). Available at: http://www.aqf.edu.au/AbouttheAQF/AQFQualifications/tabid/98/Default.aspx, accessed 14 May 2012.

Baxt, R. (1995) Professions and the challenge of competition: why the Hilmer Report and its endorsement create new opportunities for the professions, *Corporate & Business Law Journal*, 8, pp. 1–26.

Berkovic, N. (2011) Fewer law graduates are choosing practice as a career. *The Australian*, 1 July. Available at: http://www.theaustralian.com.au/business/legal-affairs/fewer-law-graduates-are-choosing-practice-as-a-career/story-e6frg97x-1226085138499, accessed 14 May 2012.

Boag, A., Poole, M., Shannon, L., Patz, C. & Cadman, F. (2010) *Breaking the Frozen Sea: The Case for Reforming Legal Education at the Australian National University* (Canberra, Law School Reform Committee).

Browne Report (UK Government Independent Review) (2010) *Securing a Sustainable Future for Higher Education: An Independent Review of Higher Education Funding and Student Finance* (London, UK Government).

Cain, M. (1994) The symbol traders, in: M. Cain & C.B. Harrington (Eds) *Lawyers in a Postmodern World: Translation and Transgression* (Buckingham, UK, Open University Press), pp. 15–48.

Campbell, I., Malone, J. & Charlesworth, S. (2008), 'The elephant in the room': working-time patterns of solicitors in private practice in Melbourne, Working Paper No 43 (Melbourne, Centre for Employment and Labour Relations Law).

Cantrell, D.J., Paluck, E.L., Lord, H. & Smith, A. (2007), Walking the path of the law: how Yale law school graduates navigate career choices, Working Paper No 07-28 (Boulder, CO, Colorado Law School). Available at: http://ssrn.com/abstract=1026618, accessed 14 May 2012.

Carmignani, A. & Giacomelli, S. (2009) *Too Many Lawyers: Litigation in Italian Civil Courts*. Available at: http://ssrn.com/abstract=1431986, accessed 12 March 2012.

Cashman, P. (2012). Adversarialism and civil dispute resolution: new legal, ethical and regulatory challenges arising from commercializing the practice of law and the funding of civil litigation. Paper presented at 'Is Adversarialism Dead? New Foundations for Legal Process and Lawyers Ethics', Australian and New Zealand Legal Ethics Colloquium, 9–10 February 2012, University of Otago, Otago, New Zealand.

Chanen, J.S. (2006) The great divide, *American Bar Association Journal*, 92(5), pp. 45–49.

Comaroff, J. & Comaroff, J.L. (2001) Millennial capitalism: first thoughts on a second coming, in: J. Comaroff & J.L. Comaroff (Eds) *Millennial Capitalism and the Culture of Neoliberalism* (Durham, NC, Duke University Press), pp. 1–56.

Cooper, D., Jackson, S., Mason, R. & Toohey, M. (2011) The emergence of the JD in the Australian legal education marketplace and its impact on academic standards, *Legal Education Review*, 21(1), pp. 23–48.

Coronil, F. (2001) Toward a critique of globalcentrism: speculations on capitalism's nature, in: J. Comaroff & J.L. Comaroff (Eds) *Millennial Capitalism and the Culture of Neoliberalism* (Durham, NC, Duke University Press), pp. 63–87.

Council of Australian Law Deans (2009) *Standards for Australian Law Schools* (Canberra, Council of Australian Law Deans). Available at: http://www.cald.asn.au/docs/CALD%20-%20standards%20project%20-%20final%20-%20adopted%2017%20November%202009.pdf, accessed 14 May 2012.

Cunningham, C.D. (2011) Should American law schools continue to graduate lawyers whom clients consider worthless? *Maryland Law Review*, 70(2), pp. 499–512.

Daly, A. (2011). Is there an excess supply of law graduates in Australia?, in: Australian Conference of Economists, 40th Australian Conference of Economists, Canberra, Australia, 11–14 July. Available at: http://www.ace2011.org.au/ACE2011/Conference_Papers/ACE2011/11_-_Conference_Papers/Conference_Papers.aspx?hkey=cd34f4ff-b393-4315-a3a7-d98e311aaa72, accessed 12 May 2012.

Dawkins, J.S. (1988) *Higher Education: A Policy Statement* ('the White Paper') (Canberra, Australian Government Publishing Service).

Dean, K. & Collings, O. (2012) Global flurry creates opportunities for smaller legal players, *Australasian Legal Business*, 1 March. Available at: http://au.legalbusinessonline.com/news/breaking-news/global-flurry-creates-opportunities-for-smaller-legal-players/107942, accessed at 14 May 2012.

Deloitte Access Economics (2011) *Broader Implications from a Downturn in International Students* (Canberra, Universities Australia). Available at: http://www.universitiesaustralia.edu.au/resources/618/1100, accessed 14 May 2012.

Dilloff, N.J. (2011) The changing cultures and economies of large firm practice and their impact on legal education, *Maryland Law Review*, 70(2), pp. 341–363.

Farmer, J. (1994) The application of competition principles to the organisation of the legal profession, *University of New South Wales Law Journal*, 17(1), pp. 285–297.

Firmspy (2011) FS editorial: Too many law grads in a deleveraged era? We ask 3 law faculty deans. Available at: http://firmspy.com/grads-students/5439/fs-editorial-too-many-law-grads-in-a-deleveraged-era-we-ask-3-law-faculty-deans, accessed 14 May 2012.

Friedman, M. & Friedman, R.D. (1962) *Capitalism and Freedom* (Chicago, University of Chicago Press).

Friedman, M. & Friedman, R. (1980) *Free to Choose: A Personal Statement* (New York, Harcourt Brace Jovanovich).

Giroux, H.A. (2004) *The Terror of Neoliberalism: Authoritarianism and the Eclipse of Democracy* (Boulder, CO, Paradigm Press).

Guthrie, B. (2012) Re: Law graduates and work sectors query, E-mail to L. Shannon, 27 March.

Hardt, M. & Negri, A. (2000) *Empire* (Cambridge, MA, Harvard University Press).

Hayek, F.A. (1960) *The Constitution of Liberty* (London, Routledge & Kegan Paul).

Hayek, F.A. (1976) *The Road to Serfdom* (London, Routledge & Kegan Paul).

Hilmer Report (1993) Independent Committee of Inquiry into Competition Policy in Australia, *National Competition Policy* (Canberra, Australian Government Publishing Service).

Jacob, M. & Hellström, T. (Eds) (2000) *The Future of Knowledge Production in the Academy* (Buckingham, UK, Society for Research into Higher Education & Open University Press).

Keating, P.J. (1992) *One Nation: Statement by the Prime Minister*, 26 February (Canberra, Australian Government Publishing Service).

Kelk, N., Luscombe, G., Medlow, S. & Hickie, I. (2009) *Courting the Blues: Attitudes towards Depression in Australian Law Students and Lawyers* (Sydney, Brain and Mind Institute). Available at: http://www.cald.asn.au/docs/Law%20Report%20Website%20version%204%20May%2009.pdf, accessed 14 May 2012.

Larcombe, W. & Malkin, I. (2011) The JD first year experience: design issues and strategies, *Legal Education Review*, 21(1), pp. 1–22.

Law Council of Australia (2011) *RRR Law: Speaking Points for Alexander Ward, President, Law Council of Australia at the Law Society of Northern Ireland Lecture/Meeting with Young Solicitors Group* (Canberra, Law Council of Australia). Available at: http://www.lawcouncil.asn.au/shadomx/apps/fms/fmsdownload.cfm?file_uuid=B51173AA-A95E-12F7-3739-4E6A4809EC40&siteName=lca, accessed 14 May 2012.

Levit, N. & Linder, D.O. (2010) *The Happy Lawyer: Making a Good Life in the Law* (Oxford, Oxford University Press).

Lyotard, J.L. (1984) *The Post Modern Condition: A Report on Knowledge* (Manchester, Manchester University Press).

Macfarlane, J. (2008) *The New Lawyer: How Settlement Is Transforming the Practice of Law* (Vancouver, UBC Press).

Mark, S. & Gordon, T. (2009) Innovations in regulation – responding to a changing legal services market, *The Georgetown Journal of Legal Ethics*, 22, pp. 501–533.

Mark, S., Gordon, T. & Shackel, R. (2012) *Regulation of Legal Services in the E-World: A Need to Short Circuit Hot Spots in Ethics and Novel Practices?* (unpublished paper) (Sydney, NSW Office of the Legal Service Commissioner).

Martin Report (1964) Committee on the Future of Tertiary Education in Australia, *Tertiary Education in Australia: Report to the Australian Universities Commission* (Melbourne, Government Printer).

McClelland, R. (2011) *National Legal Profession one step closer*, Media Release, 9 September. Available at: http://pandora.nla.gov.au/pan/21248/20111214-1249/www.attorneygeneral.gov.au/Mediareleases/Pages/2011/Thirdquarter/9-September-2011-National-Legal-Profession-one-step-closer.html, accessed 14 May 2012.

McDougall, K. & Mortensen, K. (2011) Bush lawyers in New South Wales and Queensland: a spatial analysis, *Deakin Law Review*, 16(1), pp. 75–109.

McGowan, H. (2012) 'Out there' and 'in here': Legal ethics in regional Australia, in: *Is Adversarialism Dead? New Foundations for Legal Process and Lawyers' Ethics*, Australian and New Zealand Legal Ethics Colloquium 9 February, Otago, New Zealand.

McGregor, C. (2012) No longer outpost, world on way here, *The Australian*, 24 February, p. 33.

McInnis, C. & Marginson, S. (1994) *Australian Law Schools after the 1987 Pearce Report* (Canberra, Australian Government Publishing Service).

Merritt, C. (2012a) Big three not worried by new arrivals, *The Australian*, 24 February, p. 33.

Merritt, C. (2012b) Merger of equals but Brits develop an Aussie accent, *The Australian*, 29 June, p. 31.

Moran, S. (2012) IMF's income drops by $3.6m, *The Australian*, 2 March, p. 34.

Mundy, T. (2008) *Recruitment and Retention of Lawyers in Rural, Regional and Remote NSW: A Literature Review* (Lismore, Northern Rivers Community Legal Centre). Available at: http://www.nrclc.org.au/SiteMedia/w3svc728/Uploads/Documents/RecruitmentRetentionOfLawyers.pdf, accessed 12 May 2012.

Nelson, R. (1997) Ideology, practice and professional autonomy: social values and client relations in the large law firm, in: R. Abel (Ed.) *Lawyers: A Critical Reader* (New York, New Press), pp. 70–73.

Norton, A. (2012) *Mapping Australian Higher Education* (Melbourne, Grattan Institute).

OECD (1996) *The Knowledge-Based Economy* (Paris, Organisation for Economic Co-operation and Development).

OECD (2011) *OECD Education at a Glance 2011: OECD Indicators* (Paris, Organisation for Economic and Co-operation and Development). Available at: http://www.oecd.org/dataoecd/61/2/48631582.pdf, accessed 14 May 2012.

Parker, C. (1997) Converting the lawyers: the dynamics of competition and accountability reform, *Australia and New Zealand Journal of Sociology*, 33(1), pp. 39–55.

Parker, C. (2010) An opportunity for the ethical maturation of the law firm: the ethical implications of incorporated and listed law firms, in: K. Tranter, F. Bartlett, L. Corbin, M. Robertson & R. Mortensen (Eds) *Reaffirming Legal Ethics: Taking Stock and New Ideas* (Abingdon, Oxon, Routledge), pp. 96–128.

Patterson, A. (2006) *Bendable or Expendable: Practices and Attitudes towards Work Flexibility in Victoria's Biggest Legal Employers* (Melbourne, Law Institute of Victoria).

Pearce Report (Pearce, D.C., Campbell, E. & Harding, D.E.) (1987) *Australian Law Schools: A Discipline Assessment for the Commonwealth Tertiary Education Commission)*. (Canberra, Australian Government Publishing Service).

Polanyi, K. (2001) *The Great Transformation: The Political and Economic Origins of our Time,* 2nd edn. (Boston, MA, Beacon Press).

Rice, S. (2011) Access to a lawyer in rural Australia: thoughts on the evidence we need, *Deakin Law Review*, 16(1), pp. 13–46.

Roberts, P. (1998) Rereading Lyotard: knowledge, commodification and higher education, *Electronic Journal of Sociology*, 3(3). Available at: http://www.sociology.org/content/vol003.003/roberts.html, accessed 10 May 2012.

Schultz, U. (2003) Introduction: Women in the world's legal professions: overview and synthesis, in: U. Schultz & G. Shaw (Eds) *Women in the World's Legal Professions* (Oxford, Hart), pp. xxxviii–xl.

Segal, D. (2011) What they don't teach law students: lawyering, *New York Times*, 19 November. Available at: http://www.nytimes.com/2011/11/20/business/after-law-school-associates-learn-to-be-lawyers.html?_r=1&pagewanted=all, accessed 14 May 2012.

Storper, M. (2001) Lived effects of the contemporary economy: globalization, inequality, and consumer society, in: J. Comaroff & J.L. Comaroff (Eds) *Millennial Capitalism and the Culture of Neoliberalism* (Durham, NC, Duke University Press), pp. 88–124.

Sydney University Careers Centre (2012) *Graduation Destination Report 2009*. Available at: http://sydney.edu.au/careers/staff/downloads/gds_2009_FACULTYOFLAW.pdf, accessed 12 May 2012.

Tarwirri (Indigenous Law Students and Lawyers Association of Victoria) (2012) *About Tarwirri*. Available at: http://tarwirri.com.au/index.php/about/, accessed 12 May 2012.

Thornton, M. (2006) The dissolution of the social in the legal academy, *Australian Feminist Law Journal*, 25, pp. 3–18.

Thornton, M. (2012) *Privatising the Public University: The Case of Law* (Abingdon, Oxon, Routledge).

Thornton, M. & Bagust, J. (2007) The gender trap: flexible work in contemporary legal practice, *Osgoode Hall Law Journal*, 45(4), pp. 773–811.

Trounson, A. (2012) Decline to flow through to unis, *The Australian*, 1 February, p. 23.

Wald, E. (2010) Glass ceilings and dead ends: professional ideologies, gender stereotypes, and the future of women lawyers at large law firms, *Fordham Law Review*, 78(5), pp. 2245–2288.

Weisbrot, D. (2002) What lawyers need to know; what lawyers need to be able to do: an Australian experience, *Journal of the Association Legal Writing Directors*, 1(1), pp. 21–43.

Whealing, J. (2012a) London calling for Slater & Gordon, *Lawyers Weekly*, 31 January. Available at: http://www.lawyersweekly.com.au/news/london-calling-for-slater-gordon, accessed 18 May 2012.

Whealing, J. (2012b) Minters' Mongolian move, *Lawyers Weekly*, 1 February. Available at: http://www.lawyersweekly.com.au/news/minters-mongolian-move, accessed 14 May 2012.

Is access to the profession access to justice? Lessons from Canada

AVNER LEVIN* & ASHER ALKOBY**
*Law & Business Department, Ryerson University, Toronto, Canada
**Ted Rogers School of Management, Ryerson University, Toronto, Canada

ABSTRACT *Canada, and within it the Province of Ontario, has not had a new law school in over 30 years. A combination of factors discussed in this paper has caused access to the profession to be quite limited. At the same time, the cost of legal services has increased, putting legal representation outside the reach of the lower and middle classes. In addition, diversity within the legal profession has not improved, leading to the perception of a profession dominated by 'old white males'. The paper discusses whether in light of these factors, greater access to the legal profession, in terms of absolute numbers coupled with the removal of societal barriers, would lead to improved access to justice for Canadians.*

Introduction

When the Federation of Law Societies of Canada announced in 2011 that it had approved the proposals to create two new law schools in Canada, it was the first such announcement since 1976, when the Faculty of Law at the University of Calgary opened its doors.[1] It follows that for three decades the number of law schools in Canada remained unchanged while the population of the country increased by a third. In Ontario, where one of the new law schools will be located, a new law school has not opened since 1969, when the University of Windsor started its law program. By the time the new law school, at Lakehead University in northern Ontario, opens its doors in 2013, forty-four years will have passed.

Against this background, and in an international context, it comes therefore as quite a surprise to realize that lawyers in Ontario are concerned about the 'flooding of the profession' and about an 'articling crisis' (Gray, 2011; Todd, 2011). The frequent response given by the Canadian regulators of the legal profession to the claim that Canada needs more lawyers is that there may not be enough articling positions for graduating students (Lunau, 2009). The attempts by the Law Society of

Upper Canada to address the articling placement shortage during 2010–2012, we argue, could provide no more than a limited response to the fundamental problems of accessibility and affordability of legal services in the province.

This paper follows the structure set out by the workshop 'Too Many Lawyers? Facts, Reasons, Consequences and Solutions' (International Institute for the Sociology of Law, Oñati, Spain, 19–20 April 2012), where it was first presented. Facts and figures on the legal profession in Ontario, as well as some recent developments in the debate on barriers to entry into the profession, are discussed first. The second part provides reasons for the problems faced by the legal profession in Ontario, followed by a discussion of the current and future consequences of the challenges identified. We conclude with an overview of some suggested solutions. We submit that in contrast to the lawyerly conventional wisdom in the province: there are too few lawyers in Ontario. The modest revision to the articling process being considered by the provincial regulator would largely fail to address the more fundamental challenges the legal profession faces: affordability of legal education, accessibility of legal services, and diversity within the legal profession.

Facts[2]

There are six law schools operating at present in Ontario. In 2011 they graduated 1,330 students (Law Society of Upper Canada, 2011, p. 10). Each year, 220 students on average are admitted to a law school in Ontario, with actual year sizes ranging from 160 to 300 among schools. Ontario is similar to the other Canadian provinces in this regard (Law School Admission Council, 2012). The number of practicing lawyers in Ontario is just under 32,000 in 2011 (Law Society of Upper Canada, 2011, p. 10). For a population of just under 13 million that is roughly a ratio of one lawyer for every 402 Ontarians (Statistics Canada, 2011). This ratio puts Ontario above some jurisdictions, such as South Africa (McQuoid-Mason, 2012), at par with other jurisdictions, such as the United Kingdom, New Zealand (Economides, 2012) and France, but well below the United States with its ratio of one lawyer per 260 residents (Leichter, 2011) and Israel with its ratio of one lawyer to roughly 170 residents (BdiCoface, 2011; Katvan, 2012). Put differently, 20,000 lawyers need to join the profession in Ontario to bring it to American per-capita levels.[3]

Comparatively, therefore, it is difficult to argue that Ontario is 'flooded' by lawyers. The perception of 'flooding' seems to be linked to the sense that Ontario is undergoing an 'articling crisis' because an increasing number of students are unable to secure articling placements upon graduation. But a closer look at the facts reveals a more complicated picture. Articling is mandatory in Ontario in order to be licensed and to practice law (we discuss the recently decided-upon alternative below). While, informally, applicants interview with law firms in a process that starts as early as first-year law school, it is the Law Society of Upper Canada (LSUC) that formally places applicants in articling positions. More than a third of the current articling placements in Ontario are with large law firms (namely a firm with more than 50 lawyers) and a quarter are with medium-sized firms – 11–50 lawyers (Law Society of Upper Canada, 2011, Appendix 4, 5). The smaller law firms place roughly a fifth of the successful applicants (Law Society of Upper Canada, 2011, Appendix 4, 5). Corporate (in-house) legal departments place only 1%, while the public sector and judiciary together place 16% (Law Society of Upper Canada, 2011, Appendix 4, 5).

As of 2009 there were just over 8,200 law firms (of all sizes) practicing in the Province of Ontario. In response to a survey conducted by LSUC, more than 7,000 replied that they do not place articling students within their firms (Law Society of Upper Canada, 2011, Appendix 4, 7). Taking into consideration the number of firms that replied to the survey, the percentage of firms that do not take in articling students is 91%.

Although LSUC does not track articling positions,[4] it does track the employment of lawyers at the time they are called to the Bar. In 2010, 55.5% of the candidates called to the bar had secured employment, a decrease from all-time highs of around 80% in 2001 (Law Society of Upper Canada, 2011, Appendix 4, 9), and lending to the perception that the profession is flooded, although in 2011 the percentage increased to 69%, which is a bit higher than the traditional Ontario portion of two-thirds (Law Society of Upper Canada, 2011, Appendix 5, 10).

Of particular interest are the facts related to the diversity of the articling cohort. Applicants are asked by LSUC voluntarily to disclose their membership in one or more of the following groups: Aboriginal, Francophone, GLBT, Disabilities, and Visible Minorities. The latter is an umbrella designation, also referred to as Racialized Communities, which LSUC further breaks down into Arab, Black (African-Canadian, African, Caribbean), Latin American, Hispanic, Chinese, East-Asian (Japanese, Korean), South Asian (Indo-Canadian, Indian), South-East Asian (Vietnamese, Cambodian, Thai, Filipino) and West Asian (Iranian, Afghan). Slightly more than a quarter of the 2010/2011 articling cohort self-identified as belonging to one (or more) of the groups above (Law Society of Upper Canada, 2011, Appendix 5, 4). Sixteen percent, just under two-thirds of the entire equity-seeking group, identified as visible minorities (Law Society of Upper Canada, 2011, Appendix 5, 4).

During the 2010/2011 placement year (i.e. from July 2010 until June 2011) LSUC tracked, on a monthly basis, the number of applicants without articling positions. The ratio peaked during the winter of 2011, with 1,762 looking for articling positions, and 223 not finding one, a portion of 12.6% (Law Society of Upper Canada, 2011, Appendix 5, 6). This portion is a dramatic increase from 5.8% in 2007/2008 (Law Society of Upper Canada, 2011, Appendix 4, 4). By the end of the year the portion had dropped slightly to 10% (Law Society of Upper Canada, 2011, Appendix 5, 6). Amongst applicants that did not self-identify (meaning they could have been members of one of the groups, but chose not to disclose that)[5] the portion at the end of the year was lower, and stood at 7.6% (Law Society of Upper Canada, 2011, Appendix 5, 6). Of those that did identify, 13.6% of the members of the LGBT group could not find an articling position, and almost 15% of the visible minority group could not find an articling position as well (Law Society of Upper Canada, 2011, Appendix 5, 6).

Since LSUC does not track applicants over more than one year, there is no information on the career paths of applicants that fail to secure positions in a given year. It is possible that some move into non-legal careers, and that some may continue to seek articling in years to come. Finally, grades are not an indicator of placement, and the distribution of unsuccessful articling applicants roughly correlates to the normal grade distribution ('bell curve'; Law Society of Upper Canada, 2011, Appendix 7).

To conclude, although the legal services market in Ontario does not appear to be saturated when compared with other jurisdictions, the facts suggest that there is a growing number of graduates who are unable to complete the mandatory articling requirement. Members of equity-seeking groups, the numbers further indicate, are more unlikely to secure an articling position than the rest of the cohort. In addition, a decline is also observed in the number of new lawyers that are able to find employment after completing the licensing requirements. The next section discusses the possible reasons for these developments.

Reasons

Differential access to legal education remains the primary gatekeeper to the profession. In Canada, similar to the United States, but unlike many other jurisdictions, law is not an undergraduate program. Aspiring lawyers need to complete at least two years of post-secondary education before they are eligible to apply to law school (Federation of Law Societies of Canada, 2011, p. 48). Typically, owing to the limited numbers of law school enrolments, almost all applicants complete a four-year undergraduate degree. Canadians, as a result, view the study of law as the study of a profession, and legal education is perceived as necessarily leading to the practice of law. In other jurisdictions, where law is an undergraduate degree, students may choose to study law out of academic interest, and may contemplate and choose a different occupation after completing their legal studies.[6] In Ontario, as is the case in several other North American jurisdictions (Silver, 2012), even the pursuit of a post-graduate law degree, such as the LL.M., is often attempted by internationally trained legal professionals as a gateway into the Canadian practice of law, despite the clear requirements for a J.D. or LL.B. set out by the Federation of Law Societies of Canada (Federation of Law Societies of Canada, 2011).[7]

Since articling is mandatory, and since all law school graduates are assumed by default to want to enter the profession, lawyers consider it a failure of the system and a crisis when graduates fail to find a position. In other jurisdictions there are alternatives to articling, or no articling requirement at all, leading to lessened concerns over the inability of graduates to find articling positions.

The increase in the cost of tuition is another barrier to entry into the profession. For several reasons, not least of which was the successful lobbying by professors of law, tuition cost has increased significantly in Ontario since it was deregulated in 1997/1998. In that last academic year of government oversight, tuition stood at $3,808 at the University of Toronto's Faculty of Law (King *et al.*, 2004, p. 39). For 2011/2012, students paid $25,389 at the same institution. While such tuition is comparable to US law school tuition (Kritzer, 2012), it is at the top of the list by Canadian standards. Also, that is an increase of 567%. The cost of living in Toronto increased by roughly 30% over the same period (Statistics Canada, 2012). Despite the availability of scholarships and loans, the high cost of tuition corrals and discourages students from learning law except for the purpose of working in the profession (presumably so that they may at least pay off their student loans).

The high cost of tuition has also contributed to the increase in the annual salaries of articling students. Salaries for the ten-month articling period at the big downtown Toronto firms (in which the bulk of current articling positions are found) were roughly $75,000 in 2011.[8] This has made positions with smaller law firms, who are often unable to afford similar compensation levels, less attractive to students and has led LSUC to contemplate capping articling salaries at $45,000 (Law Society of Upper Canada, 2011, p. 45). Reducing the cost of articling positions, it was suggested, could also incentivize big firms to offer more articling positions. Meanwhile, it is mostly large firms that can afford to train and pay students-at-law, and, even then, firms that employ hundreds of lawyers hire only two dozen or so students each year.[9]

All these reasons create, in combination, a funnel. It seems to us that almost no-one in Ontario decides to study law out of a purely societal or academic interest.[10] Students already have an undergraduate degree, and undertake significant debt to enter law school as a result of the deregulation of tuition fees in professional programs. These students expect, quite understandably, to enter the legal profession. While law schools have been graduating more students, law firms have been eliminating articling positions and concentrating them within the already-competitive big downtown firms. The result, within the Ontario context, is an 'articling crisis'.[11]

A combination of factors therefore appears to have contributed to the articling and employment shortages in the Ontario legal profession. The structure of the legal education system, the mandatory articling requirement – which is difficult for many students to secure in the current market conditions – and the cost of tuition in many universities offering a law degree have all created an entry funnel into the profession and have made alternative career choices to legal practice difficult to pursue.

Consequences

The diversity of the profession

A major consequence of the way in which the profession is now accessed has been the experience of visible minority and Aboriginal lawyers. There is a significant variation in the numbers of visible minorities and Aboriginal lawyers relative to the size of their communities. In 2006, there was one lawyer in Ontario for every 377 people.[12] In comparison, there were, for example, one black lawyer for every 750 members of the black community, one for every 627 South Asians, one for every 755 members of the Chinese community, and one for every 749 Aboriginal persons. These numbers were of course affected, and continue to be affected, by the number of university graduates in the respective groups (Orenstein, 2010, p. 9). The numbers indicate that the legal profession is yet to mirror Ontario's changing demographics.

Further to that, equity-seeking groups encounter barriers not only in entering the profession, but within it as well. Women lawyers, and especially visible minority women, earn significantly less than their white counterparts (Orenstein, 2010, pp. 26–29).[13] Women and visible minority lawyers are less likely to be partners in law firms and more likely to work in government. A 2011 study examined the representation in leadership among judges, governing bodies and law schools, partners in law firms, and Crown and deputy Crown attorneys in Ontario and the Greater Toronto Area (GTA). It was found that, overall, only 6.8% of the legal practitioners in leadership positions were visible minorities. Representation of partners in law firms varied substantially between firms. Some firms had almost 11% visible minorities in partner positions, while other firms had as low as 1% (Cukier, 2011). Diversity on the bench is even lower (Makin, 2012; Cukier, 2011), and the impact of the lack of diversity in legal leadership positions on the diversity of the lower levels of the professional pyramid cannot be over-estimated (R4, 2012, pp. 9–10).[14]

The resulting call to diversify the legal profession, and to promote the advancement of individuals belonging to equity-seeking groups to leadership positions within the profession, can rest on different rationales. The 'business case' for diversity has gained some advocates in recent years, although the research supporting it, whether in Canada, the United States, or the United Kingdom is not conclusive (Cukier, 2011; Wilson, 2011; Braithwaite, 2010). Of more interest to the legal profession from the perspective of the regulating body, however, is the argument that creating more inclusive and equitable legal workforce advances the cause of justice and the rule of law.

Articling and diversity

As part of a separate project (Alkoby & Levin, 2012), we interviewed influential figures in the local legal community who started an initiative they called Legal Leaders for Diversity and Inclusion (LLD, 2012) to promote diversity in the legal profession.[15] Several reasons were raised by participants as possible explanations for the difficulty of diversity to gain traction in the profession. First, it is noteworthy that some participants did not acknowledge that the articling crisis and diversity in the profession are causally connected, but rather viewed these as distinct issues (R3, 2012, p. 9; R6, 2012, p. 6; R7, 2012, p. 12; R9, 2012, p. 13; R10, 2012, p. 7).[16] Second, participants considered the problem of the diversity of the articling class as one part of the larger problem of diversity in the profession (R1, 2012, p. 9; R3, 2012, p. 13; R7, 2012, p. 18). This larger problem was seen, in turn, as originating in decisions made by equity-seeking individuals during their secondary education, in their choice of undergraduate programs, and in their elimination of law as a career option (R3, 2012, p. 13; R4, 2012, p. 7). Third, participants observed (anecdotally) that self-identifying students were not interested in pursuing the corporate commercial route and therefore in the articling positions made available by the big Bay Street firms (R3, 2012, p. 6; R6, 2012, p. 6; R9, 2012, p. 14). This, in turn, meant that they would be competing for a much smaller pool of positions that focused on areas of practice in which students felt they could give back to their communities, such as human rights law, criminal law and immigration law (R3, 2012, p. 7; R4, 2012, p. 13; R9, 2012, p. 14).[17] Fourth, participants observed (anecdotally again) that students interested in mainstream corporate law careers in the big downtown firms preferred not to form their professional identity around their sexual orientation or racialized community (R1, 2012, p. 5). These students wanted to be judged on merit, and did not self-identify to LSUC when seeking placements (R9, 2012, p. 5; R10 2012, p. 2). Fifth, while some participants believe that cultural affinities still play a significant, if unconscious role, in articling offers (R4, 2012, p. 7; R6, 2012, p. 6; R8 2012, p. 3) others do not. According to those who do, the phenomenon of 'like likes like' (i.e. that members of a certain community identify and relate to each other more strongly than they do to members of other communities) plays a significant role within the legal profession, in which the dominant community is still that of older white males (R2, 2012, p. 16; R4, 2012, p. 8). Interestingly, one of the recent initiatives of the LLD group is the creation of mentoring relationships between prominent members of certain communities and law students of similar background (Paez, 2012).

The double bottle-neck

The plausibility of this last fifth point increases given that the delivery of legal education in Ontario has not evolved since the late 1960s. A system has developed that serves the interest of the large corporate commercial firms, at the expense of the smaller firms and independent lawyers. A lucrative legal career on Bay Street (the popular nickname for the big Toronto firms) is today's Holy Grail for law students, attracting the best and the brightest and removing other legal careers from consideration. This is a state of affairs that Bay Street has little incentive to change. Consequently, clients in areas of law traditionally served by the smaller firms have suffered increased legal costs, increased delays and limited competition over their business. While the factors that determine legal costs, and the market for legal services, are economically complex (Woolley, 2008), it is clear that access to the legal system, let alone access to justice, has been increasingly out of the reach for the average Ontarian.

Ironically, the last decade has seen somewhat of an increase in the number of law school graduates seeking to enter the profession, on account of increased class sizes in several schools. However, this increase has not translated into better legal services for the reasons enumerated above. An articling bottle-neck exists in Ontario, at the same time that law school graduates are being corralled toward legal careers. Consequently, when a graduate of a Canadian legal program is unable to find an articling position, this is viewed as a crisis, whereas in other jurisdictions, such as Japan, the expectation and tradition have been that quite a few graduates would not actively seek articling (Chan, 2012).

Furthermore, if the inability of 10% of articling-seeking students to find a position is indeed a crisis, then the inability of 15% of the visible-minority group to find a position should be viewed as a dire crisis. Restated (somewhat sensationally) this fact means that the chances of a student to secure an articling position are reduced by 50% if the student self-identifies as a visible minority. That is indeed quite a problem.

And, if the anecdotal observation of participants that self-identifying students are less interested in placements with large law firms is correct, then the difficulty of these students to find a placement is related to the fact that the smaller law firms (10 lawyers and under) place only 20% of the articling cohort for the year. Legal clinic and public sector placements (not including clerkships) amount to only 10% of placements overall. In 2008, 1,171 lawyers in Ontario were registered principals (out of approximately 31,000 lawyers). This is a 4% participation rate of the profession in the training of new lawyers (Licensing and Accreditation Task Force, 2008, p. 14). The current structure of the articling program and its requirements, coupled with the interests of self-identifying students, leads therefore to a higher percentage of unsuccessful self-identifying students. Articling in this sense acts as a double bottle-neck in Ontario. It prevents entry to the profession as a whole, and it causes more difficulties for self-identifying applicants specifically.

As a result, the large law firms, which are the popular target for seekers of diversity in the legal profession, have an articling class that is less diverse than the corresponding law school class. The smaller law firms are limited in their current ability to offer articling placements and a meaningful alternative to the Bay Street experience, as are the legal clinics and the public sector. For the general population seeking affordable legal representation on non-corporate-commercial issues such as family law, immigration law, criminal law, small claims and others, the outcome is increasingly difficult. Half of the respondents to a recent survey assessing civic legal needs in Ontario (discussed below) stated that they did not think they could afford a lawyer or qualify for legal aid (Ontario Civil Legal Needs Project, 2010, p. 40).

The paralegal profession

The emergence of a thriving paralegal profession in Ontario is another consequence of the current state of the legal profession and its failure to provide for affordable access to justice. Following several years of political debate, reminiscent of the struggles around defining the legal profession in other jurisdictions such as Israel (Ziv, 2012), the Ontario government decided to have paralegals regulated and licensed by LSUC, and to allow them to provide their services in many of the areas identified above, such as small claims and criminal law, but at a significantly lower cost. There are just over 4,000 paralegals in Ontario, with about 800 entering the profession every year (Law Society of Upper Canada, 2012, p. 2). Notably, in order to work as paralegals, candidates must pass a licensing exam, but there is no articling post-graduate program. Instead, students are placed for 120 hours in a 'legal services environment' as part of their college or university program (Law Society of Upper Canada, 2010a, p. 3). LSUC's statistical information on paralegals for the years 2009 and 2010, based on self-reporting, suggests that this group is a more diverse group than the legal profession in terms of the percentages of visible minorities (Law Society of Upper Canada, 2010b). Seven percent of paralegals self-reported as black, compared with 4% of the Ontario 2006 population; 3% self-reported as Chinese, compared with 5% of the Ontario 2006 population; 9% self-reported as South-Asian, compared with 7% of the Ontario 2006 population; and 2% self-reported as

Aboriginal, the same percentage as that of the Ontario 2006 population. Contrast these percentages with the numbers above for the legal profession.

Whether any law school graduates that fail to secure articling positions end up working as paralegals is unknown, although the recently completed five-year review of the paralegal profession seems to indicate that members are on the whole graduates of college-level programs (Law Society of Upper Canada, 2012b, p. 8).

Solutions

There are many possible solutions to Ontario's current 'crisis' in the legal profession. Of course, they depend on a shared understanding and definition of the crisis in question. To those that perceive the crisis to be the inability of all articling applicants in any given year to secure placements, the solution is to increase the number of articling positions available, or to change the structure and requirements of the articling program. LSUC had attempted such solutions in recent years, and although an attempt has been made to assist principals (Law Society of Upper Canada, 2011, Appendix 3), the recent consultations mentioned above demonstrate that these solutions have been insufficient and that articling positions remain concentrated in the big firms and the public sector (Law Society of Upper Canada, 2011).

Among the options considered in the LSUC Consultation Report were the elimination of articling altogether (this has been a persistent theme for some members of the profession despite repeated affirmation of the need for articling, as recently as 2010); the introduction of a practical legal training course as part of law school or after graduation, similar to the practice in Australia and South Africa (McQuoid-Mason, 2012, pp. 3–4; Thornton, 2012); and a hard salary cap on articling positions of $45,000 (Law Society of Upper Canada, 2011, pp. iv–v). We discuss the recent outcome of the consultations below, and the discussions were framed as an attempt to address the issue of the shortage of articling placements, in keeping with the principles of competence (how to ensure that licensees receive proper transitional training) and fairness (how to ensure that licensees receive training that is transparent, objective, impartial and fair). The consideration of access to justice and how to improve it was not central to the debate, although it is the Society's principal duty under the governing legislation.

The Law Society Act states that the Society's duties are "to maintain and advance the cause of justice and the rule of law" and "to act so as to facilitate access to justice for the people of Ontario" (Government of Ontario, 1990, sections 4.2.1, 4.2.2). The function of ensuring competence "should be proportionate to the significance of the regulatory objectives sought to be realized" (Government of Ontario, 1990, section 4.2.5). Clearly, if the quality of legal services to Ontarians is maintained (by ensuring that licensees are competent), an important public interest is served. However, there are many, albeit perhaps unpopular (within the profession), ways to maintain quality, such as, for example, re-certification (Green, 2012, pp. 18–19). Care must be taken that maintaining quality does not become a proxy for gatekeeping the profession, aggrandizing legal education, and aspiring for artificial professional homogeneity, as was the case until recently in jurisdictions such as England and Israel (Katvan, 2012; Sherr, 2012). Furthermore, if access to justice means, at least in a narrow, yet important, sense, access to assistance that meets the civil and criminal justice needs of everyday Ontarians, then the barriers to entry into the profession and the accessibility of legal services should be the focus of attention regarding possible solutions.

The Ontario Legal Civil Needs Project's findings are instructive in this regard. The main reason why people in Ontario choose not to seek legal assistance was their perception of the affordability of the services (Ontario Civil Legal Needs Project, 2010, p. 31). In the words of Canada's Chief Justice Beverly McLachlin:

> Access to justice is quite simply critical. Unfortunately, many Canadian men and women find themselves unable, mainly for financial reasons, to access the Canadian justice system. Some of them become their own lawyers, or try to ... Hard hit are average middle-class Canadians. Those with some income and a few assets may be ineligible for legal aid and therefore without choices. Their options are grim: use up the family assets in litigation; become their own lawyers or give up. The result may be injustice. (Ontario Civil Legal Needs Project, 2010, pp. 8–9)

The report further identified particularly vulnerable groups that face barriers in accessing legal services, including Francophones, people whose first language is not English or French, members of equity-seeking groups (particularly persons with disabilities), members of racialized communities, people with limited literacy, people living in remote or rural communities, seniors and women (Ontario Civil Legal Needs Project, 2010, p. 43).[18]

LSUC is not indifferent to these findings, and some of the proposals tabled for discussion in connection with the articling shortage included providing an incentive to lawyers who accept legal aid to hire articling students by increasing the amount they may bill legal aid if they use an articling student, and the establishment of a form of 'Ontario Legal Corps' made up of lawyers and articling students to provide legal representation to various equity-seeking groups (Law Society of Upper Canada, 2011, 15). The latter proposal, which the LSUC Report labels 'ambitious', would be funded by the membership, through an annual levy of $250 per lawyer licensee. Such a model of funding, in itself, is problematic because of its attempt to place the obligation to access to justice with individual lawyers rather than the profession (Woolley, 2008). Moreover, while this version of extended legal aid may make legal services more accessible to low-income families, it would also perpetuate the bifurcation of the justice system, in which a second-tier legal service is made available to those who cannot afford competitive legal fees.[19]

Instead, if one recalls that Ontario is not really 'flooded' with lawyers as some other jurisdictions are, easing the current restrictions on entry to the profession could, in and of itself, improve the affordability of legal services and facilitate access to justice in that sense, and in a deeper sense, for Ontarians.[20] In other words, for those who see the articling bottle-neck as the symptom of more fundamental issues, other solutions come to mind. One possible solution is to reduce the cost of legal education, either by re-regulating the existing law programs or by allowing for new, cost-competitive law programs to be opened. Law students will thus be able to develop an interest in a variety of legal careers and careers outside the law, all of which would benefit society more than the current focus on white-shoe firms. Otherwise, opening up more articling spaces in the way LSUC proposes is not likely to result in more small-firm or public interest placements, because debt-ridden graduates would continue to seek lucrative yet scarce corporate articling positions.[21]

For those seeking to improve diversity in the legal profession, all of the suggestions above contribute somewhat, yet still fail to get at the fundamental barriers to entry into the legal profession. Participants in our study on diversity-enhancing strategies in the legal profession were divided as to what would be the most effective solution in this regard, since there were different views on where the 'real' problem exists. For some, the problem starts as early as high school, when potential lawyers belonging to equity-seeking groups elect not to pursue an undergraduate education, or to pursue undergraduate programs that lead to other careers. Such choices are indicative of broader societal issues and 'solving' them may be beyond the reach of advocates for diversity in the legal profession.

For others, the problem to be solved is the supposed disinclination of equity-seeking law students to pursue articling positions on Bay Street, and to limit themselves to less-lucrative careers. Since articling positions with smaller law firms are more difficult to secure, students end up seeking a career that both pays less and is more difficult, ironically, to enter directly. However, it is difficult to tackle this problem, to the extent that it exists, without verifiable data.

Advocates of diversity within the legal profession have not focused, so far, on the discrepancy between self-identifying and other applicants in obtaining articling placements. They have focused instead on attempts to foster diversity through the procurement of legal services. In England, for example, the Law Society has championed a Protocol on the Procurement of Legal Services (Braithwaite, 2010, p. 447), and there are many diversity-, equity- and inclusion-related initiatives within the Canadian legal profession (Chow, 2011). We discussed above one leading Canadian initiative (LLD, 2012). LLD's approach is non-confrontational, preferring to imply diversity as a preference rather than leverage their business as a threat. The LLD approach is opposed to and criticized by an alternative, less mainstream approach, known as A Call to Action Canada (ACTAC, 2009). Modelled after a popular American approach (A Call to Action), ACTAC advocates diversity as a more explicit condition for procurement and calls for corporations to commit to procure a portion of their legal services from women and minority-owned firms, through a website the organization has set up, as is becoming common practice in the United States (ACTAC, 2012).

Other advocates of diversity, the various associations of equity-seeking groups,[22] have focused on advancing and supporting their members as a way of fostering greater diversity in the legal profession. As mentioned above, that is a recent LLD initiative as well. They have not targeted the articling process or the hiring practices of the big law firms, although some are formulating suggested solutions to the articling 'crisis' which will address the equity gap (Canadian Association of Black Lawyers, 2012). The role that these associations play in the more general discussions the profession is holding over articling and the diversity of the profession is the subject of research we are conducting at present.

Finally, there are of course solutions that involve the re-definition of the legal profession, or the re-definition of activities that are limited to members of the profession, or the narrow application of 'unauthorized practice of law' (UPL) rules in a manner that would open up such activities to broad societal participation. Several jurisdictions have experimented, or are in the process of experimenting, with such reformulations, most notably England, in which non-lawyer investments in law-firms will now be permitted, and the giant retailer Tesco has announced its intention to open up such legal shops (Sherr, 2012; Menkel-Meadow, 2012). In other jurisdictions, such as Israel, the classification of certain activities as legal and therefore the exclusive domain of the legal profession has been the subject of diligent litigation by the Israeli Law Society (Ziv, 2012). Of course, the struggle between lawyers and paralegals in Ontario could be perceived as a struggle over the definition of such activities and UPL; and comparisons with other professions, such as the medical profession, and their definition and regulation of 'unauthorized' activity are instructive as well (Ziv, 2012, section IV). As Ziv (2012, p. 3) points out, the wider the reach of UPL rules, the greater the pressure to enter the exalted ranks of those authorized to practice.

Conclusion

Late in 2012, LSUC approved an alternative to the traditional method of articling (Law Society Gazette, 2012). The Law Practice Program (LPP) will run for three years as a pilot, after which time it will be evaluated (a two-year extension to the pilot is possible). In so doing, LSUC opted for the practical legal training course option identified in its consultations, over the options of abolishing articling completely or assisting articling students and principals in other ways (Law Society of Upper Canada, 2012a).[23] The Advocate Society (to which litigators, the self-perceived elite of the profession, belong), and the various lawyer associations interested in advancing their membership, spoke out against the LPP in the fear it will become an inferior pathway into the profession (Advocates Society, 2012; Federation of Asian Canadian Lawyers, 2012).

The fractious debate indicates the deep misgivings within the profession, and in particular among the equity-seeking groups, as to whether the LPP will help or hinder diversity in the profession. Arguably, the body regulating the profession should take further action, beyond its review of the articling process, to facilitate access to justice however such access is defined. It could lobby the provincial government to increase legal aid, and assist not only Ontarians with a lower income through the extension of legal aid, but through a more meaningful effort to make legal services accessible to all. But perhaps more significantly, it should consider accrediting more universities who wish to open new faculties of law, and increase the number of lawyers in Ontario as a result. LSUC could also do more to ensure that the various diversity-promoting groups and initiatives are supported and endorsed, so that women, visible minorities, LGBT individuals, and other equity-seeking groups are represented in the legal profession and that they are more likely to be found in leadership positions.

LSUC has a legislated duty "to act so as to facilitate access to justice for the people of Ontario" (Government of Ontario, 1990, section 4.2). For the lay-person 'access to justice' means affordable legal representation. For the aspiring lawyer in Ontario, 'access to justice' means the equal chance to study and practice law. The articling process, and the profession's entry barriers imposed by the law society, must reflect and serve this duty and how it is understood. Not only in the immediate and important sense of the civil needs and affordability of legal services and legal representation in Ontario (for there is growing consensus among legal professionals in Ontario that the difficulties that applicants face in securing articling impede Ontarians' access to justice, and that the Law Society must take corrective action in order to comply with its legal obligations), but equally, and perhaps more importantly, in the deep sense of a just society. In a very fundamental way access to justice correlates with access to the profession not because more lawyers will bring down legal costs, but because in a just society there should be no discriminatory barriers, and the legal profession (and indeed most professions) should reflect society as it is composed of diverse constituencies and groups.

The transformation of the legal profession in Israel, as discussed by Limor Zer-Gutman, Eyal Katvan and Neta Ziv, is instructive in this regard (Katvan, 2012; Ziv, 2012; Zer-Gutman, 2012). The profession in Israel, following the lowering of barriers to entry in 1995, is on the whole more diverse and more representative of Israeli society, as opposed to the previous judicial-professional elite (Zer-Gutman, 2012; Katvan, 2012, pp. 6–7). Significantly, there are no data to indicate that opening up the profession has resulted in a lower quality of legal services or in an increase in unethical or unprofessional activity (Zer-Gutman, 2012). These findings from Israel support the argument made by Russ Pearce and Sinna Nasseri (2012). As they persuasively argue, there is societal virtue to be found in lowering the barriers that at present impede entry into the legal profession. A society in which legal education is readily available, and not the domain of a privileged few, is a society in which liberal democratic values flourish, in which human rights are valued, and in which members of society are not alienated from the legal system on some prejudicial basis. It is a society in which access to justice is not conditional on access to legal education and to the legal profession. It is a society to which Ontario and Canada should aspire.

Acknowledgements

The authors thank the Centre for Labour Management Relations and the Law Research Centre at Ryerson University for their funding and support of the research presented in this paper. An earlier draft of this paper was presented at the workshop 'Too Many Lawyers? Facts, Reasons, Consequences and Solutions' for the International Institute for the Sociology of Law, in Oñati, Spain, on 19–20 April 2012.

Notes

[1] In English; a law school program in French was launched by the University of Moncton in 1978.

[2] While we have attempted to introduce jurisdictional comparators, the constraints of space have by and large limited this paper to a discussion of Ontario and its internal debate over the legal profession.

[3] A recent study claims that even in the United States, there are too few lawyers from an economic efficiency perspective, and that barriers to entry into the profession set by the American Bar Association keep the number of lawyers artificially low. Deregulating the profession, the authors argue, would make legal services more accessible and more affordable. $64 billion of the $171 billion spent on lawyers every year in the United States, they claim, is a premium produced by 'market distortions' (Winston *et al.*, 2011). See also Green (2012) and Pearce & Nassery (2012).

[4] The Law Society of British Columbia, by contrast, is able to track articling positions better because candidates must seek a position before entering the admissions stream (Todd, 2011).

[5] Anecdotal evidence, some of which is discussed below, indicates that many young aspiring professionals prefer to form their identity around their knowledge and skills rather than their membership in one of the aforementioned groups.

[6] It should be noted that the instruction of law as an undergraduate degree has been criticized as well, and that several jurisdictions, such as Japan and Spain, are in the process of transforming law into a post-secondary degree (Carballo Piñiero, 2012; Chan, 2012).

[7] The attitude of American law societies towards such international newcomers, described by Silver (2012) eloquently as a form of "colonial hangover", is an accurate portrayal of the traditional Canadian attitude as well.

[8] At Gowlings, one of the big firms, salary was $75,400. See http://www.iwantgowlings.com/ArticlingProgram/keyFacts.asp?id=3

[9] Firms do not readily disclose their articling class size and information is typically compiled by law students. See, for example, http://lawandstyle.ca/precedent-2013-summer-job-watch/ and http://lawandstyle.ca/summer_job_watch_student_job_offers_on_the_rise/ for summer hires, typically a proxy for articling numbers, for 2008–2013.

[10] The discussions among law students on websites such as http://lawstudents.ca are telling.

[11] Although Alice Woolley (2008, p. 114) argues (albeit in passing) that "after admittance to law school the barriers to entering the Canadian profession are relatively insignificant". For the reasons discussed in this paper, we disagree.

[12] As noted above, the ratio for 2011 was one lawyer for 402 students. The 2006 ratio is for comparative purposes with the visual minority groups.

[13] The difference in the median earnings of racialized and white lawyers, for example, is $4,000 per year for lawyers between 25 and 29 years old, and it grows to more than $40,000 by the ages of 40–44 years.

[14] Respondent R4 (see *infra* note 15) commented it is common practice to match bar to bench routinely in terms of gender, ethnicity, etc.

[15] Respondents were coded for confidentiality purposes and are cited by their code and transcription document page number. A list of participants and all transcriptions are on file with the authors and are available upon request (subject to the approval of any such request by the university's research ethics board).

[16] But see R1 (2012, p. 8), which created a new articling position designated for equity-seeking groups.

[17] In some jurisdictions, such as South Africa, 'access to justice' is synonymous with access to criminal legal representation (McQuoid-Mason, 2012, pp. 2–3).

[18] A report on British Columbia's civil legal needs had similar findings (Ensminger, 2011). Woolley argues affordable legal representation is a hard policy goal to achieve, because of the complex market for legal services (Woolley, 2008).

[19] On a more cynical note, an annual levy of $250 seems a small price to pay for keeping the number of lawyers in the province artificially low.

[20] Of course, the correlation between an increase in the number of lawyers and a decrease in legal costs is yet to be demonstrated and may be difficult to ascertain, for the reasons discussed by Woolley (2008).

[21] Though, interestingly, there seems to be little correlation between the practicality of legal education and the choice of practice. In Australia, the model of practical legal education, roughly half of eligible lawyers choose not to enter private practice (Thornton, 2012, p. 5).

[22] See, for example, the South Asian Bar Association, http://www.sabatoronto.com/saba/; the Hispanic Ontario Lawyers Association, http://www.h-ola.ca/; the Iranian Canadian Lawyers Association, http://www.icla.ca/010~Home/; the Canadian Association of South Asian Lawyers, http://www.casal.ca/web/; the Korean Canadian Lawyers Association, http://www.kclaw.ca/; the Association of Chinese Canadian Lawyers of Ontario, http://www.fccpontario.com/professionalsections/sectionlegal.asp.

[23] In its final report, the Articling Task Force in fact split into a majority and minority, with the majority recommending the LPP and the minority recommending a pre-licensing program alongside the abolishment of articling.

References

ACTAC (2009) *A Call to Action Canada*. Available at: http://www.acalltoactioncanada.com, accessed 22 July 2012.

ACTAC (2012) *Canadian Women and Minority Law Firms*. Available at: http://www.cwmlf.ca/, accessed 22 July 2012.

Advocates Society (2012) The Advocates' Society Calls for delay of debate and vote on changes to lawyer articling and licensing, *The Advocates Society*, 22 October. Available at: http://www.advocates.ca/new/about-the-society/news/tas-calls-for-deferral-of-debate-and-vote-on-articling.html, accessed 23 December 2012.

Alkoby, A. & Levin, A. (2012) Strategies for enhancing diversity in the legal profession: the Canadian approach, *Law & Society*.

BdiCoface (2011) *2011 Lawyers*. Available at: http://www.bdicode.co.il/Page_HEB/836/%D7%A2%D7%95%D7%A8%D7%9B%D7%99%20%D7%93%D7%99%D7%9F%202011, accessed 22 July 2012.

Braithwaite, J. (2010) The strategic use of demand-side diversity pressure in the solicitors' profession, *Journal of Law and Society*, 37(3), pp. 442–465.

Canadian Association of Black Lawyers (2012) *Articling Taskforce Consultation Questions*. Available at: http://www.lsuc.on.ca/WorkArea/DownloadAsset.aspx?id=2147487566, accessed 22 July 2012.

Carballo Piñiero, L. (2012) Legal education in Spain: challenges and risks in devising access to the legal professions, *International Journal of the Legal Profession*, 19(2–3), pp. 339–355, this issue.

Chan, K.-W. (2012) Setting the limits: who controls the size of the legal profession in Japan, *International Journal of the Legal Profession*, 19(2–3), pp. 321–337, this issue.

Chow, J. (2011) A call to diversify the legal profession, *University of British Columbia Law Review*, 44, pp. 25–54.

Cukier, W. (2011) *DiverseCity Counts 3: A Snapshot of Diverse Leadership in the GTA* (Toronto, Diversity Institute, Ryerson University).

Economides, K. (2012) Measuring the (over-)supply of lawyers: inter-professional, international or regional comparisons?, in: *Too Many Lawyers? Facts, Reasons, Consequences and Solutions* (Oñati, Spain, IISL).

Ensminger, C.J. (2011) Accessing justice: the legal profession's role in serving the public's diverse legal needs, *University of British Columbia Law Review*, 44, pp. 71–89.

Federation of Asian Canadian Lawyers (2012) FACL's submissions to LSUC's Articling Task Force on 'Pathways Report', *Federation of Asian Canadian Lawyers*, 11 December. Available at: http://www.facl.ca/wp-content/uploads/2012/11/FACL-Submissions-re-Pathways-Report.pdf, accessed 23 December 2012.

Federation of Law Societies of Canada (2011) *Common Law Degree Implementation Committee Final Report* (Ottawa, Federation of Law Societies of Canada).

Government of Ontario (1990) Law Society Act, *R.S.O.* Vol. Chapter L.8.

Gray, J. (2011) Law profession faces articling crisis. *The Globe and Mail*, 1 November. Available at: http://www.theglobeandmail.com/report-on-business/industry-news/the-law-page/law-profession-faces-an-articling-crisis/article4250405/, accessed 22 July 2012.

Green, B. (2012) The flood of US lawyers: natural fluctuation or professional climate change?, *International Journal of the Legal Profession*, 19(2–3), pp. 193–207, this issue.

Katvan, E. (2012) The 'overcrowding the profession' argument and the professional melting pot, *International Journal of the Legal Profession*, 19(2–3), pp. 301–319, this issue.

King, A., Warren, W. & Miklas, S. (2004) *Study of Accessibility to Ontario Law Schools* (Ontario, Queen's University).

Kritzer, H. (2012) It's the law schools stupid! Explaining the continuing increase in the number of lawyers, *International Journal of the Legal Profession*, 19(2–3), pp. 209–225, this issue.

Law School Admission Council (2012) *Official Guide to Canadian Law Schools*. Available at: http://www.lsac.org/jd/choose/canadian/, accessed 23 December 2012.

Law Society Gazette (2012) *Articling Debate: New Licensing Programs Approved*, 22 November. Available at: http://www.lawsocietygazette.ca/news/articling-debate-new-licensing-programs-approved/, accessed 23 December 2012.

Law Society of Upper Canada (2010a) *Fair Registration Practices Report – Paralegals* (Toronto, LSUC).

Law Society of Upper Canada (2010b) *Statistical Snapshot of Paralegals in Ontario* (Toronto, LSUC).

Law Society of Upper Canada (2011) *Articling Task Force Consultation Report* (Toronto, LSUC).

Law Society of Upper Canada (2012a) *Articling Task Force Final Report* (Toronto, LSUC).

Law Society of Upper Canada (2012b) *Report to the Attorney General of Ontario* (Toronto, LSUC).

Leichter, M. (2011) *Lawyers per Capita by State*. Available at: http://lawschooltuitionbubble.wordpress.com/original-research-updated/lawyers-per-capita-by-state/, accessed 22 July 2012.

Licensing and Accreditation Task Force (2008) *A Report to Convocation* (Toronto, Law Society of Upper Canada).

LLD (2012) *Legal Leaders for Diversity and Inclusion*. Available at: http://www.ryerson.ca/about/generalcounsel/pdfs/LLD%20PosterJune%2082011.pdf, accessed 22 July 2012.

Lunau, K. (2009) Where's a lawyer when you need one?, *Maclean's*, 2 February. Available at: http://www2.macleans.ca/2009/02/02/wheres-a-lawyer-when-you-need-one/, accessed 22 July 2012.

Makin, K. (2012) Of 100 new federally appointed judges 98 are white, *The Globe and Mail*, 17 April. Available at: http://www.theglobeandmail.com/news/politics/of-100-new-federally-appointed-judges-98-are-white-globe-finds/article4101504/, accessed 22 July 2012.

McQuoid-Mason, D. (2012) Access to justice in South Africa: are there enough lawyers?, in: *Too Many Lawyers? Facts, Reasons, Consequences and Solutions* (Oñati, Spain, IISL).

Menkel-Meadow, C.J. (2012) Too many lawyers? Or should lawyers be doing other things?, *International Journal of the Legal Profession*, 19(2–3), pp. 147–173, this issue.

Ontario Civil Legal Needs Project (2010) *Listening to Ontarians* (Toronto, Law Society of Upper Canada).

Orenstein, M. (2010) *Racialization and Gender of Lawyers in Ontario* (Toronto, Law Society of Upper Canada).

Paez, B. (2012) Osgoode Hall students from diverse backgrounds and corporate counsel team up, *The Law Student and Associate Recruitment Guide*, 14 November. Available at: http://www.lexpert.ca/Student/articleview/osgoode-hall-students-from-diverse-backgrounds-and-corporate-counsel-team-up -158/

Pearce, R.G. & Nasseri, S. (2012) The virtue of low barriers to becoming a lawyer: promoting liberal and democratic values, *International Journal of the Legal Profession*, 19(2–3), pp. 357–378, this issue.

R1 (2012) Interview by Alkoby & Levin. Strategies for Enhancing Diversity in the Legal Profession: The Canadian Approach, on file with authors.

R2 (2012) Interview by Alkoby & Levin. Strategies for Enhancing Diversity in the Legal Profession: The Canadian Approach, on file with authors.

R3 (2012) Interview by Alkoby & Levin. Strategies for Enhancing Diversity in the Legal Profession: The Canadian Approach, on file with authors.

R4 (2012) Interview by Alkoby & Levin. Strategies for Enhancing Diversity in the Legal Profession: The Canadian Approach, on file with authors.

R5 (2012) Interview by Alkoby & Levin. Strategies for Enhancing Diversity in the Legal Profession: The Canadian Approach, on file with authors.

R6 (2012) Interview by Alkoby & Levin. Strategies for Enhancing Diversity in the Legal Profession: The Canadian Approach, on file with authors.

R7 (2012) Interview by Alkoby & Levin. Strategies for Enhancing Diversity in the Legal Profession: The Canadian Approach, on file with authors.

R8 (2012) Interview by Alkoby & Levin. Strategies for Enhancing Diversity in the Legal Profession: The Canadian Approach, on file with authors.

R9 (2012) Interview by Alkoby & Levin. Strategies for Enhancing Diversity in the Legal Profession: The Canadian Approach, on file with authors.

R10 (2012) Interview by Alkoby & Levin. Strategies for Enhancing Diversity in the Legal Profession: The Canadian Approach, on file with authors.

Sherr, A. (2012) Tesco law and Tesco lawyers – will our needs change if the market develops?, in: *Too Many Lawyers? Facts, Reasons, Consequences and Solutions* (Oñati, Spain, IISL).

Silver, C. (2012) Coping with the consequences of 'too many lawyers': securing the place of international graduate law students, *International Journal of the Legal Profession*, 19(2–3), pp. 227–245, this issue.

Statistics Canada (2011) *The Canadian Population in 2011: Population Counts and Growth* [electronic] (Ottawa, Government of Canada).

Statistics Canada (2012) *E-Stat Table 326-0021 – Consumer Price Index* [electronic] (Ottawa, Government of Canada).

Thornton, M. (2012) The new knowledge economy and the transformation of the law discipline, *International Journal of the Legal Profession*, 19(2–3), pp. 265–281, this issue.

Todd, R. (2011) The elusive brass ring, *Canadian Lawyer Magazine*. Available at: http://www.canadianlawyermag.com/3846/the-elusive-brass-ring.html, accessed 22 July 2012.

Wilson, B. (2011) A dividend diversity: the impact of diversity on organizational decision making, *University of British Columbia Law Review*, 44, pp. 9–24.

Winston, C., Crandall, R.W. & Maheshri, V. (2011) *First Thing We Do, Let's Deregulate All the Lawyers* (Washington, DC, Brookings Institute).

Woolley, A. (2008) Imperfect duty: lawyers' obligation to foster access to justice, *Alberta Law Review*, 45(5), pp. 107–142.

Zer-Gutman, L. (2012) Effects of the acceleration in the number of lawyers in Israel, *International Journal of the Legal Profession*, 19(2–3), pp. 247–263, this issue.

Ziv, N. (2012) Unauthorized practice of law and the production of lawyers, *International Journal of the Legal Profession*, 19(2–3), pp. 175–192, this issue.

The 'overcrowding the profession' argument and the professional melting pot

EYAL KATVAN
Academic Center of Law and Business, Law School, Ramat-Gan, Israel

ABSTRACT *In 2012, fourteen law schools operated in Israel: four within universities and ten at private colleges. The number of law students at colleges and accredited attorneys who graduated from the colleges greatly exceeds the number of university law students and alumnae. There is consensus among the leadership of the Israel Bar that law colleges (the newcomers) are responsible for Israel's overpopulation of lawyers and for the legal profession's decline in prestige. Twenty years after the first law colleges were established, the time has come to inquire whether this argument of overcrowding of the profession presents a new 'discovery' or rather the recycling of a standard dynamic between professionals and legal education institutions. The present article examines this issue by evaluating several options: is the profession's 'over-crowdedness' argument an attempt to protect the public, an attempt to prevent competition and to elevate status or rather – as has not been previously suggested – is it an artificial argument aimed (perhaps also unconsciously) at creating a professional melting pot?*

Introduction

A well-known Israeli sketch portrays established immigrants deriding recent arrivals. Later, as the recent arrivals become established in the country, they in turn deride the immigrants arriving with the next wave, and so on. The sketch reflects a type of solidarity felt by 'veterans' vis-à-vis the newcomers, a solidarity that forms 'veterans' into a group apparently lacking in hierarchies. To some extent, the sketch also reflects the prevalent attitude among professional legal veterans toward law students and recently accredited attorneys, as well as that of the established law schools toward the new players in the field of legal education in Israel.

In 2012, fourteen law schools operated in Israel. Four of these are faculties within universities[1] and ten comprise part of colleges[2] – two of which are state funded[3] and the rest private. The number of law students at the colleges and of college alumnae who are accredited attorneys greatly exceeds the number of university law students and graduates. Consensus exists at present among the leadership of the Israel Bar that law colleges (the newcomers) are responsible for Israel's overpopulation of lawyers and for the legal profession's decline in prestige (see, e.g., Danus, 2008; Shihor-Aronson & Danus, 2011). Twenty years after the first colleges were established, the time has come to inquire whether the argument of the profession's overcrowding presents a new 'discovery' or the recycling of a standard dynamic between legal professionals and legal education institutions.

This article aims to address this issue by asking whether the argument about the 'overcrowding of the profession' is: An attempt to protect the public (a common public interest approach)? An attempt to prevent competition and to elevate status (a critical approach; Abel, 1988a, pp. 187, 227; Ziv, 2008, 2009)? Or – as has not been previously suggested (at least not until recently; see Garth 2013) – rather an artificial argument aimed (perhaps also unconsciously) at creating a professional melting pot?

I begin by describing the dynamics of the opposition to the legal profession's newcomers in Israel, from the Ottoman period through the present day. I then present empirical findings that illustrate the gaps between law students enrolled in colleges and law students enrolled in the universities. These discrepancies illustrate the need for achieving cohesion between the two groups and transforming them into a more homogeneous group. Subsequently, I present the analogy between immigrating into the country and entering the profession to clarify how various rituals are intended to create a melting pot. Finally, based on these findings, I posit that, whereby the professional saturation argument is indeed consistent with many of the explanations offered for it in studies to date, the ritual opposition to newcomers to a profession (students and teaching institutions alike) might indeed be mainly motivated by a desire to achieve group cohesion.

Historical perspective: overcrowding of the legal profession

Since inception, the State of Israel has been an immigration-absorbing country. Some immigrants worked in the various professions in their countries of origin, mostly Russia and Eastern Europe, as well as Germany in the 1930s. Already in the beginning of the twentieth century (when Palestine was still under the Ottoman rule), lawyers considering immigration inquired with the Zionist institutions in Palestine whether they would be able to find work. The answer they received generally was negative. The common assumption that there was not enough work for lawyers in Palestine was even more acute during the period of the British Mandate in Palestine (1917–1948). In 1922, the Advocates Ordinance was enacted, which contained instructions concerning the accreditation of new lawyers. Those who studied in the Jerusalem Law Classes (a law school established by the British in 1920) did not need to take external exams. Those who had studied in foreign countries needed to take specific tests to prove their knowledge of the laws in Mandatory Palestine. The legal committee established by virtue of the Ordinance to handle lawyers' accreditation made it difficult for foreign lawyers to become accepted (Strassman, 1985, pp. 250–253; Roda, 1945, pp. 149, 152, 156; Saker, 1961, p. 234). This practice seems to have served the interests of the British, who sought to limit immigration by limiting the entry of Jewish professionals seeking refuge primarily from Nazi Germany in the 1930s (Examinations for foreign lawyers, 1935). The Chief Justices (British judges who headed in turn the judicial pyramid in Palestine) also complained about the overcrowding of lawyers. In general, these notions were expressed during new lawyers' graduation ceremonies (Granting of diplomas to new lawyers, 1940; see also13 new lawyers, 1941).

The fear of saturating the profession concerned both those already serving in the legal profession in Palestine and potential immigrants in the field. Moshe Zmora, ultimately the first Chief Justice of the State of Israel, immigrated in 1922. In a letter to his wife, he noted that "there are already seven Jewish lawyers and the country doesn't need any more" (Zmora, 2002, p. 12). In 1926, given the economic crisis that afflicted the country, the argument of the overcrowding of the profession arose once again:

> The crisis afflicting the country ... damaged heavily the legal profession. This has been particularly felt in light of the proliferation of lawyers and the great competition that developed as a result. Therefore, a noticeable decline of the profession was felt both in the spiritual sense ('every man does what is right in his own eyes') and in the material sense (given the lack of a tariff for the lawyer's fees). (Strassman, 1985)

Criticism regarding the overpopulation of lawyers appeared in the press as well. Nevertheless, professionals were cautious in their arguments about overcrowding of the profession because, indirectly, such voices could be interpreted as opposition to the absorption of immigrants and cooperation with the British.

The establishment of the State changed this position of the local jurists, who made their opposition to the absorption of immigrant lawyers public (Envy of attorneys, 1949). Apparently, this opposition was rooted in an ideology of concern for the public at large, which the lawyers representing this view were supposed to serve. By contrast, the foreign lawyers argued that the opposition was rooted exclusively in 'fear of professional competition' (Examination of foreighn lawyers' licenses, 1948; Lawyers from abroad, 1951).

In 1961, thirteen years after the establishment of the State, the Israeli Bar Law was enacted.[4] The Israeli Bar became the body dealing with the professional qualification process and supervision of interns. These extensive involvements and others granted the Israeli Bar an unprecedented status of professional autonomy by international standards (Salzberger, 2002).

The heads of the Israeli Bar were able to guard the gates of the profession as not only those who sought to prevent the entrance of new lawyers, but also those who held the authority to do so. Some of the legislators understood this on the eve of the vote on the Israeli Bar Law. Knesset (the Israeli Parliament) Member (MK) Baruch Azania, for example, objected to granting such broad authority to the Bar Association: "There is a danger that young people who are already 'riding the bus' of the profession will shut the door before young people who didn't yet have a chance to get on" (Criticism in the Knesset, 1959, p. 7). As expected, MK Azania's fears also proved to have been justified, not because the path leading to the professional inception of law school graduates was blocked, but rather because the argument of the overcrowding of the profession became a factor acting to unify the Bar, especially on the eve of elections (Hon, 1959). Indeed, some thirty years later, a similar criticism was voiced by one of the lawyers responding to the proposals to prevent the establishment of additional institutions for law degrees:

> The request is especially strident when it comes from young lawyers. It reminds us of the episode of the passenger who pushes his way forcibly onto the bus and as soon as he is firmly planted on the steps yells to the driver and to those standing outside that the bus is already full and there is no more room. (Steinhart, 1988)

At the end of the 1960s, additional items appeared in the press about the saturation of the profession, mostly written by heads of the Israeli Bar (Peri, 1968).[5] In that period, only two law schools operated – one in Jerusalem and one in Tel-Aviv – demonstrating that the saturation argument was inherent in the professional rhetoric, regardless of the ratio of lawyers per capita, which was relatively stable between the establishment of the State and the mid-1970s. Thus, the argument of the overcrowding of the profession seems to have been a standard claim that was raised already in the early days of the profession in Mandatory Palestine and continues to be voiced to this day.

Similar to the argument of the overcrowding of the profession, opinions have been voiced in academic circles maintaining that the new teaching institutions would lead to overcrowding of the profession. In 1969, shortly after the separation of the School of Law and Economics from the Hebrew University and its establishment as part of Tel-Aviv University, an additional law school was established at Bar-Ilan University. This new institution caused concern in the Bar Association (Ben-Amir, 1969), and this time also at the Hebrew University Law Faculty. Professor Reuven Yaron, Dean of the Law Faculty, said that "two law faculties are sufficient for training jurists" (Ben-Amir, 1969, p. 23). By contrast, Dr Amnon Rubinstein, Dean of the Law Faculty at Tel-Aviv University, argued: "As far as I'm concerned, Bar-Ilan University can open a law faculty. We don't want a monopolistic position in the teaching of law". Dr Rubinstein was not concerned with the surplus of lawyers: "We train jurists, not lawyers" (Ben-Amir, 1969, p. 23). The Director General of the Ministry of Justice, Zvi Tarlo, also opposed placing limitations on entry into the profession: "Israel is a country of immigration and absorption. The restrictions will hurt working people, immigrants, and members of the Oriental communities, and will turn lawyering into a profession of the elite" (Ben-Amir, 1969, p. 23).

The argument concerning the exclusion of various populations from the study of the law was raised not long after the establishment of the State. One MK sought to assist students who studied in the Advanced School of Law and Economics in Tel-Aviv. Students of this institution did not receive recognition for many years because, among other reasons, of difficulties raised by the Mandatory authorities, who attempted to strengthen the status of the Mandatory law school in Jerusalem (which apparently sought to train local jurists in the spirit of English law; Likhovsky, 2001), as well as difficulties raised after the establishment of the State by Hebrew University (Cohen, 2009). MKs sought to relieve the situation of students in Tel-Aviv so that every suitable and talented youth in Israel can learn this profession. By this I mean the children of laborers, of immigrants, and also of the Oriental communities. One of our failures is that missing in the profession are the children of all the communities and of the various social strata in the country (Strassman, 1985).

This was apparently the first time that the argument of the exclusion of various segments of the population from the study of law was voiced.[6] Ultimately, the new school became the Law Faculty at Tel-Aviv University. Rubinstein, who headed the Faculty in Tel-Aviv, which had just severed its relations with the Hebrew University, became the Knesset member who led the move to make legal studies inclusive (in 1990). Indeed, for more than twenty years, three faculties of law operated in Israel;[7] it was only in the 1990s that the first law colleges were established. Their establishment was the result of the tribulations of rejected law school applicants stemming from the very low supply of available law students slots, certainly by comparison with the demand. Thus, only students whose qualifications were particularly high were admitted – a fact that many considered to disadvantage candidates from underprivileged neighborhoods, new immigrants, and other groups.

The move to establish additional institutions for the study of law emerged also from the desire of veteran professionals to find a solution for some of their children, who sought to study law but were excluded by the high entrance requirements. Moreover, some of the veteran law faculties sought to cooperate with the Israeli Bar for the establishment of an additional law school. When that move did not succeed, MK Rubinstein initiated legislation that would allow the establishment of colleges subject to the approval of the Bar and of the veteran faculties. Placing the authority to regulate these colleges into the hands of these two players made it possible to pass the law. After some time, when the Knesset saw that both the Bar and the veteran faculties were raising obstacles for the newcomers, they removed the authority from these institutions (cf. Abel, 1988a, pp. 235, 197: "the central irony . . . is the fact that, in constructing its project of supply control on the foundation of the university, the profession ultimately lost control over supply to the university"). Apparently, MK Rubinstein perceived the move to make legal studies universal as being part of a general move to open the gates of higher education in Israel.[8] Indeed, during that period, the 'universalization' trend started to accelerate, partly because of a limited supply of slots for students at the universities, which resulted in the exclusion of weak segments from academic studies (Pesler, 2005; Ben Yaakov, 2000; Valensky, 1996, 2004) and in a 'perturbing homogeneity' among law students.[9] The effect of the move was dramatic, as Rubinstein himself noted in the Committee on Constitution, Law and Justice in which the bill was debated: "As soon as the bill was submitted, we received notification from the Law Faculty in Jerusalem that it increased the number of students by one third."[10] But these processes represented too little too late. The homogeneity that had characterized the profession for many years was widely acknowledged (see, e.g., the statement of the former Chief Justice Benish, 2010). The move to set up the colleges was intended to meet the need to diversify.

During 1990–1991, the first three law colleges were established. In 1995, the Council for Higher Education Law was enacted, which allowed the colleges to cut the umbilical cord that attached them to the faculties of law, and made it possible for them to grant diplomas. Between 1994 and 1995 the first two colleges, established in conjunction with the faculties of law, were closed, and instead their founders opened independent colleges. Several other colleges were established in the following years. In recent years, additional tracks for legal studies opened at two private colleges, as well as at two state-funded colleges: Safed (in the North) and Sapir (in the South). The latter perhaps reflect an answer to claims that the colleges that opened did not realize the objectives for which they were established, namely to give excluded groups an opportunity to acquire legal education. Indeed, the colleges continue to charge tuition that is threefold that of what the universities charge, and most of them operate in the center of the country. The opening of legal studies at Safed and Sapir Colleges addressed this problem, for not only were these colleges that charge university rates but both are located in the periphery, in Israel's north and south.

Hence, over the years, the argument of the overcrowding of the profession has been repeated by the professionals, and more recently also by the law faculties. In the past twenty years, the same argument has been raised with respect to the new colleges training the human capital that has joined the profession.[11] The heads of the Bar even joined in supporting the deans of the university law faculties, who in a closed meeting sharply attacked the quality of students and of the education provided in the colleges, couching their concerns as stemming from concern for the public.[12] Thus, the veterans of academia and the veterans of the profession joined forces in calling for the colleges to be shut down, arguing for the need to 'protect the public'.

Mind the gap: empirical findings

I posit that the 'overcrowding of the profession' argument is intended to strengthen cohesion, forming part of the professional melting pot. As mentioned, in the past, new immigrants were considered to disrupt the homogeneity in the legal profession. In recent years, law college students have faced the same stigma. Hence, the question is whether these students are indeed different from university law students, and thereby 'disrupt' homogeneity across the profession.[13]

Empirical findings confirm this claim and illustrate both the discrepancies between the two groups at their starting points and the equality between them (in certain parameters) after entering the profession. This equality is achieved over time by creating new professional bodies, unified around the argument of the overcrowding of the profession.

My argument relies on two data sources: one is a survey I conducted in 2010 together with Limor Zer-Guttman among lawyers in Israel, which was answered by 2,000 respondents working within the profession;[14] the other is a dedicated survey I conducted in 2011 among law students at the end of their first year of study or the beginning of their second year, in two law colleges and one university law school. Respondents reflect the demographic reality among law students today.

The lawyers' questionnaire included 107 questions divided into four categories: (a) demography (e.g., age, professional seniority and education); (b) gender (e.g., number of female partners in the office); (c) professional occupation (e.g., type of employment, type of professional occupation); and (d) professional ethics and reputation (e.g., whether the respondent has a disciplinary past). The law students' questionnaire was primarily demographic, comprised of twenty-seven questions.[15] The purpose of the data collection relevant to the present study was to examine whether differences and gaps existed between the demographic attributes of college and university law students. The data (Tables 1 and 2) indicate that a substantial portion of law college students began their studies at an older age, and have had more extensive life experience than their peers in the universities, including the parameter of both parenting and previous academic studies.

My findings confirm the notion that at least a portion of law college students start studying when they are more 'mature'. According to Daicoff (1997, p. 1356):[16]

> Law students' and lawyers' stated reasons for entering the field of law are relevant because they indicate what is important to law students and lawyers. Studies of these motives provide information about a specific set of lawyer attributes: their values, goals, and ideals.

The lawyers' questionnaire presented twelve possible main motives for choosing the profession.[17] In most respects, the motives noted by law college students and university law students were similar; however, differences emerged between the two groups on two parameters: (a) personal interest/experience in law (selected by 22.6% of law college students vs. 15.4% of university law students); and (b) by default only (selected by 2.4% of law college students vs. 8.4% of university students).

These differences indicate that at least a portion of law college students joined the field of law with some life experience or at least after having grappled with legal matters. Thus, the motive of most of them to study law is not a default action, contrary to university students who perhaps lack the maturity and the understanding of 'what they want to do when they grow up'. Likewise, a substantial portion of law college students and graduates held previous degrees before their law studies. However, not all law college students fall into this category. As Dean Uriel Reichman (of a private college) noted, for example, "in the [Tel-Aviv University] faculty, some 15% of students are Jews of Middle Eastern heritage,[18] and we have 30%. We also have much greater openness toward Arab students. In the [Tel-Aviv University] law school there are almost no Arab students".[19] Indeed, directors of the law colleges claim that they serve the needs of marginalized populations (Levi-Weinrib, 2010).[20]

However, the data demonstrate substantial similarity regarding birth country, with the overwhelming majority of law students today in the two colleges and in the university being native Israelis (87% and 83.6%). Moreover, the three sampled institutions have a similar proportion of students who emigrated from Eastern Europe (12.85% and 9.2%). The various institutions are also marginally similar with respect to percentages of students' parents being born in Israel.

Apparently, there are no significant differences these days between the country of origin of college and university students. However, a no less significant (albeit hidden) finding regarding parents' education attests to the gap between law college and

Table 1. *First-year law student characteristics by institution: parenthood, age, and previous academic degrees*

	College 1	College 2	University
Parenthood	11.4%	57.2%	4%
Average age	27.4 (men: 28.6, women 26.3)	34.3 (men: 38.3, women: 32.3)	24.3 (men: 26.1, women: 22.7)
Prior academic degrees	–	–	–
2 Bachelors degrees	–	2.9%	1.4%
1 Bachelors degrees	6%	22.6%	8.5%
Masters	–	11.3%	–
Doctorate	–	1.25%	–

Notes: The survey's questionnaires were administered to students in the classrooms. Respondent numbers: 71 university students (32 men, 39 women); 70 students at College 1 (34 men, 36 women); 243 students in College 2 (124 men, 112 women; 7 did not specify gender).

Table 2. *Lawyers' characteristics before commencing legal studies, by training institution (colleges/universities): parenthood, previous degree(s)*

	Colleges	Universities
First child born	37.5%	8.8%
Previous degree/s	33.8%	25.8%

Notes: This table is based on data from the lawyers' survey.

university law students today; whereas the parents of most university law students have academic degrees, the parents of most law college students do not.

This finding is most significant (Ermisch & Pronzato, 2010). In Israel, parents' education is among the most influential parameters on their children's education. The psychometric test (Israel's SAT test) is no longer mandatory for admission into

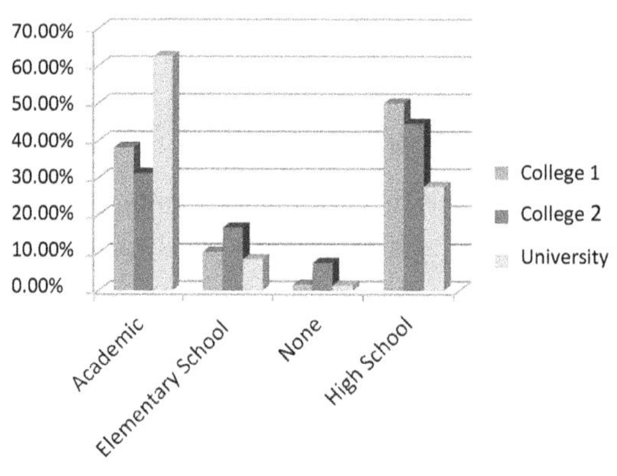

Figure 1. *(Student's) fathers education*
Note: Data regarding mother's education is almost identical to the father's education.

academic institutions, but rather an auxiliary factor in cases where matriculation exam grades are insufficient for meeting various institutions' admission standards. Thus, applicants whose matriculation exam grades are inadequate for admission to their desired department tend to take the SATs. Nevertheless, the motivation to take the SATs depends also on the parents' education. The more educated the parents are, the greater the motivation to take the SATs is and the greater the applicants' access to the tests is. Moreover, the applicants' success on the SATs also depends to a great extent on the parents' education (Dvir *et al.*, 2009; see also Beenstock, 2005). It is not surprising, therefore, that the law colleges, where the matriculation grade required for admission is lower, so that fewer applicants must take the SATs, attract more students whose parents do not hold academic degrees (not to mention those whose parents have no high school diploma; see also Zussman *et al.*, 2009). This gap between university and college students is concealed, but it is very important.[21]

In sum, the empirical findings point to significant gaps and heterogeneity between college and university law students. Were it not for the colleges, various groups would most likely be excluded from the professions, including those whose parents had no higher education, students of 'Sephardi' origin, and older, more experienced students who study law while working to support their families and maintaining their ongoing careers (cf. Abel, 1988a, p. 201). Such groups were indeed excluded until the establishment of the law colleges, which challenged the profession's homogeneity. Graduates of the colleges are integrated into the legal labor market despite various gaps between the groups, and despite the resistance toward them. Interestingly, findings show great similarity in respondents' satisfaction with legal practice. For example, 21.1% of college graduates are very satisfied, vs. 20% of university graduates; 4% of college graduates are not satisfied at all, vs. 3.4% of university graduates. In light of these levels of satisfaction, lawyers' concern with professional glut (that is, with the number of lawyers being accredited each year) is striking. Potentially, precisely because lawyers find satisfaction in their work, they are more worried about the newcomers to their market. Nevertheless, results indicate that university graduates are more worried about the situation than are college graduates. University-trained lawyers are also less likely to recommend their friends to study law and work in the field than their college-trained peers (56.3% of college graduates recommend that their friends study law, vs. 40.6% of university graduates; 52.1% of college graduates do not recommend that their friends work in the legal field, vs. 62.2% of university graduates).[22]

Hence, the question arising is, what role does the 'overcrowding of the profession' argument play in a situation in which a substantial portion of legal practitioners are themselves college graduates who oppose colleges' continued training of more lawyers for reasons of apparent professional overcrowding?

Immigration and professional integration: manifest and latent functions of the overcrowding argument

The warnings against the overcrowding of the profession are well-known. The public interest argument claims that the proliferation of lawyers harms service to the public as a result of unbridled competition between professionals and ethical offenses on the part of the newcomers – although Zer-Gutman (2012) shows that, in fact, veterans commit many such offenses. Naturally, from the perspective of the professionals, the undesirable outcome is also manifest in reduced income and reduced professional prestige (see, e.g., Larson, 1977). To the extent that the 'overcrowding of the profession' argument touches on the new players in the field – that is, the law colleges – it also appears to be based on the rationale of preventing the public harm liable to occur from the absence of meaningful criteria for admission to legal studies, deficient training, and dubious foundations of the students admitted – in addition to the fear of competition.

Yet there is an additional aspect to the overcrowding of the profession debate – perhaps an unconscious one – resulting in the consolidation of a collective identity and group cohesion, in a reality of elevated homogeneity (Abel, 1988a, p. 186). This argument is based on a known conception present in other areas, for example the opposition to integrating women into military positions that have been reserved for men, for fear that "the integration of women will hurt bonding between male soldiers, which is considered to be vital for the performance of their military functions" (Almog, 1996, p. 638).[23] It seems that, initially, the opposition to newcomers, especially to law college graduates, was based on the fear that the public would discover that lawyers are not necessarily illustrious individuals and that people from the periphery, Sephardi Jews of Middle Eastern ancestry, and those whose matriculation and SAT grades were not the highest also can become successful lawyers.

Once extraneous groups already joined the profession, the natural conclusion was that the integration of newcomers should be promoted according to the codes and patterns that have already been defined by the dominant group. In this sense, the legal profession is similar to the state, with the Bar Association as its government. This analogy is derived from another research project that I have been pursuing in recent years, investigating the medical examination of immigrants to Palestine between the two world wars (Katvan, 2011). In that research, I investigated the manifest and latent functions of the immigrants' examinations. By nature, the manifest functions are easy to reveal: protecting the health of inhabitants and of the immigrants themselves from disease and epidemics. But various evidence indicates that these examinations, carried out on a massive scale, were in fact quite superficial (Fairchild, 2003) and only a few were responsible for preventing individuals from entering the country. In other words, if the manner in which the examinations were carried out was not adequate to protect public health, what was their purpose? I posited that the examinations formed part of the social melting pot image achieved by absorption and welcoming ceremonies (Katvan, 2011). Indeed, I propose that the 'overcrowding of the profession' argument comprises a parallel latent and even unconscious function. This argument is to a large extent artificial, perhaps similar to the Bar examinations – which the vast majority of law degree graduates pass, indicating that they do not achieve the real objective of preventing entrance to the profession by allowing entrance to only a select few. When limitations to joining the profession do not achieve their objectives in the sense that more and more applicants turn to legal studies and seek admissions to the Bar, doubts arise not with regard to the effectiveness of the limitations (see Abel, 1988a, p. 195), but with regard to their rationale. After passing the examinations, women and men, Sephardi and Ashkenazi,[24] Arabs and Jews become part of an (at least apparently) undifferentiated profession, and they can jointly oppose the next wave of law students.

However, bar exams are only one example of such exclusionary rituals and symbols. As noted above, the internship period, the professional accreditation, and even the accreditation ceremony all bear potential to achieve cohesion and uniformity. Court dress and robes are clearly the best-known example in this regard, intended to create a uniform, cohesive and unique identity, differentiating lawyers for the sake of both the practicing professionals and the public at large (Isani, 2006, p. 51; McKenzie Leiper, 2007; Brundage, 2008, p. 209). Even after accreditation, the Israeli Bar maintains rituals such as professional advancement courses, conferences and professional journals, among others. The argument of the overcrowding of the profession assists these initiatives in serving as a cohesive factor.

The argument of the overcrowding of the profession was voiced in (pre-State) Israel even when fewer than ten lawyers were practicing in the country, and it is voiced today, when there are more than 50,000 registered lawyers in a country of seven million inhabitants. In this sense, Israel serves as a good test-case for analyzing the issue. What is the validity of the overcrowding argument in light of the fact that Israel has a record number of lawyers? If we accept the claim that overcrowding of the profession is evident in the number of lawyers, then the profession is indeed overcrowded – so what is the objective of struggling against an overcrowded profession in this situation?

Moreover, the argument of the overcrowding of the profession originates with both the more established professionals (some of whom did not meet the requirements demanded from those whose acceptance they now oppose),[25] and with the less established ones, graduates of the colleges, who are also concerned about the arrival of new lawyers. These facts also suggest the possibility that the arguments are superficial. Indeed, the arguments about overcrowding of the profession serve as a common denominator for all professionals who have already joined the profession. Indeed, selectivity – even if it is imaginary – strengthens intraprofessional cohesion.

This selectivity does not begin upon commencement of legal practice but rather already with the selection and admission ritual of new candidates to law studies (Guinier, 2003; see Abel, 1988a, p. 194). Axiomatically, academic-legal knowledge is the central foundation in the definition of the profession (Abbott, 1988, pp. 196–197). When facing a parallel situation in the United States, in 1881 the American Bar Association preferred extended legal training in law schools over other types of training, and even that only in 'reputable schools':

> The proponents of such measures, which they clearly saw would limit entry into the profession, often argued that such restrictions would meet the vexing problems of 'overcrowding'. For the prosperous lawyers of the association, this overcrowding did not hold much of an economic threat. Rather

> for them it seemed to bring wrong kind of people into law and led to the sort of scoundrelism at the lower ranks of the profession that they believed brought disgrace to the entire fraternity. The rising standards of education at the reputable schools, however, never cut the growing number of students entering the law schools. In part, the appearances and flourishing of part-time and nighttime law schools accounts for this. (Haber, 1991, p. 222)

Legal studies also play a significant role in the formation of professional identity (Nystrom, 2010), which is why this stage is perceived by the profession – which seeks to influence its content – to be so important by the profession (Abel, 1988a). Indeed, this is the beginning of the melting pot (see Yaar, 2007, p. 72) and part of the process of shaping the identity of jurists according to the general codes in which the profession is interested, including the learning of new tools and, no less important, of a new language and terminology that contain much ceremony – the language of the law (Barzilai, 2007). As noted above, the legal profession is like a state; the state also has a language that it seeks to impose on its citizens. If citizens who speak foreign languages arrive in the country, the state loses an important unifying indicator. Indeed, one of the criticisms being voiced against part of the newcomers to the profession, aimed primarily at students of the law colleges, is that their language is slurred. Language is no doubt part of the professional's socialization process – of creating a lawyer (Mertz, 2007). And the responsibility is placed upon the institutions that accept and qualify them, those mediators, the legal training institutions – that is, the colleges. When there was a tacit understanding between the profession and the universities about the desired model of future jurists, no problems arose. Nevertheless, the rules of the game changed with the entrance of the colleges into the arena. As Professor Ron Shapira noted,

> The covert deal between them [between law professors and the legal profession] in the past was that the professors of law will serve as the guardians of the barricades of the legal profession, and in return will benefit from shares of the economic bounty of members of the profession and from social prestige.... At a time of crisis, when the monetary temptation from breaching the walls increased, the professors of law preferred to join the besiegers, and the deal reached a state of efficient violation. (Shapira, 2004, p. 844)

It was the law colleges that caused the breach in the walls.

Summary

Historical examination demonstrates that the argument of the overcrowding of the profession is not new (Helmholz, 2011), but rather has been raised repeatedly ever since lawyers began working in Mandatory Palestine. In each instance it was targeted at the newcomers to the profession, especially at those whose attributes were different from those of the veteran professionals. The dynamics presented in this paper indeed call into mind the comedy scene mentioned in the opening of the article. Indeed, it seems that since time immemorial, the profession's veterans tried to reject newcomers by arguing that the field was too narrow to include them and that the existing institutions were sufficient for the provision of law degrees. As far as the institutions that confer law degrees are concerned, they have addressed the issue of overcrowding of the profession only indirectly, in the sense that they rejected the possibility of establishing new institutions, which they considered unnecessary. Since the early 1990s, the veteran professionals and academic institutions joined forces and accused the colleges of causing overcrowding within the legal profession. This was the second time in Israel's history that legal professionals joined forces to accuse others as a 'group'; the first time involved an attempt to thwart new immigrants who had studied abroad and sought to ply their trade in Israel. During the more recent phase, criticism was targeted at law college students – the children and grandchildren of new immigrants, who were excluded from the homogeneous fabric of members of the profession.[26] In both cases, the criticism was aimed at the new practitioners' quality of academic training and linguistic skills. The historical dynamics illustrate how the players involved tried to shape the profession in their image (and language). This is what the British did, and with the establishment of the State, this is what Israeli lawyers did through their opposition to the acceptance of new immigrants into the profession (however, in 1967 the Bar assisted new immigrants to assimilate, by teaching them Israeli law in a special college). The legal establishment benefitted from the fact that there were only a few institutions that provided law degrees in Israel, which conferred academic dignity and lessened competition within the profession.

In sum, lawyers have been zealously guarding the boundaries of the profession, and continue doing so (Abbott, 1988). This zeal has produced a relatively homogeneous group, whose members appear to have similar characteristics (see also Abel, 1988a, p. 187).[27] This fact can explain why the organized members of the profession, from the days of the British Mandate to present-day Israel, have been united on two related matters: the war against those who trespass the boundaries of the profession (see Ziv, 2012) and 'the overcrowding of the profession'.[28] This is not merely an attempt to protect the livelihood of lawyers and to guard against competition. This is an attempt to protect cohesion among professionals who are generally not motivated by ideals. As Abel (1988b, p. 10) stated: "In order to become a profession they [the producers of a service] must seek social closure." In the reality of a continuously overcrowded profession, the argument of 'too many lawyers' serves to achieve an artificial 'social closure'. As discussed above, the Bar's examinations and accreditation ceremonies form part of this ritual. The overcrowding argument is, therefore, a standard discourse, part of the legal jargon, a narrative that reflects on one hand an attempt at separation and on the other the intent to strengthen the self. Similar to lawyers' trial robes, the 'overcrowding of the profession' argument is addressed at both legal professionals and at the public at large. Among the professionals, it involves the creation of cohesion and uniqueness, and aims to enhance the status of members. It serves their self-interest by bonding various individuals over a topic agreed upon by all – the fear of the overcrowding of the profession.

Empirical findings show that to this day, law college students differ from university law students in many attributes. They bring a different skill set and background to the profession, which reduces the homogeneity to which the profession had been accustomed for many years. Precisely because of the fear of damage to homogeneity (and "the sense of professional community", as Abel (1988a, p. 188) stated), the 'overcrowding of the profession' argument acquired added poignancy. Once members of the profession understood that such 'overcrowding' and the significant rise in the ratio of lawyers per capita is inevitable, the argument became merely symbolic. Indeed, gradually, law college graduates will become the majority of legal professionals in Israel. Yet the argument of the overcrowding of the profession continues to be voiced, with the accusation pointed at the law colleges. This insistence provides further proof that the argument is mostly artificial, both because some of those who voice it today are themselves graduates of the law colleges, and because the rhetoric of the need to shut down the colleges is clearly impractical. In other words, I do not claim that the profession is not overcrowded, but rather note that in the past the argument of the overcrowding of the profession has been voiced also when the ratio of lawyers in the population was much lower. In previous years, there was no need to achieve homogeneity but perhaps just a unifying factor among individuals. Today, this argument does not prevent new lawyers from joining the profession, but it serves the veterans in achieving cohesion with those who have newly joined the ranks of the profession, under conditions of much greater heterogeneity. In this situation, there is no alternative but to accept the newcomers, even if with a certain opposition, so that they internalize the professional codes and become integrated into the profession on the terms of the veterans. With the massive entry of law college graduates into the market, to the point that they have become – or will soon become – the majority among the professionals, the opposition to the newcomers is puzzling. Nevertheless, such opposition must be regarded as even more vital, precisely within a reality in which many lawyers are being integrated into the profession: the need exists to increase bonding and group cohesion and avoid the stratification of classes within the profession, at least outwardly. This need is particularly acute when lawyers hail from different backgrounds and additional gaps might form, such as in the areas of specialization and employment patterns,[29] so that assimilation and the strengthening of the common denominator are especially important. The 'overcrowding of the profession' argument achieves this cohesion objective. At the same time, the melting pot continues its operation, and indeed, a new professional fabric is created continuously, which continues to oppose the possibility of the new lawyers joining the profession.

Acknowledgements

I thank Professor Daphne Barak-Erez, Professor Dudi Schwartz, Dr Boaz Shnoor, Dr Limor Zer-Guttman and Professor Neta Ziv, the Onati Workshop Participants on 'Too Many Lawyers' and the anonymous readers for their important comments. I also thank my research assistant, Meytal Aharon, for her excellent assistance on this article.

Notes

[1] Tel-Aviv University, Bar-Ilan University, the Hebrew University, and Haifa University.

[2] In Israel the prestigious institutions are the universities, whereas the private institutes are less so.

[3] In other words, subsidized by the state, so that tuition is the same as at the universities.

[4] Yuval (1955, p. 2) has argued that at that time already, the ratio of lawyers in Israel per capita was among the highest in the world: "Across the State of Israel already 1,200 independent lawyers are working, in other words, 1,250 citizens per lawyer. This division already places Israel at the head of the nations by the ratio of lawyers in it."

[5] President of the Israel Bar, Rothenstreich: "The country has been long suffering from an explosion in the population of lawyers, and the situation is getting worse and worse." Arad (1967, p. 5), quoting Rothenstreich: "For 2.5 million citizens there are 4,000 lawyers in Israel. In other words, one lawyer for every 6,250 citizens."

[6] Regarding the way the issue developed in the United States, see Kidder (2003).

[7] In 1992, the fourth faculty of law was established at Haifa University.

[8] Knesset session (14 March 1990) concerning the Bar Association Bill (Amendment: Higher Legal Education) 1990.

[9] Draft Law: Bar Association Bill (Amendment No. 17) 1990, 1983 bill (16 March 1990) 150. In the explanatory text, an admission rate of 15% of candidates was cited. "As a result, the student composition in the law faculties is homogeneous to a point that raises deep concern."

[10] *Ibid.* See also in *Halishka*, The legal system has fossilized (1991, pp. 11–12: interview with Emeritus Judge Bejski). Soon afterwards, Professor Mautner, former Dean of the Faculty of Law at the Tel-Aviv University, recommended opening a special admission program in light of the homogeneity among law students in the Faculty (Mautner, 2004). Cf. Abel (1988a, p. 204). See also Johnson (2011), about the importance of diversity among law students.

[11] Interestingly, the language used to oppose the law colleges' students is similar to the type used in the United States in the beginning of the twentieth century to exclude Jewish immigrants from entering the legal profession (Auerbach, 1977).

[12] "Our sense is that to some degree we are like the Bar Association, servants of the public. We are not a commercial body, we are not for profit. We have a certain input that can be of benefit" (Zarchin, 2011). See also Salzberger (2010): "Lecturers who teach in the faculties of law and moonlight in the colleges ... will admit that these are students of a different quality...."

[13] Studies conducted in the United States illustrate how the demographic attributes of law students in the 1970s and 1980s were different from those of their colleagues in other fields. Jurists were considered to come from a higher socio-economic background (Daicoff, 1997, p. 1355).

[14] The survey was mailed at the end of the December 2010 as an online link to 25,000 addressees of the Israel Bar's mailing list. The response rate of 8% was considered to be a reasonable one among Israeli professionals. It seems that the sample population reflects the population of lawyers with respect to such measures as seniority, as well as in the division between respondents who are university graduates (842) and college graduates (857).

[15] For example, sex, age, previous education, marital status, number of children, father's and mother's level of education and country of birth, economic status, reasons for choosing law studies.

[16] See also Ogloff *et al.* (2000).

[17] Namely: family pressure; influence of a family relative who is a lawyer; personal interest/experience in law; intellectual attraction; prestige; potential for higher earning capacity; desire to contribute to others/society; desire to integrate into the legal academia; desire to engage in politics; default; and 'other'. Respondents could select one main motive.

[18] Commonly referred to as 'Sephardi' Jews.

[19] Protocol No. 232 of the Constitution, Law and Justice Committee (18 February 1991) concerning amendment No. 18 to the Bar Association Law [Hebrew].

[20] Professor Dudi Schwartz (Ono College) explains that the colleges allow marginalized populations such as Ethiopians and the ultra-Orthodox to study. Nevertheless, some argue that today the universities also meet these needs. And compare with Levi-Weinrib (2009). Professor Eli Salzberger (Haifa

University) notes that that there is adequate representation of all social strata at the University of Haifa law school, including 20% Muslims. Regarding financial status, we found a certain advantage to university students. Respondents were asked to specify their economic status on a five-point scale ranging from 1 (difficult economic situation) to 5 (excellent economic situation); among university students, the lowest stratum (1) is almost unrepresented but there is over-representation in the highest stratum (5).

[21] In this sense, the colleges still provide an important solution to the need that arose decades ago for admission of populations that would otherwise have no access to the legal profession. The sheer fact that these students can pursue academic studies can lead to a reduction in social gaps, encourage social mobility and affect the education of future generations.

[22] See also Organ (2011).

[23] Women have been excluded initially from study as well (Mossman, 2006, pp. 77–78).

[24] Jews of European ancestry, the traditional 'veterans' of the Israeli legal profession.

[25] Some pointed to a portion of veterans as themselves not reflecting the required standard: "The absurdity is that it is precisely those whose professional level is controversial who lead the battle on behalf of the lawyer's professional level" (Atias, 1990, p. 45). This argument indeed had a basis.

[26] This situation is exactly parallel to that in the United States at the beginning of the twentieth century, when the dominant phenomenon was that of the children of immigrants entering the profession: "Many of these new entrants were sons of immigrants, who might have been kept out of the profession if it had still trained its new lawyers as apprenticeships" (Haber, 1991, p. 223; see also Abel, 1988a, pp. 192, 199, 201).

[27] "In Weber's view, it was the key to professional exclusivity, allowing groups of people with common characteristics to pursue collective interests by restricting access to their knowledge, education, credentials, and markets. Thus, by defining itself a 'legally privileged group', a profession is designed to exclude those whom its members see as 'outsiders'" (McKenzie Leiper, 2007, p. 21).

[28] See Abel (1988a, p. 210): "The project of controlling the production *of* producers tends to unite all those within the charmed circle of qualified professionals."

[29] Although, at least according to the lawyers' survey, the 'two hemispheres' theory (Heinz & Laumann, 1982) does not exist in the legal profession in Israel. University and college graduates do not differ dramatically in areas of legal practice.

References

13 new lawyers (1941) *Davar*, 1 August, p. 8.

Abbott, A. (1988) *The System of Professions: An Essay on the Division of Expert Labor* (Chicago, University of Chicago Press), [About the possible connections and relationships needed to decode and explain the relations between the universities and the professions.].

Abel, R.L. (1988a) United States: the contradictions of professionalism, in: R.L. Abel & P.S.C. Lewis (Eds) *Lawyers in Society (vol. 1, The Common Law World)* (Berkley, University of California Press), pp. 186–243.

Abel, R.L. (1988b) *The Legal Profession in England and Wales* (New York, Blackwell).

Almog, S. (1996) About women, the military, and equality, *Mishpat Umemshal*, 3(2), pp. 631–647.

Arad, A. (1967) Level education – without a lawyer's license, *Davar*, 10 November, p. 5.

Atias, A. (1990) Personal opinion about the idea of establishing law schools, *Din Vaomer*, 1990(3), p. 45.

Auerbach, J.S. (1977) *Unequal Justice: Lawyers and Social Change in Modern America* (Oxford, Oxford University Press).

Barzilai, G. (2007) The ambivalent language of lawyers: between liberal politics, economic liberalism, silence, and dissent, in: T.C. Halliday, L. Karpik & M.M. Feeley (Eds) *Fighting for Political Freedom: Comparative Studies of the Legal Complex and Political Liberalism* (Oxford, Hart Publishing), pp. 247–277.

Beenstock, M. (2005) The effect of parents' education and earnings upon the education and earnings of their children, Hebrew University of Jerusalem, 2 January. Available at: http://economics.huji.ac.il/facultye/beenstock/Structural%20estimation%20of%20integenerational%20correlation.pdf, accessed 11 July 2012.

Ben-Amir, Y. (1969) My learned friend, you are superfluous, *Davar*, 19 December, p. 23.
Benish, D. (2010) Statement at the graduation ceremony of the Faculty of Law at the Academic Center of Law and Business in Ramat Gan, *AleiMishpat*, 8, pp. 7–12.
Ben Yaakov, A. (2000) About the first steps of the colleges, in: D. Landau (Ed.) *The Book of Colleges* (Jerusalem, Ministry of Education and Culture), pp. 3–5.
Brundage, J.A. (2008) *The Medieval Origins of the Legal Profession: Canonists, Civilians, and Courts* (Chicago, University of Chicago Press).
Cohen, U. (2009) The pursuit of academic legitimacy: the School of Law and Economics in Tel Aviv from 1948–1935, *Mehkarei Mishpat*, 25(1), pp. 179–212.
Criticism in the Knesset regarding the Bar Association bill (1959) *Maariv*, 19 May, p. 7.
Daicoff, S. (1997) Lawyer, know thyself: a review of empirical research on attorney attributes bearing on professionalism, *American University Law Review*, 46, pp. 1337–1427.
Danus, M. (2008) Proliferation of institutes: the reason for the decline of professional prestige, *Hapraklitim*, 22, pp. 12–20.
Dvir, K., Maagan, D. & Shapira, L. (2009) Psychometric testing in Israel, 1991–2006, *Working Papers Series, No. 43* (Jerusalem, Central Bureau of Statistics).
The envy of attorneys (1949) *Maariv*, 8 June, p. 2.
Ermisch, J. & Pronzato, C. (2010) Causal effects of parents' education on children's education, ISER Working Paper Series no. 2010-16 Available at: http://www.iser.essex.ac.uk/publications/working-papers/iser/2010-16.pdf, accessed 11 July 2012.
Examination of foreign lawyers' licenses (1948) *Maariv*, 8 June, p. 4.
Examinations for foreign lawyers postponed (1935) *Doar Hayom*, 16 March.
Fairchild, A.L. (2003) *Science at the Borders: Immigrant Medical Inspection and the Shaping of the Modern Industrial Labor Force* (Baltimore, MD, The Johns Hopkins University Press).
Garth, B.G. (2013) Crises, crisis rhetoric, and competition in legal education: a sociological perspective on the (latest) crisis of the legal profession and legal education, *Stanford Law & Policy Review*, 24 October, 2012; UC Irvine School of Law Research Paper No. 2012–70. Available at: SSRN: http://ssrn.com/abstract=2166441
Granting of diplomas to new lawyers (1940) *Davar*, 5 May, p. 3.
Guinier, L. (2003) The supreme court, 2002 term: comment: admissions rituals as political acts: guardians at the gates of our democratic ideals, *Harvard Law Review*, 117(1), pp. 113–224.
Haber, S. (1991) *The Quest for Authority and Honor in the American Professions 1750-1900* (Chicago, University of Chicago Press).
Heinz, J.P. & Laumann, E.O. (1982) *Chicago Lawyers: The Social Structure of the Bar* (New York, Russell Sage Foundation).
Helmholz, R.H. (2011) Regulating the number of proctors in the English ecclesiastical courts: evidence from an early tudor tract, in: K. Pennington & M.H. Eichbauer (Eds) *Law as Profession and Practice in Medieval Europe* (Farnham, UK, Ashgate Publishing), pp. 173–186.
Hon, S. (1959) Four factions are running around the lawyers' union, *Maariv*, 10 May, p. 2.
Isani, S. (2006) Visual semiotics of court dress in England and Wales: failed or successful vector of professional identity?, in: A. Wagner & W. Pencak (Eds) *Images in Law* (Aldershot and Burlington, Ashgate Publishing), pp. 51–69.
Johnson, K.R. (2011) The importance of student and faculty diversity in law schools: one dean's perspective, *Iowa Law Review*, 96(5), pp. 1549–1577.
Katvan, E. (2011) Who is the landlord? Quarantine and medical examinations for immigrants at the gates of Eretz-Israel (1918–1929), *Korot: The Israel Journal of the History of Medicine and Science*, 20, pp. 37–72.
Kidder, W.C. (2003) The struggle for access from Sweatt to Grutter: a history of African American, Latino, and American Indian law school admissions, 1950–2000, *Harvard Blackletter Law Journal*, 19, pp. 1–42.
Larson, M.S. (1977) *The Rise of Professionalism: A Sociological Analysis* (Berkeley, University of California Press).
Lawyers from abroad ask to ease their entry into the profession (1951) *Davar*, 20 December, p. 4.

The legal system has fossilized (1991) *Halishka*, pp. 8–15.
Levi-Weinrib, E. (2009) Prof. Eli Salzberger: the legal profession in Israel is facing its greatest crisis, *Globes*, 9 January. Available at: http://www.globes.co.il/news/article.aspx?did=1000414953#FromSearchArticles, accessed 11 July 2012.
Levi-Weinrib, E. (2010) Those who ask to close the law colleges have a vested interest, *Globes*, 9 January. Available at: http://www.globes.co.il/news/article.aspx?did=1000595426#FromSearchArticles, accessed 11 July 2012.
Likhovsky, A. (2001) Colonialism, nationalism and legal education: the case of mandatory Palestine, in: R. Harris, A. Kedar, P. Lahav & A. Likhovski (Eds) *The History of Law in a Multi-Cultural Society* (Farnham, UK, Ashgate), pp. 75–93.
Mossman, M.J. (2006) *The First Women Lawyers: A Comparative Study of Gender, Law and the Legal Professions* (Oxford, Hart Publishing).
Mautner, M. (2004) The special admissions program in the Faculty of Law of Tel-Aviv University and its consequences, in: A. Maor (Ed.) *Corrective Preferment and Ensured Representation in Israel* (Tel-Aviv, Ramot), pp. 457–480.
McKenzie Leiper, J. (2007) *Bar Codes: Women in the Legal Profession* (Vancouver, University of British Columbia Press).
Mertz, E. (2007) *The Language of Law School* (Oxford, Oxford University Press).
Nystrom, S. (2010), Becoming a professional – a melting pot of experience, presented at the 6th European Research Conference, Adult Learning in Europe – Understanding Diverse Meanings and Contexts, Linköping, Sweden, 29 September.
Ogloff, J.R.P., Lyon, D.R., Douglas, K.S. & Rose, V.G. (2000) More than 'learning to think like a lawyer': the empirical research on legal education, *Creighton Law Review*, 34(1), pp. 73–244.
Organ, J. (2011) What do we know about the satisfaction/dissatisfaction of lawyers? A meta-analysis of research on lawyer satisfaction and well-being, *University of St. Thomas Law Journal*, 8(2), pp. 225–274.
Peri, Y. (1968) There are not enough crimes in Israel, *Davar*, 20 November.
Pesler, A. (2005) *Universalization in Higher Education: Process of Conceptual and Structural Change in Higher Education in Israel (1975–2000)*, unpublished PhD thesis, School of Education Bar-Ilan University.
Roda, N. (1945) *Returning to One's Homeland*, (Jerusalem, Ahiasf).
Saker, H. (1961) *Zionist Essays* (Tel-Aviv, Am-Oved).
Salzberger, E. (2002) The conspiracy of Israeli jurists: about the Israeli Bar Association and its allies, *Mishpatim*, 32(1), pp. 43–93.
Salzlberger, E. (2010) The law colleges did not contribute to the level of academic education, *TheMarker*, 21 October. Available at: http://www.themarker.com/law/1.592410, accessed 11 July 2012.
Shapira, R. (2004) Menahem Mautner: about legal education, *Iyunei Mishpat*, 27(3), pp. 821–856.
Shihor-Aronson, A. & Danus, M. (2011) A country rich in poor lawyers, *Hapraklitim*, 37, pp. 16–21.
Steinhart, H. (1988) More about the numerous clauses in law degrees…, *Orech Din Meida*, 25, p. 2.
Strassman, G. (1985) *The Robed: History of the Legal Profession in the Land of Israel* (Tel-Aviv, Israel Bar Association).
Valensky, A. (1996) Opening the gates: democratization of higher education, in: O. Baranes (Ed.) *The Third Jump: Changes and Reforms in the Educational System in the 1990s* (Jerusalem, Ministry of Education and Culture), pp. 70–82.
Valensky, A. (2004) *Academia in a Changing Environment: The Higher Education Policy of Israel, 1952–2004* (Bnei Brak, Hakibbutz Hameuchad).
Yaar, E. (2007) Continuity and change in Israeli society, in: H. Herzog, T. Kochavi & S. Zelniker (Eds) *Generations, Spaces, Identities: Current Views of Society and Culture in Israel* (Jerusalem, Van Leer Jerusalem Institute and Hakibbutz Hameuchad Publishing House), pp. 72–104.
Yuval, M. (1955) Too many lawyers…, *Davar*, 19 December, p. 2.
Zarchin, T. (2011) Deans of the universities: the level at the colleges is low, *Haaretz*, 27 July. Available at: http://www.haaretz.co.il/news/law/1.1181321, accessed 11 July 2012.
Zer-Gutman, L. (2012) Effects of the acceleration in the number of lawyers in Israel, *International Journal of the Legal Profession*, 19(2–3), pp. 247–263, this issue.
Ziv, N. (2008) Who moved my gown, *Mehkarei Mishpat*, 24(1), pp. 439–489.

Ziv, N. (2009) The lawyer's role in a contemporary democracy, tensions between various conceptions of the lawyer's role, regulation of Israeli lawyers: from professional autonomy to multi-institutional regulation, *Fordham Law Review*, 77(4), pp. 1763–1794.
Ziv, N. (2012) Unauthorized practice of law and the production of lawyers, *International Journal of the Legal Profession*, 19(2–3), pp. 175–192, this issue.
Zmora, E. (2002) *Zionist Jewish Women* (Tel-Aviv, Gvanim).
Zussman, N., Forman, O., Kaplan, T. & Romanov, D. (2009) Differences in the quality of higher education between the universities and colleges: assessment based on labor market outcomes, *Working Papers Series, No 42* (Jerusalem, Central Bureau of Statistics).

Setting the limits: who controls the size of the legal profession in Japan?

KAY-WAH CHAN
Faculty of Business and Economics, Macquarie University, North Ryde, Australia

ABSTRACT *Japan is well-known for its small number of lawyers. In the late 1990s, there was a justice system reform movement. This resulted in a governmental agenda to substantially increase the lawyers' number. The profession's population then rapidly increases. The pace of the reform has however recently been slowed down, although the full implementation of the reform and its target has not yet been achieved. Why had the number of lawyers remained small for five decades after the World War II despite Japan's economic development? Why was there a justice system reform movement in the late 1990s? Why has the pace of reform been slowed down recently? Who controlled/controls the size of the legal profession in Japan? This paper will analyse these issues.*

Introduction

Many countries have seen substantial growth in the number of lawyers in the three decades from 1970 (Galanter, 2011, pp. 70–72). Different theories have been put forward to explain the expansion in the lawyer profession. Sander and Williams (1989) attributed the phenomenon to the increase in both demand and supply. Dean Clark (1992) focused on 'demand' and considered that "long term social and economic trends" led to an increase in "demand for normative ordering" and therefore "demand for law and lawyers". As compared with many other advanced economies, Japan is relatively late in seeing substantial growth in the number of lawyers (*bengoshi*). It had a paucity of *bengoshi* (Miyazawa, 2007a, pp. 46–47), which has only commenced to substantially expand since 2001 (Figure 1). A pre-determined quota regulates the number of entrants to the profession. Legal professionals (*hôsô*) in Japan are divided into three branches: *bengoshi*, judges and prosecutors. To qualify as a legal professional, an aspiring candidate needs to pass the National Legal Examination (NLE), and then take a training programme and pass the graduation examination at the Legal Training and Research Institute (LTRI),

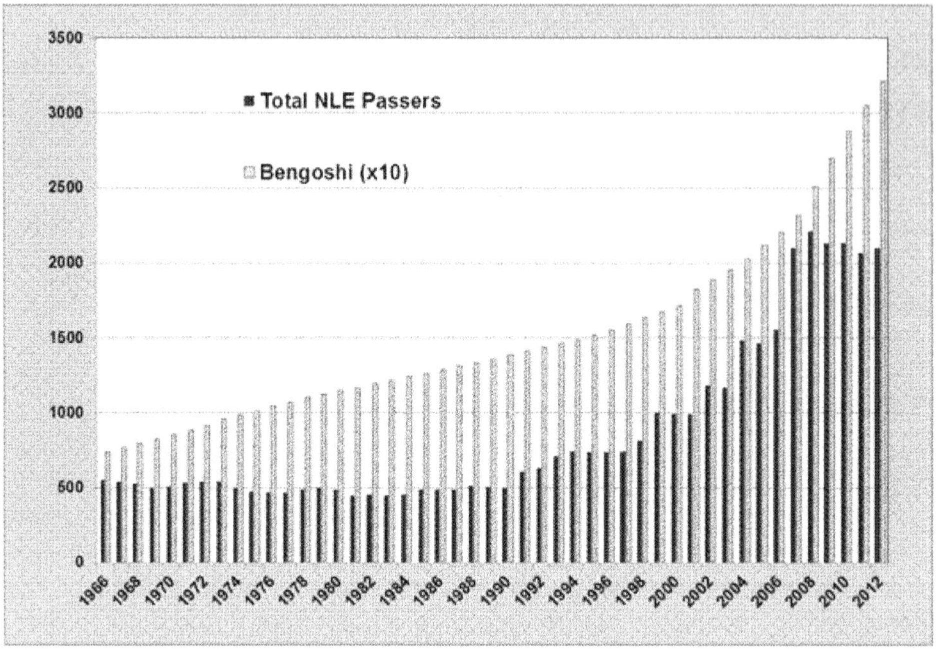

Figure 1. *Number of* bengoshi *and National Legal Examination passers (1966–2012)*
Sources: The Japan Federation of Bar Associations (2011, p. 72; 2012); Rokumoto (2007, pp. 213–214). See also the website of the Ministry of Justice (several years).

operated by the Supreme Court. Until recent years, basically nobody failed the graduation examination (Rokumoto, 2007, p. 205). The large majority of LTRI graduates become *bengoshi* (Japan Federation of Bar Associations, 2011, p. 93). Therefore, supply in the form of the quota on the number of NLE passers determines the size of the *bengoshi* profession. This supply, however, may have no connection with social demand.

The development of the NLE can be divided into four periods (Figure 1). First, from the late 1960s to 1990, the number of passers remained stagnant. Then, in the 1990s, with the first round of reforms, the number of passers started to increase. This expedited the increase in the number of *bengoshi* from the mid-1990s. The third period (the late 1990s to 2001) is characterised by the justice system reform movement and deliberations. Reform recommendations made in 2001 included a significant increase in the number of legal professionals. In the fourth period (post-2001), such reform was to be implemented. The number of passers increased substantially but recently the increase has slowed.

This development of the NLE is affected by the interaction of a number of factors, namely the complex relationship and hierarchy of legal professionals; changes in the role (or perceived role) of law in Japanese society; the institutional factor of the political environment in the country; and its economic development in the midst of globalisation. This paper analyses how one or more of these forces influenced the development of the NLE in the four periods described above.

Late 1960s to 1990: absence of reform

During this period, the number of *bengoshi* did not substantially increase because the number of NLE passers remained stable (Figure 1). This is attributable to the limited role of law in Japanese society, political stability and the hostile relationship between *bengoshi* and the judiciary.

As shown by Ota (1997/1998, pp. 182–197), there was an under-supply of *bengoshi*. While academics recognised the shortage and called for an increase (Rokumoto, 2004, p. 112), the business sector and the ruling party were not interested in any change until the 1990s (Saegusa, 2009, p. 373). The paucity benefited them. The legal system historically was mainly a tool for the Japanese government to govern the people (Miyazawa, 2007b, p. 127). It was not user-friendly for ordinary people. They rarely used the system to "challenge the government or big business" or to resolve disputes among themselves (Miyazawa, 2007b, p. 127). The Liberal Democratic Party (LDP) had been in power almost continuously. There was no need to codify their policies. Governing by administrative guidance instead of laws was flexible. Large enterprises had no objection because of their close relationship with the LDP and the bureaucracy (Saegusa, 2009, p. 367). They also did not require laws to regulate their relationships because of the role of *keiretsu* and the main bank systems in the post-war Japanese economic system (Chan, 2011a, pp. 186–187). Japanese business leaders throughout much of the 1980s considered that the high number of lawyers in the US led to litigiousness, and hindered businesses' competitiveness (Foote, 2005, p. 220). The issue of the number of NLE passers was left in the hands of the *hôsô*. In 1970, the National Diet laid down a condition that any reform of the justice system must be implemented with unanimous agreement among the judiciary, the Ministry of Justice (MOJ) (which represented the prosecutors' interests) and the Japan Federation of Bar Associations (JFBA) (which represented the *bengoshi*'s interests) (Watanabe *et al.*, 2000, p. 219).

Status quo was maintained because it was almost impossible for *bengoshi* and the judiciary to reach any consensus. At that time, the mainstream of the *bengoshi* profession had, as Taniguchi (2007, p. 91) said, an "antagonistic relationship" with the judiciary. This was attributable to the complex relationship and hierarchy of the *hôsô*. First, Japan has a continental European model career judiciary system. Judges are not recruited from experienced lawyers. Movement between the two professions is rare. Consequently, there is a strong feeling of distinction between the two groups, which is reinforced by Japanese culture and the mentality of "*soto uchi* (outsiders versus insiders)" (Prasol, 2010, p. 227). Second, pre-war, the prosecutors were at the "apex" of the hierarchy, followed by judges and then *bengoshi* (Vanoverbeke & Maesschalck, 2009, p. 15). Traditionally, Japanese society had respect for officials (Oda, 2009, p. 78), including judges and prosecutors. Legally, *bengoshi* also had a lower status (Hamano, 2002, p. 251). The pre-war MOJ held supervisory power over *bengoshi*. Until 1923, *bengoshi* had a separate qualifying examination from judges and prosecutors, who set the questions and marked the papers (Ito, 2009, pp. 75 and 85). Prosecutors and judges could become *bengoshi* without taking the qualifying examination (Oda, 2009, p. 78). Until 1937, *bengoshi* were not required to go through a post-examination training, unlike the aspiring judges and prosecutors (Ito, 2009, pp. 77 and 85). Even after its implementation, the training was separate from that for judges and prosecutors (Ito, 2009, pp. 77 and 85). Third, due to historical reasons, judges and prosecutors are generally considered as representing the 'authority' or 'prerogative power' while *bengoshi* "often take pride in acting for citizens" (Oda, 2009, p. 73). The pre-war judges and prosecutors were more or less the legal professionals who "used the justice system as a tool for serving state power" while some *bengoshi* had the attitude of "criticiz[ing], protest[ing] and resist[ing] the imperial system" (Osaka, 2007, pp. 3–4). Some members of the predecessor of the *bengoshi* profession (*daigen'nin*) did act as defence counsel for people who were prosecuted for involvement in the liberty and popular rights movement (Röhl, 2005, p. 806). They also actively participated in the movement (Toshitani, 1985, p. 30). Similarly, some *bengoshi* actively defended people against abuse of state power and the government's purge on communists and socialists in the pre-war era (Hamano, 2002, p. 252). The *bengoshi* profession developed an anti-establishment attitude, which continued for "a long time" after World War II (Taniguchi, 2007, p. 91). They called themselves the *zaiya hôsô* (meaning the legal profession who were out of office), as opposed to the *zaichô hôsô* (meaning the legal professions in office: judges and prosecutors) (Hamano, 2002, p. 252). When *bengoshi* attained professional independence after WWII, they still portrayed themselves as legal experts who would confront the government (Miyazawa, 1994, pp. 290–291).

This confrontational attitude was reinforced in the 1960s. After "intense lobbying" by the JFBA, a Committee was set up in 1962 to investigate judicial reform, including the issue of *hôsô-ichigen* (Vanoverbeke & Maesschalck, 2009, p. 21), which was a wish that the profession long held. It basically means an adoption of the common law model of judicial recruitment from experienced lawyers. Accomplishment of this would have a significant symbolic meaning for the complete levelling of the respective status of the *bengoshi* and judges. The judiciary was not in favour of the system (Vanoverbeke & Maesschalck, 2009, p. 21). The Committee considered that the time was not ripe (Takahashi, 2009, p. 54). The JFBA reacted strongly, published a critique and pursued a confrontational attitude towards the *zaichô hôsô* (Takahashi, 2009, p. 54).

In the 1970s, the hostile attitude intensified. Some active members in the radical student movement in the 1960s had joined the judiciary (Haley, 2007, p. 121). Conservative media and politicians criticised a number of "liberal" court decisions against the government in politically sensitive cases (Miyazawa, 2007a, p. 42). They particularly criticised the judges who belonged to the Young Jurists Association (YJA) for "allegedly left-leaning political positions" (Miyazawa, 2007a, p. 42). The YJA was established in 1954 by legal professionals "who opposed the anti-communist ideology" (Vanoverbeke & Maesschalck, 2009, p. 23). By 1971, over 200 judges had joined the YJA (Haley, 2007, p. 121). The Supreme Court responded with an "anti-leftist" policy towards "left-leaning" judges (Kobayashi, 2010, pp. 25 and 36–44), and demanded they withdraw from the YJA (Vanoverbeke & Maesschalck, 2009, p. 23). Those who refused tended to suffer in their subsequent judicial careers (Abe, 1995, p. 316). In this manner, the General

Secretariat of the Supreme Court proceeded to tighten control over personnel administration (Watanabe *et al.*, 2000, p. 219). While the judiciary became conservative and "right-leaning", the JFBA became more "left-leaning" (Kobayashi, 2010, p. 25). From the 1960s to 1990, left-wing *bengoshi* dominated in the team that handled the issue of judicial reform inside the JFBA (Kobayashi, 2010, p. 26). Since the 1970s, they kept opposing reform proposals from the judiciary (Kobayashi, 2010, pp. 76–77). Therefore, no consensus could be reached among the *hôsô*. This impeded any reform in the NLE.

The 1990s: first round of reform

After the mid-1990s, an increase in the number of *bengoshi* was expedited. Then, there was a steep increase at the beginning of this century. Such changes were caused by the first round of reform on the quota of NLE passers in the 1990s. This reform is attributable to economic and political development in Japan, the relationship between *bengoshi* and the judiciary, and a perceived change in the role of law due to the political and economic development. The MOJ initiated the reform as a result of the economic development in Japan. Out of fear of a revival of the pre-war hierarchy within the legal profession, the JFBA agreed to an increase in NLE passers. Due to political changes and economic development, the LDP and business sector changed their attitude and demanded expansion of the legal profession.

At the time of the bubble economy in the 1980s, many LTRI apprentices chose to become *bengoshi* (Kobayashi, 2010, p. 54). That affected the judiciary and particularly the Public Prosecutor's Office (PPO) (Kobayashi, 2010, p. 54). In the late 1980s, the MOJ (to which the PPO belongs) proposed to increase the number of NLE passers and reform the examination system to make it easier for younger candidates to pass the NLE (Watanabe *et al.*, 2000, p. 225). It considered that the LTRI graduates were reluctant to become prosecutors because of their advanced age when they passed the NLE (Shinya, 2000, p. 151). The 'culprit' was the extreme difficulty of the NLE. Many NLE examinees did not work and lost years of income in their preparation for the NLE. Further, cram schools became influential from the 1980s and NLE takers commonly took their preparatory courses (Rokumoto, 2007, p. 208), which could be costly. Therefore, NLE passers might strongly desire to quickly recoup the income loss and cram school expenses, and not be interested in becoming prosecutors. *Bengoshi* earn a high income and, unlike prosecutors, do not have a fixed retirement age.

The MOJ succeeded in setting the agenda through presenting the reform proposal in a broader perspective (Miyazawa, 2007b, pp. 109–110; Vanoverbeke & Maesschalck, 2009, p. 28). It proposed an increase in the number of NLE passers and the introduction of a scheme to favour examinees with no more than three attempts to make it easier for younger candidates to pass the NLE (*Asahi Shimbun*, 1990a, p. 3).

The Supreme Court supported the MOJ but the JFBA strongly opposed the above-mentioned scheme (Watanabe *et al.*, 2000, p. 225). The existence of different standards for passing the NLE made them worry about a revival of the pre-war hierarchy in the *hôsô* (Kobayashi, 2010, p. 56).

At the same time, over the issue of increase in *hôsô*, there was a change in the culture within the *bengoshi* profession, which had a "left-wing" and "right-wing" split in the latter half of the 1980s (Kobayashi, 2010, p. 74). As compared with 1977, survey results showed an increase in *bengoshi* who favoured an expansion of the profession in the localities where their offices were situated (*Asahi Shimbun*, 1991). Rapid economic growth also facilitated the emergence of commercial lawyers who were supportive of an expansion of the profession (Kobayashi, 2010, p. 60). The JFBA agreed to the increase in order to prevent the implementation of differential treatment. The three *hôsô* reached an agreement in October 1990 to adopt a step-by-step increase of NLE passers and, if there was no improvement in resolving the passers' advanced age problem within five years, a scheme of differential treatment (*Asahi Shimbun*, 1990b, p. 3). However, by 1994 improvement according to the agreed criteria became clearly unattainable (Miyazawa, 2007b, p. 110).

The board of the JFBA then intended to avoid the implementation of the differential treatment by agreeing to a further increase in NLE passers (Miyazawa, 2007b, p. 110). Another disagreement broke out between the JFBA and the *zaichô hôsô*. To avoid asking the Ministry of Finance for a budget increase (Miyazawa, 2007b, p. 111), the Supreme Court and MOJ proposed to shorten the LTRI training period to accommodate the increase in LTRI apprentices (*Asahi Shimbun*, 1995a, p. 3; 1997d, p. 5). *Bengoshi* suspected that it was an attempt to revive the pre-war practice of separate training for *bengoshi* and the *zaichô hôsô* (*Asahi Shimbun*, 1995b, p. 4; 1997d, p. 5) and strongly opposed it. The negotiations seemed to reach a deadlock.

External forces outside the *hôsô* came into play. The attitude of the business sector and the LDP towards the legal system changed. They started to call for an expansion of legal professionals (Watanabe *et al.*, 2000, p. 220; *Asahi Shimbun*, 1995b, p. 4; Vanoverbeke & Maesschalck, 2009, p. 30). Their attitude change was related to the political and economic changes in Japan and a consequential change in the vision of the LDP and the business sector about the role of law in Japanese society. In the 1980s, Prime Minister Yasuhiro Nakasone wanted to reduce governmental expenditure through deregulation (Miyazawa, 2007b, p. 115). In addition, the LDP lost power in 1993 after having been the ruling party since 1955 (Karan, 2005, p. 290). Despite a resumption of power in 1996, it needed to consider the possibility of another loss of power (Ramseyer & Rasmusen, 2006, p. 1880). The continual implementation of their policies could be ensured if they were codified and Japan became a law-based society (Foote, 2005, p. 221). At the same time, the prolonged recession after the burst of the bubble economy in the early 1990s exposed the weaknesses of the post-war Japanese economic system, which was characterised by extensive regulation, governmental guidance and monitoring, the *keiretsu* grouping and main bank system, and growth-oriented strategy in the business sector (as opposed to the shareholders-oriented and market-based model as commonly practised in the US). The business sector became frustrated with the bureaucrats' administrative guidance (Foote, 2005, p. 221), looked to the American model, and advocated deregulation. The LDP, the business sector and many scholars gradually reached a consensus. Japan should become an "after-the-fact review/remedy type of society" (Foote, 2005, p. 221) that is market-based and regulated by laws and rules. This requires a user-friendly and efficient legal system and therefore an expansion of the number of legal professionals.

In September 1997, the Justice Minister reportedly mentioned to journalists that the reform could proceed under the MOJ and the Supreme Court only (*Asahi Shimbun*, 1997f, p. 3). In other words, the JFBA could be ignored. This was said to be his personal view (and not representing the MOJ's position) (*Asahi Shimbun*, 1997e, p. 2) but it indicated the frustration about the JFBA's attitude. In addition, some National Diet members, irrespective of their political parties, considered that justice-system reform did not need the *hôsô*'s consensus (Watanabe & Yamanaka, 1997, p. 4). It was therefore possible for the National Diet to withdraw the condition it laid down in 1970 requiring such a consensus.

The management of the JFBA became worried about losing the support of public opinion and compromised (Watanabe & Yamanaka, 1997, p. 4). On 28 October 1997, the three *hôsô* ultimately reached an agreement to increase the number of NLE passers and reduce the LTRI apprenticeship (*Asahi Shimbun*, 1997g, p. 3). By that time, there was already a movement for a radical justice system reform. Unlike the situation until then, the *hôsô* did not have control over reform discussions.

Late 1990s–2001: justice system reform movement and deliberations

This round of NLE reform was part of a large-scale justice system reform that was initiated by the business sector in response to economic development (discussed above). The reform momentum was sustained by the support of and demands from the business sector, the LDP and political leaders. Both Prime Ministers Keizo Obuchi and Junichiro Koizumi were reformists. The Justice System Reform Council (JSRC) was successfully created. It produced a drastic reform plan.

On 22 January 1997, the Japan Association of Corporate Executives (*Keizai Dôyûkai*) publicly stressed the necessity of a rapid expansion of *hôsô* (*Asahi Shimbun*, 1997a, p. 3). The LDP would not ignore the business sector's demands (Chan, 2011a, p. 186) and established its Special Research Committee on the Justice System in June 1997 (*Asahi Shimbun*, 1997c, p. 3). This marked a deviation from the traditional practice of relying on the three *hôsô* in relation to issues concerning the justice system (*Asahi Shimbun*, 1997c).

On 16 June 1998, the Committee issued a report with comprehensive recommendations concerning justice system reform. These included an expansion of the *hôsô* and investigations into issues such as the introduction of a new law school system. Importantly, it also recommended an expansion of the justice system discussions beyond the *hôsô* and the establishment of a justice system reform council. Clearly, the LDP was assuming leadership in this round of reform. Dissatisfaction grew in the LDP about the slow pace of agreement among the three *hôsô* (*Asahi Shimbun*, 1998, p. 2). National Diet members negatively commented that the JFBA could not respond to the changes of the time (*Asahi Shimbun*, 1997b, p. 7).

The JSRC was established directly under the Cabinet in July 1999 (Rokumoto, 2007, p. 216). Each of the three *hôsô* branches had only one representative among the thirteen members appointed to the JSRC. Further, the representatives for the judges and prosecutors were in fact retirees (Vanoverbeke & Maesschalck, 2009, p. 33). The academy, with five members, formed the largest group (Prime Minister's Office, n.d.). The business sector also had two representatives (Prime Minister's Office, n.d.). Another JSRC member, a novelist, was critical of the JFBA (Vanoverbeke & Maesschalck, 2009, p. 33). Therefore, irrespective of the three *hôsô* branches' positions, the JSRC was successful in proposing a substantial increase in the number of NLE passers.

This time, the Ministry of Education, Culture, Sports, Science and Technology (MEXT) also played a role in the design of the reform, albeit not having representation in the JSRC. It actively pursued the introduction of the law school system. Its Universities Deliberative Council issued a report on 26 October 1998, stating that it was necessary to examine the law school system as part of the graduate school reform measures. On 27 April 2000, upon the JSRC's request, the Investigation Council Concerning the Idea on Law Schools (Tentative Name) was established under the MEXT. The Ministry's keen interest in the issue was probably due to the aging of the Japanese society, as indicated by the reference to this issue in the above-mentioned 1998 report. Between 1947 and 1997, Japan saw a significant rise in life expectancy but a substantial decline in fertility rates (Karan, 2005, p. 165). The declining birth-rate caused a shrinkage in undergraduate enrolment, which might be compensated by developing postgraduate programmes. Moreover, the need for postgraduate professional and business studies also related to the weakening of the post-war Japanese practice of lifetime employment and the seniority-based wage and promotion system for regular workers in big enterprises. Under such a system, businesses did not need candidates with "special skills or training" but those with the potential to be moulded into what was required in the posts (Prasol, 2010, pp. 214–215). Mid-career recruitment was rare. Promotion was not based on merit and qualifications. Professional and business postgraduate programmes were not needed. Now, however, non-regular employees increased (Japan Institute for Labour Policy and Training, 2012, pp. 38–41). Some enterprises introduced a performance-based remuneration system (Ohtake, 2007, p. 2). A secondary job market was activated. These changes meant that there was an increased need for postgraduate professional and business studies.

This time, the JFBA did not oppose the increase in the number of NLE passers. The LDP, business sector and many scholars already had a consensus on the need for such an increase. The management of the JFBA should have been well aware that resisting such change was impossible. It took the opportunity to pursue other reform proposals such as *hôsô-ichigen* (Miyazawa, 2007b, p. 123). However, in the JSRC, only the *bengoshi* representative was eager concerning this issue (Kobayashi, 2010, p. 192). Several JSRC members (including an ex-judge and an ex-prosecutor) opposed the idea (Kobayashi, 2010, p. 192). The key focus of the JSRC in fact was on introducing the law school system and implementing a substantial increase in the number of legal professionals. Kobayashi (2010, p. 191) considered the high number of academics in the JSRC as an indicator that the introduction of law schools was a priority in the reform agenda. Furthermore, both the chairperson and vice-chairperson were academics. The chairperson was known for his suggestion regarding the introduction of the law school system (Miyazawa, 2007b, p. 125). The MEXT was able to push forward the law school system although it was less powerful than the MOJ (Saegusa, 2009, p. 388).

In June 2001, the JSRC issued the *Recommendations of the Justice System Reform Council – For a Justice System to Support Japan in the 21st Century* (the Report). It recommended a substantial increase in the *hôsô* through increasing the number of NLE passers step-by-step to 1,500 persons in 2004 and then to at least 3,000 persons by 2010. Postgraduate law schools were to be established and, subject to an exception (discussed below), only their graduates could sit for the new NLE. The reform proposal did not include *hôsô-ichigen*. It only recommended a diversification of the sources of supply and adoption of measures to promote the appointment of *bengoshi* to the judiciary.

Post-2001: implementation of the reform

Following the issuance of the Report, the reform momentum had been maintained for several years. The number of *bengoshi* substantially increased. However, the pace of reform subsequently slowed and its scale was reduced. This is attributable to political developments in Japan and a change in its business sector's interest in the reform.

Sixty-eight law schools opened in 2004 and were subsequently joined by six additional law schools. A new NLE was introduced for their graduates. The first new NLE was held in 2006. To phase out the old system, the old NLE was basically kept until 2010. From 2011, people who are not law school graduates can take a preliminary examination and, if they pass, can take the new NLE. The number of NLE passers initially sharply increased, but declined after reaching its peak in 2008 (Figure 1).

As Miyazawa commented (2007b, p. 157), there was "ample opportunity" for the politicians, bureaucrats and parties with vested interests to "chip away at and minimize" the reform during its implementation. An important factor for maintaining the reform momentum was the prime minister's leadership (Miyazawa, 2007b, p. 157). The justice system reform received support from the former Prime Minister, Keizo Obuchi, who passed away in the midst of the reform movement in 2000. His successor, Yoshiro Mori, served a relatively short term (until April 2001). The next Prime Minister, Junichiro Koizumi, was a reformist and stayed in the post until September 2006, after law schools were opened. However, subsequently, the prime ministership in Japan became unstable. In the three years after Prime Minister Koizumi completed his terms, the LDP had three prime ministers before its loss of power to the Democratic Party of Japan (DPJ) in 2009. Then, the DPJ also had three prime ministers before its defeat in a lower house election in December 2012. In addition, after 2008, Japan was affected by the global financial crisis, the EU crisis and the strongest earthquake it had suffered in recorded history (CNN, 2011) and tsunami. The natural disaster led to huge financial and human losses as well as a nuclear reactor crisis. These crises, for the government, are more imminent and serious than justice system reform.

The LDP's attitude towards the scale of the NLE reform also seemingly changed. In August 2007, then Justice Minister Kunio Hatoyama commented that it was excessive to have 3,000 NLE passers (*Sankei Shimbun*, 2007, p. 28). On 16 October 2007, LDP's Justice System Research Council decided to examine whether to reconsider the extent of the increase in NLE passers (*Yomiuri Shimbun*, 2007). Justice Minister Hatoyama in January 2008 said that an increase in the number of legal professionals would influence quality, and that the Ministry would consider this issue (*Sankei Shimbun*, 2008a, p. 3). Such a change in attitude could also be due to the change in the prime ministership. The LDP Cabinets after Koizumi have revised the approach towards deregulation (Kinoshita, 2010, p. 284). As opposed to Koizumi's and his successor, Abe's, reformist direction (structural reform towards a self-responsibility society), the Fukuda administration (September 2007–September 2008) reverted to the traditional model of the government playing the "guardian" role (*Yomiuri Shimbun*, 2008, p. 3). In March 2008, the Fukuda Cabinet decided to halt the acceleration of the increase in the number of NLE passers (*Yomiuri Shimbun*, 2008). Within the LDP, some members also began to demand a reconsideration of the pace of increase (*Weekly Toyo Keizai*, 2010, p. 56).

Further, as Miyazawa (2007b, p. 127) predicted, there was a possibility that the LDP and the business sector would stop their pursuit of justice system reform when their immediate goals were achieved. The business sector's needs indeed have, to some degree, been satisfied. The increase in the number of *bengoshi* in recent years has facilitated the expansion of the commercial legal practice sector (Chan, 2011a, pp. 191 and 195). Foreign lawyers' operations in Japan have also been liberalised. Corporate in-house *bengoshi* have increased (JFBA, 2011, pp. 160–161). The business sector may also have reservations regarding further substantial expansion of the *bengoshi* profession due to the change in the public's attitude towards the role of law (in other words, their legal culture). A survey conducted in 2009 found that, when asked about the action that they would take if an acquaintance failed to repay a large amount of money borrowed after the agreed deadline expired, the second most popular choice (multiple answers possible) picked by the respondents was "consultation with a *bengoshi*" (41.9 per cent) (Cabinet Office, 2009). When asked about the action that they would take regarding disputes with siblings over the distribution of a deceased father's estate, the most popular choice (multiple answers possible) was "consultation with a *bengoshi*" (47 per cent). In contrast, in a survey conducted in 1983, when participants who did not think that their rights had been infringed in the past were asked about the type(s) of action that they would take if their rights were infringed, only 6.7 per cent of the respondents picked "consultation with a *bengoshi*" (Cabinet Office, 1983) (multiple answers possible). The choices varied between these two surveys but comparison can be made because all these questions permitted multiple answers. This comparison shows a change in society's legal culture. To the large enterprises, a further expansion of the legal profession may be detrimental because it would enhance the general public's access to legal services and to the power to challenge them.

With the gradual implementation of reform and the increase in the number of *bengoshi*, there was growing opposition within the *bengoshi* profession against the increase in NLE passers. On 18 July 2008, the JFBA proposed a slow-down in the pace of expansion of the legal profession (*Tokyo Shimbun*, 2008, p. 1). Many local bar associations also demanded a reconsideration of the plan for growth (Chan, 2011b, pp. 74–75).

Although the then Chief Cabinet Secretary criticised JFBA's proposal/demand (*Sankei Shimbun*, 2008b, p. 25), it is obvious that there was a "lack of political leadership at the highest level" (Miyazawa *et al.*, 2008, p. 350). This provided an opportunity for the three *hôsô* to be the sole decision-making parties (Miyazawa *et al.*, 2008, p. 350). In reality, it is predominantly in the hands of the Supreme Court and particularly the MOJ.

The justice ministership, like the prime ministership, also keeps changing. In any case, the "main actor in policy-making" in a ministry in Japan is the administrative vice-minister who is the highest-ranking civil servant in that ministry and often "more powerful" than the minister (Vanoverbeke & Maesschalck, 2009, p. 16). Persons serving this post in the MOJ almost all come from the PPO (Vanoverbeke & Maesschalck, 2009, p. 16). The judiciary and MOJ are apparently not supportive of the substantial increase (Okada, 2010, p. 6). They already showed a "cautious" attitude towards "hasty" reform during the justice system reform discussions of the late 1990s (Sato, 2002, p. 78). As Kinoshita (2010, pp. 284–285) pointed out, a substantial increase in the number of *bengoshi* would cause an increase in civil and criminal litigation and necessitate a rapid increase in the number of prosecutors and judges, which the PPO and the judiciary do not want. The LTRI has a maximum annual capacity of 3,000 new apprentices (Osaka, 2007, p. 3). Replacement or abolishment of the LTRI would meet opposition from the Supreme Court, which insisted on maintaining the LTRI (Miyazawa *et al.*, 2008, p. 345). It would not want to lose its involvement in legal training (*Tokyo Shimbun*, 2004, p. 5). In fact, the judiciary and the MOJ already took such a stand during the time when the JSRC was holding deliberations on the reform (Miyazawa *et al.*, 2008, p. 345). Through the LTRI, the Supreme Court has a gatekeeper role. The Supreme Court therefore would not support a drastic increase in NLE passers. In its report produced to the JSRC, the Supreme Court (1999) stated that it did not agree to reform that began with a substantial increase in the number of legal professionals and left it to the market.

Further, as Okada (2010, p. 11) commented, the government agencies which regulate quasi-legal professions in Japan might have a dislike towards the substantial increase in the number of *bengoshi* because this would result in *bengoshi*'s encroachment into these quasi-legal professions' jurisdictions. Quasi-legal professions include judicial scriveners (regulated by the MOJ), tax attorneys (regulated by the National Tax Agency, the Ministry of Finance) and patent attorneys (regulated by the Japan Patent Office, the Ministry of Economy, Trade and Industry). Among these professions, judicial scriveners' practice areas are closest to *bengoshi*'s practices. They handle the work of drafting legal documents for filing with courts, and real estate and corporate registration matters (Oda, 2009, pp. 80–81). *Bengoshi* can also conduct such work. Hitherto, they were not interested because they had more lucrative and 'higher-status' matters to handle. A substantial increase in *bengoshi* will pose a serious threat to judicial scriveners and, albeit probably to a lesser extent, the other quasi-legal professions. *Bengoshi* are entitled to register as tax and patent attorneys without the need for passing the relevant certification examinations. Furthermore, the governmental agencies have respective supervisory power over the quasi-legal professions but not the *bengoshi*. Continual expansion of the number of *bengoshi* might cause a decline in these quasi-legal professions and replacement of them by *bengoshi*. This would worry their respective supervisory governmental agencies. The MOJ is one such agency.

The number of NLE passers declined after reaching its peak in 2008 and it remains far below the JSRC's target of 3,000 for 2010 (Figure 1). The exact number of NLE passers is decided by the National Legal Examination Committee (NLE Committee) and the MOJ (Kinoshita, 2010, p. 285). The Justice Minister chose the NLE Committee members (Kinoshita, 2010, p. 284). Kinoshita (2010, p. 284) concluded that the parties which really have an influence on the decision regarding the number of NLE passers were the Justice Minister and the ruling party. However, as discussed above, the bureaucrats inside the Ministry could also exert a strong influence.

Conclusion

The discussion above has explored the interaction of forces behind the development of the *bengoshi* population in Japan, namely the internal factors of the complex relationship and hierarchy of the *hôsô*, and the external forces of changes in the role of law in Japanese society, the political environment in the country and its economic development in the midst of globalisation.

Growth remained slow for almost three decades from the 1960s due to a lack of interest of the business sector and the LDP in any change and the antagonistic relationship between *bengoshi* and the *zaichô hôsô*.

However, economic growth affected such a framework. It caused a shortage of supply of prosecutors in the 1980s. The MOJ initiated and pushed forward reform proposals. The objective was not to increase the number of prosecutors but to fill the vacancies. Once the need was met, it might not be supportive of any further increase in the number of NLE passers. This is exactly the situation in the implementation of the justice system reform in the twenty-first century. Such reform movement was not initiated by the Ministry. It has no intention of expanding the number of prosecutors. This is the same for the judiciary. This is evidenced by the small extent of the increase in numbers of prosecutors and judges. The numbers of prosecutors and judges only increased by 26–27 per cent between 2001 and 2011 while the same decade saw a 67 per cent increase for *bengoshi* (JFBA, 2011, p. 98).

The justice system reform movement in the late 1990s was initiated by the business sector and the LDP. The collapse of the bubble economy and the prolonged recession exposed the weakness of the post-war economic model in Japan. Political and business leaders began to look to the American market-based model. They reached consensus on the need of deregulation. To support such transformation, a user-friendly legal system is needed. Furthermore, the temporary out-of-power experience made the LDP aware of the need to prepare for another loss of power. Once codified, its "policies" could continue to be implemented despite a future loss of power (Foote, 2005, p. 221). Therefore, due to political and economic developments, both the politicians and the business sector pushed for justice system reform.

When the justice system reform momentum commenced in the late 1990s, it also became clear that Japanese society was rapidly aging. This would cause a decline in student enrolment and seriously affect the education sector. The development of professional postgraduate programmes, such as postgraduate law schools, can help to compensate for a decline in undergraduate enrolment. The interests and wishes of the LDP, the business sector, the universities and the MEXT matched. The JSRC was established. It proposed a drastic reform plan, which included a significant increase in the number of NLE passers. Japan seemed on track to have a substantial expansion in the number of its legal professionals.

However, while the MEXT is keen to develop the law school system, it lacks co-ordination (Miyazawa *et al.*, 2008, p. 348) and has "continuing bureaucratic infighting" with the MOJ (Aronson, 2011, p. 37).

With the disappearance of both political leadership and the business sector's pressure on NLE reform due to political changes and seemingly the satisfaction of the business sector's needs, the issue of the number of NLE passers was again in the hands of the three *hôsô*. In reality, this means control is predominantly in the hands of the Supreme Court and particularly the MOJ. Both want to maintain the LTRI and a highly competitive NLE (Miyazawa *et al.*, 2008, p. 350). Reform has been scaled down. The *bengoshi* who oppose an increase in their number are gradually getting what they want. Nevertheless, as shown in the analysis above, the size of the *bengoshi* profession in reality is controlled by the judiciary and the MOJ, due to their gatekeeping roles via the LTRI and the NLE, respectively. Their wishes, however, as shown by the justice system reform movement in the late 1990s, can be overridden by the wishes of the business sector, which is powerful and influential in policy making in Japan.

Acknowledgments

The author would like to thank the participants at the Workshop "Too many lawyers? Facts, reasons, consequences, and solutions" held at the Onati International Institute for the Sociology of Law on 19–20 April 2012 and the two anonymous reviewers for their valuable comments, which have been considered or incorporated when earlier versions of this paper were revised. The author has deep gratitude to one reviewer for the suggestions on extracting and highlighting at the beginning of the paper the "forces" at play which explain the development of the National Legal Examination.

References

Abe, M. (1995) The internal control of a bureaucratic judiciary: the case of Japan, *International Journal of the Sociology of Law*, 23, pp. 303–320.

Aronson, B.E. (2011) The brave new world of lawyers in Japan revisited: proceedings of a panel discussion on the Japanese legal profession after the 2008 financial crisis and the 2011 Tôhoku Earthquake, *Journal of Japanese Law*, 16(32), pp. 31–64.

Asahi Shimbun (1990a) Regarding the reform of the National Legal Examination, the executives of the Japan Federation of Bar Associations proposed to agree on unconditional increase of the number of passers, *Asahi Shimbun* (Morning Edition), 15 July, p. 3 (in Japanese).

Asahi Shimbun (1990b) The three branches of the legal profession agreed on an increase of 900 passers in five years for the National Legal Examination and making it easier for young persons to pass, *Asahi Shimbun* (Morning Edition), 19 October, p. 3 (in Japanese).

Asahi Shimbun (1991) The number of *bengoshi*, *Asahi Shimbun* (Evening Edition), 3 September, p. 1 (in Japanese).

Asahi Shimbun (1995a) The Interim Report of the Council on the Reform of the Training System of the Legal Professions and Related Matters: the majority favoured a doubling of the National Legal Examination passers and it also supported the restriction on the number of attempts, *Asahi Shimbun* (Morning Edition), 14 February, p. 3 (in Japanese).

Asahi Shimbun (1995b) The final stage of the National Legal Examination reform debate: an agreement should be sought from the citizen's perspective, *Asahi Shimbun* (Morning Edition), 31 October, p. 4 (in Japanese).

Asahi Shimbun (1997a) On judicial reform, the Japan Association of Corporate Executives put forward suggestions of recruiting specialised judges from the talents in the private sector, *Asahi Shimbu* (Morning Edition), 23 January, p. 3 (in Japanese).

Asahi Shimbun (1997b) The Deregulation Committee of the Liberal Democratic Party's Administrative Reform Promotion Headquarter: endless criticisms on the actual situation of the legal professions, *Asahi Shimbun* (Morning Edition), 19 February, p. 7 (in Japanese).

Asahi Shimbun (1997c) The Liberal Democratic Party's Special Research Committee on the Justice System had its first meeting: having a justice system reform led by the politicians, *Asahi Shimbun* (Morning Edition), 13 June, p. 3 (in Japanese).

Asahi Shimbun (1997d) Editorial: the legal professional training that is for the citizens, *Asahi Shimbun* (Morning Edition), 13 August, p. 5 (in Japanese).

Asahi Shimbun (1997e) Justice Minister Matsu'ura said justice system reform could be conducted by just two branches of the legal professions and there was no need to involve the Japan Federation of Bar Associations, *Asahi Shimbun* (Morning Edition), 6 September, p. 2 (in Japanese).

Asahi Shimbun (1997f) The Japan Federation of Bar Associations protested against the Justice Minister Isao Matsuura's comments and its President said such comment was an insult, *Asahi Shimbun* (Morning Edition), 7 September, p. 3 (in Japanese).

Asahi Shimbun (1997g) The three parties formally agreed on the reform of the number of passers etc. regarding the National Legal Examination system, *Asahi Shimbun* (Morning Edition), 29 October, p. 3 (in Japanese).

Asahi Shimbun (1998) The Liberal Democratic Party demanded the establishment of a Justice System Reform Council and aimed to establish leadership by the politicians, *Asahi Shimbun* (Morning Edition), 17 June, p. 2 (in Japanese).

Cabinet Office (1983) *Public Opinion Survey Concerning Human Rights Protection* [online] (in Japanese). Available at: http://www8.cao.go.jp/survey/s58/S58-09-58-09.html, accessed 26 February 2012.

Cabinet Office (2009) *Public Opinion Survey Concerning Comprehensive Legal Support* [online] (in Japanese). Available at: http://www8.cao.go.jp/survey/h20/h20-houterasu/index.html, accessed 26 February 2012.

Chan, K. (2011a) The reform of the profession of lawyers in Japan and its impact on the role of law, in: Y. Dezalay & B.G. Garth (Eds) *Lawyers and the Rule of Law in an Era of Globalization* (Oxford, Routledge), pp. 185–216.

Chan, K. (2011b) Justice system reform and legal ethics in Japan, *Legal Ethics*, 14(1), pp. 73–108.

Clark, R.C. (1992) Why so many lawyers? Are they good or bad?, *Fordham Law Review*, 61, pp. 275–302.

CNN (2011) *Anxiety in Japan Grows as Death Toll Steadily Climbs*, 14 March [online]. Available at: http://edition.cnn.com/2011/WORLD/asiapcf/03/13/japan.quake/index.html?iref=NS1, accessed 23 February 2012.

Foote, D.H. (2005) Forces driving and shaping legal training reform in Japan, *Australian Journal of Asian Law*. 7(3), pp. 215–240.

Galanter, M. (2011) More lawyers than people: the global multiplication of legal professionals, in: S.L. Cummings (Ed.) *The Paradox of Professionalism: Lawyers and the Possibility of Justice* (New York, Cambridge University Press), pp. 68–89.

Haley, J.O. (2007) The Japanese judiciary: maintaining integrity, autonomy, and the public trust, in: D.H. Foote (Ed.) *Law in Japan: A Turning Point* (Seattle, WA, University of Washington Press), pp. 99–135.

Hamano, R. (2002) How did the image of *bengoshi* change, in: Y. Wada, S. Ota & M. Abe (Eds) *Negotiations and Dispute Resolution* (Tokyo, Nippon Hyoron Sha), pp. 248–273 (in Japanese).

Ito, A. (2009) *Study on the Bengoshi Profession* (Tokyo, Sangakusya) (in Japanese).

Japan Federation of Bar Associations (JFBA) (2011) *Lawyers White Paper 2011 Edition* (Tokyo, Japan Federation of Bar Associations) (in Japanese).

Japan Federation of Bar Associations (JFBA) (2012) *Members of the Japan Federation of Bar Associations* (Tokyo, Japan Federation of Bar Associations) (in Japanese) [online]). Available at: http://www.nichibenren.or.jp/jfba_info/membership/about.html, accessed 8 February 2012.

Japan Institute for Labour Policy and Training (2012) *Labor Situation in Japan and its Analysis: General Overview 2011/2012* (Tokyo, Japan Institute for Labour Policy and Training).

Justice System Reform Council (JSRC) (2001) *Recommendations of the Justice System Reform Council – For a Justice System to Support Japan in the 21st Century* (Tokyo, Justice System Reform Council).

Karan, P.P. (2005) *Japan in the Twenty-First Century: Environment, Economy, and Society* (Lexington, KY, The University Press of Kentucky).

Kinoshita, T. (2010) *An Economic Analysis of the Post-War Justice System: Small-Scale Justice and its Transition* (Tokyo, Nihon Keizai Hyouronsha) (in Japanese).

Kobayashi, M. (2010) *Who Made This Kind of the Japan Federation of Bar Associations* (Tokyo, Heibonsha) (in Japanese).

Liberal Democratic Party Special Research Committee on the Justice System (1998) *Firm Guidelines for the Justice Administration in the 21st Century* (reprinted in *Hôritsu jihô zôkan shirîzu shihôkaikaku*, I, pp. 333–336) (in Japanese).

Ministry of Justice (2006) *Results of the New National Legal Examination in 2006* (in Japanese) [online]. Available at: http://www.moj.go.jp/content/000006357.pdf, accessed 29 March 2012.

Ministry of Justice (2010) *The Change of the Number of Applicants and Passers in Part 2 of the Old National Legal Examination* (in Japanese) [online]. Available at: http://www.moj.go.jp/content/000057099.pdf, accessed 29 March 2012.

Ministry of Justice (n.d.-a) *Results of the New National Legal Examination in 2007* (in Japanese) [online]. Available at: http://www.moj.go.jp/content/000006382.pdf, accessed 29 March 2012.

Ministry of Justice (n.d.-b) *Results of the New National Legal Examination in 2008* (in Japanese) [online]. Available at: http://www.moj.go.jp/content/000006423.pdf, accessed 29 March 2012.

Ministry of Justice (n.d.-c) *Results of the New National Legal Examination in 2009* (in Japanese) [online]. Available at: http://www.moj.go.jp/content/000006465.pdf, accessed 29 March 2012.

Ministry of Justice (n.d.-d) *Results of the New National Legal Examination in 2010* (in Japanese) [online]. Available at: http://www.moj.go.jp/content/000053691.pdf, accessed 28 March 2012.

Ministry of Justice (n.d.-e) *Results of the New National Legal Examination in 2011* (in Japanese) [online]. Available at: http://www.moj.go.jp/content/000103954.pdf, accessed 22 December 2012].

Ministry of Justice (n.d-f) *Examinee Numbers of Passers in Part 2 of the Old National Legal Examination in 2011* (in Japanese) [online]. Available at: http://www.moj.go.jp/content/000073033.pdf, accessed 24 December 2012.

Ministry of Justice (n.d.-g) *Results of the National Legal Examination in 2012* (in Japanese) [online]. Available at: http://www.moj.go.jp/content/000102108.pdf, accessed 22 December 2012.

Miyazawa, S. (1994) *The Reality of the Legal Process* (Tokyo, Shinzansha), (in Japanese).

Miyazawa, S. (2007a) Law reform, lawyers, and access to justice, in: G.P. McAlinn (Ed.) *Japanese Business Law* (Alphen aan den Rijn, Netherlands, Wolters Kluwer), pp. 39–89.

Miyazawa, S. (2007b) The politics of judicial reform in Japan: the rule of law at last?, in: W.P. Alford (Ed.) *Raising the Bar: The Emerging Legal Profession in East Asia* (Cambridge, MA, East Asian Legal Studies, Harvard Law School), pp. 107–162.

Miyazawa, S., Chan, K. & Lee, I. (2008) The reform of legal education in East Asia, *Annual Review of Law and Social Science*, 4, pp. 333–360.

Oda, H. (2009) *Japanese Law*, 3rd edition (Oxford, Oxford University Press).

Ohtake, F. (2007) Introduction: future of the performance-based pay system in Japan, *Japan Labor Review*, 4(2), pp. 2–6.

Okada, K. (2010) The groundlessness of the arguments on control of the population of the legal professions: the target of 3000 passers must be realized now, *The Lawyers*, 7(12), pp. 6–11 (in Japanese).

Osaka, E. (2007) Debate over the concept of the competent lawyer in Japan: 'What skills and attitudes does Japanese society expect from lawyers?', *International Journal of the Sociology of Law*, 35(1), pp. 1–17.

Ota, S. (1997/1998) Lawyers in Japan – an economic analysis, *Yearbook Law and Legal Practice in East Asia*, 3, pp. 177–198.

Prasol, A. (2010) *Modern Japan: Origins of the Mind – Japanese Traditions and Approaches to Contemporary Life* (Singapore, World Scientific).

Prime Minister's Office (n.d.) *Members of the Justice System Reform Council* [online]. Available at: http://www.kantei.go.jp/foreign/policy/sihou/singikai/members_e.html, accessed 24 February 2012.

Ramseyer, J.M. & Rasmusen, E.B. (2006) The case for managed judges: learning from Japan after the political upheaval of 1993, *University of Pennsylvania Law Review*, 154(6), pp. 1879–1930.

Röhl, W. (2005) Legal education and legal profession, in: W. Röhl (Ed.) *History of Law in Japan since 1868* (Leiden, Brill), pp. 770–827.

Rokumoto, K. (2004) *Law and Society in Japan* (Tokyo, Yuhikaku) (in Japanese).

Rokumoto, K. (2007) Legal education, in: D.H. Foote (Ed.) *Law in Japan: A Turning Point* (Seattle, WA, University of Washington Press), pp. 190–232.

Saegusa, M. (2009) Why the Japanese law school system was established: co-optation as a defensive tactic in the face of global pressures, *Law and Social Inquiry*, 34(2), pp. 365–398.

Sander, R.H. & Williams, E.D. (1989) Why are there so many lawyers? Perspectives on a turbulent market, *Law and Social Inquiry*, 14, pp. 431–479.

Sankei Shimbun (2007) Becoming a litigious country would lead to ruin: Justice Minister Hatoyama having concern about the rapid increase in *bengoshi*, *Sankei Shimbun*, 5 September, p. 28 (in Japanese).

Sankei Shimbun (2008a) The Ministry of Justice had concern about the decline of quality if 3000 persons passed the National Legal Examination annually and would have a review study, *Sankei Shimbun* (Tokyo Edition), 26 January, p. 3 (in Japanese).

Sankei Shimbun (2008b) The President of the Japan Federation of Bar Associations and the Chief Cabinet Secretary having verbal warfare over the increase in legal professionals, *Sankei Shimbun* (Tokyo Edition), 26 July, p. 25 (in Japanese).

Sato, I. (2002) Judicial reform in Japan in the 1990s: increase of the legal profession, reinforcement of judicial functions and expansion of the rule of law, *Social Science Japan Journal*, 5(1), pp. 71–83.

Shinya, T. (2000) The present situation and issue of reform of the prosecutor system, *Hôritsu jihô zôkan shirîzu shihôkaikaku*, I, pp. 148–156, (in Japanese).

Supreme Court (1999) *Thinking about the Justice System in the 21st Century: The Court's Fundamental Thoughts about Justice System Reform* (in Japanese) [online]. Available at: http://www.kantei.go.jp/jp/sihouseido/dai8append/append2.html, accessed 23 March 2012.

Takahashi, H. (2009) Career judiciary, judicial reform, and practicing attorneys, *Journal of Japanese Law*, 14(27), pp. 39–57.

Taniguchi, Y. (2007) The development of an adversary system in Japanese civil procedure, in: D.H. Foote (Ed.) *Law in Japan: A Turning Point* (Seattle, WA, University of Washington Press), pp. 80–98.

Tokyo Shimbun (2004) Editorial: the new National Legal Examination – according to the principles of reform, *Tokyo Shimbun,* 15 December, p. 5, (in Japanese).

Tokyo Shimbun (2008) Japan Federation of Bar Associations worried about the lowering of quality under the plan of 3000 entrants per year and proposed a slow-down of the increase in legal professionals, *Tokyo Shimbun,* 19 July, p. 1, (in Japanese).

Toshitani, N. (1985) *Thinking about Japanese Laws* (Tokyo, University of Tokyo Press) (in Japanese).

Universities Deliberative Council (Ministry of Education, Culture, Sports, Science & Technology) (1998) *About the Image of Universities of the 21st Century and Reform Measures from Now On – Universities that will Shine in its Individuality in a Competitive Environment*, (in Japanese) [online]. Available at: http://www.mext.go.jp/b_menu/shingi/12/daigaku/toushin/981002.htm, accessed 15 March 2012.

Vanoverbeke, D. & Maesschalck, J. (2009) A public policy perspective on judicial reform in Japan, *Journal of Japanese Law*, 14(27), pp. 11–38.

Watanabe, C. *et al.* (2000) The details of the justice system reform and the point reached, *Hôritsu jihô zôkan shirîzu shihôkaikaku*, I, pp. 219–238 (in Japanese).

Watanabe, M. & Yamanaka, T. (1997) The issue of reduction of the training period in the National Legal Examination reform was the key factor affecting whether there would be agreement among the three branches of the legal professions, *Asahi Shimbun* (Morning Edition), 24 September, p. 4 (in Japanese).

Weekly Toyo Keizai (2010) Japan Federation of Bar Associations was really divided in two: continuing the large increase or having a change, *Shûkan Tôyô Keizai* [*Weekly Toyo Keizai*], 22 May, pp. 54–57 (in Japanese).

Yomiuri Shimbun (2007) The Liberal Democratic Party Justice System Research Council decided to examine the reconsideration of the increase in the number of National Legal Examination passers, *Yomiuri Shimbun*, 16 October (in Japanese) [online]. Available at: http://www.yomiuri.co.jp/politics/news/20071016ia21.htm, accessed 16 October 2007.

Yomiuri Shimbun (2008) Putting a brake to the expansion of the legal profession's population: the foundation of the justice system reform shakes, *Yomiuri Shimbun*, 26 March, p. 3 (in Japanese).

Legal education in Spain: challenges and risks in devising access to the legal professions

LAURA CARBALLO PIÑEIRO
Department of Common Law, University of Santiago de Compostela, Santiago de Compostela, Spain

ABSTRACT *The establishment of the European Higher Education Area has not only triggered changes in legal education in Spain but also in access to the legal professions. This paper briefly addresses the implementation of the new educational system in order to understand the scope of the modifications that the legal professions are undergoing. The new educational model has been viewed as a specific opportunity to tackle the lack of professional control of lawyers, which was considered an anomaly within the European Union. A new entry system was implemented in 2011, and this paper also discusses the risks and challenges that this poses. To this end, the main traits of the legal profession and legal education prior to 2011 are first presented, following which the new system is described and its strengths and weaknesses compared to the former system are highlighted. The change of model, accompanied as it is by the current economic downturn, is not only likely to produce a fall in the number of junior lawyers but also to endanger less well-off students' access to the profession. On the plus side, it brings legal education up to date and establishes the basis for enhancing interaction between stakeholders and thus for improving the quality of lawyers' education.*

Introduction

Legal education in Spain is undergoing a process of change, triggered by its integration into the European Higher Education Area (EHEA), and this includes entry to the legal professions. This paper will chiefly focus on lawyers, as they are the legal professionals to be most affected by the reforms that are underway. Until 2011 there was no professional control for lawyers and this has now become an issue which goes hand-in-hand with the question of how lawyers ought to be trained. Given the previous absence of control over entry to the profession, the answer to the question posed in the Oñati Workshop "Too Many Lawyers? Facts, Reasons, Consequences and Solutions" coordinated by Eyal Katvan, Carole Silver and Neta Ziv, could only be a resounding 'Yes!' in a country with one of the highest lawyer/inhabitants ratios in Europe after Lichtenstein, Italy, Greece and Luxembourg. The data presented here are provided by the Spanish Institute of Statistics (INE – *Instituto Nacional de Estadística*) and a study published by the General Council of Spanish Lawyers (CGAE, *Consejo General de la Abogacía Española*) in 2008,[1] which give a ratio of 2.63 lawyers per 1,000 inhabitants (CGAE, 2008, p. 46). These are the facts.

The reasons lie in the total absence of any control over entry to the profession other than the market, and the consequence is a probable surplus of lawyers, but one which is evenly distributed across the country, representative of Spanish society and with whose services most clients claim to be satisfied. The current perception of lawyers' work is positive and their role as social mediators, i.e. helping clients to avoid litigation, is appreciated. In a survey conducted in 2008, interviewees showed a high level of satisfaction with lawyers' services, with regard not only to the treatment they received (8.3 on a scale of 10) but also with their handling of their workload and dedication (7.5) (CGAE, 2008, p. 127).[2] And indeed, the fact that only 60% of cases actually reach the courts (CGAE, 2008, pp. 146–147, 161) confirms the reorientation of legal services from litigation to legal advice (Toharia & García de la Cruz, 2005, pp. 14–16). Was the Spanish system therefore really a case for reform?

The 'but' that we are concerned with refers to the training of lawyers. Indeed, there was already unease about this matter among professionals (CGPJ, 1997, pp. 37–38) as obtaining a law degree was almost tantamount to being admitted to the profession. In contrast with other legal professions with specific training and an entry system, becoming a lawyer in Spain only required a degree in law and enrolment in a bar association. The next part of this paper will deal with the features of this profession up to 2011, the year in which a major reform came into force. This reform was undertaken in the aftermath of Spain's joining the Bologna process aimed at establishing the EHEA in 2006[3] (Pulido, 2007).

The driving forces behind the Bologna process are twofold, namely mass higher education and its increasing internationalization, with significant policy issues being the unification of the credit system[4] in order to make degrees easily readable and comparable across the EHEA, thus facilitating the mobility of higher education staff, graduates and students' throughout Europe as well as attracting students from outside the EHEA. In general, the Bologna process aims at facilitating the recognition of qualifications on the grounds of flexibility and portability among different educational models and professional sectors. Also on the policy agenda are the establishment of a two-tier degree structure and the introduction of a quality assessment system; it is worth pointing out here that any major structural changes involved were to be undertaken by the states taking part in this process, since the Bologna process is not a European Union initiative.

However, the main change brought about by the Bologna process was a methodological shift: as will be seen, the Spanish university system was characterized by a formalistic education with a rote-learning approach. As outlined on the Spanish Ministry of Education and Science website,[5] the Bologna process stresses competencies and skills as well as knowledge, with a view to increasing employment opportunities within the European Union and converting European higher education into a magnet for students and professors from other parts of the world, for which it is necessary to switch from acquiring existing knowledge to learning how to manage the constant flux of information with which we now live. This is particularly true when it comes to legal education; beyond competencies and skills, which require their own share of teaching time, the superimposition of legal orders provides a growing number of rules with different binding forces and a complicated classification within the Kelsenian pyramid, rendering the rote-learning method, which has dominated for so long in Spanish law faculties, useless (among many others, Mullerat, 2002, pp. 283–306; Silver, 2009, pp. 2–15; Smits, 2011, pp. 44–48; Toharia, 2002, pp. 118–120).

The third part of this paper therefore focuses on the Bologna process and how the structural and methodological changes that it seeks have been implemented in Spain. It has in fact been seen as an opportunity to implant the specific training lawyers lacked, as well as to establish professional control. As mentioned above, the reform has just entered into force and adaptation to the new educational system is still underway in Spain, so there are no data as to whether these changes have achieved the goals sought by the reform. However, what is feasible is to advance an opinion as to whether the new system is really an improvement on the former one.

Finally, the issue addressed in the fourth part of this paper is what changes are to be expected in the legal profession as a consequence of the new system; whether it will reduce the number of lawyers, and whether access to justice will be affected as a result, questions which cannot be answered without taking into account the ongoing economic downturn. The Spanish government, meanwhile, is adopting new measures concerning the university system and the judicial system which are a real threat to the legal profession and need to be taken into consideration while analyzing how the system in force from 2011 will work.

Becoming a lawyer in Spain before 2011

Before 2011 a law degree was all that a graduate needed to become a fully qualified lawyer. A Spanish *abogado* is equivalent to a lawyer in the United States, combining the skills of solicitors and barristers (Hendel, 2011, pp. 38–42) which are exercised in a monopoly system. They are corporately organized into *colegios profesionales*[6] equivalent to bar associations, so that after obtaining a law degree a Spanish *licenciado* simply needed to enroll in an association and pay the fees to be a lawyer. Legally speaking, Spanish law graduates did not need to pass a professional exam (similar to the bar exam), undertake a pupilage or pursue any kind of practical training after obtaining their *títulos* or degrees. Hence, a major feature of the Spanish system was the lack of professional control.

Lawyers, along with *procuradores de los tribunales*[7] (who represent individuals in court and whose role is complementary to the lawyers' tasks of providing clients with legal advice and defense) were, in fact, the only legal professionals without any sort of professional control. Becoming a judge, an attorney general, a judicial secretary, a notary or a state advocate is a long process in Spain; passing the qualifying exams requires extensive preparation, and successful applicants still have to undergo a training period at a corporate school. The system for lawyers, however, was set up on the basis that a law degree already provided the competencies and skills necessary to practice.

However, this assumption was not mirrored by the Spanish university system, where a law degree granted access to a variety of professions and jobs; in other words, it was not tailored to training lawyers. The versatility of Spanish law graduates explains the high supply and demand characterizing these degrees. Spain has both public and private universities and most of them offer law degrees: 73 of the 56 public universities and 18 private universities, in fact (INE, 2012). This figure is even more striking when compared to the number of law faculties in other countries with higher populations, such as Germany with 44 law faculties, France with 68 and Italy with 58 (Salvador, 2012). Many Spanish law faculties were founded in the 1990s as part of a public policy to promote university education which built a campus in almost every administrative province in Spain.[8] Low costs and the prestige associated with establishing a law faculty did the rest, leaving the map of Spain covered in facilities with too many expenses and too few students, to which anyone wishing to study law was admitted.[9]

In addition to the high number of law faculties, studying law was neither expensive[10] nor demanding; students were simply required to pass a number of courses that were taught according to a doctrinal approach following Lilly's classification (1995, p. 1430). Law students were thus exposed to an analytical examination of the legal system and its rules, seeking the underlying principles but with almost no opportunity to apply them and thus to show their skills. As mentioned above, law degrees in Spain were not designed to teach students how to be lawyers; indeed, most graduates chose other professional options such as positions in the growing public administration. In 2003, for example, there were 13,500 new law graduates but only 6,000 actually joined the bar; moreover, only 84% did so as active lawyers while 16% were dormant, meaning that only 37% of law graduates, around 5,000 individuals, ended up practicing as lawyers (CGAE, 2008, p. 98).

As a result of this combination of factors, the legal profession was characterized by a low-cost, formalistic education with no follow-up training period on the one hand, and the lack of a controlled entry system on the other. Both features were to blame for the high number of lawyers which used to be characteristic of Spain, and they also contributed to another trait of the legal profession: legal services have always been understood in the broad sense in Spain, i.e. including more than litigation as suggested by Menkel-Meadow (2012).

This state of affairs raised many fears among those involved in the legal system, who complained about the poor quality of lawyers' work on the one hand and the excessive litigation produced by there being too many lawyers seeking work and disregarding ethical questions in favor of survival on the other. The two consequences of having too many lawyers would appear to be endemic; they can be found in a speech on advocacy given by José de Covarrubias, a lawyer and the equivalent to a Secretary of State for Justice, in 1789 (pp. 23–83), and Spanish legal practitioners were in general agreement with Calamandrei's critical statements in *Troppi Avvocati* (translated into Spanish in 1926). However, the last century witnessed a reaction to the many criticisms of graduates' lack of specific training as lawyers, and this led to the establishment of legal practice schools, mainly linked with bar associations although some were run by law faculties.[11] In addition to this, an optional exam for newcomers was established following a general meeting of Spanish bar associations in 1997.

The main topic of the meeting was Law 1/1996 on legal aid which developed Article 119 of the Spanish Constitution and classified it as a public service. In addition to providing support to lawyers, Spanish bar associations play a key role in the administering of legal aid. The aforementioned law sets out who has a right to legal aid, how to obtain it and which services are paid for, and the first step is to apply to a bar association, which is responsible for the initial assessment. The bar associations serve more than a million people each year through the roughly 35,000 lawyers who offer legal aid services: 29% of practicing lawyers in Spain (CGAE, 2008, p. 105). Such figures give an accurate idea of how relevant and active this service is, and bar associations look after it very carefully for obvious reasons.[12] Most young practitioners begin their careers there, and since it is a blind service, meaning that the client cannot choose, the less well-qualified could try to make a living in this way. Bar associations therefore seek to maintain the service's quality by firstly requiring all lawyers involved to be listed by the corresponding bar, and secondly, by running updating courses which are compulsory for lawyers wishing to stay on the lists. An 'optional' exam was another measure set up by bar associations to ensure the best possible service.

These efforts to improve lawyers' training seem to have had a positive outcome, since they are no longer viewed as rent seekers who foster litigation out of thin air. Toharia in fact dismantled this myth, emphasizing the covenant culture of Spanish lawyers (1987, pp. 114–125) as the data already provided on the number of cases reaching the courts confirms. Furthermore, following the liberalization of fees in Spain, the argument that the market is not playing its part in regulating the number of lawyers is not convincing either. Bar associations used to intervene in the market by publishing fee tables which helped to keep prices up in an overcrowded profession, as Calamandrei emphasized (1926, pp. 85–93). Nowadays this regulatory conduct is held to be contrary to antitrust rules and lawyers are free to agree on their fees with their clients, only resorting to bar association fee tables in cases of disagreement.[13] Hence, those not capable of attracting clients will not remain in the market, particularly as the Spanish do not appear to be a litigious nation (Toharia, 1987, pp. 75–113; Toharia & García de la Cruz, 2005, pp. 14–16), unlike in the past (Kagan, 1981).

Still, the lack of professional control stressed Spain's isolation within the European Union where this matter was concerned. The White Paper on Justice issued in 1997, which was the basis for a thorough reform of the Spanish judicial system, is of special interest. This report was drawn up by the governing body of Spanish judges, the *Consejo General del Poder Judicial* (CGPJ), and tackled the role of lawyers as key collaborators in justice according to Articles 17.3 and 24 of the Spanish Constitution. A section dedicated to professional control does not even mention the number of lawyers but it does mention their legal education and suggests a mandatory pre-practice training period as well as a lifelong learning program in order to match other European jurisdictions (CGPJ, 1997, pp. 37–38). These were the internal forces and interests that were pushing for reform, which was eventually undertaken due to external forces, namely Spain's joining the Bologna process.

The Bologna process and its impact on legal education in Spain

The Bologna process has had a major impact on Spanish law faculties, where the law curriculum has been adapted to the new system based on ECTS, the division between undergraduate and postgraduate education and quality assessment. Once the Bologna process came into force, it was no longer only about law but also about teaching skills and thus behavioral learning and assessment. Since then legal education has begun to play a role in Spain[14] and it has also been acknowledged that the increasingly complex legal system can no longer be taught at university. As a matter of fact, law faculties cannot turn completely to practice either, since on the one hand this is in a constant state of flux, and on the other it is easily mastered, at least when the practitioners have a good theoretical grounding. The issue is therefore providing this basis, whose scope ought to be informed by reality and so avoid hyper-complicated speculative theories in favor of a more practical approach; i.e. taking into account what is going on in the economy and society (Bizcarrondo, 2002, p. 275; Pérez, 2002, pp. 197–268; Ribstein, 2011, pp. 1672–1676). In other words, it was time to shift from a rote-teaching model of positive rules to learning what legal culture is, as proposed by Merryman (1985), Friedman (1994) and others (Toharia, 2002, pp. 115–118).

Along with this methodological change, the reform brought about another major change, i.e. the law curriculum was liberalized. Indeed, the Spanish educational system has swung from a position where there was barely any room for divergence to almost total freedom for universities in the setting up of their degrees. On the basis of the credit system, Spanish law curricula might potentially differ completely from one university to another, so they can be tailored not only to meet the market's needs, but also to attract the best students. Not surprisingly, law faculties have not availed themselves of such freedom and the outcome is, once again, a fairly homogeneous set of subjects organized in the old style, which means that there are still a significant number of similarities between the law curriculum established in 1953 and the current ones.

One factor leading to this inertia is the quality assessment process in which law faculties are engaged, which favors standardization as suggested by the experiences of other countries (Sherr, 2001). This standardization was partly induced by the Spanish Agency for Teaching Quality Assessment (ANECA – *Agencia Nacional de Evaluación de la Calidad*) which advised the committees in charge of devising the new curriculum on the following specific guidelines provided for different institutions, but in particular by a White Paper, drawn up by a team of professors from several law faculties and financed by ANECA (2005), which identified competencies, skills and abilities with which a law degree should equip students. Another factor favoring standardization lies in the socio-economic context in which law faculties operate: Spanish students tend to study at the nearest university to their family homes, so that while law faculties do not need to compete for students from other regions, they are also discouraged from specializing insofar as their students wish to be able to choose from among the full range of jobs available to law graduates. This does not mean that there is no room for specialization, but this is restricted to joint degrees: these are a real success within the Spanish education system, in particular the combination of Law and Business Administration.

The new system has also brought about major changes in the structure of degrees, which are now split into two, bachelor's degrees and master's degrees. Spain has thus shifted from a structure in which students needed nothing more than a law degree to become lawyers to another in which after a four-year degree they are bachelors in law but are not entitled to practice as lawyers. However, a law degree does enable qualified individuals to apply for junior posts in the public and private sectors and to do other jobs related to practicing law, such as notary assistants, clerks or paralegals.

The Bologna process therefore seems to paint a picture in which a bachelor in law has to study a master's degree in order to be admitted to the legal profession, and this is in fact what has happened; the Bologna process has triggered the long-awaited internal reform by establishing both specific training for lawyers and professional control. The question now is whether it has really improved the previous state of affairs or whether the formalistic educational model is actually being absorbed into the new structure. Indeed, the establishment of the master's degree for lawyers has already been very controversial. Key issues were the avoiding of conservative trends, in particular the temptation to turn postgraduate studies into the fifth year of the former *licenciatura* by placing too little emphasis on the acquisition of practical know-how, and focusing on litigation issues and not on the mediation role of lawyers.

A Regulation was issued in 2011[15] which completed Law 34/2006 by establishing an entry system for professional practice to counteract both trends. It contained a list of competencies and skills to be acquired by lawyers at the end of their one-year study period, related to a variety of topics and highlighting the importance of settling disputes out of court by resorting to alternative methods of conflict resolution and proper legal advice, negotiation skills, ethical and social liability issues, and law firm management.[16] It would appear from these learning outcomes that the new master's degree aims to develop a specific professional identity with a view to training competent lawyers with a responsible approach to clients and the public in general, i.e. 'learning to be a lawyer' and so meeting the goals sought by the legal reform.

Further policy issues resolved by this piece of legislation concerned the questions of who is to be admitted to training and which institutions should offer the corresponding postgraduate courses. The first was settled by clearly stating that only applicants with a bachelor's degree in law or *licenciados* would be considered,[17] while the second was resolved by perpetuating the former system; law faculties as well as legal bars might offer postgraduate studies. This dual system has been heavily criticized by law faculties[18] willing to take the lead in this matter, on the basis of a formalistic argument; the fact that master's degrees can only be offered within the university system. On the contrary, involving both institutions avoids the temptation to turn lawyer-oriented master's degrees into the fifth year of the former law degree, as well as turning them into a means of controlling the supply of new professionals. Weber's theory becomes reality within the new entry system, but only to a certain extent since bar associations are not the only controlling parties; they have to balance their interests with those of law faculties and professors, and vice-versa. Cooperation between the two institutions is strongly encouraged by the Regulation[19] and this seems to have been the trend so far (Tomás, 2009): only one of the 41 master's degrees is offered by a legal practice school without university involvement.[20]

An internship period is also laid down,[21] i.e. a six month period working with a judge, a lawyer or an attorney general, or with entities which require legal services such as penitentiaries, police stations or other organizations pursuing general interests.[22] Taking into account the limited range of legal services that the latter internships might offer and their consequent lack of interest to applicants, the provision specifies that students can only spend part of their internships at these facilities but not exactly how long, and it might well be asked how spending time at such places would improve students' legal training. The rule does have a positive side in that it also aims to avoid an articling crisis. It should also be noted that rotation is not mandatory as it is with the German *Rechtsrefendariat*, and so students in Spain may actually spend their entire internships at the same place (with the exception of the latter facilities of course).

Applicants have to take a final written exam, which is the same for everyone throughout Spain.[23] Every *Comunidad Autónoma* has to set up a selection committee whose members are also legally predetermined and which oversees the fairness of the examination procedure and ensures that it is properly carried out.[24] The exam is divided into two parts and applicants must pass the first to qualify for the second. The first part is a multiple choice test,[25] whose grade depends not only on the test result itself but also on up to 20% of the grades obtained on previous postgraduate courses, with the aim of recognizing students' other work. The second part requires candidates to resolve a case of their choice from among several alternatives.[26] The final grade simply acknowledges that the candidate has either passed or failed.[27]

We are currently in a period of transition, since the new system has not yet fully replaced the former. It must be borne in mind that the first bachelors to graduate under the new model are still in the law faculties, so courses are being run for those who obtained their degrees under the former system. Law 24/2006 originally included *all* law graduates, but after a great deal of pressure students enrolled on the previous degree courses, i.e. those graduating as *licenciados*, obtained an exemption from the law in force so as not to be subject to the new model. The rule has just been modified[28] and some universities have decided not to offer the new master's degree while others have kept it on to test its efficacy; taking into account that these master's degrees are nowadays playing the role of the courses previously offered by legal practice schools, it seems that most of them have enough students to be running.

While it is still too soon to evaluate the functioning of the new system, it is possible to identify some issues which may hamper the achieving of its aims, although progressive improvements should be expected as the methodological shift introduced by the Bologna process is consolidated. At the moment both law professors and their students are uneasy about it (Pérez, 2002, pp. 230–239), and this challenge must be faced if a Gattopardian move is to be avoided; training lawyers requires getting rid of formalistic teaching and going beyond rote-learning.

A quick look at the programs available on the Internet shows a large number of courses all called Civil, Criminal, Labor or Administrative Clinics along with subjects devoted to deontological issues and negotiation and drafting skills. It was clear that the system would not change overnight but it is regrettable that the curriculum drafters have not even tried to move away from the traditional compartmentalized approach taken by civil law systems. A holistic approach is more suitable for the teaching of skills and competencies sought by the legislation in force, in addition to providing prospective lawyers with a taste of reality.

Furthermore, the new postgraduate courses have a significant weak point. They do not even attempt to broach the question of legal clinics, in which students deal with clients and bring their cases before court (Wilson, 2009, pp. 829–830), something that does not happen when they are working with practicing lawyers because they are not allowed to represent clients in court. As previously mentioned, legal aid is provided by lawyers for a fee paid by the state, so students are left out of this equation. This does not mean that legal clinics are unknown in Spain, and in fact an International Journal of Legal Clinical Education Conference was held in Valencia in 2011[29] but there have only been a couple of experiences throughout the country.

In addition to all this, the reform of the legal educational system seems to have stopped halfway through: apart from lawyers and *procuradores de los tribunales*, there have been no further movements to re-regulate entry to other legal professions, despite suggestions in this direction (Galindo, 2012) and the governing body of judges' acknowledgment that it is necessary (*Diario La Ley*, 2011). They have not been targeted, yet legal professions such as notaries, judges, judicial secretaries or attorney generals are all already highly regulated. On the 31 January 2011 the selection committee responsible for examining candidates who wish to become judges or attorney generals[30] issued an agreement[31] which merely provided a syllabus, with no focus at all on skills and competencies; qualifying is once again relegated to passing exams and the consequent admission to a specific school linked with these professions (Espiniella, 2007).

This entry system has at least two drawbacks: firstly, it merely focuses on knowledge, distorting completely the educational objectives established by the new educational trends inasmuch as prospective judges, attorney generals, public notaries and so forth will study for examinations in which they are asked about positive rules and not assessed on their skills. Taking into account the natural interaction between the legal professions and undergraduate studies (Pérez, 2002, p. 201), this rote-learning approach is likely to delay the successful application of new educational methodologies.

Secondly, there is no recognition of candidates' efforts; if they fail the exam they start from scratch in the labor market without being able to provide any credentials apart from a bachelor's degree. In fact, most of those who do not already have a specific master's degree will take the postgraduate degree aimed at prospective lawyers, delaying their preparation for the examinations. In other words, demand for these master's degrees is likely to lead to a situation unforeseen by the legal rules in which master's degree for lawyers will be taken by all legal professionals, rather than the more specific degrees. This is not necessarily negative, but it remains to be seen whether this master's will be faithful to its task of training prospective lawyers.

On the positive side, the new system will change the way in which junior lawyers are hired. Instead of employing recently qualified lawyers law firms will hire students on the master's courses; in this way companies can begin training their employees during this time and, of course, trying them out as prospective lawyers. This will be a positive outcome for the whole system, as law firms will have an interest in actively promoting high quality master's degrees. In fact, in addition to the interaction between bars and universities, law firms are also expected to become increasingly involved in law faculty affairs.

All in all, it will be interesting to see whether law faculties and bar associations are able to meet the market's demands (Ribstein, 2011, pp. 1651–1652). The liberalization of the legal curriculum includes a review at least once every six years, and this opportunity to improve prospective lawyers' legal education ought to be taken. Unfortunately, lack of competition is also a feature of the new system. The quality assessment put in place does not help; on the contrary, it fosters standardization, as already mentioned. Competition might result from the number of applicants passing the final exam and in this sense it is regrettable that the final grade is only pass or fail. It is a step forward compared to the former situation inasmuch as it provides for an objective parameter of comparison, but it is doubtful that this will be enough, taking into account the system's inertia.

The new model in context

The competencies and skills learning approach and specific training for lawyers are benefits brought about by the new model triggered by the Bologna process. Both have fulfilled historical demands by radically changing access to the legal profession. At the same time they may have triggered other less welcome changes, in particular as regards the number of lawyers and their socio-economic backgrounds, which would also be a by-product of the economic downturn that Spain is still experiencing. As discussed later on, the new educational model may also cause a reduction in the number of lawyers and endanger access to university for less well-off students as a result of an increase in tuition fees and the introduction of *numerus clausus* at law faculties, the former mainly a consequence of the worrying financial situation of the public university system and the latter the outcome of the new educational methods. A radical judicial reform undertaken by the government is now to be added to all this, one which threatens to change the Spanish judicial system, up to now understood as a public service, and thus the key role attributed to lawyers within it, putting access to justice at risk.

The Bologna process has been heavily criticized in Spain because of the resulting rise in university fees. This would seem to be a valid criticism, taking into account the fact that to qualify as lawyers law students now have to obtain two degrees instead of one, and pay the corresponding tuition fees. Most well-known universities in Spain are public and tuition fees are therefore low, although they have already risen significantly.[32] Furthermore, current government policy paves the way for a deepening of the social breach insofar as the legal grounds for increasing tuition fees have already been issued,[33] theoretically granting universities the power to increase them if they wish. Unfortunately this freedom is in fact empty rhetoric, inasmuch as the universities' financial survival is currently at stake, so it is easy to predict a significant fee increase in the near future. This will affect the access of students from low- and middle-income families to university and undermine the latter's role as a means to achieve social cohesion in a democracy.

In 2011 a project called *Eurostudent* was set up within the European Union to assess the social and living conditions of the university population, and its findings were published by the Spanish Ministry of Education (see Ariño & Llopis in Barañano *et al.*, 2011). In the study, Ariño & Llopis (2011, pp. 19–32) analyses the relationship between the social dimension and university participation, coming to the conclusion that university democratization is a long way from being a reality in Spain, given the fact that there are still many socio-economic hurdles for specific groups of students trying to reach university. The aforementioned legislation on access to the profession of lawyer acknowledges this situation inasmuch as it contains a reference to scholarships for applicants. Implementing this scholarship policy in the current economic situation is certainly another matter, but it is a decisive one for the social backgrounds of future lawyers. Unfortunately, the government has not yet issued specific rules on the issue, but the outlook is not good, bearing in mind that there has already been a significant fall in the scholarship budget as well as an increase in the prerequisites to be met in order to obtain one.[34]

A further consequence of the Bologna process is likely to be a reduction in the number of lawyers. The changes in teaching methodology that the process promotes has led to the introduction of *numerus clausus* in most law faculties, since the new methodology can only really work with small classes. Most law faculties have reduced the number of new entrants accordingly, taking into account their human resources,[35] as the educational reform has not been accompanied by an increase in university budgets.

It might be argued that a reduction in the number of lawyers is to be welcomed. In fact, a hypothetical lack of lawyers sounds like science fiction, since most lawyers practicing in Spain are still only in their forties (CGAE, 2008, p. 39). However, a lack of human resources in the long run may lead to justice being denied to the most underprivileged in society, opening the front door to inequality (Pearce & Levine, 2009). The increasing demand for legal services over recent decades, measured in terms of the percentage of the population resorting to lawyers' services – 23% in 1978, 38% in 2002, 53% in 2003 and 54% in 2008 (CGAE, 2008, p. 137) – ought to be taken into account when assessing an eventual shortfall of lawyers.

The economic downturn is likely to end the trend for requiring more legal services in Spain, in particular because the government has already set in motion a dramatic increase in court fees,[36] which will at any rate discourage individuals from resorting to the courts. Indeed, this judicial reform shakes the justice model which has so far been understood as an (almost) free state service and a means for achieving social justice. From now on, citizens will be charged for this service, and this endangers the survival of many lawyers in rural areas in particular, which will only further increase hurdles in access to justice in Spain.

Nowadays, lawyers working alone or with less than three partners are still in the majority in Spain. According to data gathered in 2008, 71% of practicing lawyers work as non-dependants, 16% as partners or associates in a firm and 13% as company, trade union lawyers or others (CGAE, 2008, p. 21). Law firm structures are closely linked to the legal services they offer, and the fact that in Spain the majority are small shows that most legal services are still provided on an individual basis; a very good sign, as it means that Spanish people have easy access to legal services even in small towns and rural areas. This can be confirmed by taking into account two features of the former system: the high number of lawyers and the low fees. Low barriers to entering the profession not only means a high number of lawyers but also affordable fees for most citizens within a system guided by bar associations setting minimum and maximum prices if legal aid is not granted. The first feature guarantees the even distribution of lawyers across the country and according to population, and this is the reason why 68% of Spanish lawyers work in Madrid, Barcelona, Andalucía, Catalonia and Valencia, apart from these cities and regions' economic and industrial power (CGAE, 2008, p. 21). This feature, in combination with the practical abolition of court fees, made access to justice affordable for everyone. In this regard, the reform undertaken by the government is shaking the grounds of the judicial system,[37] for which it will be challenged in the Spanish Constitutional Court.[38]

There are also plans to discharge functions from the courts in favor of other legal professionals like public notaries or those in charge of property registration, thus casting doubt on the need to employ a lawyer as well. Alternative methods of conflict resolution are being reinforced at the same time, driven by European harmonization in this area but also as a consequence of the changing role of judges in the Spanish legal system, which has shifted from a judge-centered model into a state service from which specific tasks might be left out (Cappelletti, 1981; Reale, 2011). In a context in which most citizens will be unable to afford to resort to the judicial system, ADR methods look like a good alternative, although it is highly debatable whether this carrot will be eaten in the absence of a stick.

All in all, Spanish lawyers are facing dramatic changes, along with those being experienced by academia and the justice system. They are expected to benefit from a more tailored legal education, but one which is significantly more expensive than previously, while trends brought about by post-industrialization and internationalization will doubtless become more marked, namely the predominance in lawyers' daily work of mediation and risk-prevention over litigation, and the merging of law firms due to increasing specialization on the one hand but in particular to market pressures on the other. In the short run, the relative raising of barriers to becoming a lawyer put forward by the recent legal reforms is likely to cause a fall in their numbers which will be intensified by other legal measures undertaken by the government on the grounds of the need to counteract the economic downturn. The establishing of high court fees is particularly troublesome since it seriously hampers access to judge-made justice in

Spain and clearly undermines its role in a democratic society (Galanter, 2010; Resnik, 1995; Santos, 2009, pp. 81–128) while reducing the legal profession's workload at the same time. Indeed, it creates a vicious circle, since the likely reduction in the number of lawyers triggered by the increase in court fees will only intensify problems of access to justice.

Conclusion

It is too soon to assess the only partially implemented system, apart from stating that there is now a basis for improvement. The reform has been driven by the Bologna process as well as by the acknowledgement that Spain was the only EU country whose sole requirement for becoming a lawyer was having a law degree. Professional control is now part of the Spanish system as a consequence of changes in legal education. Paradoxically, this may lead to a lowering of standards instead of improving the quality of lawyers insofar as the new system, hand-in-hand with the economic downturn, is likely to produce fewer lawyers than before and thus lower fees for bar associations. The legal profession could be said to be at a crossroads, and with it the whole judicial system. Nevertheless, the dynamism shown in recent years by bar associations in taking the lead to enhance the quality of legal services shows that they are aware of their role in Spanish society as well as in the global market. A clear example of this is the agreement between CGAE, acting in coordination with all Spanish bar associations, and International Transparency Spain to set up a *pro bono* lawyers register available to all professionals willing to cooperate with public interest litigation, in particular in cases where the transparency of public powers is in question.[39] This action was motivated by the desire to have a major impact on society and it is to be expected that the new educational model will be driven by the same dynamism, and that it will particularly benefit from the interaction among all stakeholders.

Acknowledgements

This paper has benefitted from the discussion held at the Oñati Workshop mentioned in the text and comments from the two anonymous reviewers, who the author wishes to thank, as well as all participants at the aforementioned workshop and, in particular, their co-organizers; all opinions and errors are her own. The work has also benefitted from financial help from FEDER and the Consellería de Educación e Ordenación Universitaria (Xunta de Galicia).

Notes

[1] The data provided by this study come from a nationwide survey devised by the company Metroscopia and conducted by Toharia, statistically representative of the Spanish population and made up of 1,000 adults of both sexes. The margin of error is roughly 3.2% and the confidence level is 95.5%. Further details and the survey questions and answers are provided in the study (CGAE, 2008, pp. 163–178).

[2] The 2010 survey ordered by the CGAE is published in their review, available at: http://www.cgae.es/portalCGAE/archivos/ficheros/1317831396000.pdf, and provides similar figures confirming Spanish citizens' high opinion of lawyers, as well as a further survey restricted to the provision of legal aid, published in 2012 with the V Report of the Legal Aid Observatory (137–154), available at: http://www.abogacia.es/wp-content/uploads/2012/07/V-Informe-del-Observatorio-de-Justicia-Gratuita.pdf, accessed 18 December 2012.

[3] *Ley 34/2006, de 30 de octubre, sobre el acceso a las profesiones de Abogado y Procurador de los Tribunales, Boletín Oficial del Estado* (hereafter, BOE) No. 260, 31 October 2006.

[4] This unification was achieved via the *Tuning* project which is based on the European Credit Transfer and Accumulation System (ECTS). Available at: http://www.unideusto.org/tuningeu/, accessed 18 December 2012.

[5] See http://www.mec.es/universidades/eees/index.html, accessed 18 December 2012.

[6] In Spain there are 83 *Colegios de abogados*, all of them members of the CGAE. In 2008 there were 118,775 practicing lawyers and 38,000 who were dormant (CGAE, 2008, p. 12).

[7] *Estatuto General de los Procuradores de los Tribunales*, passed by Royal Decree 1281/2002, 5 December.

[8] A university may offer law degrees on different campuses, one result of which is that the Spanish Ministry of Education website gives 175 facilities in different places. See http://www.mecd.gob.es/educacion-mecd/areas-educacion/universidades.html, accessed 7 December 2012.

[9] There are several routes to university, but to be admitted to a law faculty it was neither necessary to pass a specific exam nor to prove oneself to be a good student.

[10] Prices are fixed by regional governments within the guidelines provided by the *Conferencia General de Política Universitaria*, a state organization which covers them all. Law is one of the cheapest degrees, with a cost of around €10 per credit unit, according to data gathered in 2011 (Facts and Figures of the Spanish University System, 2011–2012, p. 58).

[11] There are 46 legal practice schools linked with bars, 11 with universities, 10 with both universities and bars, and four with private universities.

[12] They have instituted an Observatory which provides regular reports on the health of the legal aid system in Spain, with detailed statistics and analysis by independent experts: available at: http://www.abogacia.es/2012/07/03/informes-del-observatorio-de-la-justicia-gratuita/, accessed 18 December 2012.

[13] Article 44 of the *Real Decreto 658/2001, de 22 de junio, por el que se aprueba el Estatuto General de la Abogacía Española* (General Statute of Lawyers).

[14] This role can be illustrated by mentioning the founding of specific legal journals on the matter, such as the *REJIE: Revista Jurídica de Investigación e Innovación Educativa*, available at: http://www.eumed.net/rev/rejie.

[15] *Real Decreto 775/2011, de 3 de junio, por el que se aprueba el Reglamento de la Ley 34/2006, de 30 de octubre, sobre el acceso a las profesiones de Abogado y Procurador de los Tribunales* (Royal Decree 775/2011 passing the Regulation of Law 34/2006).

[16] Article 10 of the Royal Decree 755/2011.

[17] Article 3 of the Royal Decree 755/2011.

[18] See critiques by the XVIII Conference of Law Faculty Deans held in La Rioja on 10 February 2011, available at: http://www.unirioja.es/facultades_escuelas/fcjs/asambleadecanos/conclusiones10022011.pdf, accessed 18 December 2012.

[19] See Article 4 Royal Decree 755/2011 following Law 34/2006.

[20] See a list available at: http://www.abogacia.es/wp-content/uploads/2012/07/prueba-01.pdf, accessed 15 December 2012.

[21] See Article 14 Royal Decree 755/2011.

[22] See Article 15 Royal Decree 755/2011.

[23] See Article 17.1 Royal Decree 755/2011.

[24] See Article 19 Royal Decree 755/2011.

[25] See Article 17.2 and 3 Royal Decree 755/2011. The Spanish Ministry of Justice has already issued a mock exam discussed with various professionals and available at: http://www.mjusticia.gob.es/cs/

Satellite/es/1200666550200/Tramite_C/1288776144635/Detalle.html#informacion. The test will focus on deontology, professional liability, legal aid, law firm organization and statutes in general. Applicants' ability to resolve basic cases by applying their legal knowledge will be assessed by 25 questions.

[26] See Article 17.3 Royal Decree 755/2011.

[27] See Article 20.2 Royal Decree 755/2011.

[28] See *Disposición Adicional Tercera* of Royal Decree-Law 5/2012, 5 May, (BOE No. 56, 6 March 2012).

[29] Further information available at: http://www.numyspace.co.uk/~unn_mlif1/school_of_law/IJCLE/index.htm.

[30] Article 305 *Ley Orgánica del Poder Judicial.*

[31] BOE No. 31, 5 February 2011.

[32] A list of all currently available master's degrees and their prices can be downloaded from http://www.abogacia.es/wp-content/uploads/2012/07/prueba-01.pdf, accessed 18 December 2012.

[33] *Real Decreto-ley 14/2012, 20.4, de medidas urgentes de racionalización del gasto público en el ámbito educativo* (Royal Decree-law 14/2012, on urgent measures to rationalize public spending in the educational field), BOE No. 96, 21 April 2012.

[34] See Royal Decree-law 14/2012 in combination with *Real Decreto 1000/2012 de 29 de junio, que establece los umbrales de renta y patrimonio familiar y las cuantías y régimen de las becas y ayudas al estudio universitario* (Royal Decree 1000/2012, establishing income and family assets' thresholds, and amounts and regulations on scholarships and grants for university studies). BOE No. 260, 5 July 2012.

[35] For example, my faculty now only admits 180 first-year students while figures had reached 400 in previous years.

[36] See *Ley 10/2012, de 20 de noviembre, por la que se regulan determinadas tasas en el ámbito de la Administración de Justicia y del Instituto Nacional de Toxicología y Ciencias Forenses* (Law 10/2012, regulating specific fees within the Judicial System and the National Toxicology and Forensic Sciences Institute), BOE No. 280, 21 November 2012.

[37] See Art. 7 of Law 10/2012 on court fees made up of a fixed and a variable quantity. For example, a regular civil proceeding will cost €300 plus 0.5% of the value of the subject-matter of the proceedings. When assessing these fees, it must be taken into account that the minimum salary in Spain is €641.40 per month and legal aid is only granted to those earning less than twice this amount. See Royal Decree 1888/2011, of 30 December, fixing an inter-professional minimum salary for 2012. BOE No. 315, 31 December 2011.

[38] See http://www.diariojuridico.com/actualidad/noticias/el-psoe-recurrira-la-ley-de-tasas-judiciales-ante-el-tribunal-constitucional.html.

[39] Information is available at the following websites: www.abogados.es and www.cgae.es.

References

ANECA – Agencia Nacional de Evaluación de la Calidad (2005) *Libro Blanco Grado en Derecho.* Available at: http://www.aneca.es/modal_eval/docs/libroblanco_derecho_def.pdf, accessed 28 July 2012.

Barañano, M., Finkel, L. & Rodríguez, E. (2011) Procedencia socio-familiar, in: A. Ariño & R. Llopis (Eds) *¿Universidad sin clases? Condiciones de vida de los estudiantes universitarios en España (Eurostudent IV)* (Madrid, Ministerio de Educación), pp. 87–116. Available at: https://sede.educacion.gob.es/publiventa/descargas.action?f_codigo=14909&codigoOpcion=3, accessed 28 July 2012.

Bizcarrondo Ibáñez, A. (2002) El nuevo perfil del abogado, *Anuario de la Facultad de Derecho de la Universidad Autónoma de Madrid*, 6, pp. 271–282.

Calamandrei, P. (1926) *Demasiados abogados*, translated by J.R. Xirau (Madrid, Librería General de Victoriano Suárez).

Cappelletti, M. (Ed.) (1981) *Access to Justice and the Welfare State* (Florence, European University Institute).

CGAE – Colegio General de la Abogacía Española (2008) *La Abogacía española en daños y cifras 2008*. Available at: http://www.cgae.es/portalCGAE/archivos/ficheros/1225374383601.pdf, accessed 28 March 2012.
CGPJ – Consejo General del Poder Judicial (1997) *Libro Blanco de la Justicia* (Madrid, Consejo General del Poder Judicial).
Covarrubias, J. (1789) *Discurso sobre el estado de la abogacía en los tribunales de la nación* (Madrid).
Diario La Ley (2011) El CGPJ abre el debate sobre el acceso a la carrera judicial y se plantea solicitar que los opositores sean master, *Diario La Ley* [online], *Sección Hoy es Noticia*, p. 7551, 20 January. Available at: http://diariolaley.laley.es, accessed 27 July 2012.
Espiniella Menéndez, A. (2007) La adaptación de la asignatura de Derecho internacional privado al EEES en la Universidad de Oviedo, in: D. García San José (Ed.) *Innovación docente y calidad en la enseñanza de Ciencias Jurídicas en el Espacio Europeo de Educación Superior* (Oviedo, Laborum), pp. 63–86.
Friedman, L.M. (1994) Is there a modern legal culture?, *Ratio Juris*, 7, pp. 117–131.
Galanter, M. (2010) Access to justice in a world of expanding social capability, *Fordham Urban Law Journal*, 77, pp. 115–128.
Galindo Ayuda, F. (2012) La formación de los jueces, *Diario La Ley*, p. 7896. Available at: http://diariolaley.laley.es, accessed 27 July 2012.
Hendel, C.J. (2011) Doing business in Spain, including selecting and managing international counsel, *NYSBA International Law Practicum*, 24(1), pp. 38–42.
INE (2012) *Estadística de la Enseñanza Universitaria en España. Curso 2010–2011*, 28 May.
Kagan, R.L. (1981) *Lawsuits and Litigants in Castile: 1500–1700* (Chapel Hill, NC, The University of North Carolina Press).
Lilly, G.C. (1995) Law schools without lawyers? Winds of change in legal education, *Vanderbilt Law Journal*, 81, pp. 1421–1470.
Menkel-Meadow, C. (2012) Too many lawyers? Or should lawyers be doing other things?, in: E. Katvan, C. Silver & N. Ziv (Coords) (Eds) *Oñati Workshop: Too Many Lawyers? Facts, Reasons, Consequences and Solutions* Oñati, pp. 19–20, April.
Merryman, J.H. (1985) *The Civil Law Tradition. An Introduction to the Legal Systems of Western Europe and Latin America* (Stanford, CA, Stanford University Press).
Mullerat, R. (2002) El futuro de la abogacía y la formación del abogado, *Anuario de la Facultad de Derecho de la Universidad Autónoma de Madrid*, 6, pp. 283–306.
Pearce, R.G. & Levine, S.J. (2009) Rethinking the legal reform agenda: will raising the standards for bar admission promote or undermine democracy, human rights, and the rule of law?, *Fordham Law Review*, 77, pp. 1635–1663.
Pérez Lledó, J.A. (2002) Teoría y práctica en la enseñanza del Derecho, *Anuario de la Facultad de Derecho de la Universidad Autónoma de Madrid*, 6, pp. 197–268.
Pulido San Román, A. (2007) *Las Universidades hacia el 2020: un ejercicio de prospectiva*. Available at: http://www.antoniopulido.es/documentos/con070621.pdf, accessed 9 July 2012.
Reale, Ma.C (2011) 'Judge-only' justice v. collaborators: introduction, *Oñati Socio-Legal Series*, 1(9), *Social Science Research Network*. Available at: http://ssrn.com/abstract=1986720, accessed 27 July 2012.
Resnik, J. (1995) Many doors? Closing doors? Alternative dispute resolution and adjudication, *The Ohio State Journal of Dispute Resolution*, 10(2), pp. 211–265.
Ribstein, L.E. (2011) Practicing theory: legal education for the twenty-first century, *Iowa Law Review*, 96, pp. 1649–1676.
Salvador Cordech, P. (2012) Editorial. Per la renovació de l'ensenyament del dret a Espanya, *InDret*, 2. Available at: www.indret.com, accessed 9 July 2012.
Santos, B. de S. (2009) *Sociología jurídica crítica. Para un nuevo sentido común en el derecho* (Madrid, Trotta).
Sherr, A.H. (2001) The case of the common law in European legal education, *Social Science Research Network*. Available at: http://ssrn.com/abstract=1881609, accessed 9 July 2012.
Silver, C. (2009) Educating lawyers for the global economy: national challenges, *Social Science Research Network*. Available at: http://ssrn.com/abstract=1519387, accessed 26 July 2012.
Smits, J. (2011) European legal education, or: how to prepare students for global citizenship?, in: B. Akkermans & A.W. Heringa (Eds) *Educating European Lawyers* (Cambridge, Intersentia), pp. 43–64.

Toharia Cortés, J.J. (1987) *'¡Pleitos tengas!..' Introducción a la cultura legal española* (Madrid, Centro de investigaciones sociológicas).

Toharia Cortés, J.J. (2002) Las nuevas realidades sociales y la enseñanza del derecho, *Anuario de la Facultad de Derecho de la Universidad Autónoma de Madrid*, 6, pp. 115–125.

Toharia Cortés, J.J. & García de la Cruz Herrero, J.J. (2005) *La Justicia ante el espejo: 25 años de estudios de opinión del CGPJ* (Madrid, Consejo General del Poder Judicial).

Tomás Martínez, G. (2009) El futuro de la formación inicial de la abogacía en el nuevo marco profesional y académico, *Diario La Ley*, p. 7227. Available at: http://diariolaley.laley.es, accessed 27 July 2012.

Wilson, R.J. (2009) Western Europe: last holdout in the worldwide acceptance of clinical legal education, *German Law Journal*, 10(7), pp. 823–846.

The virtue of low barriers to becoming a lawyer: promoting liberal and democratic values

RUSSELL G. PEARCE* & SINNA NASSERI**
*Fordham University, School of Law, New York, USA
**New York, USA

ABSTRACT *This article offers a new perspective on how to determine whether barriers to practicing law are appropriate. It identifies a connection between those barriers and the role of legal services providers ('lawyers') in permitting individuals to obtain their basic political and economic rights in a liberal democracy. Democratic values require making legal services as equally available as possible to all citizens, while liberal values dictate that each individual has access in order to enforce human rights, compete in a market economy, and engage in a legal system grounded in the rule of law. Liberal and democratic values therefore require the lowest barriers to becoming a lawyer, consistent with the minimum requirements of competence and the recognition that the level of competence required will vary according to the type of legal services provided and the segment of the market served. Any contrary regulatory approach requires strong empirical support to overcome the presumption of low barriers that liberal and democratic values create. Accordingly, the article rejects as unpersuasive arguments for high barriers based on promoting the public good, avoiding rent-seeking, protecting consumers, advancing judicial efficiency, redressing lawyer misconduct, and preserving lawyers' high incomes.*

1. Introduction

With regard to the question of whether a society has 'too many lawyers?', our concern is not that a society has too many lawyers, but rather that it has too few. The preliminary thesis we present is relatively simple: lawyers provide vital functions in a liberal democracy and the values of a liberal democracy require making the barriers to becoming a lawyer as low as reasonably possible.[1] We do not restrict our consideration to those persons who today are formally denominated as lawyers. Instead, we employ the term to refer more broadly "to occupations that require nearly full-time expertise and commitment to analyzing, explaining, and arguing the law, whether they are expressly termed 'lawyers' or not" (Pearce & Levine, 2009, p. 1637). We use the term 'liberal democracy' to describe a political system that is democratic in the sense that the basis for governance is majority rule of equal citizens and liberal in the sense that it seeks to promote and protect individual freedom (Pearce & Levine, 2009, p. 1637). One component of liberalism is rule of law. Although rule of law is subject to a range of definitions, this Article "will focus in particular on the equal application of legal rules to all members of a society, whether or not they are part of the ruling elite" (Pearce & Levine, 2009, pp. 1636–1637). Given their commitment to individual freedom, liberal democracies rely on market economies.

In a liberal democracy, lawyers serve as 'civics teachers' (Green & Pearce, 2009). They provide necessary assistance to people in managing their personal and business affairs, in participating in political life, and in accessing the system of justice. In doing these things, lawyers have a particular responsibility for encouraging popular support for liberal democratic values. While some lawyers are public officials, most provide their services to private clients through the market. In order to promote the democratic value of equal access to knowledge and power, and the liberal values of protecting human rights and rule of law (which may conflict with democratic values), as many citizens as possible should be able to become a lawyer and as many citizens as possible should be able to afford to retain a lawyer when needed. The best way to achieve this goal is to permit only those barriers to law practice consistent with the minimum standard of consumer protection. Although the precise calibration of the appropriate barriers is beyond the scope of this article, they would provide a floor that would permit the market to determine the number of lawyers a liberal democracy needs, with exceptions for additional government-subsidized services for low- and middle-income persons. The appropriate level of these subsidies is also beyond the scope of this article, which focuses specifically on the effect of barriers to permission to practice law absent such subsidies.

We next consider five common arguments in support of high barriers to becoming a lawyer. These are: the lawyer's commitment to the public good, the danger of rent-seeking, the requirement of highly expert generalists to protect consumers, the need for judicial efficiency and redress of lawyer misconduct, and the protection of lawyers' livelihoods. We find these arguments unpersuasive. Low barriers satisfy the legitimate concerns that these arguments implicate. Beyond those concerns, these arguments rely on claims that have little or no empirical support. Given the virtues of low barriers, the burden of demonstrating the value of high barriers is on their proponents. Absent persuasive evidence for high barriers, therefore, societies should prefer low barriers in the interest of democratic and liberal values.

In performing this analysis, we rely more heavily on US sources because we are more familiar with them and because US commentators have traditionally focused on a political role for lawyers beyond valuing excellence and integrity in their work (Pearce, 2001, p. 386). Nonetheless, we do seek to consider sources outside the United States and argue that our claims apply in general to liberal democracies. We identify both the United States and South Africa as nations that create barriers that undermine liberal democracy and contrast the approach in the United Kingdom, which appears to be on the road to developing a system of low barriers more consistent with liberal democratic values.

2. The virtue of low barriers

Dean Roscoe Pound (1953, p. 5) described lawyers as "pursuing a learned art as a common calling in the spirit of public service – no less a public service because it may incidentally be a means of livelihood." This description captures how the provision of legal services has both public and private dimensions. As this section explains, the public dimension of the delivery of legal services is connected to the exercise of political and economic rights in a democracy. At the same time, in a liberal democracy, the delivery of most legal services occurs through the market, and not through government action. To maximize the availability of legal services – and to best promote liberal democratic values – the barriers to providing legal services should be as low as possible consistent with the minimum standards of consumer protection.

The public dimension of lawyers' work

In his 1921 and 1928 reports on legal education for the Carnegie Foundation, Alfred Z. Reed described the importance of low barriers. He explained that becoming a lawyer was "admission to our governing class" (Reed, 1921, p. 56). Reed observed that:

> Practicing lawyers do not merely render to the community a social service, which the community is interested in having them render well. They are part of the governing mechanism of the state. Their functions are in a broad sense political. This is not due primarily to the circumstance a large proportion of our legislative and administrative officials and virtually all of our judges, are chosen from among this practically ruling class.... It springs even more fundamentally from the fact, early discovered, that private individuals cannot secure justice without the aid of a special professional order to represent and to advise them. (Reed, 1921, p.3).

In identifying lawyers' work as having a vital political dimension, Reed offered a perspective that historically dominated the thinking of American legal ethicists. In the United States, the first legal ethicists built

> on the insights of the Framers and of leading jurists like Justice Story and Chancellor Kent [to] posit] that lawyers, as professionals, were skilled at perceiving and promoting the public good and would ensure that society balanced the interests of individuals with the public good. (Pearce & Wald, 2012, p. 517)

In 1854, George Sharswood, one of the fathers of American legal ethics, explained that lawyers served both liberal and democratic goals. In democratic government, lawyers "'fill the highest public stations', including dominance of the legislative process, and exclusive administration of the judicial system as advocates and judges" (Pearce, 1992, p. 255). As private practitioners and community leaders, they "counsel[ed] the ignorant, defend[ed] the weak and oppressed, and ... [stood] forth on all occasions as the bulwark of private rights against the assaults of power" (Sharswood, 1907, pp. 53–54). Whether "providing counsel to clients, [or] making arguments in court to judge and jury" (Pearce, 1992, p. 255), lawyers "diffuse[ed] sound principles among the people" (Sharswood, 1907, pp. 30, 54) and brought the law "home so nearly to every man's fireside" (pp. 30–31).

Later, when the American Bar Association (ABA) codified legal ethics, this understanding of lawyers' central political role continued. The ABA's 1908 *Canons of Ethics* asserted that "[t]he future of the republic, to a great extent depends upon [lawyers'] maintenance of justice pure and unsullied". The ABA's 1969 *Model Code of Professional Responsibility* declared that "[l]awyers, as guardians of the law, play a vital role in the preservation ... and [t]he continued existence of a free and democratic society". The ABA's 1983 *Model Rules of Professional Conduct* called lawyers "public citizen[s] having special responsibility for the quality of justice" and "play[ing] a vital role in the preservation of society".

Another classic exposition of this perspective is the 1958 American Bar Association–American Association of Law Schools joint report on Professional Responsibility, for which the famous legal philosopher Lon Fuller was the reporter. Bruce Green and Russell Pearce (2009) have described the Report's conception of the lawyer's role as a 'civics teacher'. The Report describes

> [p]rivate practice [as] a form of public service when it is conducted with appreciation of, and a respect for, the larger framework of government of which it forms a part, including under the term government ... voluntary forms of self-regulation. (ABA & Association of American Law Schools, 1958, p. 1162)

As a counselor and litigator, the lawyer maintains "the integrity of those fundamental processes of government and self-government upon which the successful functioning of our society depends" (p. 1162).[2] Indeed, "democratic and constitutional government is tragically dependent on voluntary ... co-operation in the maintenance of its fundamental processes and forms" (p. 1162). In both private and public roles, lawyers promote "voluntary cooperation" and "help shape the growth and development of public attitudes toward fair procedures and due process", in order to prevent the "inevitable tendency for practice to drift downward to the level of those ... whose experience of life has not taught them the vital importance of preserving just and proper forms of procedure" (p. 1216).

Perhaps the best-known inquiry into the role of lawyers in a liberal democracy has been that of Alexis de Tocqueville. He famously struggled with the question of how the United States could successfully maintain a liberal democracy without declining into a tyranny of the majority. He identified the key role of lawyers and observed that they "form the political upper class ... of society" (Tocqueville, 1840, p. 268). On one hand, "their interest ... naturally pulls them toward the people" (p. 270). Lawyers would only have such a prominent role in a democracy, and not an aristocracy or oligarchy where others would fill the role of the "political upper class" (p. 268). On the other hand, lawyers would not have the same powerful role without a commitment to the liberal values of rule of law and individual rights. Tocqueville observes that lawyers

> are the masters of a necessary and not widely understood science; they serve as arbiters between the citizens; and the habit of directing the blind passions of the litigants toward the objective gives them a certain scorn for the judgment of the crowds. (Tocqueville, 1840, p. 264).

Tocqueville described how lawyers promoted both liberal and democratic values:

> There is hardly a political question in the United States which does not sooner or later turn into a judicial one.... As most public men are or have been lawyers, they apply their legal habits and turn of mind to the conduct of affairs. Juries make all classes familiar with this. So legal language is pretty well adopted into common speech; the spirit of the law ... infiltrates through society right down to the lowest ranks, till finally the whole people contracted some of the ways and tastes of a magistrate. (Tocqueville, 1840, p. 270)

Many other commentators have identified a similar function of lawyers. The structural-functionalist (Abel, 1989, p. 15) approach of Emile Durkheim (1957) and Talcott Parsons (1954, pp. 370, 384), for example, identified lawyers as intermediaries between the people and the law, and suggested a role that is central in a liberal democracy. Commentators in legal scholarship today continue to explore the political dimensions of lawyers' work from a variety of perspectives.[3] Halliday *et al.* (2007, p. 4), for example, have noted that lawyers have a strong history of supporting "freedoms of the person, speech, movement, property and association". They find that

> [h]istorical and sociological studies demonstrate the legal professions often were active builders of the institutions of liberal politics. In a variety of ways, legal professions sought the moderation of state power via judicial independence, the creation and mobilisation of a politically engaged civil society, and the vesting of rights in subjects as citizens who would be protected by judiciaries. (Halliday *et al.*, pp. 1–2)[4]

Nonetheless, at the same time, other commentators ignore or minimize the political role of lawyers. They view lawyers from a guild perspective that focuses largely on the integrity and excellence of lawyers' work (Pearce, 2001, p. 382, n. 5); a Marxist perspective of lawyers as marginal to politics (Abel, 1989, p. 15); a Weberian view of lawyers as market actors seeking a "competitive advantage within a relatively free market" through professional organization (p. 15), or a skeptical understanding that because lawyers pursue their own self-interest and not the public good they have withdrawn from their political role (Pearce, 2006, p. 1339).

While a more detailed response to these commentators is beyond the scope of this article, we hold with those commentators who find a central role for lawyers in a liberal democracy. We make this argument as a descriptive matter – and for purposes of this article do not reach the debate regarding whether lawyers have an adequate ideological commitment to the public good, or serve their own interests or those of business clients (Pearce, 1995; Halliday & Karpik, 1997, p. 53). We agree with Reed, Fuller, Tocqueville and others that lawyers do indeed play a significant political role. As a result of both their expertise and their work, lawyers tend to serve in disproportionate numbers as formal political leaders (Shepherd, 2003, pp. 652–654; Halliday, 1989, p. 375; Heinz *et al.*, 1993, pp. 127–132). They also serve as informal leaders both in their communities and through their everyday work, in which they are civics teachers who help shape how clients and community understand liberal democratic values (e.g. Pearce, 2006; Green & Pearce, 2009) Accordingly, both in their public and private capacities, lawyers in fact serve as intermediaries between the people and the law. In this role, lawyers influence how well a liberal democracy provides democratic participation in political and economic institutions and protects human rights and rule of law, whether lawyers consciously seek those goals or not.

Why lawyers' political role requires low barriers in a liberal democracy

Given this role, liberal democratic values require that the opportunity to become a lawyer and to obtain the services of lawyer be widely available. Democratic values require that citizens have an equal opportunity to become a lawyer and join the political leadership class. Democratic values also weigh in favor of providing citizens with an equal opportunity to gain from lawyers the legal knowledge and assistance they need to participate effectively in political and economic life. Liberal values weigh in the same direction. Citizens need to access the legal knowledge and assistance of lawyers to vindicate their individual rights, especially when those rights conflict with the will of the majority. Rule of law further requires that citizens have access to lawyers in order to obtain equal justice from the legal system, even when justice conflicts with the will of the majority. Broad access to becoming a lawyer and to obtaining a lawyer's services helps disseminate liberal democratic values throughout the population.

In applying this analysis to the qualifications for becoming a lawyer, we return to the work of Alfred Z. Reed. First, he recognized that barriers to becoming a lawyer should be as low as possible. He explained that "democratic ideals" necessitated "that participation in making and administration of the law shall be kept accessible to Lincoln's plain people" (Pearce & Levine, 2009, p. 1655). As a result, the "general education requisite for admission to ... public service [as a lawyer should not exceed] the level that can be reached by the average man" (Reed, 1921, pp. 52–53). Second, Reed observed that the market for legal services was differentiated. Accordingly, the delivery of legal services should not be subject to a unitary legal profession (p. 60). Consumers of legal services have a range of needs and a range of resources. This differentiated market, in Reed's view, demanded "lawyers of differing skills and qualifications serving different purposes and different elements in society" (Stevens, 1983, p. 114).

Reed's principles accord with liberal democratic values. To make the ability to provide or to obtain legal services as broadly available as possible, the only barrier to legal practice should be the minimum standard of consumer protection – that the provider can provide the legal services competently and honestly.[5] Although the precise calibration of such minimum standards is beyond the scope of this article,[6] delivery of simple legal services might require only a few weeks or months of legal training, or it might require allowing a lawyer to create procedures for, and supervise, non-lawyer service providers. More complicated services, such as representation in court, would require mastery of court procedures, as well as some minimum amount of general legal knowledge. A competitive market would provide additional protection to consumers. Efficient markets provide consumers with the best quality services at the lowest cost. An efficient legal services market would include products, such as private referral or rating services, to help consumers evaluate the quality of lawyers (Pearce, 1995, p. 1273).

In addition, liberal democratic values would suggest that the range of acceptable requirements could depend upon the level of education and resources in a society. In Stevens, 1983, p. 184 n. 42, the nineteenth-century United States, for example, where free public education through high school was not generally available (Goldin, 1999, p. 4), lawyers representing clients in court had to satisfy only minimal standards and did not even need a high-school education (Barton, 2011, pp. 111–113). During this period, many distinguished lawyers, such as Abraham Lincoln and John Marshall, lacked formal legal education, and the legal system as a whole functioned reasonably well (Barton, 2011; Pearce & Levine 2009, pp. 1654–1660).

3. Unpersuasive defense of high barriers

Using the examples of the United States and South Africa, this section explains how high barriers transgress liberal and democratic values. Next, it evaluates arguments commentators have used to justify these harms and finds little support for them.

Harms of high barriers

The United States and South Africa offer examples of liberal democracies with high barriers to becoming a lawyer. The barriers undermine both democratic and liberal values. They make it more difficult than necessary for people to become lawyers and skew membership in the legal profession toward those with privilege in society. Similarly, high barriers make it more challenging for those without privilege to obtain legal services (Barton, 2011, pp. 144–146). This deprives them of an equal opportunity to participate in both democratic government and the market economy, to obtain justice from the courts, and to protect their human rights. High barriers also undermine popular commitment to liberal democratic values.

In the United States today, the barriers to becoming a lawyer include a four-year college degree, the Law School Admission Test (LSAT), three years of law school, a bar exam, and a moral character requirement.[7] The cost of the three years of law school tuition (without even considering living costs) averages $105,000 for private school and $60,000 for public school (Law school tuition soars, 2011). These requirements are the same for all lawyers, from those who prepare the simplest wills to those who litigate the most complicated antitrust cases. Several states also allow for the practice of 'reading law', in which lawyers integrate work experience in a legal office with independent study of the law (Moeser & Huismann, 2012, pp. 8–12) According to a 2003 estimate, only a few hundred students nationwide were pursuing this route to the bar (McDonald, 2003). The ABA and National Conference of Bar Examiners strongly discourage this practice, maintaining that "Neither private study, correspondence study, law office training, age, nor experience should be substituted for law school education" (Moeser & Huismann, 2012).

High barriers in the United States lead to two key types of harms. First, they restrict the type of people who become lawyers (Winston *et al.*, 2011, p. 82). In the legal profession, persons with privilege are over-represented and those who are less privileged are under-represented. For instance, racial minorities made up more than one-third of the United States population in 2010 (Hixson *et al.*, 2011, p. 2), but only 11.6% of lawyers (Chambliss, 2011, p. 10).[8] And the American legal education system skews the same way: racial minorities[9] and low-income people[10] are under-represented among law students. For example, a UCLA Law School study found that "of people in their twenties, those from families with incomes over $200,000 were about fifty times more likely to end up as students at [the] law school than were those from families below the poverty line" (Sander, 1997, p. 475).

Second, high barriers restrict the type of people who are able to purchase legal services. According to Deborah Rhode (2004, p. 5), "about four-fifths of the civil legal needs of the poor, and two-to three-fifths of the needs of middle-income individuals, remain unmet". Further, "[o]nly one lawyer is available to serve approximately 9,000 low-income persons, compared with one for every 240 middle- and upper-income Americans" (Rhode, 2003, pp. 47–48).

South Africa has similar high barriers and similar harms. In South Africa, the barriers include a college degree, brief practical training, and an apprenticeship (Pearce & Levine, 2009, p. 1650). Though seemingly less restrictive than the barriers in the United States, South African barriers constrain diversity in the legal profession and limit the populace's access to justice.

The white minority dominates the legal profession in South Africa. Although blacks, coloreds, and Asians are 90.6% of the population, they represent only 25% of lawyers (Pearce & Levine, 2009, p. 1650). The high barriers to entry cause this disparity for many reasons. Although blacks are approximately 50% of current law students (p. 1652), this number is still below their percentage of the population and indicates that equality in the legal profession is far from realization. Similarly, for example, the requirement of an apprenticeship with a practicing attorney has "had the practical effect of keeping non-white law graduates from obtaining admission" because "candidate attorneys [must] find a lawyer or law firm [willing to] offer them [a clerkship]" and "the legal profession historically has been comprised overwhelmingly of white attorneys in a racially segregated legal system" (p. 1652, n. 67).

In addition to attorneys, South Africa provides a limited number of alternative legal services practitioners: "approximately 350 'community advice centers', and 56 'paralegal advice offices', some of the staff of which have completed 'an intensive three month training program', provide advice 'at the community level', especially 'in rural areas'" (Pearce and Levine, 2009, p. 1650).

Even with this additional group that falls within our definition of lawyers, South Africa fails to meet the test of liberal and democratic values in providing legal services. David McQuoid-Mason (2012, p. 26) estimates that as much as 70% of the population is unable to afford a lawyer. Strikingly, for example, "about 10,000 people a year are … sentenced to terms of imprisonment without being legally represented" (McQuoid-Mason, 2012, p.7).

All these statistics illustrate how high barriers function to reinforce the privileged position of white South Africans and to create a barrier to equality for black and colored South Africans.

Why efforts to justify these harms are unpersuasive

In countless books and articles, commentators have sought to justify high barriers. This article briefly considers these arguments and explains why they are unpersuasive.

The lawyer's commitment to the public good. Some commentators argue that high barriers are necessary to limit lawyers to those who will, in Roscoe Pound's (1953, p. 5) terms, "purs[ue their legal careers] as a common calling in the spirit of public service".[11] Commentators have identified a range of qualifications that arguably promote this spirit, including a liberal arts education (ABA, 1929, pp. 605, 621–624), a multi-year Socratic legal education (Robinson, 2011), or a required professional responsibility course.

Undoubtedly, commitment to public service has potential benefits in a liberal democracy. If lawyers as civics teachers view their work as a "calling in the spirit of public service," they are probably more likely to work to promote both democratic and liberal values. On the other hand, the arguments for each of the proposed requirements are based on supposition. There is no persuasive evidence that a liberal arts education, Socratic legal education, or professional responsibility course make it more likely that lawyers will view their work as a "calling in the spirit of public service" (Pound, 1953, p. 5).[12]

Moreover, anecdotal evidence is to the contrary. Some of the greatest members of the US legal profession, such as Chief Justice John Marshall (Stevens, 1983, p. 11, n. 14; Federal Judicial Center, 2012) or Abraham Lincoln (Stevens, 1983, p. 19, n. 72, p. 25; Law school tuition soars, 2011), never completed a liberal arts education, Socratic legal education, or a professional responsibility course.[13] Anecdotal evidence also suggests that these educational barriers have proven ineffective in inculcating 'the spirit of public service'. Bar leaders, for example, complain of a "crisis of professionalism" (Pearce, 1995, p. 1263) resulting from lawyers' declining commitment to the public good.

Accordingly, there is no evidence to support arguments that high barriers promote an ethic of public service.

Danger of rent-seeking. Some commentators worry that lawyers are "parasitic rent-seekers" (Galanter, 1994, p. 636) who seek to manipulate law and the legal system to their own benefit or the benefit of their clients and who accordingly exert a negative influence on economic growth (Magee, 2010, p. 2). They argue, for example, that rent-seeking lawyers promote excessive lawsuits, too many laws and regulations, and economic inefficiency (p. 3). High barriers could reduce the number of lawyers and therefore the opportunity for rent-seeking (p. 3) or could exclude those with a propensity for becoming rent-seekers from the pool of lawyers.

As an initial matter, the factual grounding for the claim that lawyers are rent seekers is weak. Economists and sociologists have examined this claim at length and the evidence is equivocal at best.[14] But even assuming that lawyers are rent-seekers, the arguments for high barriers are unpersuasive. As noted above, high barriers have not proven effective in identifying lawyers with a greater or lesser commitment to the public good and would therefore be unlikely to exclude lawyers who have an inclination to rent-seeking. Similarly weak is the argument that high barriers will minimize rent-seeking solely by reducing the number of lawyers (Magee, 2010, p. 3). Other economists have argued, for example, that high barriers and the resulting oligopoly on the provision of legal services promote rent-seeking. They suggest that high barriers create "socially perverse incentives for attorneys in their collective behavior as an interest group to support inefficient regulatory, liability, patent, and other policies that preserve and enhance their wealth" (Winston *et al.*, 2011, p. 5). Lowering barriers would make the market for legal services more efficient by "allow[ing] a greater number of qualified participants to spur competition in the legal services market and reduce legal fees, creating substantial economic welfare benefits" (p. 85).

Consumer protection requires a profession of highly expert generalists. Some commentators argue that the high barriers associated with highly expert generalists are necessary to protect consumers. They reject the idea of differentiated legal services and a differentiated legal services market. They argue that all legal problems are complex and require the attention of an attorney who has undergone extensive training.[15] Accordingly, even legal matters that appear to be relatively simple, like an uncontested divorce, implicate countless rights and liabilities (Robinson, 2011). Only a highly trained professional can navigate this complex web to prevent possible unintended and profound consequences (Robinson, 2011). Commentators argue that as a result of this complexity, the information asymmetry between lawyers and consumers of legal services, as well as the potential for irremediable harm, require protecting consumers through *ex ante* barriers rather than through market competition and *ex post* remedies (Barton, 2011, pp. 147–150).

This argument suffers from a number of weaknesses. First, as Benjamin Barton (2011, p. 148) observes, "[n]either information asymmetry nor irremediable harms is present in most areas of legal practice". Second, the limited empirical evidence that exists does not support the claim that high barriers provide necessary consumer protection. Studies in England and Wales, for example, found that "nonlawyers provided better legal service in civil matters such as welfare benefits, debt, housing, and employment than solo and small-firm practitioners provided" (Winston *et al.*, pp. 86–87).[16] In a US study, Herbert Kritzer (1998, pp. 76, 108, 148, 190) compared lawyers and non-lawyers in representing clients in administrative proceedings and found that "formal training (in the law) is less crucial than is day-to-day experience".[17] Another study in California of "people who had obtained assistance in litigating pro se, [found that] a higher percentage of those who had obtained help from paralegals were satisfied than of those who received help from lawyers" (Selinger, 1996, pp. 879, 910).

Third, the argument for a unified legal profession of highly expert generalists necessarily relies on the assumption that the legal services market is unitary. This assumption is false. Consumers with different resources and needs seek different levels of legal services in today's market. Indeed, treating the legal services market as undifferentiated and requiring only one level of services leaves many individuals without any access to legal services. In a liberal democracy, legal services are sold on the market. In the market, low- and middle-income consumers will never be able to afford the same quality of services as wealthy individuals and organizations.

Some commentators nevertheless prefer to treat legal services as a unitary market because in theory low- and middle-income people would receive the same quality of legal services as more privileged consumers.[18] In reality, though, the legal services market is not unitary. Accordingly, the choice is not between equal or inferior services for low- and middle-income consumers. The choice is between no services in a unitary market or affordable services in a differentiated market (Rhode 2004, p. 5, 2003, pp. 47–48) Of course, in all markets, wealthy individuals and organizations are able to purchase higher quality goods and services than low- and middle-income persons. The answer is not to deny low- and middle-income persons services altogether but to provide the greatest amount of access possible through the market and to pursue institutional strategies to maximize the possibility of equal justice. (Pearce, 2004). As Deborah Rhode (2004, p. 4) notes, "Equal justice may be an implausible aspiration, but more accessible legal institutions are within our reach."

Judicial efficiency and redress of lawyer misconduct. We group these arguments because they are similar and have similar responses. In essence, commentators have claimed that low barriers would permit legal services providers who do not understand procedural law to interfere with the efficient administration of justice (Mystal, 2011) and also to provide legal services without being subject to liability for malpractice and discipline (Elefant 2011). These objections have little merit. Requiring legal services providers to understand procedural law before they can practice in court would fall squarely within the minimum requirements of even a low barrier to practice. So, too, would liability for malpractice and discipline.

Protection of lawyers' livelihoods. Some commentators endorse high barriers and limiting the number of lawyers in order to protect relatively high incomes for lawyers. They argue that the legal market is saturated,[19] and that steps should be taken to reduce the supply of lawyers in order to protect the profession's average wage (Greenbaum, 2010). Critics[20] (See Grassley, 2011; Mystal, 2010) have singled out the ABA in particular for "continu[ing] to allow unneeded new schools to open and refus[ing] to properly regulate the schools" (Greenbaum, 2010). They argue that the ABA should use its accreditation power more forcefully to restrict the amount of new law schools and to close some existing schools.[21]

This argument suffers from three weaknesses. First, limiting freedom to pursue an occupation and to purchase services freely violates the principles of liberal democracy. Second, even if it did not, low – and not high – barriers would actually benefit lawyers in the long run. Lowering barriers would likely lead to competition that would encourage the legal services industry to innovate to include low and middle-income consumers and potentially create more jobs.[22] Lowering barriers would also reduce the cost of legal training and therefore would similarly "make it possible for [lawyers] to afford to work at salaries that would permit the development of new law practices that could serve the large number of low and middle income consumers who cannot currently afford to purchase legal services" (Pearce, 2012b). Last, while lower barriers and increased competition would probably decrease the income of some lawyers, lower barriers would also

> benefit lawyers and people who are thinking about becoming a lawyer in other ways. By reducing earnings premiums, deregulating entry into the legal profession would reduce the likelihood that some individuals make a socially and privately suboptimal career choice to become a lawyer in pursuit of high earnings. (Winston *et al.*, 2011, p. 90).

4. Experiments in lower barriers

As a counter to the negative examples of the United States and South Africa, we offer the positive examples of developments in England and Wales. With a history of somewhat lower barriers and recent developments that significantly lower barriers, the experience of England and Wales tentatively suggests that moving in the direction of liberal democratic values can prove workable. We also draw attention to parallel developments in Australia and increasing interest in low barriers in the United States.

First, the general requirement in the United Kingdom for being a lawyer who can provide a wide range of services, such as a solicitor or barrister, is more in accord with liberal and democratic values. In contrast to the United States, which requires three years of expensive graduate education, England and Wales only require an undergraduate degree in law (or college degree plus a year of legal training), together with practical training and an apprenticeship (Law Society, 2012). Moreover, in England and Wales, undergraduate education is more widely available and less expensive than in the United States. South Africa has general requirements similar to those in England and Wales, but its barriers are less liberal and democratic both because a smaller percentage of the population attends college and because, as noted above, the racial majority is significantly under-represented in legal education.[23]

Second, especially since the 1980s, England and Wales have made it significantly easier for those who are not solicitors and barristers to provide legal services; i.e. to fit within this article's definition of a lawyer. As a historical matter, the United Kingdom, including England and Wales, never erected the high barriers to providing transactional representation that the United States created in the twentieth century. As a result,

> in the UK, there have been very few restrictions on offering legal advice and assistance. Most legal services can be offered by anyone for free or for a fee. Some important legal services are "reserved" in the sense that only authorised practitioners may offer them. However, the list is relatively short: conveyancing (real property transfer), probate, preparation for litigation, advocacy and notary work. By contrast, the number of authorised practitioners who may offer these services is relatively large and includes not only lawyers but also, depending on the work, licensed conveyancers, legal executives, patent agents, banks and insurance companies. (Whelan, 2009, pp. 465, 471)

Indeed, today "the single largest providers of legal advice are probably the Citizen Advice Bureaus, which are actually staffed by lay volunteers" (Kritzer, 1999, p. 744). Tesco, the UK analog to Wal-Mart, began to offer low-priced legal services pertaining to "divorce, employment and business online" in 2004 (Whelan, 2009, p. 491).[24]

Moreover, in an effort to promote economic liberalism,[25] the trend since the 1980s has been to broaden the extent of legal services offered by those who are neither solicitors nor barristers. In 1985, for example, the government abolished "the solicitors' conveyancing monopoly" (Whelan, 2009, p. 472). Predictably, as "[l]icensed conveyancers [came to] undertake work that had yielded fifty percent of their collective income", the result was "[i]ncreased competition [and] lower prices" (p. 473). Today, the liberalization continues. Following the Clementi Report and the Legal Services Act of 2007, people who are not solicitors will be able "to invest in and own law firms" (Flood, 2011, p. 514). Moreover, the new regulatory structure permits the creation of Alternative Business Structures that can "provide any type of legal services, both reserved and unreserved, as well as other related services such as insurance, surveying and so on[; can] raise capital by listing on the stock exchange" and can consist of both solicitors and other service providers, or even no solicitors at all (Whelan, 2009, pp. 481–482).

This framework better serves liberal and democratic values. Lower barriers for becoming a legal services provider make more democratic the opportunity to become a formal or informal political leader. By making it easier to obtain legal services, lower barriers make more democratic the provision of legal services and the opportunity to participate effectively in political and economic life. This was the driving force behind the legal services reforms of the past decade in the United Kingdom. Lord Falconer, then serving as Secretary of State for Constitutional Affairs, outlined in a 2005 White Paper his 'vision of a legal services market ... that is responsive, flexible, and puts the consumer first". Since "legal services are crucial to people's ability to access justice", they "must therefore be regulated and made available in such a way as to meet the needs of the public – individuals, families, and businesses" (Department for Constitutional Affairs, 2005, p. 7). Wider availability of legal services also serves the liberal end of assisting citizens in vindicating their individual rights and obtaining equal justice from the legal system. Last, this broad access holds the potential to better disseminate liberal and democratic values. We do recognize, however, that not all commentators view these developments as wholly positive and the long-term effects have yet to be measured.[26]

Australia has also loosened restrictions on the provision of legal services in light of these concerns. In 2004, the Australian state of New South Wales passed the Legal Profession Act (LPA), which allows legal service providers to "incorporate and provide legal services either alone or alongside other legal service providers who may, or may not be 'legal practitioners'".[27] The purpose of the 2004 LPA is to foster liberal and democratic values: it aims to regulate legal practice "in the interests of the administration of justice and for the protection of law clients and the public generally" (LPA 2004, 1.1:3). Australia's reforms have had a substantial impact: Slater and Gordon, a large law firm with 20 offices nationwide, made Australian history in 2007 by placing millions of shares of the company up for trade on the Australian Stock Exchange.[28] Early indications suggest that the quality of legal services has not diminished (Mark, 2009; Mark & Gordon, 2009).

At the same time, the United States boasts a lively academic discourse about lowering barriers. McGinnis and Mangas (2012) suggest that undergraduate institutions offer a major in law, which (combined with a year of apprenticeship after graduation[29]) would allow students to sit for the bar without incurring the exorbitant costs of graduate education. They expressly argue that an undergraduate degree in law would provide the benefits of a liberal arts education through "an interdisciplinary education, mixing elements of social science and humanities with legal doctrine" (p. 42). In addition to an undergraduate degree, their model would also permit alternative JD programs. Like McGinnis and Mangas, Pearce (2012a, b) promotes an undergraduate law degree, a one-year intensive course for those who complete a different undergraduate degree, and a shortened JD degree rather than the current three-year program.

Similarly, within the last two decades, many legal scholars have argued for lowering barriers more generally. Thomas Morgan (1977, 2010), Deborah L. Rhode (1996) and Russell G. Pearce (1995), and more recently Larry Ribstein (2007, 2010), Gillian Hadfield (2011), Benjamin Barton (2011) and Renee Newman Knake (2012), among others,[30] have argued for significant deregulation of the legal profession. Knake's influential work, for example, argues that the prohibition on corporation ownership of law practices both violates the United States Constitution and impedes access to services for low- and middle-income consumers.[31] Knake (2012, p. 9) predicts a shift to permitting corporate ownership, citing the ongoing litigation against the corporate ownership ban in New York, New Jersey, Connecticut and North Carolina. Morgan (2010), Pearce (1995), Hadfield (2011), Barton (2011) and Ribstein (2007, 2010) argue that law firms already function as profit-seeking businesses and accordingly deregulation will increase access to, and improve the quality of, legal services without corrupting the legal profession.

Nonetheless, proponents of high barriers continue to have great influence. The leadership of the American bar persists in promoting high barriers in developing countries (Pearce & Levine, 2009) and Japan, South Korea, and Taiwan are engaged in transitions to graduate legal education (McGinnis & Mangas, 2012, pp. 26–28). We hope that the framework presented in this article offers a new way of evaluating such proposals in terms of their effectiveness in either promoting or undermining liberal and democratic values.

5. Conclusion

Low barriers to becoming a lawyer, consistent with minimum standards of competence in differentiated markets for legal services, best promote liberal and democratic values. Low barriers make it easier to become a lawyer and to purchase legal services. In doing so, they provide more equal access to political and economic institutions, and greater protection for human rights and the rule of law. High barriers, as in the examples of the United States and South Africa, favor those who are already privileged in society and disadvantage those who are less privileged, without demonstrably improving the quality of legal services. Proponents of high barriers have failed to offer persuasive evidence to the contrary.

We acknowledge that there is only very limited empirical research, if any, on basic issues we have raised, including exactly what specific minimum standards are necessary for consumer protection and the precise ways in which lower barriers promote liberal and democratic values. In the absence of definitive research on these topics, we conclude that the weight of liberal and democratic values favors low barriers and requires that any defense of high barriers must satisfy the burden of persuasion.

Determining a more calibrated approach requires further research into both the efficacy of barriers to the delivery of services and their implications for liberal and democratic values. First, research could identify the specific training required to resolve competently different types of legal problem, as well as to promote commitment to ethics and the public good among legal services providers. For example, research could prove or disprove whether an undergraduate liberal arts education is essential to providing all types of legal services or to maintaining a commitment to ethics and the public good. Second, research into jurisdictions that increase or decrease barriers, or between jurisdictions with higher and lower barriers, could help illuminate the extent to which barriers correlate with more equal access to legal or economic power. For example, although England and Wales have historically provided less economic mobility than the United States, they have in recent years surpassed the United States (DeParle, 2012). Economic mobility is, of course, a liberal and democratic goal. Given the importance of lawyers to both political and economic opportunity, our thesis would predict this result in light of the significantly lower barriers to providing legal services in England and Wales. But whether low barriers to legal services have indeed had a meaningful influence on this result requires further investigation.

Acknowledgments

Russ Pearce presented drafts of this article at the Oñati International Institute for the Sociology of Law workshop on *Too Many Lawyers: Facts, Reasons, Consequences, and Solutions* and a Chicago-Kent Law School faculty workshop. We are very grateful to the participants in these workshops for their extremely helpful comments and suggestions. We also owe a special thanks to John McGinnis for his helpful insights. Last, we could not have completed this article without the extraordinary contributions of reference librarian Laurence Abraham and research assistants Ross Miller and Ademisope Mojiminiyi.

Notes

[1] The legitimacy of liberal and democratic values is beyond the scope of this Article. See, for example, Pearce (2006, pp. 1358–1365).

[2] Cf. Abel (1987, p. 467), explaining that "[t]o assert a legal claim is to perform a vital civic obligation".

[3] See Pearce (2001, pp. 385–387, 2006, pp. 1354–1356), Pearce & Wald (2011), Green & Pearce (2009, p. 1212), Breyer (2000, pp. 8, 11, 15, 16, 18, 21–22), Simon (2000, pp. 63, 80, 118–120), Wendel (2010, pp. 89–92), Ziv (2009, pp. 1767–1770) and Luban (2009, p. 9).

[4] See also Abel (1987, p. 454), noting that "[l]itigation is an important form of political activity: courts exercise political authority, modify substantive laws, and allocate resources".

[5] Of course, minimal standards of consumer protection would also require methods for addressing lawyers' violation of ethical and legal obligations (Barton, 2011, pp. 147–151).

[6] Indeed, we note that some commentators, such as Milton Friedman, rejected any occupational licensing requirements on the ground that they artificially increased the price and reduced the quality of professional services (Friedman, 1962, pp. 137–160).

[7] These barriers would have been even more prohibitive earlier in the twentieth century. The percentage of persons aged 25 years and over with an undergraduate or advanced degree has increased from 2.7% in 1910 to 3.9% in 1930, 7.7% in 1960, and 30.1% in 2011 (National Center for Educational Statistics, 2011).

[8] Levin & Alkoby (2012) identify similar results in Canada.

[9] In Fall 2010, only 7.2% of law school matriculants were black (LSAC, 2010), although 12.9% of America's population was black (http://www.lsac.org/LSACResources/Data/matrics-by-ethnicity.asp; Rastogi *et al.*, 2011, p. 3). Similarly, Hispanics and Latinos made up only 6.1% of matriculants (LSAC, 2010) while comprising 16% of the population (Ennis *et al.*, 2011, p. 2).

[10] Sander's (1997, p. 475) UCLA study found that for law students at the school, "the median income of student's parents was more than double the national median".

[11] Consider the claim by Halliday & Karpik (1997, p. 53) that the credibility of those who seek to link political goals and the public good may be undermined by a strong commitment to corporate markets and the intense pursuit of material interest.

[12] See generally Barton (2005) and Winston *et al.* (2011, pp. 83–84: "In the case of legal services, it is not clear that occupational licensing has measurably improved service quality because no evidence exists to justify the ABA's initial accreditation policies"). Wald & Pearce (2011, p. 405) argue that "Law schools have been instilling a very specific brand of professional identity, forming students into autonomously self-interested lawyers" who "believe that their duties to the public interest and to public service are fulfilled by their representation of private client interests such that they have no other responsibility to further the rule of law and access to justice." See also Kronman (2000, p. 32) and Hamilton & Monson (2011).

[13] Even some of the key arguments that helped persuade the ABA to adopt high barriers would be considered bigoted and unpersuasive today. In 1929, Henry Drinker, a leader in the field of legal ethics, argued that higher barriers would ensure that only the "right kind of people" (Levine, 2005, pp. 8–9) entered the legal profession and would exclude potential lawyers who "came up from the gutter", such as "Russian Jew boys" (ABA, 1929, pp. 605, 621–624).

[14] See Galanter (1994, pp. 647–656) and Cross (2005, pp. 9–10).

[15] See Mystal (2011), Robinson (2011), Elefant (2011), NY Times Editorial (2011) and Winston (2011).

[16] See also Cantrell (2004, pp. 883, 888–891) and Moorhead (2003, pp. 784–789).

[17] See also Cantrell (2004, pp. 887–888).

[18] For example, the ABA has opposed the use of some self-help services for consumers, professing worry about their quality: "The stated concern is that ignorant consumers will suffer from assistance offered by individuals who do not meet the competence and ethical standards established for licensed attorneys." The upshot of this resistance "is that a majority of surveyed courts lack formal services to assist pro se litigants" (Rhode, 2004, p. 83).

[19] See, for example, Rampell (2011: "The climate is hard partly because of the weak economy, but also partly because the nation's law schools are churning out more lawyers than the economy needs even in the long run"); Greenbaum (2010: "[T]housands of lawyers now find themselves drowning in the unemployment line as the legal sector is being badly saturated with attorneys"); Lowrey (2011: "The demand for lawyers has fallen off a cliff, both due to the short-term crisis of the recession and long-term changes to the industry, and is only starting to rebound"); and Lat (2010: "I share the concern that perhaps too many schools are cranking out too many debt-saddled graduates, releasing them into an already saturated legal job market").

[20] See Grassley (2011) and Mystal (2010).

[21] See Greenbaum (2010) and Mystal (2010).

[22] See Winston *et al.* (2011, p. 94), Somin (2011) and McGinnis & Mangas (2012).

[23] Notwithstanding these lower barriers, the United Kingdom continues to face challenges in providing women and people of color with equal access to becoming a lawyer (Sommerlad *et al.*, 2010).

[24] Although Tesco had previously "experimented over the years in offering legal services by contracting with outside lawyers" (Knake, 2012, pp. 6, 40), the 2007 Legal Services Act allowed them to start providing these services themselves. For a consumer-oriented comparison between various forms of will-writing, including do-it-yourself wills and hiring a lawyer, see Legal Services Board (2011).

[25] See Whelan (2009, pp. 472–75) and Webb (2004, p. 81).

[26] For example, Avrom Sherr (1998, p. 2) writes that "deregulation ... [and] competition within and among the professions" are responsible for the legal profession's "move away from the altruism of the professional ideal towards a more open commercialism". Moorhead (2010, p. 227). argues that changing norms of legal practice, marked by deregulation and greater specialisation, bring negative consequences for both lawyers and clients: "Work is de-skilled and broken up into different activities which can be handled by lower level operatives. Many working within this new system find it easier to begin areas of highly complex work. However, long hours and the repetitive nature of the work have caused many young solicitors stress and worries about whether they have made the right choice of career." He further suggests that the new approaches result in multiple lawyers handling the various elements of a client's case and undercut the possibility of a sustained relationship between lawyer and client that can inform the lawyer's advocacy.

[27] Mark (2009, p. 47) defines legal practitioners as those with a full license to practice law. See also Knake (2012, pp. 10, 39).

[28] See Mark (2009, p. 55), Knake (2012, p. 39) and also Grech & Morrison (2009).

[29] Interestingly, in systems that require apprenticeship, commentators have noted that such a requirement tends to favor those who are privileged on the basis of class, gender, race, or national origin (Levin & Alkoby, 2012, pp. 15–16; Sommerlad *et al.*, 2010, pp. 31–36; Sommerlad & Stapleford, 2009).

[30] Knake (2012, pp. 37–38) notes the contributions of Edward Adams, John Matheson, Mitt Regan, and Charles Wolfram.

[31] To Knake (2012, p. 7), "It is not difficult to imagine other alternative law delivery models that might be developed if a company like Google could take the next step to directly own or invest in a law practice, or if Wal-Mart could add a legal assistance window next to the banking center or health care provider located in its stores."

References

Abel, R. (1987) The real tort crisis – too *few* claims, *Ohio State Law Journal*, 48(2), pp. 443–467.

Abel, R. (1989) *American Lawyers* (New York, Oxford University Press).

ABA (1908) *Canons of Professional Ethics* (Chicago, American Bar Association).

ABA (1929) Proceedings of the section of legal education and admissions to the Bar, *Annual Reports of American Bar Association.*

ABA (1969) *Model Code of Professional Responsibility* (Chicago, American Bar Association).

ABA (1983) *Model Rules of Professional Conduct* (Chicago, American Bar Association).

ABA & Association of American Law Schools (1958) Professional responsibility: report of the joint conference, *American Bar Association Journal*, 44(12), pp. 1159–1162, 1216–1217.

Barton, B.H. (2005) The ABA, the rules and professionalism: the mechanics of self-defeat and a call for a return to the ethical, moral, and practical approach of the canons, *North Carolina Law Review*, 83(2), pp. 411–480.

Barton, B.H. (2011) *The Lawyer-Judge Bias in the American Legal System* (New York, Cambridge University Press).

Breyer, S. (2000) *The Legal Profession and Public Service* (Washington, DC, National Legal Center for the Public Interest).

Cantrell, D.J. (2004) The obligation of legal aid lawyers to champion practice by nonlawyers, *Fordham Law Review*, 73(3), pp. 883–902.

Chambliss, E. (2011) The demographics of the profession, in: *IILP Review 2011: The State of Diversity and Inclusion in the Legal Profession* (Chicago, Institute for Inclusion in the Legal Profession), pp. 10–32.

Cross, F. (2005) Identifying the virtues of the common law, *University of Texas School of Law Working Paper Series: Law and Economics*, Working Paper No. 063, pp. 9–10.

DeParle, J. (2012) Harder for Americans to rise from lower rungs, *New York Times*, 5 January, p. A1.

Department for Constitutional Affairs (2005) *The Future of Legal Services: Putting Customers First* [pdf]. Available at: http://webarchive.nationalarchives.gov.uk/+/http://www.dca.gov.uk/legalsys/folwp.pdf, accessed 23 July 2012.

Durkheim, E. (1957) *Professional Ethics and Civic Morals* (New York, Routledge).

Elefant, C. (2011) No need to deregulate lawyers if we debunk an economist, *MyShingle*, 25 October. Available at: http://myshingle.com/2011/10/articles/myshingle-solo/no-need-to-deregulate-lawyers-if-we-debunk-an-economist/, accessed 12 July 2012.

Ennis, S.R., Rios-Vargas, M. & Albert, N.G. (2011) *The Hispanic Population: 2010*, US Census Bureau 2010 Census Briefs. Available at: http://www.census.gov/prod/cen2010/briefs/c2010br-06.pdf, accessed 30 July 2012.

Federal Judicial Center (2012) *Biographical Directory of Federal Judges: John Marshall*. Available at: http://www.fjc.gov/public/home.nsf/hisj, accessed 17 July 2012.

Flood, J. (2011) The re-landscaping of the legal profession: large law firms and professional re-regulation, *Current Sociology*, 59(4), pp. 507–522.

Friedman, M. (1962) *Capitalism and Freedom* (Chicago, University of Chicago Press).

Galanter, M. (1994) Predators and parasites: lawyer-bashing and civil justice, *Georgia Law Review*, 28(3), pp. 633–681.

Goldin, C. (1999) *A Brief History of Education in the United States* (Cambridge, MA, National Bureau of Economic Research).

Grassley, C. (2011) Letter to the American Bar Association, 11 July. Available at: http://www.grassley.senate.gov/about/upload/2011-07-11-Grassley-to-ABA.pdf, accessed 30 July 2012.

Grech, A. & Morrison, K. (2009) Slater and Gordon: the listing experience, *Georgetown Journal of Legal Ethics*, 22(2), pp. 535–540.

Green, B.A. & Pearce, R.G. (2009) 'Public service must begin at home': the lawyer as civics teacher in everyday practice, *William and Mary Law Review*, 50(4), pp. 1207–1038.

Greenbaum, M. (2010) No more room at the bench, *Los Angeles Times*, 8 January. Available at: http://articles.latimes.com/2010/jan/08/opinion/la-oe-greenbaum8-2010jan08, accessed 30 July 2012.

Hadfield, G.K. (2011) Producing law for innovation: promoting innovation and growth through legal reform, in: R. Litan *et al.* (Eds) *Rules for Growth* (Kansas City, Ewing Marion Kauffman Foundation), pp. 23–53.

Halliday, T.C. (1989) Legal professions and the state: neocorporatist variations on the pluralist theme of liberal democracies, in: R.L. Abel & P.S.C. Lewis (Eds) *Lawyers in Society, vol. 3: Comparative Theories* (Berkeley, University of California Press), pp. 375–426.

Halliday, T.C. & Karpik, L. (1997) Politics matter: a comparative theory of lawyers in the making of political liberalism, in: T.C. Halliday & L. Karpik (Eds) *Lawyers and the Rise of Western Political Liberalism: Europe and North America from the Eighteenth to the Twentieth Centuries* (Oxford, Clarendon Press), pp. 15–64.

Halliday, T.C., Karpik, L. & Feeley, M. (2007) The legal complex in struggles for political liberalism, in: T. C. Halliday, L. Karpik & M. Feeley (Eds) *Fighting for Political Freedom*, Oñati International Series in Law and Society (Oxford and Portland, OR, Hart), pp. 1–40.

Hamilton, N. & Monson, V. (2011) Legal education's ethical challenge: empirical research on how most effectively to foster each student's professional formation (Professionalism), *St. Thomas Law Review*, 9(2), pp. 325–402.

Heinz, J.P., Laumann, E.O., Nelson, R.L. & Salisbury, R.H. (1993) *The Hollow Core: Private Interests in National Policy Making* (Cambridge, MA, Harvard University Press).

Hixson, L., Hepler, B.B. & Kim, M.O. (2011) *The White Population: 2010*, US Census Bureau 2010 Census Briefs. Available at: http://www.census.gov/prod/cen2010/briefs/c2010br-05.pdf, accessed 30 July 2012.

Knake, R.N. (2012) Democratizing the delivery of legal services, *Ohio State Law Journal*, 73(1), pp. 1–46.

Kritzer, H. (1998) *Legal Advocacy: Lawyers and Nonlawyers at Work* (Ann Arbour, University of Michigan Press).

Kritzer, H.M. (1999) The professions are dead, long live the professions: legal practice in a postprofessional world, *Law & Society Review*, 33(3), pp. 713–759.

Kronman, A. (2000) The law as a profession, in: D. Rhode (Ed.) *Ethics in Practice* (New York, Oxford University Press).

Lat, D. (2010) A law school is coming to Shreveport – Hallelujah!, *Above the Law blog*, 11 August, 11:23 a.m. Available at: http://abovethelaw.com/2010/08/a-law-school-is-coming-to-shreveport-hallelujah/, accessed 30 July 2012.

Law school tuition soars (2011) *New York Times*, 17 July. Available at: http://www.nytimes.com/imagepages/2011/07/17/business/17legalGraphic.html?ref=business, accessed 31 July 2012.

Law Society (2012) Routes to qualifying. Available at: http://www.lawsociety.org.uk/careers/becoming-a-solicitor/routes-to-qualifying/, accessed 8 September 2012.

Legal Services Board (2011) *Research Report: Understanding the Consumer Experience of Will Writing Services*. Available at: http://www.legalservicesboard.org.uk/what_we_do/Research/Publications/pdf/lsb_will_writing_report_final.pdf, accessed 22 July 2012.

Levin, A. & Alkoby, A. (2012) Is access to the profession access to justice? Lessons from Canada, *International Journal of the Legal Profession*, 19(2–3), pp. 283–299, this issue.

Levine, S. (2005) Rediscovering Julius Henry Cohen and the origins of the business/profession dichotomy: a study in the discourse of early twentieth century legal professionalism, *American Journal of Legal History*, 47(1), pp. 1–34.

Lowrey, A. (2011) Law of averages: why the law school bubble is bursting, *Slate*, 18 March. Available at: http://www.slate.com/articles/business/moneybox/2011/03/law_of_averages.html, accessed 30 July 2012.

LPA (2004) *New South Wales Legal Profession Act 2004. 1.1:3*. Available at: http://www.austlii.edu.au/au/legis/nsw/consol_act/lpa2004179/, accessed 23 July 2012.

LSAC (2010) *Matriculants by Ethnicity*. Available at: http://www.lsac.org/LSACResources/Data/matrics-by-ethnicity.asp, accessed 30 July 2012.

Luban, D. (2009) *Legal Ethics and Human Dignity* (Cambridge, Cambridge University Press).

Magee, S.P. (2010) The optimum number of lawyers and a radical proposal for legal change, in: *An American Illness: Essays on the Rule of Law* (Washington, DC, School of Law, George Mason University), 3–4 December.

Mark, S. (2009) Views from an Australian regulator symposium: the future is here: globalization and the regulation of the legal profession, *Journal of the Professional Lawyer*, 49(1), pp. 45–63.

Mark, S. & Gordon, T. (2009) Innovations in regulation – responding to a changing legal services market, *Georgetown Journal of Legal Ethics*, 22(2), pp. 501–533.

McDonald, G. (2003) The self-made lawyer, *The Christian Science Monitor*, 23 June. Available at: http://www.csmonitor.com/2003/0603/p13s01-lecs.html, accessed 16 July 2012.

McGinnis, J.O. & Mangas, R.D. (2012) An undergraduate option for legal education. Available at: http://www.masonlec.org/wp-content/uploads/2012/11/McGinnis-undergraduate4.pdf, accessed 7 January 2013, forthcoming *Internal Journal of Law and Economics*.

McQuoid-Mason, D. (2012) Access to justice in South Africa: are there enough lawyers?, in: *Too Many Lawyers? Facts, Reasons, Consequences and Solutions* (Oñati, Spain, IISL).

Moeser, E. & Huismann, C. (Eds) (2012) *National Conference of Bar Examiners and American Bar Association Section of Legal Education and Admissions to the Bar, Comprehensive Guide to Bar Admission Requirements 2012*. Available at: http://www.ncbex.org/assets/media_files/Comp-Guide/CompGuide.pdf, accessed 12 July 2012.

Morgan, T. (1977) The evolving concept of professional responsibility, *Harvard Law Review*, 90(4), pp. 702–743.

Morgan, T. (2010) *The Vanishing American Lawyer* (New York, Oxford University Press).

Moorhead, R. *et al.* (2003) Contesting professionalism: legal aid and nonlawyers in England and Wales, *Law & Society Review*, 37(4), pp. 765–808.

Mystal, E. (2010) *No. More. Law schools!, Above the Law blog*, 8 August, 12:43 p.m. Available at: http://abovethelaw.com/2010/01/no-more-law-schools/, accessed 30 July 2012.

Mystal, E. (2011) *New York Times* op-ed advocates letting everybody play 'lawyer', *Above the Law*, 25 October. Available at: http://abovethelaw.com/2011/10/new-york-times-op-ed-advocates-letting-everybody-play-lawyer/, accessed 12 July 2012.

National Center for Education Statistics (2011) Table 8: Percentage of persons age 25 and over and of persons 25 to 29 years old with high school completion or higher and a bachelor's or higher degree, by race/ethnicity and sex: Selected years, 1910 through 2011, *Digest of Education Statistics*. Available at: http://nces.ed.gov/programs/digest/d11/tables/dt11008.asp, accessed 7 January 2013.

NY Times Editorial (2011) Addressing the justice gap, *New York Times*, 23 August. Available at: http://www.nytimes.com/2011/08/24/opinion/addressing-the-justice-gap.html, accessed 12 July 2012.

Parsons, T. (1954) *Essays in Sociological Theory* (New York, The Free Press).

Pearce, R.G. (1992) Rediscovering the republican origins of the legal ethics codes, *Georgetown Journal of Legal Ethics*, 6(2), pp. 241–282.

Pearce, R.G. (1995) The professionalism paradigm shift: why discarding professional ideology will improve the conduct and reputation of the bar, *New York University Law Review*, 70(6), pp. 1229–1276.

Pearce, R.G. (2001) Lawyers as America's governing class: the formation and dissolution of the original understanding of the American lawyer's role, *University of Chicago Law School Roundtable*, 8(2), pp. 381–421.

Pearce, R.G. (2004) Redressing inequality in the market for justice: why access to lawyers will never solve the problem and why rethinking the role of judges will help, *Fordham Law Review*, 73(3), pp. 969–980.

Pearce, R.G. (2006) The legal profession as a blue state: reflections on public philosophy, jurisprudence, and legal ethics, *Fordham Law Review*, 75(3), pp. 1339–1365.

Pearce, R. (2012a) Two of three Carnegie reports support the undergraduate law degree, *Legal Ethics Forum*, 8 February. Available at: http://www.legalethicsforum.com/blog/2012/02/two-of-three-carnegie-reports-support-the-undergraduate-law-degree.html, accessed 9 July 2012.

Pearce, R. (2012b) Why Occam's razor cuts in favor of making law an undergraduate degree, *Legal Ethics Forum*, 6 February. Available at: http://www.legalethicsforum.com/blog/2012/02/why-occams-razor-cuts-in-favor-of-making-law-an-undergraduate-degree.html, accessed 9 July 2012.

Pearce, R.G. & Levine, S.J. (2009) Rethinking the legal reform agenda: will raising the standards for bar admission promote or undermine democracy, human rights, and rule of law?, *Fordham Law Review*, 77(4), pp. 1635–1663.

Pearce, R.G. & Wald, E. (2011) The obligation of lawyers to heal civic culture: confronting the ordeal of incivility in the practice of law, *University of Arkansas Law Review*, 34(1), pp. 1–53.

Pearce, R.G. & Wald, E. (2012) Rethinking lawyer regulation: how a relational approach would improve professional rules and roles, *Michigan State Law Review*, 2012(2), pp. 513–536.

Pound, R. (1953) *The Lawyer from Antiquity to Modern Times*, (West Publishing Co.).

Rampell, C. (2011) The lawyer surplus, state by state, *New York Times Economix blog*, 27 June, 11:00 a.m. Available at: http://economix.blogs.nytimes.com/2011/06/27/the-lawyer-surplus-state-by-state/, accessed 30 July 2012.
Rastogi, S., Johnson, T.D., Hoeffel, E.M. & Drewery, M.P. (2011) *The Black Population: 2010*, US Census Bureau 2010 Census Briefs. Available at: http://www.census.gov/prod/cen2010/briefs/c2010br-06.pdf, accessed 30 July 2012.
Reed, A.Z. (1921) *Training for the Public Profession of the Law: Historical Development and Principal Contemporary Problems of Legal Education in the United States, with Some Account of Conditions in England and Canada* (New York, Carnegie Foundation for the Advancement of Teaching).
Reed, A.Z. (1928) *Present-day Law schools in the United States and Canada* (New York, Carnegie Foundation for the Advancement of Teaching).
Rhode, D.L. (1996) Professionalism in perspective: alternative approaches to nonlawyer practice, *Journal of the Institute for the Study of Legal Ethics*, 1(1), pp. 197–214.
Rhode, D.L. (2000) *In the Interests of Justice: Reforming the Profession* (Oxford, Oxford University Press).
Rhode, D.L. (2003) Equal justice under law: connecting principle to practice, *Washington University Journal of Law and Public Policy*, 12, pp. 47–62.
Rhode, D.L. (2004) *Access to Justice* (New York, Oxford University Press).
Ribstein, L. (2007) Want to own a law firm?, *The American*, 30 May. Available at: http://www.american.com/archive/2007/may-0507/want-to-own-a-law-firm/, accessed 24 July 2012.
Ribstein, L. (2010) The death of big law, *Wisconsin Law Review*, 3(3), pp. 749–815.
Robinson, W.T. (2011) Legal help for the poor, *New York Times*, 26 August. Available at: http://www.nytimes.com/2011/08/31/opinion/legal-help-for-the-poor-the-view-from-the-aba.html, accessed 30 July 2012.
Sander, R.H. (1997) Experimenting with class-based affirmative action, *Journal of Legal Education*, 47(4), pp. 472–503.
Selinger, C.M. (1996) The retention of limitations on the out-of-court practice of law by independent paralegals, *Georgetown Journal of Legal Ethics*, 9(3), pp. 879–914.
Sharswood, G. (1907) *An Essay on Professional Ethics*, 5th edn (Philadelphia, T. & J.W. Johnson Co).
Shepherd, G.B. (2003) Defending the aristocracy: ABA accreditation and the filtering of political leaders, *Cornell Journal of Law & Public Policy*, 12(3), pp. 637–663.
Sherr, A. (1998) Inculcating and educating professional codes and professional behaviour, *University of London – Institute of Advanced Legal Studies Working Paper Series*.
Simon, W. (2000) *The Practice of Justice: A Theory of Lawyers' Ethics* (Cambridge, MA, Harvard University Press).
Somin, I. (2011) Clifford Winston's case for abolishing the requirement that lawyers must get law school degrees and pass the bar exam, *The Volokh Conspiracy*, 27 October. Available at: http://www.volokh.com/2011/10/27/clifford-winstons-case-for-abolishing-the-requirement-that-lawyers-must-get-law-school-degrees-and-pass-the-bar-exam/, accessed 31 July 2012.
Sommerlad, H. & Stapleford, J. (2009) Barriers to entry and progression in the solicitors' profession in England and Wales, in: L. Cooper & S. Walters (Eds) *Learning/Work: Turning Work and Lifelong Learning Inside Out* (Cape Town, HSRC Press).
Sommerlad, H., Webley, L., Muzio, D., Tomlinson, J. & Duff, L. (2010) *Diversity in the Legal Profession in England and Wales: A Qualitative Study of Barriers and Individual Choices* (London, Legal Services Board).
Stevens, R. (1983) *Law School: Legal Education in America from the 1850s to the 1980s* (Chapel Hill, NC, University of North Carolina Press).
Tocqueville, A.D. (1840) *Democracy in America*, trans. from French by J.P. Mayer & G. Lawrence, 1969 (Garden City, NJ, Doubleday).
Wald, E. & Pearce, R.G. (2011) Making good lawyers, *St. Thomas Law Review*, 9(2), pp. 403–445.
Webb, J. (2004) Turf wars and market control: competition and complexity in the market for legal services, *International Journal of the Legal Profession*, 11(1–2), pp. 81–102.
Wendel, W.B. (2010) *Lawyers and Fidelity to Law* (Princeton, NJ, Princeton University Press).
Whelan, C. (2009) The paradox of professionalism: global law practice means business, *Penn State International Law Review*, 27(2), pp. 465–494.

Winston, C. (2011) Are law schools and bar exams necessary? *New York Times*, 17 July. Available at: http://www.nytimes.com/2011/10/25/opinion/are-law-schools-and-bar-exams-necessary.html, accessed 30 July 2012.
Winston, C., Crandall, R.W. & Maheshri, V. (2011) *First Thing We Do, Let's Deregulate All the Lawyers* (Washington, DC, Brookings Institution Press).
Ziv, N. (2009) The lawyer's role in a contemporary democracy, tensions between various conceptions of the lawyer's role, regulation of Israeli lawyers: from professional autonomy to multi-institutional regulation, *Fordham Law Review*, 77(4), pp. 1763–1794.

‘I love my American job’: professional prestige in the Indian outsourcing industry and global consequences of an expanding legal profession

SWETHAA BALLAKRISHNEN*,**
*Sociology, Stanford University, USA
**Affiliated Fellow, Program on the Legal Profession, Harvard Law School, USA

ABSTRACT *A crucial consequence of the explosion of legal work is the expansion of the locations where this work is actually being done. With client pressures and rising global credibility of a competent end product, international offshoring has become an obvious extension of the global value-chain. Relying on lawyers in the developing world to meet deadlines has moved from being a possible alternative to a potential imperative for legal strategists. This paper looks at one (possibly unintended?) consequence that this diversification of workflow introduces in the domestic legal profession of the supplying nation by examining the ways in which this process shapes prestige stratification within the Indian legal profession. Using field data from the Indian legal outsourcing industry (collected as part of the Harvard Law School Program on the Legal Professions Study on legal process outsourcing firms), it suggests the ways in which association to the West has emerged as a marker of prestige and how, while important, traditional understandings of prestige markers are not enough to explain this transformative function. Universality of professional prestige has traditionally not taken into consideration the effect of globalization as a prestige factor in and of itself. The article offers that, in addition to the markers used (e.g. level of skill, monetary rewards, etc.), and especially while trying to understand the emerging industrialized world, an approach more reflective of the ‘halo’ effect of the West is crucial.*

1. Introduction

The recent and exponential expansion of the international legal workforce represents a definite clash of directional interests.[1] On the one hand, we are wary of an overpopulation of the profession and, at the same time, global demands dictate that the legal workforce becomes broader, wider and more efficient. Particularly over the last two decades, the increasing significance of technology on production and the institutional restructuring of international trade and regulatory barriers have, together, configured various options for 'global' work and 'multinational' work environments.[2] Naturally, these logistical rearrangements have had significant effects on how work is being done, how people think of their jobs,[3] and how workflow chains have been structured.[4] But for a professional community like the legal profession that guards its boundaries tightly around jurisdictional legitimacy, what exactly does this expanding workforce and space mean?

In some sense, it means this: In 2002, if a multinational corporation headquartered in Manhattan needed 10 hours of legal research and drafting, the general counsel of the firm would either walk down the corridor and have a team of in-house lawyers do the job or pay a junior associate in a law firm – probably a few blocks away – about 450 dollars an hour to do the work over the next week. Now, more than a decade of processes-oriented service innovation later, market-savvy and efficiency-aggressive General Counsels (GCs) are more likely to send their work to offshore firms where the job can be done for a fraction of the cost and time. Thus, to the extent we think of lawyering as a part of production and the legal service provided as a product, the means of production have been changed irrevocably with the advent of technology-aided legal solutions.

This newly organized world order is no doubt efficient for clients and markets alike. Yet, at the same time, this global efficiency has two important, and slightly tangential, consequences. First, because the source of market efficient solutions are typically internation, the boundaries of what we think of as the 'profession' have stretched. Second, by forming a supply chain that splits the deliverable legal service into manageable parts that can be 'shipped' to various locations, it necessarily commoditizes – and, in turn, deprofessionalizes[5] the nature of the work being done. Assuming that we think of this global legal profession to include all these lawyers and legal professions, this paper asks, broadly: what are the consequences of a globalized legal profession, given the newly emergent re-conceptualizing of these professional boundaries?

In this paper, I focus on one set of consequences of this expanding legal workforce: the professional conception and consequent rise in prestige accorded to the legal process outsourcing (LPO) industry in India.[6] In particular, I consider how factors of expansion and deprofessionalization have been important in shaping the experience of professionals in this industry. In general, we would assume that commoditized lawyering would be a 'hard sell' for a predominantly professional workforce since value for professional jobs, while tied to monetary rewards, has long been equally tied to other factors like the importance of the work, prestige of the work and the purity of the legal practice. Thus, while this watered-down version of legal process delivery might well be economically beneficial (and therefore likely to be in demand), one would assume that it would nevertheless be detrimental to the professional prestige valuation of the job done. However, evidence from interview field data and content analysis of media reports alike seems to suggest that, over the very short years since its introduction in the Indian legal professional market, these jobs are being seen as more prestigious or full of value than when they were first introduced. To try and explain part of this puzzle, I enquire into the reasons that have resulted in this increased prestige that these otherwise non-prestige-worthy jobs seem to attract. Specifically, what has been the role of globalization in general in creating a new prestige paradigm that favorably attaches itself to the way these jobs are being received in India? In turn, how has this expanding and overtly Western production of the delivery of a legal product changed the way lawyers and legal professionals in India think of their jobs and the prestige associated with it? And what consequences does this have for the way we understand the formation (and reformation) or the boundaries of the global legal profession?

2. Why prestige: existing frameworks and the need for a new one

Research on the impact of globalization on local labor markets has shown that the effects of foreign industry exposure are never straightforward. While on the one hand they do bring fresh opportunity and revenue,[7] they also simultaneously introduce various stratification[8] and multi-level, socio-cultural consequences.[9] In turn, these processes help construct what we think of as the boundaries of a 'global' profession and its resultant consequences.[10]

The impact of Western influences in shaping global attitudes and preferences has been studied in a range of contexts.[11] For the most part, however, research on the global offshoring of jobs has been portrayed as a transformation of low-wage, low-prestige jobs to what are considered high-wage, high-prestige jobs in the outsourced country (Friedman, 2005).[12] This simplistic transformation story is problematic in the particular case of the legal outsourcing industry for a couple of reasons. First, it relies on an economic assumption that these high-wage jobs automatically attract a better quality of worker (and, subsequently, higher prestige) in the outsourced country, without pursuing other non-monetary factors, which might account for this transformed job value. Second, and in particular, this blanket explanation for transformation does not extend itself sufficiently to explain outsourcing patterns that demand a professionally qualified workforce. This is crucial because professionals rely on various profession-specific factors (e.g. purity, skill) independent or in addition to monetary rewards to value prestige (Abbott, 1981). The research on the globalization of the professions, for instance, has been restricted to the commoditization and the subsequent deprofessionalization of these services. This is because ideas of professional decline remain preoccupied with sophistication, knowledge and ownership of 'real' work.[13] In the particular context of the legal profession, routine work is consistently seen as low prestige (e.g. specializations that focus on routine work are consistently deemed low prestige; Wallace & Kay, 2008). Yet, there is some reason to believe that this focus on prestige that is limited to traditional markers like the quality of work loses some favor in certain contexts. Thus, third, this simplification, even if true, loses some nuance by not entirely examining the effect of globalization in reshaping the traditional markers of prestige. To understand how prestige is constructed in this new workforce, it remains important both to outline the existing markers of prestige and to juxtapose them against the new ones suggested here.

Existing and traditional markers of prestige

Justifications for occupational prestige have traditionally been functional. The classic explanation for stratification within the occupations has been that societies value and reward jobs with important functions and that the most important people get the most important jobs (Davis & Moore, 1945; Parsons, 1940). This in turn, is relevant because individuals with important jobs have other relational rewards – both with others who had similar jobs (e.g. status) as well as with those who had different jobs (e.g. deference, derogation). Naturally, this component of 'importance' was likely to lead to other instrumental advantages (pay, benefits, etc.) but this was not why they were deemed superior in the first place. Departing from this view of prestige as an achievement variable, subsequent research – in industrialized (Inkeles and Rossi, 1956) and non-industrialized (Hodge *et al.*, 1966) alike – has extended this dependence on objective order to other characteristics: relative honor (Goldthorpe & Hope, 1974), professional purity (Shils, 1968; Abbott, 1981) and individual rewards such as desirability (Jencks *et al.*, 1988). But while there has been some debate on the theoretical motivations of these prestige sources (Wegener, 1992),[14] most research converges on prestige indicators that are functional, at least at some diluted level, to either the society or the individual actor.[15]

The case of the legal profession is no different. Like other professions, it operates by right of control over techniques and abstract knowledge, influenced by differentiation in clients, intellectual jurisdictions, and settlements reached through divisions of labor (Ray, 2006). As we know, successful professions are those that continue to maintain a monopoly over a core jurisdiction in spite of key events that create and destroy these jurisdictions (Abbott, 1988). In the case of the legal profession, this fight to retain control over 'core' professional work deeply influences its prestige stratification. Specifically, two main theories of prestige dominate the study of the legal profession, both of which fit the framework of functionality. The first is the 'client-type' hypothesis (Laumann & Heinz, 1977), which focuses on the receiver of the professional service; the second is the 'professional purity' hypothesis (Abbott, 1981), which values work that is non-routine and core to the profession. Since prestigious clients are most likely to offer the most sophisticated work (Sandefur, 2001), the two theories follow a straightforward mechanism of functional importance. Using this logic, we would argue that lawyers who work on sophisticated legal matters are most likely to be seen as prestigious either because they do important or sophisticated work or work for important clients (see Erlanger, 1980 on status within the legal profession more generally). Following this reasoning, even among lawyers that do not do sophisticated work, those who perform 'pure work', which is rooted in doing specifically legal tasks (e.g. litigating lawyers), are more likely to be seen as prestigious when compared with those who perform legally 'impure' tasks like form-filling (Abbott, 1981; Sandefur, 2001).

Limitations of these traditional markers

The traditional understandings of these professions that I have outlined above, however, shed little light on new professional extensions that depend on new market demands for services (Clarke, 1999). By assuming that jurisdictional strategies are made by professionals for their peers, these constructs say little about professionals

Table 1. *Comparative prestige structures*

	US workforce perception	Offshore workforce perception
Outsourcing industry	Low prestige, low pay	High prestige, high pay
Legal outsourcing industry (2006)	Low prestige, low pay	Low prestige, high pay
Legal outsourcing industry (2009)	Low prestige, low pay	Rising prestige, high pay

Table 2. *Descriptive statistics of interviews conducted (2006, 2009)*

Interview year(s)	Firms	Interviewees (Managers, associates)	Ancillary interviews
2006	9	25	10
2009	14	41	5
Both 2006 and 2009	5	15	–
Total interviews	23	66	15
Non-overlapping interviews	18	51	15

who work in large organizations (Lowendahl, 2005), where professionally skilled employees are managed by managers whose business interests do not coincide with those of the professionals they oversee. This is particularly salient in the legal outsourcing sector, where the focus of professional purity is diluted by business value-chain processes that concentrate on servicing cost-beneficial customer requirements. In addition, there remain tensions that organizational limitations place on professional prestige. For example, research on large universities shows that, among professional employees whose primary contribution is their professional expertise, there is a constant tension between organizational commitment and commitment to the profession (Lewis, 1967). Thus, those with low professional prestige but high organizational prestige can be more committed to their work than those with high professional prestige but low organizational prestige (Lewis, 1967; Sang, 1969). In the regular outsourcing context, employees are typically low-prestige college graduates for whom the organizational prestige of working for international firms is high-prestige work (Table 1). By contrast, professionally qualified lawyers draw prestige from working in core legal organizations (e.g. firms and litigation offices) because they view these firms as access to training (human capital), connections (social capital), professional prestige and standing (Reichman & Sterling, 2010). However, in the legal outsourcing context, this advantage of social standing and human capital is compromised because the work that these outsourcing firms do is not, at the core, rooted in what have traditionally been thought of as professional tasks and functions.[16] Should these tensions hold in the Indian LPO context, the high professional prestige of the associates (i.e. being lawyers) should interfere with their low organizational prestige (outsourcing firms as 'back end' firms) to result in a very low organizational identification and commitment to these firms by its employees.

Using interview data from the Harvard Program on the Legal Professions' Project on Indian LPOs (Harvard PLP-LPO)[17] over a three-year (2006–2009)

Table 3. *Institutional map of the Indian legal process outsourcing sector*

	Pure play LPOs	Legal offices in KPO/BPO	Law firm LPO
Definition	Firm incorporated to do only legal offshoring work	Legal offshoring team within an existing BPO or KPO company	Legal offshoring firm either owned by or associated with a law firm
Average size	40–800 lawyers	10–100 lawyers (depending on the size of the BPO/KPO and their interest in legal outsourcing)	10–250 lawyers (similar to KPO, it depends on law firm's commitment and ability to manage an LPO)
Type of work	Litigation support, due diligence, legal research. In some cases, legal transcription and form filing	Litigation support, due diligence, legal research. In some cases, legal transcription and form filing	Litigation support, due diligence, legal research. In some cases, legal transcription and form filing
Clients	International clients, usually through a known network (known law firms, references, etc.)	Typically existing clients of the KPO/BPO that also need legal outsourcing work	Clients are typically referred by law firm or recruited using connections that the law firm offers

Note: BPO, business process outsourcing; KPO, knowledge process outsourcing; LPO, legal process outsourcing.

observation period,[18] it seems as though positive organizational identification by associates to these firms increased despite continual engagement in tasks with low professional purity. This unexpected result of rising prestige identification offers a novel case for understanding how these prestige markers operate independent of traditionally understood organizational and professional prestige limitations.

Table 4. *Further description of interviews*

	2006	2009
Firm characteristics		
Legal units of KPOs/BPOs	4	5
LPO units of law firms	3	3
Stand alone (pure play) LPOs	2	6
Total	9	14
Manager characteristics		
Western educated	3	13
Western work experience	5	15
Western born	1	10
Total	15	18
Associate characteristics		
Top 20 law school graduates	–	10
Prior law firm experience	–	12
Prior litigation experience	6	6
No prior work experience	4	5
Total	10	23

Note: BPO, business process outsourcing; KPO, knowledge process outsourcing; LPO, legal process outsourcing.

Table 5. *List of non-legal process outsourcing (LPO) interviews*

	2006	2009	Overall
Indian legal (non-LPO) professionals	6	3	9
Foreign clients	4	1	5
Indian regulators	–	1	1
Total	10	5	–

Table 6. *Summary analysis of interview data*

	2006	2009
Recruits		
Rise of prestige		
Demand, quality of recruits	Demand restricted to local, less elite schools	More diffused demand. Higher quality of graduates interested in the sector
Attrition	High. LPO management complains about the high attrition rate.	No mention of attrition as a problem.
Traditional advantages		
Professional purity		
Type of work	Routine, technical tasks, legal research	Routine, technical tasks, legal research
Sophistication of work	Low	Low
Importance of work	Low	Low
Client type hypothesis		
Type of client	International	International
Mobility because of client	No	No
New work opportunities abroad	No	No
Other factors		
Instrumental advantages		
Monetary rewards	Higher than comparable jobs in the legal industry	Higher than comparable jobs in the legal industry
Physical spaces	Small offices (with limited extension)	Large office spaces, Western amenities (high security buildings, posh offices, Western-style cafeteria dining)
Western 'halo'?		
Western corporate environment	Not prominent	Very prominent
Western colleagues	Few	Each office had a strong international presence, and at least a couple of managers/trainers from the West who were resident in the office and/or made frequent visits
Interaction with Western colleagues	Not recorded	Highly proximate work environment with heavy interaction

3. New markers of prestige: what is different in the Indian context?

The data from the Harvard PLP-LPO project provide a rich source to contrast the growth of the legal outsourcing sector in India. We have used these data elsewhere to show descriptively the broader socio-legal implications of this emergence,[19] but I use the data here with the limited agenda of demarcating the peculiar evolution of professional prestige within the sector.[20] My attempt here is: (a) to use the interview data from informants in the market to get a sense for the reasons for the rise in prestige of jobs within this sector;[21] (b) to contrast these data with prestige indicators that have traditionally been used to understand professional prestige; and (c) to trace the source of the difference. This context, of lawyers drawing prestige by association independent of factors that are traditionally thought of as crucial to their professional standing (e.g. academic/technical purity of work), is important because it offers nuance to Western understandings of professional stratification by introducing a possible non-functional, 'halo', explanation for prestige understandings. Empirically, it throws light on the effect of globalization as a factor of prestige and provides context to better understand employee perceptions or supply-side dynamics that feed into the global value-chain.

Have Indian LPO jobs become more prestigious?

There is no doubt that between the two time periods, there was an increased demand for these jobs. Part of this might have been attributable to the institutional maturity and expansion of these firms.[22] Also significant is the pure economical explanation: outsourcing was cost-efficient and, following a recession, more work was being sent to India than ever before.[23] Still, from the interviews in 2009, it seemed like it was not only a change in numbers that had been affected in the three years of growth – it was also a change in quality of recruits. Thus, also, while in the Phase 1 transcripts, managers and associates alike were aware of the business opportunities that the LPO model offered the West, there was little reference or expectation that it would attract higher-quality talent within the Indian legal profession. The transcripts in Phase 1 were riddled with employer complaints about their inability to retain people because of the low-quality work and expectations of the legally trained employees to do 'real' lawyer jobs.[24] By contrast, employees in the Phase 2 transcripts, who were often from higher-tier law schools than those employed in 2006, displayed an unprecedented enthusiasm for these jobs even though the substance of the work done in these firms had not become more 'real'. As one senior LPO manager commented on the recruiting successes his firm had both at top law schools and laterally:[25]

> Three years ago, we had to actively recruit and sort of make do with what we got, you know? I remember being a last slot recruiter at [name of top law school] and we would get no bites because people did not want these jobs. Now, I have resumes running through my ears – and not just *any* resumes. We get seriously good applications and we have to put them on a waitlist and reject them because we cannot expand fast enough to accommodate the demand. (emphasis added)

This increase in demand, especially by better-qualified applicants than ever before, offered the firms the advantage of being choosy about their recruits. As a result, there are now stricter entrance restrictions (screening checks, entrance tests, multi-process interviews) for jobs that are, in legal substance, not very different from the jobs in Phase 1. In turn, this demand among domestic lawyers[26] for these jobs changed the way these firms placed with other domestic legal institutions as recruiters of the available talent.[27] Finally, what made this demand pertinent and reflective of an increase in perceived prestige was that the nature of work done remained stagnant across the two periods. For a variety of regulatory concerns, tasks like litigation support and document review have remained – and are likely to remain - the 'bread and butter' of work outsourced.[28] Three main legal tasks remained prime in the offshoring sector across time periods: (a) document support, (b) litigation and transaction services,[29] and (c) legal research, contract and drafting. In other words, the work outsourced was fairly low-end process work with only few (if any) opportunities for the employment of legal sophistication. Respondents in both the 2006 and 2009 interviews agreed that the 'core work' done by these LPO firms, across hierarchy, were revenue-generating process work like legal transcription, effectuation of minor corrections, corrections to briefs and memoranda and other basic services traditionally provided by on-site paralegals and support staff in Western firms. In addition, the firms that identified as doing 'high-end work' mostly did litigation support, document review and due diligence:[30,31] work that was both mechanical and easily customizable administrative process work.[32]

Applicability of traditional accounts

This positive change in demand could not be explained by the usual traditional explanations since neither the work done nor the remuneration for it had changed drastically in the three years between our observations. The work remained fairly unsophisticated and the money – which was an advantage acknowledged by employees even in 2006 – had not been enough to alter favorably employee (or industry) perception in the past. Yet, somehow, the work had transformed from "grunge, non-law work" in a high-attrition "stop-gap" position to careers that associates felt secure in.[33] Further, there was no smokescreen to the nature of work either: employees at these LPO firms continued to confirm that they did no legal advisory or "serious law-type work". Yet, unlike their peers in 2006 who thought of this low-quality legal work as the main reason for these jobs' non-sustainability, LPO employees in 2009 thought of these jobs as "career options". Thus, core functionality or the importance of these jobs was not what was attributing value to these jobs. If anything, independent of these traditional prestige markers, these jobs were attracting superior talent and a dedicated workforce. This is not to say that the money was not an important factor for why these jobs were desirable – only that monetary advantages alone were not enough to persuade high-quality recruits to join these firms. As Suresh[34], an associate who had laterally transferred from a litigation career in the Delhi High Court to work in one of these firms said of the insufficiency of this monetary advantage:

> I would say one of the reasons is the money, and that is no way that we can ignore that. Secondly, and I believe this is one major point here – there is the brand name of these firms. Money is not alone enough, you know how lawyers have a fascination for brand and names".

The perks of an 'American job': non-traditional explanations of advantage

If these LPO firms were not engaged in important or sophisticated legal work and the money was not reason enough to explain the change in demand for these jobs, what was the explanation? The overarching non-monetary benefit on which all respondents concurred was some form of an international advantage that working for these LPO firms provided. Of these alluded international advantages, three specific forms were recurrent: the access to (a) internationally 'branded' clients, (b) Western workplace advantages and (c) foreign-trained colleagues.

Access to international clients. The fascination with 'brand and names' that Suresh alludes to above as something 'you might know' refers to what many respondents agreed to be the lure of the LPO industry: the 'global opportunities' of working with well-known international companies. In some part, the branding was relevant because of the access it offered global clients. Doing otherwise low-prestige legal tasks (i.e. document review) for an important international client was seen as an 'opportunity'. Here, an ex-law firm employee, now working at an LPO firm whose 'bread-and-butter' work was document review, offers in explanation:

> So, among other things, we would also do work for [big brand company] worldwide contract. So, what we have is an example of a work of perfection and this gives us an opportunity that you will never get in a law firm. Here, you actually see the life of how that contract proceeds, all the way to execution.

Note how document review, an otherwise menial task, escalated to a level of 'perfection' and 'opportunity' because it had a connection to a leading brand name. She says, "In some way, I am part of [big brand company] global counsel. I see what an in-house counsel sees." The catch here is not that she does what an in-house counsel does – but that, instead, she has access to what is otherwise only seen by this elite company's in-house counsel. At the same time, it is important to distinguish this company branding from just any 'big brand' company. The evidence that professionals are drawn to power and wealth at the cost of doing work that is not professionally 'pure' is not new in itself.[35] However, it seemed to be the case that they were drawing prestige not just from the 'big brand company' but the fact that they could pass as the 'global counsel' for a 'Western big brand company'.[36]

The valorization of this access to international (seemingly, Western) clients was consistently primed in these interviews. Yet, the advantage was received with enthusiasm not because of the better work these important clients promised (respondents were quick to reaffirm the '"non-legal advisory' nature of their work). Neither was it the case that these associates saw these jobs as stepping-stones to other international careers (when asked about their career prospects, none of the respondents saw these jobs as useful for transitioning into foreign firms, for example). Thus, this 'halo' prestige was sourced purely from the work being 'international'. Anand, an LPO employee who had given up a 10-year litigation practice to work for his firm, explains this advantage clearest:

> Let us face it, you know, most lawyers in India cannot so much as fantasize about getting into a legal department of top international companies like [famous US-based IT company] – that is not easy, right? Then you have an LPO hired by [famous US-based IT company] to do their everyday work. So most people are like – okay, this way, I can say I got the opportunity today to at least work with this company!

To clarify, this access to international clients per se is not new. LPO clients have always been predominantly international but the maturation of the market in 2009 had made this client base particularly salient for a combination of reasons: (a) with international market pressures to outsource, more prominent clients were seeking LPO services, making the client base more attractive to be associated with; (b) diffusion of this client knowledge by the press[37] had helped 'set' the brand name for some of these firms; and (c) India's closed legal regulatory regime made these LPO firms uniquely positioned in their access to international clients and therefore global work. With the exception of the top law firms that worked with their global elite counterparts on cross-border transactions, Indian lawyers did little transactional work for non-Indian clients. The smaller local firms and litigation practices (which were main workplace contenders for Suresh and his LPO peers) had little if any access to such 'branded, global' work, which made these LPO practices all the more attractive in the eyes of their recruits.

Access to Western work environments and 'American jobs'. Still, it was not just the access to global clients that these local firms and legal offices lacked. Respondents also claimed the relative advantage that these firms offered in terms of Western workplaces and environments. And there was evidence that this was evolving between the two periods of observation. While the 2006 interviews were held with employees and CEOs in small, 'back-end'-style offices, the 2009 interviews with the same organizations were in their new addresses: large US-law-firm-style offices in high-prestige business district spaces. These materially superior advantages compared well to most Indian law firm offices (upscale units in modern business parks, large working desks, double computer screens, etc.) and offered an effective lure for protective recruits.

Yet, it was not the physical spaces alone that had evolved – a distinctive advantage of these legal outsourcing offices was their continuing commitment to the nurturing of a Western corporate culture. The 2006 transcripts alluded to some evidence of this, but in 2009 this was a recurring theme of relative advantage. Crucial to understanding this advantage is to place it in context against the other legal offices in India. In contrast to law firms that continued to work like family-run offices of a single (or, at best, a couple of) lawyer(s), these corporate LPO units worked as professional corporate structures with definite work trajectories, transparent promotional policies and officious 'Western' business cultures, which made them attractive to the average law graduate in the country. As an employee who had left litigation practice in the Delhi courts and moved to Gurgaon (a suburb of Delhi) to work as a team manager in an LPO recalls:

> A lot of employees feel happier being in an LPO as opposed to a law firm in India because law firms in India do not work like law firms in the US or the UK. So, law firms, as you know, work like family-run businesses and especially if you work with a litigating practice, like I did, your work trajectory is proportional to what kind of family you are from and who you know. It may seem crude – but culturally, these things are very important in this country. I knew that if I stayed there, my promotions would have nothing to do with how hard I worked – but here [at this LPO X], it is like working for a corporate organization, you know? Your path is defined. You know that if you do X extra hours, you get this and you will go up this next step. I knew my talent would be recognized and that I would not be pushed down because of X, Y, Z factors that I had no control over.

In turn, these Western workplaces and work environments offered these Indian lawyers a chance at working in what they saw as a culturally superior environment for organizational growth. For instance, defending her decision to join an LPO instead of staying in the law firm she laterally transferred from, Rina, a prospective senior associate at a Mumbai LPO, reasons:

> So, you know, people can complain about this all they want – but the fact is, *outsourcing is also making American jobs available to someone like me*. I have been here almost a year now, and am going to be a senior manager.... These are totally different career choices for us and, I mean, they are wonderful because we hone skills without (having to deal with the) grind of litigation or unfairness [of] ... having to work in a law firm. I'll never go back to work in a law firm.

The 'people' Rina refers to here are the growing number of attorneys who oppose the growth of these LPO firms in India on the basis of what has been a rooted protectionist stance: a closed market for legal services.[38] Interestingly, there was no such opposition in 2006 because these firms, seen very much as supplementary to the legal profession, were not threats for local talent. The 'grind', for example, that she refers to above are the long hours that litigators in India dedicate to their job, often at little (or no) compensation for their work. And these were reasons that resonated with many respondents.

Access to foreign colleagues. Part of the international advantage in 2009 was the number of US/UK-trained lawyers these LPO firms had on-site as part- and full-time consultants. The influence this training provided was clearly important: take for instance, this transcript from a young woman who had left a law firm to join an LPO firm because she saw it as a superior opportunity:

> The intense observation that people need to make about this industry is that training by these foreign lawyers is all-round Western training that other

lawyers in India are not finding. The skill sets that LPOs emphasize because of the international exposure are unique. Take for example the attention to detail. That is one of the foremost because no Indian lawyer has ever laid emphasis on this particular attention to detail. But here, we have [name of foreign attorney] teaching us that.

But in addition to these valuable skill sets that employees found peculiar to the LPO setting, there was the recurring theme of an implied association advantage. In an otherwise largely homogenous work environment, this access to foreign-trained lawyers was seen as a key draw for new recruits. Again, like the access to foreign clients, this advantage was not seen as key because of the mobility or access to other foreign jobs that it provided. Instead, employees valued the training by these foreign colleagues in what they saw as key Western professional work ethic styles like "attention to detail". Further, respondents felt that being able to "talk to Sam* about NYC" or "ask Jenna* any questions about American law and culture", especially when they had to place a client conversation in context, made their workplace unique. Particularly salient was that these foreign-trained associates were accessible despite being in positions of power (usually senior managers, visiting supervisors). Maya, a new LPO associate's view of this advantage mirrors a consistently shared view:

"[foreign consultant] is from California and is a lawyer there. But he comes here to give us talks and training. If I have any questions, I can always just ask [foreign consultant] for advice. There is that comfort. We can use his first name and just talk to him without being worried or scared.

By contrast, at a litigation practice or a private law firm, Maya would have had limited contact with foreign consultants and clients and little freedom to be similarly approachable with her Indian bosses. This premium on association with high-prestige colleagues also had other advantages. Associates were encouraged not only to feel free to approach their American peers (most offices had open-door policies or open-office spaces and associations on a first-name basis), but also in some cases to meet them in social situations as well. Maya explained that house parties and team dinners were not uncommon, and groups would often go without prejudice to hierarchy within the organization. This association with high-status colleagues, especially to the extent that it extended to their non-office sphere (e.g. the ability to call a senior American colleague by first name in front of a family member/law school peer) added another visible prestige marker for these LPO associates.

4. The role of public perception: evidence from content analysis

While comprehensive interviews over the two time periods offered an exhaustive view of the sector, these data remain limited by some factors. First, given how nascent the sector was and how eager firms and employees alike were to 'get the word out', it is possible that the transcripts were riddled with a self-reporting bias, especially in responses about the rise in demand and the absolute increase in prestige. Second, since there are limited data available from these interviews about people outside the LPO sector (only 15 ancillary interviews between both years), we do not know what the public perception of this prestige was. Finally, given that all three researchers who collected the data were visiting from a prestigious American law school, it is possible that much of the Western bias that I am making a case about might well have been a response to what these respondents thought the interviewers would understand and appreciate as 'important'.

Given the dearth of large-scale representative data on the sector, I resorted to analyzing publicly available information about these outsourcing firms on the Internet to triangulate the existing interview data.[39] From this analysis, three broad trends emerged. First, in the years between Phase 1 and 2, there was more media coverage (7 vs. 145 cases) in more diffused channels (Table 7) than ever before.[40] Second, the tone of this reporting had changed to favor these firms. While earlier reports were preoccupied with advantages and disadvantages from a Western business standpoint (e.g. cost efficiency to Western firms), later reports were more focused on highlighting factors that might have had an impact on potential Indian recruits (e.g. 'shiny new offices'; see Table 8).[41] Third, in turn there was evidence of a deliberate reconceptualization of the sector in these later reports. Fewer complaints about the quality of work and a descriptive emphasis on these firms as superior places of work (Table 9)

Table 7. *Descriptive results of the content analysis of publicly available internet resources on Indian legal process outsourcing (N = 152)*

	Pre T1 (2006 study)		T1–T2 (2009 study)		
	2000–2004	2005	2006	2007	2008
Total cases (N = 201)	3	6	39	67	86
Coded cases (N = 152)	2	5	26	44	75
Indian sources					
Indian national news (e.g. *The Hindu Times of India*)	–	1	8	7	17
Indian business news (e.g. *The Economic Times*)	–	4	13	13	15
Indian local news (e.g. *Hindu Education Plus*)	–	–	–	4	1
Western sources					
Western news (e.g. *Washington News, Time*)	–	–	–	1	3
Western legal news (e.g. *ABA Net, AM Daily*)	1	–	1	6	2
Other sources					
Web-only articles (e.g. *Rediff Business*)	1	–	1	4	15
Press releases (e.g. *PR Newswire*)	–	–	3	6	11
Legal websites/blogs (*Law.Net*)	–	–	–	1	11
Asian news (Channel Asia)	–	–	–	2	–
Main focus of case (only 1 count/case)					
Western advantage	1	1	10	2	15
Indian recruit advantage	–	–	8	29	33
Other	1	4	8	13	27
Total cases	2	5	26	44	75

Note: (a) Both interview studies were conducted in the first few weeks of January 2006 and 2009 respectively. For ease, all 2006 cases are considered 'post T1'. Similarly, no cases in 2009 were coded. (b) In the 'Focus of case' measure above, I give counts for any case that concentrated on *only* the advantage. The maximum count per case was 1. For a more detailed summary of this focus, see Table 8. (c) For a more detailed summary of type of sources and exhaustive coding examples, see Tables 8 and 9. (d) Cases were selected using a Google Advanced search for the words 'legal process outsourcing' and 'India'.

Table 8. *Focus of the data, from publicly available internet resources on Indian legal process outsourcing (N = 152)*

	Pre T1 (2006 study)		T1–T2 (2009 study)		
	2000–2004	2005	2006	2007	2008
Western focus (totals)	2	3	11	3	20
Advantage (e.g. efficient, cost, better work)	1	1	10	2	15
Disadvantage (e.g. attrition, work quality, confidentiality)	–	–	–	–	1
Both (e.g. 'cost efficient but high attrition')	1	2	1	1	4
Indian recruitment focus (totals)	0	2	12	30	40
Advantage (e.g. lucrative, western clients, better offices)	–	–	8	29	33
Disadvantage (e.g. routine work, low prestige)	–	–	3	1	3
Both (e.g. 'pays well but low-end work')	–	2	1		4
Joint focus (West + India) (e.g. 'win-win situation')	–	–	3	5	5
Neutral (no relevant focus) (e.g. press release about a joint venture LPO)	–	–	–	6	10
Total	2	5	26	44	75

Note: (a) Both interview studies were conducted in the first few weeks of January 2006 and 2009 respectively. For ease, all 2006 cases are considered 'post T1'. Similarly, no cases in 2009 were coded. (b) 'Focus cases' counts refer to the main focus of the article/news report/press release only. For a more detailed code count of the data, see Table 9.

presumably helped lend credibility to aspiring recruits. Thus, over time, the same substantive work that was previously reported as 'routine' and 'repetitive' had become work that was 'glamorous':[42] and the associative Western 'halo'[43] had at least some part in this transformation.

These content analysis data offer an important dimension to our understanding of the dynamics of the LPO industry because they shed light on the role of public perceptions in molding the professional identity of the sector – in only five years – from 'just another job' to an enviable career prospect. This construction of public opinion by media reports offer that, even though work remained fairly standard and process driven, recruits and bystanders alike were viewing the industry differently. At a basic level, it could have just been that the increased attention that the sector was getting just offered more publicity and, therefore, more demand. In any event, working for an LPO firm had become a real legal career option for many who would have never coveted the position before: a viable alternative to domestic legal jobs.

5. Conclusion: why prestige matters

In this paper, I make a case for the pivotal role Western influences have had in shaping the trajectory of professional prestige of the legal outsourcing industry in India. From these data, there is some evidence that factors like Western clients and 'foreign' coworkers are seen as markers of global signaling in ways that have made this transformation of a workspace real. This is important because it makes for a case in which a legal deliverable, on being deprofessionalized and stripped of many of the

Table 9. *Detailed count (%) for all prominent codes in the data, from publicly available internet resources on Indian legal process outsourcing (N = 152)*

	Pre T1 (2006 study)		T1–T2 (2009 study)		
Code counts	2000–2004	2005	2006	2007	2008
Total coded cases	2	5	26	44	75
Cumulative trends					
More jobs	–	0.40	0.46	0.55	0.62
Higher demand	–	–	0.31	0.39	0.52
High quality recruits	–	–	0.23	0.32	0.48
Sector growth	–	0.60	0.23	0.45	0.57
Western (demand) advantages					
Economic efficiency	1.00	1.00	0.65	0.25	0.50
Higher quality of work than West	–	–	10	0.25	0.33
Western (demand) disadvantages					
Attrition	0.50	0.60	0.25	–	0.01
Poor quality of recruits	0.50	0.40	0.15	–	–
Indian (supply) sisadvantages					
Routine work	0.50	0.80	0.19	0.04	0.04
Low prestige work	1.00	0.80	0.12	0.04	0.04
Indian (supply) advantages					
Traditional professional prestige factors					
Professionally pure legal work	–	–	–	0.02	–
High-end work	–	–	–	–	–
High-end work for non-lawyers (e.g. patent filings by engineer)	–	0.20	0.60	0.14	0.19
'Halo' high-end law work (e.g. ambiguous reference to work done, referring to LPO as a law firm)	–	–	–	0.06	0.05
Instrumental prestige factors					
Lucrative	0.50	0.80	0.58	–	–
New offices	–	–	–	0.11	0.12
Western 'halo' factors					
Western clients	0.50	0.80	0.39	0.68	0.73
West as global opportunity	–	–	0.08	0.54	0.66
Western corporate culture	–	–	–	0.16	0.11

Note: (a) All 'counts' above are percentages of cases that were coded with a reference to the particular theme. (b) Both interview studies were conducted in the first few weeks of January 2006 and 2009 respectively. For ease, all 2006 cases are considered 'post T1'. Similarly, no cases in 2009 were coded. (c) Code counts include all codes that appear in a certain case. While each code was only coded once, each case was likely to have more than one code. These count data are different from the 'focus' data (which are limited to one count per case). If you wish to see the only focus counts, see Table 8. LPO, legal process outsourcing.

factors that offered it traditional value, gains prominence on being handled by a new workforce. Universality of professional prestige has traditionally not taken into consideration the effect of globalization as a prestige factor in and of itself. I offer here that, in addition to the markers used, and especially while trying to understand the non-industrialized world, an approach more reflective of the 'halo' effect of the West is needed.

The way prestige works in relaying value at the individual level of the worker is important because it reflects the efficiency of the larger work chain. The change in perception of this work from legal outsourcing to 'global lawyering' is pertinent because it has changed the way people think about their jobs at the individual level. At the interactional level this matters because of what these jobs have begun to signal to others with whom these people are in communication.

In some part, the way these jobs have been portrayed by the media has influenced this perception. But other factors – seemingly incidental factors like the way an office looks and the kind of food the canteen serves, etc. – have been instrumental in both creating this media perception as well as the worker's own. As a young woman in a Noida-based LPO said about her job, "I am part of [big American corporation]'s global counsel team" – and the fact that she works in a company that looks like this corporation's India office has helped cement this idea both to herself and to her local networks. She could have been doing the same work for this company from a corner of a three-bedroom apartment in Delhi (a very common set-up for early LPOs when they started), but until the offices looked like they did – in posh corporate parks, with high security and foreign colleagues – they were not capable of signaling the same tenor of prestige.

The lesson to be learned from these data, which outline a sense of professional favor for jobs independent of the quality of work, is that while researching in a developing country context, broader markers of value have to be given regard. My agenda in targeting only these unorthodox factors (e.g. Western corporate culture, American colleagues) is not to disrespect the traditional assumptions about prestige creation – but instead, to add necessary nuance while attempting to study global professions. The focus on the role of globalization and association to the West is important when trying to frame, record and analyze the consequences of an increasingly global legal profession. From the supply side, an important part of sustainable delivery of a quality legal product lies in an analysis at the individual level of the worker. If a lawyer in India who works on a contract for, say, Google, from a multi-storied office, feels like she is part of Google's 'global legal team', it is more likely she will remain invested in the job and committed to a quality end product than if she thinks of herself as a lawyer who 'just does document review'. But this is not all. As this study reflects, prestige linkages can be – and are – drawn from client names but their non-functional signal-ability can be as important in creating and maintaining a culture of assimilation within these firms. Thus, even if she is doing document review for Google, the fact that she is doing it in an office that is globally networked, along with coworkers who are internationally trained, all add to her realization of being part of a global legal workforce. In turn, being able to imagine oneself as a worker in a natural extension of an American or Western workspace is a powerful construct and an important one to consider as we study and research these professional spaces. From the demand side, trying to understand the factors that shape this focus becomes important to ensure a quality end product. Thus, creating an environment where a worker feels invested in the firm is not just useful at the level of the individual organization or worker, it reflects on the long-term sustainability of the industry as a whole. In turn, it is important to be aware of the effects of being a global demander of legal services on the quality of the end product, as we move determinately into this muddled and disparate internationalization of the legal profession.

From an institutional perspective, it is important to note that many of these factors that have evolved over time to garner prestige are (a) associated strongly with technological innovation that was (b) not initially introduced with any foresight about prestige associated with the worker. If we recall the evolution of this industry as a whole, the high-technology requirements (laptops with high security, login-specific servers, doors with screened entry, multiple desktop monitors that were meant to connect 'up' and 'down') were aimed at client-centric efficiency. But in some sense, it was this efficiency that enabled the development of prestige too: the restricted access to data made people feel more privileged; the teams that were set up with unique access with 'code names' for their projects felt similar to their law firm counterparts that worked in specific teams. Similarly, their foreign colleagues who were sent initially to increase productivity and make Western clients feel more comfortable, ended up increasing the value of association for the Indian employees, who were enriched by the diversity of their work ecosystem. Technology and security, in turn, gave these lawyers access to new codes (for example, almost every interview in 2009 had the mention of terms like 'QC' – local speak for quality control – organizational charts, six sigma, 'best practices') that were seen as access to new information and, in turn, a new professional space. Add to this media adulations, and the workspace had the capacity to transform in the imagination of these workers as one that was newly fitting of value, newly transformative in its scope. A Marxian perspective would argue that this technology meant to divide labor would have left the end worker even more alienated from these jobs. Instead, here is a case where something that started off as a deprofessionalizing process-based mechanism had, when imported to a non-Western context, the capacity to make something more professional, more prestigious (Marx, 1978). And in the construction of this prestige, the way these norms translate globally and the impact of globalization as a factor in itself has mattered.

The other reason why this is important is because it offers a case in which local norms are influenced by expectations and aspirations towards expected global norms. At the same time, it holds close the comfort of local norms and values[44] – together creating what Wilkins, Silver and other scholars of the globalization of the legal profession have called a "glocal" space for negotiation of prestige and value. In turn, this creates not just a new form of professional prestige, but a new professional space and, within it, a new professional. By no longer being a 'back-end' lawyer, this global conceptualization is affording more lawyers value and meaning to their work than ever before; and as researchers of the global legal profession, it remains integral for us to see that not all the factors offering this prestige are functional.

Of course, perhaps it is not all this nuanced and just simply a glorified economic argument. The attraction to the Western clients and ways of interaction and association might simply be because the West has invested in these firms much more than any other country. But other similar associations (e.g. like the 'brain bank' migration to the Gulf by Indian Keralites; see Khadria, 2008) have historically not been considered attractive in the same way as this association to the West: which in turn leaves something to be explored. It might just be that India is ripe for recognizing Western cues better than others because of their long history with colonial influence and are better at valuing (and reaching out) for Western markers as sources of prestige in themselves. Either way, this particular conceptualization of prestige in the developing country context places a burden on companies working with India (and other countries that might be as susceptible to finding globalized associations as halo indicators) to be cognizant and respectful of this difference.

Acknowledgements

Previous versions of this paper have been presented at the Onati Workshop on Too Many Lawyers, The Stanford South Asia By the Bay conference and the International Sociological Association Forum. I thank participants and colleagues for important comments and reactions to these drafts. All of the empirical interview data collection for this project was made possible by the Harvard Law School Program on the Legal Profession. The author specifically thanks David Grusky, Pavan Mamadi, Russ Pearce, Woody Powell, Rebecca Sandefur, Carole Silver and David Wilkins for important comments and contributions that shaped the thinking of this paper.

Notes

[1] Legal academic research has been concerned with the expansion of the Bar and its consequences. See, for example, Ayer (1979) and Stern (1994).

[2] For a broad overview of how technology affects global change, see Grubler (2003). For a review of the literature on how IT impacts organizational characteristics and outcomes, see Dewett & Jones (2001). Other scholars, like Silver (2010), however, have highlighted with caution the regulatory implications technology and the legal profession.

[3] For example, Laurel Terry (2008) argues that globalization impacts 'non-global' US lawyers because of the challenges it presents to their own career prospects and trajectories.

[4] For a brief overview of the outsourcing industry in India and its association with globalization generally, see Dossani & Kenney (2007).

[5] There has been an increasing literature on the deprofessionalization and the consequent consequences it has for the legal profession both domestically and internationally. This debate has gained particular significance in light of the (UK) Law Society's Training Framework Review (see Boon *et al.*, 2005).

[6] While the first reported instance of offshoring legal services to India occurred in 1995, legal outsourcing did not begin in earnest until the early 2000s. For a detailed review of the sector, and the importance of studying these supply-side characteristics of the process.

[7] Embracing globalization has been an important strategy for various (and particularly, Asian) organizational outcomes (see Johansson & Yip, 1994).

[8] The globalization literature is rich with this neocolonialism perspective. For instance, research on Taiwan shows that, while globalization has been useful in the creation of jobs, it has negatively affected the work and lives of people in informal and traditional economic sectors (Tsai *et al.*, 2006). In the context of the legal profession and outsourcing specifically, Jay Krishnan (2006–2007) argues that, while outsourcing has indeed offered great rewards for those Indians who have the capacity to access it, most Indians are not participants in or beneficiaries of this fairly stratified industry.

[9] These socio-cultural changes happen at different levels of analysis. In some cases, globalization can (and does) impact culture at the level of the industry as a whole. For example, research on the social work industry offers an example in which institutional processes industry-wide have been altered by the introduction of technocratization and globalization (see Dominelli & Hoogvelt, 1996). For a review of the changes in culture at the level of the organization generally, see Prasad (2003). At the individual level, these consequences are particularly pertinent because they offer us perspective on the local identity of the workplace – something that can have far-reaching consequences on the actual production of the end product. As Rachel Sherman (2006, pp. 421–422) argues, "Workplaces are increasingly embedded in a variety of global processes, such as new kinds of labor migration, capital mobility, and economic integration. The rise of service work brings the customer and hence the question of consumption into the work site. And increasing academic interest in a range of sources of identity, from gender, race, and ethnicity to citizenship and consumption, complicates the picture. These factors begin to force the study of work out of the workplace." Tony Fang (2005–2006), for instance, advocates for paying closer attention to the national paradoxes and dynamics while researching cross-cultural management in what he calls a change from "onion" (a Cold War paradigm of imposing perspectives) to "ocean" (a more inclusive way).

[10] For a review of the literature on construction and resistance encountered in the creation of global professions, see, generally, Fourcade (2006). Fourcade explores how connections to US-based standards of work and practice are used in local negotiations to gain various kinds of corporate and political legitimacy. In turn, the paper argues that this construction of the profession – in this case, of economics – is a product of complicated transnational mechanisms in which globalization is a major factor in the construction of professional boundaries (see also Malin, 2000).

[11] We know that Western culture has been pivotal in shaping popular choices (Piklington, 2002), norms about interpersonal relationships, attitudes towards sex (Karena, 2003) and perceptions about body image (Lake *et al.*, 2000). More pertinently, in the labor market context, others (Nadeem, 2009) have shown that cultural processes and identities of people and institutions alike are continuously shaped and resisted by globalized influences – especially when Western jobs are 'shipped' out for organizational and economic efficiency.

[12] This is not to say that there is no sociological research on outsourcing per se. For a review of the ways in which outsourcing, generally, has been changing the nature of work being done, see Davis-Blake & Broschak (2009). They make the argument in this review piece that outsourcing is associated with important changes in design and functioning of jobs, work groups and internal labor markets (p. 322), yet much of the research has been concentrated on the macro-levels of either defining the industry or explaining the arrangements within it. However, while the authors highlight the ways in which outsourcing affects the nature of work in the lead firms (i.e. firms that outsource), their review does not include the specific case of outsourced legal work because (a) the research they review did not focus on the offshoring of substantive professional tasks and (b) their focus on culture and micro-level perspectives were restricted to a lead firm perspective.

[13] See Haug (1973, 1975, 1977) on the IT sector, and Larson (1977, 1979) on the medical profession.

[14] Wegener (1992) posits that there is an inherent distance between the end of social hierarchy and social closure. Based on this orientation of stratification (order-hierarchy vs. conflict-closure) and social action (normative-subjective and rational-objective), he offers four classification of prestige research. I only concentrate on these theories to the extent that they apply to professional prestige.

[15] The conception of prestige at the societal level borrows from a traditional stratification framework. Burdened with the task of placing individuals in social positions and motivating them to work, societies are seen as forced to create and place people in jobs with different hierarchical rewards and requirements (Davis & Moore, 1945). When this is seen as an 'integrated value system' (Parsons, 1940), individuals within the society validate the system by valuing those jobs that are most important (and therefore, have the most rewards). From a purely functional standpoint, then, in most societies prestige is measured by functional uniqueness (no other person can perform this task) and dependence (degree to which others are dependent on you). In addition to

this functionality of importance, there might also be the ancillary function of 'purity' (Abbott, 1981) that can make a job prestigious and independent of achievement; jobs could still be prestigious because they are closest to the centers, or core, of what the society values (Abbott, 1981). At a more individual level, employees are likely to think of a job as prestigious if some salient features of the job (independent of importance, function and sophistication, that is) appeal to them. Prestige then can potentially be primed by the 'desirability' of a job (Goldthorpe & Hope, 1974; Hauser & Featherman, 1977) – or the amenities that the job offers at the individual level. While monetary compensation and pay-related amenities are key to this job desirability (Garbin & Bates, 1966), nonmonetary characteristics (vacation weeks, portion of the job that is repetitive, hazards, etc.) can also be key (Jencks *et al.*, 1988).

[16] Naturally, part of the problem could be that what is 'core' to the profession is evolving constantly, both locally and globally. For instance, technology is offering an extension that is changing the very nature of what is prestigious globally.

[17] The original collection of data was for a Harvard Law School research project (Program of the Legal Profession LPO Study) that was studying the industry broadly at the macro-level. Respondents were, in these interviews, requested to describe in detail sector and employment data, which enabled us to contrast differences over time. Table 2 gives summary information about the interviews conducted. For a review of the different players in the market at the time of these interviews, see Table 3.

[18] Descriptive data were collected first in January 2006 (Phase 1) by Shaun Mathew and Vikram Thomas on a still nascent industry. In January 2009 (Phase 2), I went back to track many of the original respondents to do a comparative study. A broader institutional perspective of these findings and change in supply side mechanisms between these periods is the subject of a different research paper (Ballakrishnen & Wilkins, 2012, unpublished): I only focus here on the data relating to prestige.

[19] Idem.

[20] Tables 4 and 5 offer a detailed overview of the firm and employee characteristics of the preliminary and ancillary interviews. Note that all firm and institution characteristics in the tables (Table 4, particularly) were coded after data collection rather than during. I stress particularly on the 'Western' attributes of the managers and associates because it was a theme that, though not initially primed for in these interviews, emerged. All interviews were conducted face to face in English, typically, in the firm's premises, and were subsequently tape-recorded and transcribed. Interviews were typically 30-45 minutes long post-briefing of the project, although some lasted up to an hour. All data were open-coded for themes using the qualitative methods program *HyperResearch*.

[21] Based on interviewees' descriptions of the LPO structures, work done and perceived prestige of these firms, these open-coded transcripts were further amalgamated into emergent codes in three broad areas: (a) the nature of the work done (type of low-, mid- and high-end work, process-oriented work); (b) relative position of LPOs within the Indian legal labor market (institutional structure, comparison with litigating firms, comparison with law firms, effect of the financial crunch, demand for jobs by elite graduates); and (c) employee perceptions of LPO advantages (foreign clients, global exposure, opportunity, international networks, training, prestige). During this part of the coding process, passages within the transcripts with statements relating to the prestige theoretical framework (functional importance of LPOs, professional purity of the work done, individual-level advantages for employees) were selected. Based on the coding of these transcripts, recurring themes (across several cases) were identified and examined across firms and between the two timeframes

[22] While the 2006 transcripts describe small, mid-size firms (median size of about 10 lawyers + other non-law staff), most of the LPOs interviewed in 2009 had between 35–80 lawyers on their rolls, with the largest LPO seeking expansion to a 1,000-lawyer office by the end of the financial year.

[23] There were fewer than 50 LPO firms in 2006, compared with an estimated 250 firms in 2009 (Value Notes Report, 2009).

[24] Explaining one firm's advantage in the job market vis-à-vis all career avenues with the exception of these top firms, one managing partner of a Mumbai LPO explains: "The common criticism to this

field is always whether you are still a 'real' lawyer.... But you have to remember, you are starting from a position where you would have never gotten yourself into a [top] law firm in the first place – so you cannot really be comparing it to that. In all other cases, this is."

[25] This interest from lateral litigation firm employees (an interest that was not evident in Phase 1) as a sign of an increase in demand is pertinent for two reasons. First, Indian litigating firms (which is where many of these lateral recruits were from) were not affected adversely by the recession because they were not dependent on Western companies and firms for work. Second, firms that did have clients in the West who were affected by the recession were more likely to get more, rather than less, work post-recession – leading to a general increase in jobs all around. Thus, it cannot be that these recruits were joining LPOs because they were being let go from their jobs at their law firms. While the recession no doubt played a big part in sending more work to India, this rise in demand among lateral recruits was independent of any effects attributable to the recession.

[26] Of course, there is one other effect of the recession on these labor markets that I refrain from explaining here for lack of applicability: the quality of potential law firm associates returning to India from Western jobs that they were let go from during the recession. Their competition, however, is unlikely to have affected the demographic of the current interview population.

[27] Firms in *Phase 1* were wary of locating legal talent for their jobs because of their inability to respond to the legal job requirement that they felt these employees were in search for. As a result, these LPOs were very much a peripheral process industry that posed no competition to domestic legal institutions in as much as talent was concerned. By contrast, firms in Phase 2 were actively competing (with limited exception of the few domestic elite firms) for legal talent not just from better schools, but also from lawyers looking to transition within the profession from litigation and law firm practices. Most interviewees, agreed that, while they were not really competing with the very top-tier graduates that joined the 3,000-odd 'top firm' jobs in the market, their recruitment advantages were highly comparable to all other options that these graduates had (local firms, litigation practices, etc.). Take, for example, this recollection by a top partner in a Mumbai LPO about the capability of these firms to retain talent now, although they would not have been able to just a few years ago: "And now, when we are called to take part [at the job fair in the earlier mentioned law school], we only go if it is a first day of recruiting. If [name of law firm] is going on Day 1 to recruit its employees, I am going on Day 1 too. It may not be the same slot – but it better be the same day. Otherwise, I am not going. There are enough applications for me to review."

[28] Outsourced professional services typically remain low-end because of home-country ethical restrictions on professional responsibility. This has remained especially true for the legal services outsourced to India between the three years of observation, especially with heavy restrictions on outsourcing pure legal work like legal advice. Pure legal work is considered the 'practice of law'. The ABA forbids offshore lawyers to 'practice law' without it being reviewed and revised by an American lawyer. Furthermore, Indian legal regulation does not allow the practice of foreign law or the practice of law by foreign lawyers within the country.

[29] Litigation support, an area viewed by most firms as rapidly growing, includes scanning, conversion into editable text (OCR), database creation, objective coding, electronic discovery, document review, fact and motion chronology preparation, and basic 'landscape' or survey research.

[30] In this setting, LPO employees sift through the plethora of sales contracts, loan agreements and other company agreements for change-in-control clauses and other issues potentially relevant in a merger context.

[31] In some exceptions, Mathew and Thomas (2006) noted that smaller firms focused initially on supporting solo practitioners in torn claims. A lawyer they interviewed in a Mumbai LPO firm (which had closed operations by the time Ballakrishnen was back in 2009) commented that his firm helped an attorney in Pasadena, California with accident cases by doing everything from basic research to drafting the opening statement.

[32] One pure-play LPO firm in Mumbai, for instance, processes qualified domestic relations orders, which divide the assets of a plan participant in an employee pension plan upon a change in status

(e.g. divorce). This involved reviewing court orders and related state-law-governed documents and determining compliance with ERISA and the federal tax code for Fortune 500 corporations and family law counsel. This process involved collecting all relevant documentation into a docket for the client to provide to the appeals committee.

[33] For example, most associates mentioned clear trajectories within the firm and said they would only consider attrition to the extent that it was to another firm within the sector.

[34] All names have been changed to protect confidentiality of the interviewees.

[35] See, for example, Sandefur (2001) on corporate law associates who do routine work for large corporations to consume the prestige of the corporation)

[36] Respondents, especially in the Phase 2 interviews, frequently would talk at length about their US and UK clients, even if it was the case that the firm did work for other big brand companies in Asia or the Middle East. In one such interview, when it seemed particularly odd that the respondent (a senior associate who was very excited about working at this Delhi firm) had not mentioned non-Western clients, I asked about the firm's offices in another big Asian city (information that I had gathered before the interview from the Internet), his clients there and the advantage that offered him as an employee. In his response, he made no reference to the clients and limited his eagerness to the fact that the other Asian office was a good promotion prospect (senior Indian LPO employees are often sent as visiting managers to set up other offices and train staff). This hand waving directed at non-Western clients in one interview is by no means enough to charge the entire industry of a purely Western halo. But the fact that so few of these respondents mentioned non-Western clients (especially when their websites highlighted sales locations across the world) is salient.

[37] See the content analysis in section 4.

[38] There has been some brewing discontent about the operation of these legal outsourcing firms and, in 2010, a Madras High Court writ petition challenged the operation of these LPOs as a violation of the existing protectionist legislation. Irrespective of the actual outcome of the still undecided writ, it offers some evidence of the slow (but sure) transformation of public perception of the LPO sector from a back-end service provider to a core contender in the protectionist debate for domestic legal services.

[39] To triangulate this evidence with public sources of information, I used timeline data from all the English sources in the Google search results for the terms 'legal outsourcing', 'LPO' and/or 'India'. All national newspapers in India have online editions and coding their content for factors influencing prestige was relevant in that it pointed to the public information that the country was consuming in the three years between interviews. Table 7 offers descriptive information about the sources analyzed and brief information about the main focus of the cases. Table 8 gives more information about the focus of these articles – note, however, that each 'case' was only coded once for a main focus.

[40] See Table 7 for a complete review of these counts. While most data before the Phase 1 interviews were in Indian business newspapers that possibly had a select reading audience, data between 2006–2009 appeared in more pervasive sources – like national daily newspapers and educational supplements. It seems understandable, then, that there was more diffusion of knowledge about the industry in 2009 than in 2006.

[41] Note that in the pre-Phase 2 time period, there were more reports in the public media with an Indian recruitment focus (82 vs. 34 cases), a higher percentage were targeted towards advantages for Indian recruits (0.86 of all Indian cases) than about Western advantages (0.79 of all Western cases).

[42] For one, the disadvantage of what were initially labeled cumbersome technical jobs was replaced ambiguous references (e.g. "we outsource legal intelligence"), or references to high-end work that was done by engineers in the firm (e.g. high-end patent filing). To compensate for this subdued reference to low-prestige work (only 7 cases between 2006 and 2009), these later cases focused on the advantage for Indian lawyers that these firms were offering – and the nature of these advantages evolved over time. Also, reports that focused on the advantages of jobs in this new sector, primed Western work using both known clients and references to generic prestige markers (e.g. "Firm X does all the legal work for many UK law firms").

[43] There is some research on the halo factors that influence prestige in the organizational context. For instance, buyers attribute their positive perceptions of a high-prestige organization to its outputs (independent of the actual transaction), thereby increasing the output's perceived value through a "halo effect" (Sine *et al.*, 2003). In another example, Perrow (1961) found that patients relied on general hospital characteristics entirely unrelated to their medical needs (such as building design) to decide whether or not to seek particular health services at the hospital in question. Similarly, in terms of chances of obtaining recognition, a scientist gained more from affiliation with a major university than from high productivity (Crane, 1965). Seen differently, it may be that buyers prefer to transact with more prestigious organizations because the mere interaction with high prestige affords a prestige by association (Sine *et al.*, 2003). In particular, research shows that prestige may rest upon the 'image' or a 'value-laden symbol' or some other factor completely independent of the essential quality of the product/service (Perrow, 1961). The prestige that global exposure and access to international workspaces and colleagues affords these Indian lawyers extends well to this explanation.

[44] For example, a manager at a Noida-based LPO firm said, "We give our workers the security of medical insurance not just for themselves, but for their entire family: who else does that, you tell me? We understand that if the family is happy, he is happy and he will work with us. We understand them."

References

Abbott, A. (1981) Status and strain in the professions, *American Journal of Sociology*, 86(4), pp. 819–833.

Abbott, A. (1988) *The System of Professions* (Chicago, University of Chicago Press).

Ayer, J. (1979) Do lawyers do more harm than good?, *American Bar Association Journal*, 65, pp. 1053–1058.

Boon, A., Flood, J. & Webb, J. (2005) Postmordern professions? The fragmentation of legal education and the legal profession, *Journal of Law and Society*, 32(3), pp. 473–492.

Clarke, M. (1999) The professionalisation of financial advice in Britain, *Sociological Review*, 48(1), pp. 58–79.

Crane, D. (1965) Scientists at major and minor universities: a study of productivity and recognition, *American Sociological Review*, 30(5), pp. 699–714.

Davis, K. & Moore, W.E. (1945) Some principles of stratification, *American Sociological Review*, 10(2), pp. 242–249.

Davis-Blake, A. & Broschak, J.P. (2009) Outsourcing and the changing nature of work, *Annual Review of Sociology*, 35, pp. 321–340.

Dewett, T. & Jones, G.R. (2001) The role of information technology in the organization: a review, model and assessment, *Journal of Management*, 27(3), pp. 313–346.

Dominelli, L. & Hoogvelt, A. (1996) Globalization and the technocratization of social work, *Critical Social Policy*, 16(47), pp. 45–62.

Dossani, R. & Kenney, M. (2007) The next wave of globalization: relocating service provision to India, *World Development*, 35(5), pp. 772–791.

Erlanger, H. (1980) The allocation of status within occupations: the case of the legal profession, *Social Forces*, 58(3), pp. 882–903.

Fang, T. (2005–2006) From 'onion' to 'ocean': paradox and change in national cultures, *International Studies of Management & Organization*, 35(4), pp. 71–90.

Fourcade, M. (2006) The construction of a global profession: the Transnationalization of economics, *American Journal of Sociology*, 112(1), pp. 145–194.

Friedman, T.L. (2005) *The World Is Flat: A Brief History of the Twenty First Century* (New York, Farrar, Straus & Giroux).

Garbin, A.P. & Bates, F.L. (1966) Occupational prestige and its correlates: a re-examination, *Social Forces*, 44(3), pp. 295–302.

Goldthorpe, J.H. & Hope, K. (1974) *The Social Grading of Occupations: A New Approach and Scale* (Oxford, Clarendon Press).

Grubler, A. (2003) *Technology and Global Change* (Cambridge, Cambridge University Press).

Haug, M. R. (1973) Deprofessionalization: an alternative hypothesis for the future, *Sociological Review Monograph*, 20, pp. 195–211.

Haug, M.R. (1975) The deprofessionalization of everyone?, *Sociological Focus*, 8(3), pp. 197–213.

Haug, M.R. (1977) Computer technology and the obsolescence of the concept of profession, in: M.R. Haug & J. Dofny (Eds) *Work and Technology* (London, Sage), pp. 215–228.

Hauser, R.M. & Featherman, D.L. (1977) *The Process of Stratification, Trends and Analyses* (New York, Academic Press).

Hodge, R.W., Treiman, D.J. & Rossi, P.H. (1966) A comparative study of occupational prestige, in: R. Bendix & S.M. Lipset (Eds) *Class, Status and Power* (New York, Free Press), pp. 309–321.

Inkeles, A. & Rossi, P.H. (1956) National comparisons of occupational prestige, *American Journal of Sociology*, 61(4), pp. 329–339.

Jencks, C, Perman, L. & Rainwater, L. (1988) What is a good job? A new measure of labor-market success, *American Journal of Sociology*, 93(6), pp. 1322–1357.

Johansson, J.K. & Yip, G.S. (1994) Exploiting globalization potential: US and Japanese strategies, *Strategic Management Journal*, 15(8), pp. 579–601.

Karena, C. (2003) Monsoon wedding: raining on tradition, *Australian Screen Education Online*, 33, pp. 117–120.

Khadria, B. (2008) India: skilled migration to developed countries, labor migration to the Gulf, in: S. Castles & R.D. Wise (Eds), *Migration and Development: Perspectives from the South* (Switzerland, International Organization of Migration), pp. 79–112.

Krishnan, J.K. (2006–2007) Outsourcing and globalizing legal profession, *William & Mary Law Review*, 48, p. 2189.

Lake, A.J., Staiger, P.K. & Glowinski, H. (2000) Effect of Western culture on women's attitudes to eating and perceptions of body shape, *International Journal of Eating Disorders*, 27(1), pp. 83–89.

Larson, M.S. (1977) *The Rise of Professionalism* (Berkeley, University of California Press).

Larson, M.S. (1979) Professionalism: rise and fall, *International Journal of Health Services*, 9, pp. 607–627.

Laumann, E.O. & Heinz, J.P. (1977) Specialization and prestige in the legal profession: the structure of deference, *American Bar Foundation Research Journal*, 2(1), pp. 155–216.

Lewis, L.S. (1967) On prestige and loyalty of university faculty, *Administrative Science Quarterly*, 11(4), pp. 629–642.

Lowendahl, B. (2005) *Strategic Management of Professional Service Firms* (Copenhagen, Copenhagen Business School Press).

Malin, N. (Ed.) (2000) *Professionalism, Boundaries and the Workplace* (London, Routledge).

Marx, K. (1978) Alienation and social classes, in: *The Marx Engels Reader*, 2nd ed., pp. 133–135.

Mathew, S. & Thomas, V. (2006) *Winter Term Writing Project*, Harvard Law School.

Nadeem, S. (2009) Macaulay's (cyber) children: the cultural politics of outsourcing in India, *Cultural Sociology*, 3(1), pp. 102–122.

Parsons, T. (1940) An analytical approach to the theory of social stratification, *American Journal of Sociology*, 45(6), pp. 841–862.

Perrow, C. (1961) Organizational prestige: some functions and dysfunctions, *American Journal of Sociology*, 66(4), pp. 335–341.

Prasad, A. (Ed.) (2003) *Postcolonial Theory and Organizational Analysis: A Critical Engagement* (New York, Palgrave Macmillan).

Ray, M.S. (2006) 'Teams and the control of work: a case study in Arizona, in: R. Mugridge & R. Bazirijan (Eds) *Teams in Library Technical Services* (Oxford, Scarecrow), pp. 45–61.

Reichman, N. & Sterling, J. (2010) So, you want to be a lawyer? The quest for professional identity in a changing legal world, *Fordham Law Review*, 78(7), pp. 2289–2314.

Sandefur, R.L. (2001) Work and honor in the law: prestige and the division of lawyer's labor, *American Sociological Review*, 66(3), pp. 382–403.

Sang, M.L. (1969) Organizational identification of scientists, *Academy of Management Journal*, 12(3), pp. 327–337.

Shils, E. (1994 [1968]) Deference, in: D.B. Gursky (Ed.) *Social Stratification: Class, Race and Gender in Sociological Perspective* (Boulder, CO, Westview), pp. 197–203.

Sherman, R. (2006) Rethinking the ethnographic local identity, culture, and politics at work in the global economy, *Work & Occupations*, 33(4), pp. 421–422.

Sine, W.D., Shane, S. & Di Gregorio, D. (2003) The halo effect and technology licensing: the influence of institutional prestige on the licensing of university inventions author(s), *Management Science*, 49(4), pp. 478–496.

Silver, C. (2010) What we don't know can hurt us: the need for empirical research in regulating lawyers and legal services in the global economy, *Faculty Publications*, Paper 38. Available at: http://www.repository.law.indiana.edu/facpub/38

Stern, B. (1994/1995) Too many lawyers, *Experience*, 5, p. 44.

Terry, L. (2008) The legal world is flat: globalization and its effect on lawyers practicing in non-global law firms, *Northwestern Journal of International Law & Business*, 28(3), pp. 527–560.

Tsai, Y.-M. *et al.* (2006) The personal consequences of globalization in Taiwan, *Ethnology*, 45(4), pp. 275–285.

Value Notes Report (2009) *Legal Process Outsourcing: Crisis Creates New Opportunities*. Available at: http://www.sourcingnotes.com/content/view/554/1/

Wallace, J.E. & Kay, F. (2008) The professionalism of practicing law: a comparison across work contexts, *Journal of Organizational Behavior*, 29(8), pp. 1021–1047.

Wegener, B. (1992) Concepts and measurement of prestige, *Annual Review of Sociology*, 18, pp. 253–280.

Index

Note: **Boldface** page numbers refer to figures and tables, page numbers followed with "n" refer to notes.

For Product Safety Concerns and Information please contact our EU
representative GPSR@taylorandfrancis.com
Taylor & Francis Verlag GmbH, Kaufingerstraße 24, 80331 München, Germany

www.ingramcontent.com/pod-product-compliance
Ingram Content Group UK Ltd.
Pitfield, Milton Keynes, MK11 3LW, UK
UKHW050054200926
475702UK00019B/2825

* 9 7 8 0 3 6 7 0 3 0 1 4 8 *